Public Affairs Reporting Now

Public Affairs Reporting Now

News of, by and for the People

G. Michael Killenberg

AMSTERDAM • BOSTON • HEIDELBERG • LONDON • NEW YORK • OXFORD
• PARIS • SAN DIEGO • SAN FRANCISCO • SINGAPORE • SYDNEY • TOKYO

Focal Press is an imprint of Elsevier

Acquisitions Editors: Cara Anderson and Elinor Actipis
Publishing Services Manager: George Morrison
Project Manager: Kathryn Liston
Assistant Editor: Robin Weston
Marketing Managers: Marcel Koppes, Becky Pease
Interior Design: Alisa Andreola
Cover Design: Steven Stave

Focal Press is an imprint of Elsevier
30 Corporate Drive, Suite 400, Burlington, MA 01803, USA
Linacre House, Jordan Hill, Oxford OX2 8DP, UK

 Recognizing the importance of preserving what has been written, Elsevier prints its books
on acid-free paper whenever possible.

Library of Congress Cataloging-in-Publication Data
Application submitted

British Library Cataloguing-in-Publication Data
A catalogue record for this book is available from the British Library.

ISBN: 978-0-240-80825-3

For information on all Focal Press publications
visit our Web site at www.books.elsevier.com

07 08 09 10 11 12   10 9 8 7 6 5 4 3 2 1

Printed in the United States of America

Working together to grow
libraries in developing countries

www.elsevier.com | www.bookaid.org | www.sabre.org

ELSEVIER   BOOK AID
International   Sabre Foundation

To Penny

Contents

5   The Neighborhood Approach   129

6   Government News for the People   155

11   Lessons in Law and Ethics   337

Preface

Real journalism isn't a game of trivial pursuit.

Do not be fooled by the daily stream of fluffy stories about fads, fashions or fetishes. People love to revel in celebrity gossip or fantasize about extreme makeovers. But Donald Trump's social life or the South Beach Diet doesn't satisfy when people worry about a home invasion in their neighborhood or a rezoning proposal to bring a Wal-Mart super center to town or a Department of Education report that their child's school scored bottom-most in reading achievement.

Everyday life, no matter whether the issues or events arise next-door or a continent away, raises questions and concerns that the public counts on journalists to answer and, more important, confront.

Public Affairs Reporting Now: News of, by and for the People is intended to teach the best practices and provide the best advice for covering what's generically known as "public affairs reporting." It is a term that is neither inspiring nor precise, but "public affairs reporting" has long described the kind of news coverage that keeps people informed as citizens and keeps our institutions, public and private, focused on the public good. Journalists, after all, are the ultimate *public servants*—or should be.

Never underestimate the importance of journalists in a republic such as ours. Those who hold appointed or elected government positions owe their allegiance to the people, and while they cannot possibly serve the diverse interests of every citizen, public officials must never forget who governs in America—the people. Journalists play an indispensable role as surrogates for citizens too busy, too tired, too infirm or too unqualified to govern for themselves. Reporters act on the public's behalf when they scrutinize candidates for elected office; request judicial records at the courthouse; investigate the expenditure of municipal tax dollars; attend meetings of the school board; interview prisoners held in the county jail; or stand watch over a limitless range of issues and conditions that touch the lives of citizens. As they serve the public, journalists expose corruption, sound alarms, question public policy, demand accountability and expose injustice.

The subtitle comes, of course, from Lincoln's Gettysburg Address. News "of the people" means journalists can never lose their focus on the everyday lives of people. To maintain that focus, journalists must venture well beyond the institutions and figures of power for news that can only be found by entering and understanding the world most Americans inhabit. News "by the people" acknowledges that journalists cannot report the news alone. They depend on people to share their fears, hopes, aspirations, frustrations and deeply held opinions. People will not reveal themselves freely unless they sense journalists genuinely care about them. News "for the people" acknowledges that journalism, at its best and truest, arms citizens with the knowledge to govern themselves.

About this Book

Public Affairs Reporting Now is an updated and expanded version of a textbook published in 1992. Much has changed in journalism and the news beats that journalists cover, and many of those changes are identified and examined. Throughout the book, newer information has been blended with the wisdom of journalism's elders.

Each chapter provides background and instruction for students in the reporting assignments they can expect in their first years in journalism. Special areas of reporting, such as politics and science, receive ample attention, but neither students nor their instructors should expect the book to provide the depth and sophistication specialized beats require. Journalists generally must prove themselves ready for specialized beats by years of success at public affairs and general-assignment reporting.

On one level, the book is a practical, example-laden guide to the traditional beats of public affairs useful for both students and working professionals. On another level, it examines how public affairs reporters go about their work, with attention given to the implications and consequences of their behavior. As a result, emphasis is placed on multicultural perspectives, interpersonal competence and ethical issues. Students and others who draw from *Public Affairs Reporting Now*, however, should view it as a departure point, not a comprehensive set of instructions. The best reporters never stop learning and discovering new things about themselves and others.

Acknowledgments

I am indebted to Robbie Arkovich for his photographic contributions. Arkovich, a veteran police officer with a degree in photojournalism, displays his discerning eye for urban life—its ironies, moods and flavors. In Chapter 7, he adds personal commentary to his photographs. He enriched the book by his words and images.

My thanks, too, to Kate Bradshaw, my 20-something graduate assistant, who helped me bridge several generation gaps by critically reading the original textbook. Kate pointed out dated or unclear references, verified statistical information, recommended contemporary examples and questioned terminology and idiosyncratic speech if it seemed foreign to her. For each chapter, Kate produced a detailed analysis, complete with recommended changes in both content and context.

Three journalism educators—each an accomplished journalist—reviewed the manuscript and helped tighten its focus and improve its organization. They helped, as well, by catching errors of both commission and omission. The three reviewers—Chip Scanlan, Steve Weinberg and Walt Harrington—embody the highest standards of our profession.

At Elsevier, Amy Jollymore, as acquisitions editor, encouraged me to revive a 15-year-old book, and she sold the idea to her colleagues. I thank Amy for her confidence in me and her unwavering support. Cara Anderson took over the project at a crucial juncture, and she patiently allowed me extra time to finish the manuscript and then quickly put the project on a fast track for publication. Cara's able, responsive attention to all the editorial details freed me to focus on research and writing. Kathryn Liston, project manager, not only kept the book on a strict production schedule; she gave it special attention, overseeing a front cover and text design that put a professional sheen on a barebones manuscript. By words and deeds, Amy, Cara and Kathryn caringly helped me from start to finish. No book could have been in better hands.

Despite all that I owe to these fine people, my greatest inspiration and assistance has come from three decades of students, through whom I learned valuable lessons in reporting, teaching and life. Each term, I sent my students into the community, and they returned with extraordinary stories about the community and its people. They helped me understand the community in its diversity and provided street-level perspectives that influenced how I came to view and teach journalism.

To me, public affairs reporting comprises the heart and soul of journalism. I hope that all those who teach and study public affairs reporting experience the great satisfaction that comes from doing journalism in service to the public.

The Roles and Realities of Reporting

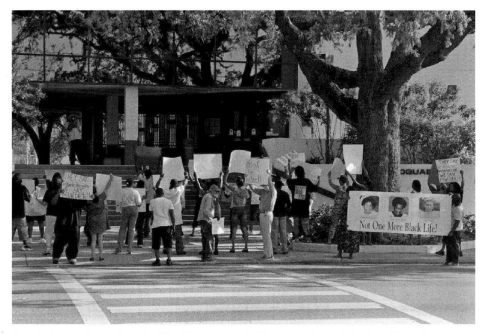

A protest, a media event—or both?   A local group, the Uhurus, marches and chants outside police headquarters in St. Petersburg, Fla., over the fatal shooting of a young black man by Pinellas County sheriff's deputies, who sometimes pursue suspects into the city. Journalists struggle over how—or if—to cover orchestrated news, dubbed *pseudo-events* by historian Daniel Boorstin. Because a pseudo-event seems less "real," is it therefore less newsworthy? On the other hand, does it reflect an underlying reality that journalists cannot disregard? (Photograph by Robbie Arkovich.)

On a raw winter night in 1899, an 18-year-old reporter named H. L. Mencken (1880–1956) struggled to compose what was to be his first published news story—a minor item from police records. "I wrote and tore up, wrote and tore up," Mencken later recounted in *Newspaper Days*. "Finally there emerged the following:"

> A horse, buggy and several sets of harnesses, valued in all at about $250, were stolen last night from the stable of Howard Quinlan, near Kingsville. The county police are at work on the case, but so far no trace of either thieves or booty has been found.[1]

Following a path familiar to generations of journalists, Mencken apprenticed on the police beat, eventually moving on to other areas of public affairs reporting. He also wrote more than 30 books and collections of essays and reported on the American political scene for nearly a half-century. Despite recent criticism focusing on Mencken's anti-Semitic statements, journalists still admire his style and craftsmanship.

Mencken, no doubt, would admire their work, too, recognizing that the world reporters now cover is vastly more dangerous, complex and ambiguous than the one he knew. The realities of reporting have changed, and so have the reporter's roles. In a few short decades, gang violence displaced stickball on city streets. Silicon Valley supplanted the factory town. And technicians, wearing protective suits against danger-ous wastes, took over jobs the garbage collectors once handled. The reporter's working knowledge came to include "crack," anthrax and global warming, as the problems and the complexities of urban life spilled over into suburban and small-town America.

Today most Americans, seldom by preference, lead an existence characterized by Big Macs served at the drive-through window instead of leisurely meals enjoyed around the dining-room table. "Haven't got time for the pain," said a popular adver-tisement, appealing to those so bent on success they could not allow a headache to slow them down. Life, indeed, rushes on, but who can budget an hour or two for the week's grocery shopping, much less fit in a meeting of the school board or the city council? In an increasingly confusing, troubling world, people depend on journalists to discover and report news of import in their lives.

While José and Marie Martinez run errands, the school board is debating whether a 9-year-old carrying the AIDS virus will attend class with 25 other third-graders, among them the Martinez's daughter, Mary. Across town, lawyers for a huge waste-hauling corporation pressure the city council to double the size of its landfill. Beyond reporting these stories—and stories on water rates, revenue bonds and purse snatch-ings—journalists are expected to scan the horizon, alert for signs of tomorrow's emerging news. It is a challenging, serious calling that requires astute, sensitive and, above all, responsible practitioners.

A Reporter's Role

A number of metaphors reflect the traditional role of our news media—"Watchdog," "Fourth Estate" and "Checking Power" among them. These terms describe an institu-tional responsibility to ensure that government performance and policy undergo rigor-ous scrutiny and critique.

Deeply rooted in our history and law, we can find ample support for the notion that democracy relies on a free and responsible press. In the 1931 Supreme Court case of *Near v. Minnesota*, for example, Chief Justice Charles E. Hughes wrote:

> . . .[T]he administration of government has become more complex, the opportunities for malfeasance and corruption have multiplied, crime has grown to most serious propor-tions, and the danger of its protection by unfaithful officials and of the impairment of the fundamental security of life and property by criminal alliances and official neglect, empha-sizes the primary need of a vigilant and courageous press. . . .

In *New York Times v. Sullivan*, the 1964 case that gave the press formidable protection against defamation lawsuits brought by aggrieved public officials, the Supreme Court said its decision rested upon "a profound national commitment to the principle that debate on public issues be robust, uninhibited and wide-open."

Ten years later, Justice Potter Stewart reflected on a free, autonomous, aggressive press as envisioned by the Founders in drafting our Constitution. "Perhaps our liberties might survive without an independent established press," he said in an address at Yale School of Law. "But the Founders doubted it, and, in the year 1974, I think we can all be thankful for their doubts." He spoke at the time the nation faced the Watergate scandal, which was brought to public attention and debate by relentless investigative journalism.

In our democracy, we depend upon journalists to keep us informed as citizens and to hold our institutions, both public and private, accountable. Unfortunately the traditional, civic-rooted role of journalism has suffered as news organizations, at times, pander to the perceived public appetite for spectacle, sleaze and sensation in search of audiences other than the Lipitor and Celebrex generation.

Competition alone does not explain journalism's diminishing role as public servant. Everyone, it seems, with a talk show plays the game of make-believe journalist. Although they bring politicians and policymakers on for chats, they provide a safe haven—a civic duty-free zone—where no one demands accountability and no one challenges or contests what the high-profile guest says or does. So politicians and policymakers intentionally book on Oprah or Maury and bow out to *60 Minutes* or the *Washington Post*.

The Internet, too, has spawned a slew of imposters who operate without allegiance to codes of ethics and values that guide responsible journalists. Americans—young, middle-aged and older—find it liberating to access news online, and they frequently search for news in nontraditional places. Sometimes they make decisions and form opinions based on the information they acquire online, trusting a Google search more than the *New York Times*. With trivial news supplanting serious reporting, and with all the make-believe, amateur and illegitimate journalists on the scene, real journalists—those who understand they serve the public and buttress democracy—need to rededicate themselves to the public good. *Journalists are the ultimate public servants*—or should be.

A Reporter's Orientation

Successful journalists understand the value of an interpersonal technique called *empathy*. Empathy involves a sincere attempt to identify with the experiences and emotions of others. Practicing empathy does not mean reporters must abandon skepticism or deny their own feelings. But empathy does require reporters to listen and evaluate with an open mind, which is not always easy. Consider this situation: Based on hearsay, the newly assigned courthouse reporter concludes that the county treasurer is a bumpkin incapable of balancing his own checkbook, much less managing a $15 million budget.

Now the reporter must interview the treasurer to explore charges by political opponents that his office is mismanaged. Without a commitment to empathy, will the reporter be able to give the man a fair hearing? Empathy cannot be feigned or misused as a manipulative interviewing tool, however; it must be genuine and honest.

In the journalist's world, empathy can coexist with skepticism and assertiveness. It is often a question of balance and moderation. Communication professor Michael Schudson offers this advice: "Journalists, like other seekers, must learn to trust themselves and their fellows and the world enough to take everything in, while distrusting themselves and others and the appearances of the world enough not to be taken in by everything."[2] The words of philosopher Max Ehrmann (1872–1945) also serve as a guide for journalists:

> Speak your truth quietly and clearly; and listen to others, even to the dull and the ignorant; they too have their story. . . . Exercise caution in your business affairs, for the world is full of trickery. But let this not blind you to what virtue there is; many persons strive for high ideals, and everywhere life is full of heroism.[3]

QUOTABLES
"We must resist the cynical impulse: News organizations must begin to exercise more self-control over their own darkest habits of thought. . . . There are great benefits to be found in assuming the worst—often quite cheaply through assuming a posture—and there are great risks in bringing cynicism under proper journalistic discipline. . . . I don't suggest that news organizations abandon their role as critics and investigators. Quite the contrary, they need to expand the areas in which they accept this challenge. But I do think they need to pause before assuming the worst, hold back when allegations are made until they develop some credible evidence supporting the charges." (pp. 192, 193)
—Jack Fuller, *News Values*, Chicago: University of Chicago Press, 1996

Unfortunately, surveys indicate that the public generally considers journalists as anything but empathic. They are seen as an arrogant, rude and insensitive lot, inflicting pain wherever they go. Movies and prime-time television programs contribute to the image by depicting reporters as little better than ruthless news vultures. In 1989, writer Janet Malcolm began an article in *The New Yorker* magazine with this blanket indictment of the press: "Every journalist who is not too stupid or too full of himself to notice what is going on knows that what he does is morally indefensible. He is a kind of confidence man, preying on people's vanity, ignorance, or loneliness, gaining their trust and betraying them without remorse."[4]

Malcolm's description of journalists unfairly and inaccurately generalizes, but her words deserve to be heard and considered, particularly when she talks about reporter-source relationships:

> The catastrophe suffered by the subject is no simple matter of an unflattering likeness or a misrepresentation of his views; what pains him, what rankles and sometimes

drives him to extremes of vengefulness, is the deception that has been practiced on him. On reading the article . . . in question, he has to face the fact that the journalist—who seemed so friendly and sympathetic, so keen to understand him fully, so remarkably attuned to his vision of things—never had the slightest intention of collaborating with him on his story but always intended to write a story of his own.[5]

Stripping away Malcolm's hyperbole, you will find the root of many reporter-source problems. Those problems frequently begin with the tendency in reporting to dehumanize "news subjects." Reporters should never treat or view people as objects to be used and discarded. It might help to remember that a story is not the reporter's alone; it belongs, as well, to the people quoted, described and represented in the story. Reporters must also remember that above all, people—presidents and postmasters alike—want to be treated with decency.

A few journalists, as *Washington Post* reporter Lou Cannon says, exhibit an "annoying self-righteousness" that they are "performing a sacred calling."[6] Some adopt a scorched-earth approach to gathering the news, burning bridges and destroying resources they might need later on. Some become unnecessarily aggressive, kicking down doors without first gently knocking. And some confuse skepticism and cynicism, forgetting that one is helpful and the other destructive.

Despite the public's poor image of reporters, journalists seldom deceive, betray or exploit deliberately. Nonetheless, even well-intentioned journalists hurt people at times. Trained, conditioned and rewarded to nail down stories and make deadlines, they sometimes overlook the feelings and needs of others. Part of that conditioning includes devotion to a seductive principle: the public's right to know. It is an ambiguous and, at times, self-serving term. Other than journalists themselves, few people argue fiercely that the public has a *right* to know. Besides, which "public" does the press serve? And if a public's right to know does exist, who says the public always wants to know? "The press justifies itself in the name of the public," said professor James Carey (1934–2006). "The canons of journalism originate in and flow from the relationship of the press to the public. The public is totem and talisman, and an object of ritual homage."[7] Even "objects of ritual homage" do not entitle reporters to ask anyone anything at any time and at any cost.

Lofty principles of journalism are invoked most passionately on public affairs beats. Waving the right-to-know banner on high, certain reporters demand answers and accountability. Indeed, the mythology of journalism casts the press and public officials in adversarial roles. Should reporters and officials constantly butt heads? Richard C. Harwood, when he was the *Washington Post's* ombudsman, questioned the value of an adversarial orientation. "[I]t does not contribute to intimate or confessional relationships in which 'truthtelling' . . . is a common transaction." Journalists should worry less about becoming too cozy with public officials, he said, and worry more about becoming too removed. "It is rather the problem of being too distant from those whose personalities, beliefs, knowledge, hopes and fears are essential to the understanding we would communicate to our countrymen."[8] Although

Harwood's thoughts apply most directly to reporters covering the centers of political power, they are relevant, as well, for reporters covering school boards or zoning commissions.

Harwood's approach does not mean reporters should stop asking hard questions and pressing for answers. In his memoir, longtime *New York Times* reporter John L. Hess said, "The press should always be pushing against the wind, rebutting the establishment truth—if not in our editorials, then in our news columns, and if not there, in our op-ed pages."[9] Push as they might, journalists soon discover that public officials are not always obligated to talk to them or provide information. Certainly public officials, much less officials in the private sector, are not inclined to cooperate with demanding, combative reporters. In the mid-1960s, journalist James Reston (1909–1995) used the metaphor "artillery of the press" to urge reporters to unleash "a relentless barrage of facts and criticism, as noisy but also as accurate as artillery fire."[10]

Reston's concept tends to reduce public affairs reporting to a form of warfare. War is dirty business; artillery shells do indiscriminate damage and sometimes hurt non-combatants. Before firing the heavy artillery, first determine whether a barrage will elicit answers and responses that are complete and forthright. After the dust clears, what will be the condition of the reporter-source relationship? Always consider whether a non-confrontational, empathic approach will work as effectively—and cause less damage. At times, however, the artillery might be needed to break through deliberate barriers set up by public officials or public figures to thwart news coverage.

Although all journalists should be concerned about a healthy, fruitful reporting environment, those on the front lines of journalism—the public affairs beats—have the most to gain; they also have the most to lose.

A Reporter's Reality

The best journalists know that skill at the mechanics of reporting is not enough to do the job well. Journalists must also understand the processes by which they see, define, convey and, indeed, influence that churning mass of information known as "news." By understanding these processes, reporters can recognize their own limitations and weaknesses. Journalists enjoy no special ability to discover the truth or achieve objectivity. "The press," said journalism scholar James Carey (1934–2006), "should not present itself as seer, but simply as doing the best it can to figure out today what is going on."[11] Carey's observation suggests that reporters must resist being lulled into a false sense of security or smugness over their powers to detect and verify news.

To come to grips with the implications of their work, reporters should begin with a careful examination of their own attitudes, values and experiences. Reporters who take time to understand themselves can better observe and analyze events and people. In an enduring passage written more than 80 years ago, journalist and commentator Walter Lippmann (1889–1974) described how people generally perceive the world: "For the most part we do not first see and then define; we define first and then see. In the great blooming, buzzing confusion of the outer world we pick out what our culture has already defined for us."[12] Lippmann's words refer to a process known as *socialization*—the way people come to accept the prevailing standards and attitudes of their culture. Socialization starts in childhood, and in its wake can be blind spots, biases and misconceptions.

By adulthood, fixed habits of association, lifestyle and belief combine to further influence what reporters see—or fail to see. Psychologist Mauricio Gaborit says people tend to attribute a higher probability to what they believe is typical, disregarding evidence that challenges their assumptions. "In general, we seek information that conforms to our prior knowledge, and often ignore outright any information that contradicts it."[13] The implications for journalists are clear. Although editors and reporters bring varied experiences and perspectives to their work, they tend to lead lives that are different and removed from those of many Americans. Occasional visits to places like a refinery, a veterans' hospital or an assisted-living center might be necessary for reporters to expand—or renew—their views of "reality."

QUOTABLES

"A suspicious public that sniffs for slanted news . . . may perceive deliberate slanting in the inescapable fact that no reporter can entirely obliterate what he or she *is*— conservative, optimist, affluent, ill-educated—from the work being written. Usually, however, slanting is in the olfactory organ of the sniffer. Slanting does, of course, occur, but usually it is a result of deliberate intent. Reporters are trained in, and take pride in, the discipline of holding themselves above palpable, immediate influence, such as whether they favor a particular candidate or party or personally dislike the president. They consider detachment from such obvious influences as a mark of their craft, their integrity." (pp. 89, 90)

—Tom Wicker, *On the Record,* New York: Bedford/St. Martin's, 2002

In his autobiography, Jack Newfield (1938–2004) of the *Village Voice* reminded journalists that socialization is a double-edged process of both seeing and being seen:

> We all carry a variety of identities in our heads. I'm an only child and a poor kid from Bed-Stuy [Bedford-Stuyvesant, a neighborhood in Brooklyn]. I'm a graduate of a mostly black high school and of the City University—when it was still tuition-free. I'm a civil rights and antiwar activist from the 1960s, and a friend and biographer of Robert Kennedy. I'm a father and a husband; a democrat and a Jew; a muckraker and an empiricist. I cherish both Martin Luther King and Sugar Ray Robinson, so, please don't understand me too quickly.[14]

On the one hand, Newfield acknowledged his own socialization. But he also underscored how others might misread him if they fail to take the time and care necessary to see him clearly and fully. Reporters must try to understand others as well as understand themselves.

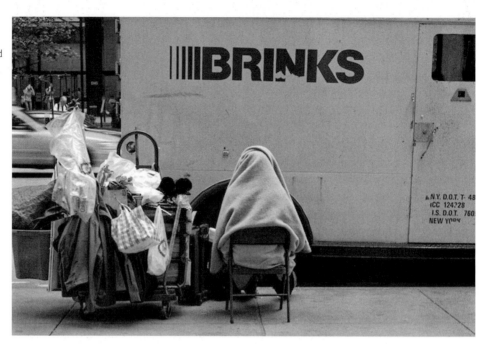

Rags, riches cross paths on a city street An armored truck stops in front of a homeless man and his worldly possessions. A journalist's powers of perception include an awareness of and sensitivity to life's ironies. (Photo by Robbie Arkovich.)

Journalists who recognize that news can be their—or someone else's—prejudiced, subjective, imperfect perceptions of reality will make efforts to compensate. An editor who once marched with civil rights protesters will attempt to listen with an open mind to a Ku Klux Klan organizer; a reporter who plays racquetball and reads John Le Carré mysteries will strive to understand the world as seen by the cab driver who bowls and buys the *National Enquirer* at the supermarket checkout line; and a reporter whose news judgment sometimes is twisted by overconfidence or zeal will remember this classic admonition from a reader of the *Los Angeles Times:* "Get a grip on yourselves, guys, and do the best job you can, but don't suffer an identity crisis while doing it. Just try to spell the names right, get your facts straight and never forget that today's big story is tomorrow's birdcage carpet."[15]

A journalist's sense of "reality" may also be influenced by the patterned, predictable methods news organizations often employ to gather information. Sociologist Gaye Tuchman sees news as a "construction of reality"—a product of reporters' work routines and contact with sources.[7] When a government reporter, for example, relies heavily for stories and information from a handful of public officials, all within the physical and attitudinal confines of the city hall, news can become a narrow, slanted construction of reality. If "news" frequently is what sources *say*, and if those sources are predominantly people in authority positions—such as police officers and city council members—stories are not likely to reflect divergent opinions and present different, perhaps conflicting, accounts of reality.

Building on Tuchman's theory, another sociologist, Mark Fishman, used coverage of a "crime wave" against New York City's elderly to illustrate the concept of news as a self-fulfilling prophecy. Once legitimized as "news," the crime wave begat even more news, such as the mayor's vow to make the streets safe for the elderly. Crime-wave coverage dominated the news for weeks, despite police statistics revealing a decrease in crimes against the city's elderly compared with the previous year.[17]

The work of Tuchman and Fishman raises a question confronting all journalists: Does the press only report the news, or does it sometimes manufacture it? While the term *construction of reality* hints of fabrication or fiction, reporters in New York City did not invent stories about rapes, murders or muggings of the elderly. But they did *selectively* concentrate on a particular variety of crime, and, in turn, "confirmed" the existence of a crime wave in the minds of politicians, police and the public. Certain stories—usually "happenings" like a hurricane or plane crash—are less subject to journalistic selectivity. But with many other stories, reporters, editors and news directors are free to define and prioritize the news. Of course, the press is expected to help set society's agenda. So when journalists target particular problems for attention, such as crime against the elderly, they perform a vital role of mobilizing public interest and action. In the process, however, journalists must regularly remind themselves of their power to determine what is "news"—and their duty to exercise that power responsibly. Fishman's case study illustrates how silly and sensational the media can be, but it also highlights the power of journalists to draw attention to issues.

Journalists also need to acknowledge that their power to learn and report the "truth" is limited. Truth is elusive, subjective and intangible; it is affected by many variables, among them the perspective, distance, emotional state and motives of those purporting to know the truth. A young man witnesses a police officer making an arrest. The witness passionately tells a reporter that the police officer, without provocation, grabbed the suspect and shoved him roughly into the patrol car. The account is the truth, as he believes it. But consider the variables. The young man came around a corner to see the end of the arrest. He watched from 20 feet away, his view partially blocked by the officer's back. What he sees angers him, further impairing his view of the truth, because a few days before a traffic cop hassled him over a broken taillight. The young man believes cops enjoy hassling civilians. He is not lying, but his version is distorted and incomplete. The 1981 film *Absence of Malice* stereotypes the work of journalists, but it does contain a memorable line delivered by Paul Newman as he scolds a reporter: "You don't come across the truth that easily. Maybe it's just what you think. What you feel. Things aren't always what they seem."

Truth can be hard to detect for other reasons. Reporters in stenographic fashion can collect detail after detail, figure after figure and quotation after quotation—all accurate—and still miss the larger truth, which remains hidden beneath a pile of "obvious" facts. Had Carl Bernstein and Bob Woodward merely reported the obvious facts of the Watergate break-in, the story would have ended with a minor police-blotter report and not revealed a scandal that resulted in a president's resignation.

QUOTABLES

"It is actually more helpful, and more realistic, to understand journalistic truth as a process—or continuing journey toward understanding—which begins with the first-day stories and builds over time. The first news stories signal a new event or trend. They may begin with an account of something simple, a meeting or car accident.

". . . Once they have verified the facts, reporters try to convey a fair and reliable account of their meaning, valid for now, subject to further investigation. The individual reporter may not be able to move much beyond a surface level of accuracy in a first story. But the first story builds to a second, in which the sources of news have responded to mistakes and missing elements in the first, and the second to a third, and so on. Context is added in each successive layer. In more important and complex stories, there are subsequent contributions on the editorial pages, the talk shows, in the op-ed accounts, and the letters to the editor or the callers to radio shows—the full range of public and private conversation.

"This practical truth is a protean thing which, like learning, grows as a stalagmite in a cave, drop by drop over time." (pp. 43, 44)

—Bill Kovach and Tom Rosenstiel, *The Elements of Journalism*, New York: Three Rivers Press, 2001

Sometimes, even the journalistic ideal of "objectivity" keeps reporters from the truth. "Objectivity may become the mere presentation of two sides of an issue in a way that distorts the proportionate importance of each," says Wesley G. Pippert, whose career with United Press International included coverage of the Watergate scandal. Pippert urges reporters to go beyond the obligatory "two-sides formula" and determine whose account suggests the "greater grasp of truth."[18] While journalists should always pursue the truth, at times they must reluctantly and realistically settle on the best *obtainable* version of the truth. But truth seeking is what journalists are supposed to do, even if their best efforts sometimes fall short. British journalist Gerald Priestland offers these encouraging words: "Although we may never arrive at the central core of the truth, we must never foreclose on it or assume that the little progress we can make towards it is not worthwhile."[19]

REAL-LIFE LESSONS

Professor David Protess and his journalism students at Northwestern University believe a reporter's quest for the truth can make the difference between death and life. Over the years, Protess and his novice investigators have helped free four death row prisoners in Illinois. In 2003, two days before his term ended, the state's governor, George Ryan, commuted the death sentences of 160 prisoners to life without parole. He credited Protess and his students for exposing flaws in the law enforcement and judicial handling of death penalty cases. "How many more wrongful convictions have to occur before we can all agree that the system in Illinois is broken?" he asked at an announcement of the blanket commutations, held at Northwestern, with Protess attending. Aaron Patterson also attended; he was summarily released from a state prison after Protess's students tracked down a key witness who recanted her testimony naming Patterson as the killer of a Chicago couple in 1986. Through extensive interviewing in the neighborhood of the double homicide, the students identified two other residents as the likely killers. After the students discovered additional exonerating evidence, Gov. Ryan released Patterson.

Here's how Protess, in his words, guided and inspired his students:

> I draw a set of concentric circles on the blackboard. In the outermost circle are secondary source documents, things like press accounts. . . . The next circle in is primary sources documents, trial documents like testimony and statements. The third circle in is real people, witnesses. We interview them to see if everything matches what's in the documents. We ask them questions that may have come up looking at the documents. And at the inner circle are what I call the targets—the police, the lawyers, others suspects, and the prisoner.[20]

The students never accept anything for granted, he said. They systematically and conscientiously verify presumed facts.

The lesson: *Do not rely solely on news accounts or officials. Go to the original material found in court records, trial testimony, police reports and other primary documents. Then go about verifying the truth of documents and statements.*

With rare exception, journalists honorably pursue the truth. However, the exceptions, particularly the Jayson Blair scandal of 2003, damage the public's confidence in the press. Blair, a *New York Times* reporter, committed journalism's mortal sin—he knowingly published untruths. He finally got caught when a Texas newspaper accused him of plagiarizing one of its articles; Blair resigned a few days later. The *Times* then started investigating Blair's previously published work. The in-house inquiry revealed that Blair, working for the world's most respected newspaper, made up quotes, interviews and facts, including the fabrication of an entire story about the parents of Iraq prisoner of war Jessica Lynch.[21] The scandal rocked the *New York Times* and led to heightened efforts to ensure the accuracy and professional behavior of its news staff. Reporters in big cities and small towns alike suffered from the fallout.

Blair dishonored all journalists, but he indirectly buttressed the resolve of the press to seek the truth. Rather than approach their work with certitude, bravado or, as Blair demonstrated, blatant disregard for the truth, reporters who keep the faith try hard to objectively analyze events, scrupulously conduct research and dutifully detect biases—their own and those of their news subjects. They know the reward will not be perfection, but their efforts will bring them closer to the journalistic ideal of accurate, honest, fair and meaningful news coverage. They also know they cannot expect the public's full trust or support. But serving the public remains the ultimate goal.

The Competent Reporter

Unlike lawyers or doctors, journalists are not required to demonstrate a level of competence or knowledge to gain a license to practice. Early in the history of American journalism, typical qualifications for the job of reporter were a high school diploma, street smarts and a gift for writing. In the 1870s, Horace Greeley (1811–1872), founder and editor of the *New York Tribune*, told a bright-eyed college graduate hoping to be hired as a reporter, "I'd a damned sight rather you had graduated at a printer's case."[22] Greeley put more stock in a practical, informal education than in a degree. At the turn of the century, H. L. Mencken shunned college and "the balderdash of chalky pedagogues" to learn about life and journalism through self-education.

Contemporary journalists are not necessarily better educated than past generations, but they are largely college graduates, many of them products of journalism schools. Today most editors and educators would say a key prerequisite for a career in journalism is a sound, broadly based education. Legendary professor Melvin Mencher says reporters need a full, regularly restocked storehouse of knowledge that they work at "seven days a week, 18 hours a day." As he asks rhetorically:

> How else will you get to know everything: the difference between robbery and burglary; what a mill levy is; who succeeded Richard Nixon in the presidency; why the rate is more informative than the raw number; what the Cultural Revolution was about; the source of the Mississippi; what rap sheets, revenue bonds, stock options, the GNP, the margin of error, pinch hitters, NATO, the 10-K, arraignments, fender-benders, inquests, commercial zoning, creation science, special assessments are.[23]

The contents and size of each reporter's storehouse inevitably will vary. Above all, the educated reporter is a literate person, and, for the 21st century, that literacy spans knowledge of communication, culture and technology.

Communication Literacy

Technical skill in grammar, punctuation and language usage, while important, only constitutes a partial inventory of communication competencies expected of journalists. Beyond the ability to craft clear and correct stories looms an even greater imperative: journalism—as an institution—must faithfully serve as a vital instrument of public communication and democratic discourse. Ironically, critics say, journalism often limits itself to the transmission of the news. In that limited role, news organizations "speak" rather than "communicate." In the words of Joseph Pulitzer (1847–1911) that resonate with present-day relevance, "[A]lways remain devoted to the public welfare; never be satisfied with merely printing the news." For news organizations devoted to the Pulitzer creed, the duty to communicate requires broader participation than providing content—no matter how excellent its quality—to its audiences; it comprises competent listening and dedicated interaction with the communities and people they serve.

When people of a community communicate, issues, concerns and attitudes surface, but they will not be heard or acted upon if journalism restricts itself to the transmission of news. Journalists must, in belief and practice, value communication. "Journalism is a conversation, not a lecture," says Jeff Jarvis, media executive with Advance Communications who also produces the popular blog BuzzMachine. "The news isn't done when we print it. That's when the public can add questions, corrections, perspectives. That will improve the news. And it also will change our relationship with the public."[24] Journalists need to acknowledge that news emerges and evolves from communication, not just from routine exchanges with news sources or conventional tips it receives from the public.

Even in everyday interpersonal communication, journalists cannot afford to assume talking and listening come naturally; nor can they underestimate the intricacies of human discourse. Reporters spend a much greater time talking and listening than they do writing. Yet, as one veteran educator says, the journalism student "strangely . . . gets little or no theory and practice in interviewing—probably the most important 'technique' which a journalist can have."[25]

Deborah Tannen, author of *That's Not What I Meant!*, says an understanding of how language works "restores a sense of control over our lives, making it possible to improve communications and relationships in all the settings in which people talk to each other: at work, in interviews, in public affairs."[26] Putting Tannen's observation in practical terms, the literate reporter is competent in the nonverbal, symbolic and psychological facets of language. Such competency is crucial if reporters are to comprehend fully and understand correctly. Grasping the "message" of a news subject's trembling voice, set jaw or raised eyebrow might be as important as recognizing a quotable comment. Journalists must develop a sensitivity to the needs and feelings of others and an understanding of the power of words, questions and other means of communication, including what anthropologist Edward T. Hall called the "silent language" of behavior and cultural differences.[27] A reporter's ignorance of or indifference to verbal and nonverbal cues may well result in an unsatisfactory interview and a botched story.

QUOTABLES

"We reporters enjoy First Amendment protections, but we don't have subpoena power. People don't have to talk to us. They do for many reasons, among them that they trust we are searching for the truth. The less we listen, the less they will talk to us."

—Ken Auletta, "Whom Do Journalists Work For?" The Red Smith Lecture in Journalism, Notre Dame, Ind., December 2005

13

Bob Steele, a former newsperson and now a widely quoted ethicist at the Poynter Institute, a school for journalists, understands from experience how communication incompetence can translate into bad journalism.

> I'm on the receiving end of several hundred interviews a year. Too often I'm troubled by the techniques of the reporter. Weak subject-matter preparation. Poorly framed questions. Leading questions. Hints of bias and closed-minded thinking. Failure to listen to my responses and to ask logical follow-up questions. Intermittent note taking (keyboard clicking tells a lot about what the reporter is looking for and what he is ignoring).[28]

How many reporters, though, never recognize the potency of language in their day-to-day communication? How many never recognize the damage done and opportunities lost? Reporters who appreciate and understand how language works can anticipate better interviews, keener perceptual power and ultimately more complete, more accurate stories.

Cultural Literacy

E. D. Hirsch Jr. created a stir when he suggested in his 1987 best seller, *Cultural Literacy*, that most Americans lack fundamental knowledge of history, politics, geography and the arts. Hirsch worried in particular about the shortcomings of contemporary students. "They know a great deal," he said. "The trouble is that, from the standpoint of their literacy and ability to communicate with others in our culture, what they know is ephemeral and narrowly confined to their own generation."[29]

Presumably, young reporters, too, are deficient in intergenerational knowledge. In some instances, the gaps are painfully apparent, as journalism instructors know from grading stories riddled with gaffes like "Joan of Ark," the "Crucifiction" and "Porky and Bess." The consequences of intergenerational ignorance, of course, are more serious than an occasional malaprop. A reporter, for example, cannot intelligently cover—much less analyze—a school integration case without knowing the significance of *Brown v. Board of Education*. And all reporters, male and female, should know about suffragists and Susan B. Anthony if they hope to interpret contemporary women's issues.

Although Hirsch deserves credit for illuminating a serious problem, some critics found his list of 5,000 essential names, dates, phrases and concepts too ethnocentric, too outdated, too mainstream or too short. In response, Rick Simonson and Scott Walker proposed a "multicultural literacy" to account for diversity in gender, race, age and nationality. As Simonson and Walker colorfully put it:

> Though Hirsch's list does include "penis envy," "macho," and "vasectomy," he fails to find significant "mastectomy," "gynecology," or "Georgia O'Keeffe." Nor does he deem it important for culturally literate Americans to know about "alcoholism," "internment camps," "Bhagavad Gita," "Pelé," "rhythm and blues," "computer crash," "El Salvador," or "One Hundred Years of Solitude."

The concept of America as a "melting pot" no longer applies, if it ever did. Differences and diversity in our society reflect a colorful, complex mosaic. "None of us," Simonson and Walker say, "can afford to remain ignorant of the heritage and culture of any part of our population."[30]

Hirsch, to his credit, made amends for some of his oversights in subsequent books, including *The New Dictionary of Cultural Literacy,* published in 2002.[31] In it, he and his co-authors not only added hundreds of entries, they had to revise many original entries to reflect recent changes in history, politics, art and, especially, science and technology. Dozens of entries cover the controversial, burgeoning field of genetics, including "in vitro fertilization," "genetic engineering" and "Dolly," a sheep celebrated in 1996 as the world's first cloned mammal. The 2002 edition also includes the cultural-political nuances of certain terms, such as "urban renewal," noting that bulldozing slums literally paved the way for effluent businesses and housing at the expense of the people it displaced.

Cultural illiteracy sometimes leads to cultural insensitivity. Betty Friedan, a leader of the women's movement of the 1960s, admitted that at the age of 57 she failed to relate to a vast segment of society—the elderly. "I had the same view of aging as everyone else in America. You know: Poor things, dreary. Not me." She served as an advocate for older citizens until her death in 2006. With reporting increasingly becoming the work of young people, sensitivity by the press to the problems and issues of aging is especially needed. Otherwise, reporters will continue to write stories peppered with patronizing stereotypes. Journalism educator Carole Rich cited this feature lead from the *Arizona Daily Star:*

> This place hops. The food's tame, the dance steps slower than they used to be, the stiffest drink comes from the water fountain. Still, the Gray Crowd jams the Armory Park Senior Citizens Center. Typically, 1,200 men and women gather daily for gossip, games, and yes—even to cast some plain old-fashioned goo-goo eyes.

"The reporter who wrote that was 26 years old," Rich said. "Certainly, he was not going to help me feel positive about getting old."[32]

Cultural illiteracy can go beyond age, gender or ethnic insensitivities to result in serious deficiencies in news coverage. In her book *Cities on a Hill*, Pulitzer Prize-winning writer Frances FitzGerald examined four enclaves she said reflected America's continuing cultural transformation—Rajneeshpuram, Ore., a town taken over by an Indian guru; Jerry Falwell's Liberty Baptist Church in Lynchburg, Va.; the Castro in San Francisco, one of the country's first gay neighborhoods; and Sun City, Fla., a retirement community whose residents, she says, are "pioneers on the frontier of age." FitzGerald contends each community heralded important societal changes that many journalists failed to detect immediately. The emergence of the Christian fundamentalist movement of the early 1980s illustrates her point. "That most journalists (myself included) knew nothing about fundamentalist theology even though Falwell and many others had been preaching it for a decade on national television suggested a blind spot. It suggested a gap in our education and a gap that had developed relatively recently."[33]

Problems compound when communication and cultural illiteracy intersect, as journalist Dorreen Yellow Bird observes in her commentary about Oprah Winfrey's visit to the Navajo reservation in Window Rock, Ariz., to document, among other things, an authentic powwow. Navajo representatives tried to explain to Winfrey's production crew that the powwow has its roots among the Plains tribes. But the crew insisted on including a staged powwow, and, in the process, Yellow Bird said, distorted Native American culture. "Harpo (Winfrey's company) missed some truly beautiful traditions of the Navajo people and instead will have the entire country believe that powwows are a Navajo tradition."[34]

The episode demonstrates the potential for harm inflicted by journalists indifferent to the feelings—and the heritage—of others. With the Internet, cell phones, expanded air travel and immigration reducing the planet to what Marshall McLuhan presciently described as a "Global Village," journalism needs reporters who are fluent in the culture, language and history of other peoples, particularly blacks and two growing segments of the American population, Hispanics and Asians. U.S. Census Bureau figures from 2005 put America's black population at 38 million, the Hispanic population at 41.8 million and the Asian population at 12.4 million. Census officials project that by 2050, the nation's Asian and Hispanic populations would represent about one-half of our total population, which passed 300 million in 2006. As the nation becomes more ethnically diverse, reporters who are bilingual and multicultural will gain greater access to stories and news subjects; moreover, they will be less apt to misjudge or misinterpret.

Technological Literacy

With an enormous amount of information now accessible online, reporters possess a powerful reference and research tool. Of course, anyone can click a mouse and embark on a scavenger hunt for information through Google, Ask.com, Yahoo! or other search engines. Journalists, however, cannot hunt randomly or haphazardly. They search with purpose and prudence, knowing the Internet harbors worthless, untrustworthy information masquerading as legitimate. Still, unskilled, unwary, undisciplined journalists waste time, squander opportunities or, worse still, fall into traps intentionally set to snare the careless or the gullible. The widespread use of computers and Web resources now carries a common label—computer-assisted reporting. The word "assisted" should resonate for competent journalists; they know the limits of Internet reporting. Even in a technologically driven world, solid journalism still relies on "legwork"—getting into the field to gather news through interviews, observation and in-person fact checking.

Computer-assisted reporting not only speeds and extends access to information; it enables reporters to analyze records more efficiently for meaning and patterns.

The hardware and software of information technology encourage the press to monitor public affairs systematically through what is known as *precision reporting*. Instead of relying on anecdotal, impressionistic evidence, reporters can use census data, crime reports and court records to produce in-depth stories that are proactive—not merely reactive—accounts of events and issues. With precision-reporting methods, the validity of stories based on assumptions and theories, such as the crime wave described in Mark Fishman's study, are put to tougher, more valid tests of accuracy and completeness.

Computer-assisted reporting requires a degree of expectancy tempered by patience, but for reporters willing and able to pore over data, the reward can be substantial. The files of the Investigative Reporters and Editors, Inc. (www.ire.org) abound with examples of reporting based on digital information retrieved and analyzed by computer. For example, the *Charlotte Observer* discovered that blacks who bought homes in communities across America were four times as likely as whites to get high interest rates for mortgage loans. Its 2005 series, "The Hard Truth in Lending," was based on analysis of records from 25 of the nation's largest lenders. The newspaper found that even blacks with incomes above $100,000 a year were charged higher rates more often than whites with incomes below $40,000. For decades, African-Americans struggled to get loans at any price. A ground-breaking 1988 computer-assisted series by the *Atlanta Journal and Constitution* that relied on computer tapes obtained from a federal agency revealed whites were five times as likely to be granted home loans in Atlanta as blacks in the same income bracket. Lenders ignored entire black neighborhoods, a practice called redlining. Ironically, the *Charlotte Observer* investigation uncovered a new subspecies of discrimination by lenders.

Technologically literate journalists also need a basic, up-to-date knowledge of science and technology no matter what beat they cover. Journalism cannot rely on its specialists alone to keep the public informed and well served; all journalists should weigh the scientific dimensions of stories they cover. The golf beat writer who admires the community's emerald-green fairways should also question the ecological impact of pesticides on local water quality and wildlife. The county government reporter who carefully monitors administration of the budget should also consider whether tax dollars adequately support energy conservation. In the lifestyle section, the home and garden writer who showcases the efforts of the community's amateur horticulturalists ought to investigate whether genetic engineering has invaded the backyard vegetable patch. The pace of discovery and change can leave even scientists and engineers gasping to stay abreast, much less ahead, of the curve. While it is unrealistic to expect journalists to acquire true expertise, we can expect them to recognize the presence of science and technology in and on our lives.

Without scientific-technical literacy, reporters may either dismiss or exaggerate the significance of developments, provided they detect developments at all. Journalism lore includes the apocryphal story of the big-city editor who decided that the 1957 launch of *Sputnik*, mankind's first artificial satellite, warranted no more than placement on page 10A. Technical developments played out over a period of time are much harder to spot and explain. Despite a brilliant career as a foreign corre-spondent, A. M. Rosenthal (1922–2006) was faulted by *New York Times* colleagues for missing the importance of Japan's technological revolution and its implications for the American economy.[35] With science and technology influencing modern life in so many ways—energy, environment and economics—society cannot afford technically illiterate or insensitive journalists.

Reporters do not acquire *communication, cultural* and *technical literacy* through happenstance or casual encounters; it takes a determined, enthusiastic effort to grow in both knowledge and experience. Journalists of all ages and backgrounds who take their work seriously constantly *read* and *discover*. They relish a trip to a bookstore for browsing and buying. They enroll in courses in other disciplines, not simply to earn electives but to gain new perspectives. They travel for enjoyment and education, uninhibited and curious about sampling other cultures. They venture into the com-munity to learn about others and themselves. Above all, they consider themselves lifelong learners, duty-bound to stay alert and informed.

Models for Journalism and Journalists

Traditionally, news has been event-centered. Even in the new millennium, coverage tends to focus on the standard menu of news—disasters, human confrontations and assorted acts of violence, drama or aberration. By such criteria, news rarely rises above the level of journalism reflected in coffee-shop conversation: "Hey, Fred. Did you see the story about the creep who killed his six kids? Can you believe it?" A paradox of our complex, turbulent society is that reporters, overwhelmed at times by waves of infor-mation and daily occurrences, resort to superficial coverage when people most need something of substance. Of course, straight "process" news, such as covering a fire or a city council meeting, remains important. But other models of reporting are needed to elevate journalism to a more important role. Three models, in particular, address the demands placed on journalists who will be covering news in the 21st century.

Humanistic Reporting

News becomes meaningful when it is related in ways ordinary people can understand. Thirty years ago, Alex Edelstein and William Ames said, "Humanistic reporting is not human interest reporting. The latter stresses unusual or unique qualities of individu-als. The former tells how one person is like another, how he shares special human qualities with the reader."[36] Humanistic reporting stresses the human condition; it is personal and involving, not abstract. In today's celebrity- and politics-driven world, we read about the drug abuse of professional athletes and the avarice of elected officials, but these stories usually lack authenticity because the subjects rarely reveal anything behind their handler-protected facades. Stories about hard-working, dedicated parents, teachers, social workers and shopkeepers do, though, ring true because we know these people. We can relate to their challenges and triumphs. Their stories also provide a fuller appreciation and respect for the everyday existence of people all around us.

If, for example, a community finds itself facing a spike in violent drug-related crime, reporters can pursue the problem at city hall, police headquarters or the Chamber of Commerce, relying on insights and understanding provided by well-meaning public officials. A humanistic approach would seek out "experts" who live day to day with crime, who see it from their front porches or who feel it in the grief of parents of a 10-year-old girl killed accidentally in a drive-by shooting.

Humanistic reporting does not ignore "what's wrong" in a community; but it does highlight "what's right" stories about the good deeds of average folks and about the institutions and organizations that work well and help solidify the community. Journalists engaged in humanistic reporting know the difference between the river and its banks, says Christopher Scanlan of the Poynter Institute, who borrows a quotation from philosopher Will Durant to make a point:

> Civilization is a stream with banks. The stream is sometimes filled with blood from people killing, stealing, shouting and doing the things that historians [and journalists] usually record; while on the banks, unnoticed, people build homes, make love, raise children, sing songs, write poetry and even whittle statues. The story of civilization is the story of what happened on the banks.[37]

Humanistic reporters walk along the banks. One of them is Michael Winerip of the *New York Times*, whose work Nat Hentoff of the *Village Voice* compared to Dickens'. "Charles Dickens seldom covered breaking news," says Hentoff. "He was more interested in what could be called chronic news—litigants covered with spider webs in the courts, children barely surviving and barely knowing why it was worth the effort, and the ballooning hypocrisy of those in charge of 'saving' these children. Michael Winerip's . . . stories hardly ever make the front page of the A section, but are sometimes of a more lasting importance than the thunderclap news of the day. Winerip, for example, has made child abuse and neglect a haunting concern."[38]

Humanistic reporting also calls for respect and caring in the gathering of news. A common public misperception of reporters is that they are callous, manipulative and untrustworthy. Actually, most reporters show great regard for the feelings and needs of news subjects. But journalists who believe they need to approach assignments with business-like detachment may leave interviewees feeling unappreciated and may never reach the level of dialogue necessary for full communication. Humanistic reporting begins well before journalists sit down to write.

Anticipatory Reporting

Preoccupation with hard news may prevent reporters from seeing past the moment and beyond the obvious. At its best, journalism should serve as society's early warning system. In 1962, Morton Mintz of the *Washington Post* alerted American women to the dangers of thalidomide, a tranquilizer then widely prescribed in pregnancy.[39] Thalidomide caused thousands of babies to be born without arms or legs. Mintz's groundbreaking reporting, however, undoubtedly spared countless pregnant women from similar heartache.

Twenty years later, Randy Shilts of the *San Francisco Chronicle* fought a lonely battle in the early 1980s to focus national attention on AIDS, which, at the time, went by the label GRIDS, or gay-related immunodeficiency diseases. Shilts, who died from AIDS in 1994, brought the disease out of the shadows, particularly after publication of his 1987 book, *And the Band Played On*, a chronicle of gay life and a global epidemic, AIDS. Shilts, however, said it took the death of movie star Rock Hudson in 1985 for AIDS to become a news story deserving continuing coverage.[40]

Early in 2001, a *Fortune* magazine reporter, Bethany McLean, blew the whistle on Enron, the energy-trading corporation heralded in news accounts as innovative, visionary and extraordinary successful, at least based on its soaring stock value. McLean questioned the glowing accounts, asking whether Enron's earnings accurately reflected its stock price. Later that year, Enron collapsed into bankruptcy, its stock plummeting from a high of $90 a share to 30 cents, revealing a massive scandal of corporate fraud that ruined the lives of stockholders and thousands of employees who, in some cases, invested their entire savings in the corporation and lost their pensions, as well. McLean, in a subsequent interview, said she hoped Enron remained vivid in the public memory. "When I think back to that time, in early 2001, the idea that one of the largest companies in the country could be involved in fraud and be bankrupt—that wasn't conceivable."[41]

Although history, and journalism, teem with examples of the "inconceivable" becoming reality, why did these stories and others initially go undetected or overlooked by the news media? One answer is that journalists often wait until a hard news "peg" or "angle," such as the death of Rock Hudson, provides the justification and impetus to pursue a story. What's more, the reporting effort necessary to tell the full story of thalidomide, AIDS or Enron is complicated and time-consuming; it is not done by spending an afternoon covering a speech, protest march or press conference. When a social problem finally appears for all to see, the press usually does a thorough job of catch-up journalism. By then, though, major damage may already have been done.

QUOTABLES

"We need journalists to watch over things for us, since we do not go where they go or see what they see. But the things they can watch for go well beyond the corrupt official, the dissembling politician, the bungling bureaucracy. The press needs to watch for places where we lose touch with the public world by letting our attention lapse, our indifference grow. It should keep itself alert to the points of contact between our felt troubles and larger issues that rise on the public screen. Training their sights on public problems, journalists can watch carefully for the best points of entry, where people can raise their voices, lend their views, make use of their talents, get involved. Knowing that a fascination with the larger world lives in all of us, they can try to keep track of the human hunger to know, which never quite dies, amid all the other appetites to which our popular culture caters." (pp. 297–298)

—Jay Rosen, *What Are Journalists For?* New Haven, Conn.: Yale University Press, 1999

Anticipatory reporting is decidedly more difficult than event-centered, episodic reporting. Reporters must occasionally pause—indeed, be given the time—to brainstorm, research and explore. In his book *Behind the Front Page*, David Broder urges newspapers and television stations to free reporters from regular assignments periodically so they can roam. "We need journalistic scout parties out there on the fringes of society," he says, "where the ideas that may ultimately change our politics and government often first appear."[42]

In most cases, those best positioned to anticipate significant developments are specialists in areas like law, medicine, human behavior, environment and economics. Journalism needs its generalists as well, but all reporters are capable of fine-tuning their antennae, no matter where they work or what they do. A *Philadelphia Inquirer* labor reporter might break a medical story about carcinogenic dangers in the American workplace; a courthouse reporter in Beloit, Wis., might alert the public to chemical hazards in the local cement plant.

Explanatory Reporting

Explanatory reporting differs from anticipatory reporting in that it often looks back instead of ahead. Reporter William Greider advises the press, "Instead of being pre-occupied with what's going to happen next, papers should ask more frequently and more coherently what really did happen."[43] When the press stops to explain and interpret, the results are impressive. Eric Newhouse, projects editor at the *Great Falls* (Mont.) *Tribune*, won the 2000 Pulitzer Prize in the explanatory journalism category for his vivid examination of alcohol abuse and the pervasive problems it creates for a community. *Tribune* staffers noticed that they kept bumping into the problem of alcohol abuse—on the police beat, health beat, school beat, social issues beat and others—so rather than report piecemeal, the newspaper decided to take a yearlong look at alcohol in Montana and explore how it affected lives, from cradle to grave. Executive editor Jim Strauss said the series did more than explain. "We analyzed the far-reaching problems of alcohol abuse and reported on solutions that offer hope for bringing that abuse under control."[44]

James Reston (1909–1995) of the *New York Times* once criticized the press for concentrating on dramatic, splashy spot news. "We are fascinated with events, but not by the things that cause events. We will send 500 correspondents to Viet Nam after the war breaks and fill the front pages with their reports, meanwhile ignoring the remainder

Cocaine, exposed to moisture, and a snorting straw The cost of cocaine far exceeds the toll it takes on its users. Explanatory reporting goes beyond merely covering arrests and drug busts to address the rising social costs of cocaine and its derivative, crack cocaine, in such areas as homelessness, prison populations and emergency-room visits. (Photo by Robbie Arkovich.)

of the world, but we will not send one or two reporters there when the danger of war is developing."[45] Reston's point applies even more so in an age of the endless news cycle, as print, broadcast, cable and Web reporters now flood the scene of a fatal school shooting in California or a refinery explosion in New Jersey, hungry for a morsel of news undiscovered by their colleagues. In time, particularly when another spot news event springs up, the news crews pack their gear and leave the scene. The contextual, complete story of the event often is left behind, along with fast-food wrappers and Styrofoam coffee cups.

Perhaps Reston overstated the problem. Public affairs reporters are on the job from Pottsville to the Pentagon, covering meetings, press conferences and pronouncements. But his central point is valid. Pressured to stay abreast of the day's news, few reporters for local newspapers or television or radio stations enjoy the luxury of time and resources needed to practice explanatory journalism of the caliber most often found in network documentaries, monthly magazines or elite newspapers. Yet on a smaller scale in everyday coverage, explanatory reporting can be accomplished by stressing *how* and *why* something happened as opposed to *what* happened. If an honor roll student takes her life, why? If a black candidate for mayor ousts the established white incumbent, how? Such questions are not always answerable. Indeed, explanatory reporting often explores a range of answers, but in doing so it begins to chip away at the half-baked, stereotypical theories, myths and rumors surrounding an event or issue.

Explanatory reporting does not focus exclusively on the big story. Ordinary subjects, when explained well and thoroughly, offer great insight and meaning. Columnist

Bob Greene, who above all is a reporter, frequently pursued ordinary subjects, such as "two 15-year-old boys growing up in a sprawling suburban shopping mall" or "a father begging someone to help his wayward son before it became too late." In Greene's view, "Those are the kinds of things that don't really qualify as 'news,' but that seem to me to have as much to do with the way we live as most of the events that warrant bold banner headlines."[46] Explanatory reporting helps people more clearly understand their lives, which is no small accomplishment.

American journalists are entering a period of great challenge and great opportunity. A highly skilled, educated and motivated cadre of public affairs reporters is needed to produce stories that cannot be based on a handful of questions or told in a few paragraphs. Print journalists face a special test of their abilities. With television, cable, radio and Web sites dramatically and instantaneously covering society's events and occurrences, newspapers, in particular, cannot afford to remain headline services. If newspapers fail to emphasize stories other than "happenings," they can expect further loss of readership. But print journalists must be mindful that readers will not tackle long, involved stories unless they are exceptionally well reported, written and presented.

Reporters in the 21st century, covering a world as diverse and confusing as ours, must operate with great sensitivity and insight. How else can journalists report and write about what commentator Roger Rosenblatt called "our surreal existence"? Reflecting on the death of Salvador Dali, the artist who sought "to systematize confusion and contribute to the total discrediting of the world of reality," Rosenblatt wondered about the "collage of incongruous images" in the news. He compared a "March for Life" by 67,000 anti-abortion protesters to the following day's "March for Death" outside the Florida prison where thousands cheered the execution of serial killer Ted Bundy. "Journalists are born surrealists," says Rosenblatt. "Every form they observe is accompanied by a distortion of that form."[47]

Reporters everywhere face confusion and challenge. Small-town America, itself an endangered species, now mirrors big-city problems. As one reporter explores crack cocaine abuse in Newark, another is pursuing the same subject in Waynesville, Mo. We must hope that both of them succeed.

Exercises

1   Ask someone whose knowledge and judgment you respect to recommend a book that influenced her or him greatly. Read the book and then discuss it together. Make the same request of other persons you respect; set a goal of reading one important book each month.

2   Volunteer for an experience that will heighten your multicultural perspective, such as work at a nursing home or inner-city preschool. Keep a diary of what you observed and learned.

(3) Test your listening and observational skills. As you talk with a friend or colleague, watch and listen for his or her unspoken language—gestures, facial expression, posture. Then discuss your interpretations to determine your ability to accurately assess another person's nonverbal communication.

Notes

1. H. L. Mencken, *Newspaper Days* (New York: Knopf, 1941), p. 7.
2. Michael Schudson, *Discovering the News* (New York: Basic Books, 1978), p. 194.
3. Max Ehrmann, *Desiderata* (Los Angeles: Brooke House, 1972).
4. Janet Malcolm, "The Journalist and the Murderer," *New Yorker*, March 13, 1989, p. 38.
5. Malcolm, "The Journalist and the Murderer," p. 38.
6. Lou Cannon, *Reporting: An Inside View* (Sacramento, Calif.: California Journal Press, 1977), p. 31.
7. James Carey, "The Press and the Public Discourse," *Center Magazine,* March–April 1987, p. 5.
8. Quoted in *Making Sense of the News* (St. Petersburg, Fla.: Modern Media Institute, 1983), p. 9.
9. John L. Hess, *My Times: A Memoir of Dissent* (New York: Steven Stories Press, 2003), p. 11.
10. James Reston, *The Artillery of the Press* (New York: Harper & Row, 1967), p. vii.
11. James W. Carey, "The Press and the Public Discourse," *Center Magazine*, March–April 1987, p. 17.
12. Walter Lippmann, *Public Opinion* (New York: Macmillan, 1922), p. 81.
13. Quoted in Jeannette Batz, "Who Needs to Know?" *Universitas*, Winter 1989, p. 6.
14. Jack Newfield, *The Education of Jack Newfield* (New York: St. Martin's Press, 1984), p. 1.
15. "We're Interested in What You Think: A Sampling of a Year's Letters to the Chairman of Times Mirror" (Los Angeles: Times Mirror Corp., 1987), p. 9.
16. Gaye Tuchman, *Making News* (New York: Free Press, 1978).
17. Mark Fishman, *Manufacturing the News* (Austin: University of Texas Press, 1980), pp. 3–13.
18. Wesley G. Pippert, *An Ethics of News: A Reporter's Search for Truth* (Washington, D.C.: Georgetown University Press, 1989), p. 5.
19. Gerald Priestland, *The Dilemmas of Journalism* (London: Butterworth, 1979), p. 113.
20. Quoted in Bill Kovack and Tom Rosenstiel, *The Elements of Journalism* (New York: Three Rivers Press, 2001), p. 89.
21. "*Times* Reporter Who Resigned Leaves Long Trail of Deception," *New York Times*, May 11, 2003, p. 1.
22. Quoted in Michael Schudson, *Discovering the News* (New York: Basic Books, 1978), p. 68.
23. Melvin Mencher, *The Sayings of Chairman Mel* (St. Petersburg, Fla.: The Poynter Institute, 1997), p. 8.
24. Steve Outing, "What Journalists Can Learn From Bloggers," Poynter Online, Dec. 8, 2004.
25. John Calhoun Merrill, *Existential Journalism* (New York: Hastings House, 1977), p. 124.
26. Deborah Tannen, *That's Not What I Meant!* (New York: Ballantine Books, 1986), p. ii.
27. See Edward T. Hall, *The Silent Language* (Garden City, N.Y.: Anchor/Doubleday, 1981).
28. Bob Steele, "Doing It Right: A Mini Case Study," Poynter Online, June 6, 2003.
29. E. D. Hirsch Jr., *Cultural Literacy* (New York: Vintage Books, 1988), p. 7.

30. Rick Simonson and Scott Walker, eds., *Multicultural Literacy* (Saint Paul, Minn.: Graywolf Press, 1988), p. xii.

31. E. D. Hirsch Jr., Joseph F. Kett and James Trefil, *The New Dictionary of Cultural Literacy* (Boston: Houghton Mifflin Company, 2002).

32. Quoted in Carole Rich, *Writing and Reporting News* (Belmont, Calif.: Wadsworth Publishing Company, 1997), p. 352.

33. Frances FitzGerald, *Cities on a Hill* (New York: Simon & Schuster, 1986), p. 15.

34. Dorreen Yellow Bird, "Oprah Missed an Important Chance," GrandForksHerald.com, June 6, 2006.

35. Joseph C. Goulden, *Fit to Print: A. M. Rosenthal and His Times* (Secaucus, N.J.: Lyle Stuart, 1988), p. 75.

36. Ron Dorfman and Harry Fuller Jr., eds. *Reporting/Writing/Editing* (Dubuque, Iowa: Kendall/Hunt, 1982), p. 79.

37. Quoted in Christopher Scanlan, *Reporting and Writing: Basics for the 21st Century* (Fort Worth, Texas: Harcourt College Publishers, 2000), p. 179.

38. Nat Hentoff, "Brave Reporters—and the Other Kind," *Village Voice*, March 14, 1989, p. 18.

39. Louis M. Lyons, *Reporting the News* (Cambridge, Mass.: Belknap Press. 1965), pp. 236–241.

40. Randy Shilts, *And the Band Played On* (New York: St. Martin's Press, 1987).

41. "Interview with Bethany McLean," JournalismJobs.com, June 2005.

42. David S. Broder, *Behind the Front Page* (New York: Simon & Schuster, 1987), p. 128.

43. *Making Sense of the News* (St. Petersburg, Fla.: Modern Media Institute, 1983), p. 5.

44. "Alcohol: Cradle to Grave," http://www.gannett.com/go/difference/greatfalls/pages/part1/index.html.

45. James Reston, *The Artillery of the Press* (New York: Harper & Row, 1966), p. 83.

46. Bob Greene, *American Beat* (New York: Penguin Books, 1984), pp. 15, 16.

47. Roger Rosenblatt, "The Journalist as Surrealist," *U.S. News & World Report*, Feb. 6, 1989, p. 10.

Reporting, standing up and on the run Broadcast interviewers set up quickly for interviews and remote reports from the field before rushing off to the newsroom or the next assignment. Backdrops, such as police headquarters, that broadcasters use in their stand-ups provide visual authenticity. (Photo by Robbie Arkovich.)

The Ways and Means of Reporting

2

Charlie Bosworth stood quietly to one side of a conference room at an Illinois State Police complex just outside St. Louis. As Bosworth watched and took notes, a dozen television and print reporters questioned police officials about a massive drug bust that had taken place a few hours earlier. In another room, the state troopers displayed the spoils of the raid: sawed-off shotguns, cash and drugs.

When the briefing ended, Bosworth went to work. Talking easily to state police officers he addressed by first name, Bosworth sought information that went beyond the press release and news conference. Other reporters received polite, standard, no-frills responses, but he obtained details—names, addresses, anecdotes, background.

Bosworth, now a best-selling author of true-crime books, served as a model of public affairs reporting in Madison County, Ill., part of the St. Louis metroplex. Cops trusted him. "He's one of the best in the business," said a state police sergeant. Judges knew he understood the law. Politicians appreciated his integrity and fairness.

Bosworth used to joke about being kept on an electronic leash—his beeper. Actually, his editors at the *St. Louis Post-Dispatch* trusted Bosworth to work independently, juggle multiple assignments, meet deadlines and, most of all, produce accurate, complete stories.

It is not a job for the meek, naive or lazy. Reporters must face tears and curses, recognize snow jobs and scoop the competition. In the course of a career—perhaps in the course of a day—a public affairs reporter will be set up, put down and chewed out. Why, then, do it? Writer Martin Mayer puts it simply: "The reporter wants to know what is happening—I mean, really happening."[1] Mark Twain once explained the lure of the job:

> No other occupation brings a man into such familiar sociable relations with all grades and classes of people. The last thing at night—midnight—he goes browsing around after items among police and jail-birds, in the lock-up, questioning the prisoners and making pleasant and lasting friendships with some of the worst people in the world. And the very next evening he gets himself up regardless of expense, puts on all the good clothes his friends have got—goes and takes dinner with the Governor, or the Commander-in-Chief of the District, the United States Senator, and some more of the upper crust of society. He is on good terms with all of them, and is present at every public gathering, and has easy access to every variety of people.[2]

Twain's feelings still apply. Reporting is an invitation to ask questions, an entree to people and places and a front-row seat to the day's big stories. That is why thousands of journalists across the country find their work exciting and satisfying.

Covering public affairs calls for resourcefulness, knowledge, curiosity, street *and* people smarts and, when warranted, aggressiveness. Public affairs reporters are expected to know what is going on, night or day. Editors count on them to generate significant stories, in depth, but only after they first cover the routine news—from sewer backups to fender benders—quickly and accurately. The job begins on the traditional news beat.

The Beat System

The beat system became a standard method of gathering news in the 1830s. Beginning with Benjamin Day's *New York Sun*, newspapers for the average citizen appeared and prospered in cities like Boston, Philadelphia and Baltimore. Stressing news rather than political commentary, the *Sun* and its imitators sold for a penny a copy, replacing the six-penny journals that fit neither the interests nor the budgets of the average person. The Penny Press era marked the advent of news in its modern sense. Salaried reporters were posted at the city hall, courthouse, police station and capitol to search out and report the news. Today beats include specialized subjects, such as transportation or agriculture, as well as traditional public places.

Beat coverage remains a relatively efficient and effective method of surveillance. Working a beat allows reporters to develop expertise, contacts and continuity in news coverage. But the system has its weaknesses.

Reporters in general tend to overemphasize official viewpoints, a tendency that is greatest on beats. According to a series of studies, reporters rely heavily on a small circle of news contacts and experts, many of them white, male, government executives.[3] Stationed as they are at police headquarters or the courthouse, reporters naturally develop cooperative, regular relationships with certain "reliable" sources.

If an empathic approach is more productive than an adversarial one, then professional "relationships" between reporters and news sources are desirable. But beat reporters who limit their relationships to a handful of official contacts risk becoming unwitting practitioners of "establishment" journalism. In extreme cases, reporters become trapped in arrangements that regress from cooperation to dependency, especially if public officials release or withhold information as a form of reward and punishment. News, then, becomes a hostage, and reporters become vulnerable to pressures they could normally resist. To avoid becoming either a pipeline or pawn of official, elite points of view, the reporter needs to draw constantly on a diversity of news sources.

Although over time it is natural that reporters and the people they cover develop associations that extend outside the beat, complications can arise. A reporter accepts the city attorney's invitation to play on a local softball team; later, both of them find it hard to separate their social and professional roles. The city attorney cannot understand why his buddy, the reporter, refuses to keep a lid on an internal investigation of the police department; the reporter cannot understand why his buddy, the city attorney, would try to stop him from telling an important story.

Some complications are hard to avoid. Reporter Kurt Rogahn of the *Cedar Rapids* (Iowa) *Gazette* encountered awkward situations on the education beat because his wife is a teacher. He explains:

> One morning I got a call from her new principal. He wanted me to come over and talk about an early childhood education institute he had just attended in Washington. It sort of put me on the spot. We don't usually do much with institutes, but I agreed to talk to him. Maybe with somebody else, I would have turned him down on the phone. I think it's a good illustration of what can happen when you know sources.

On the other hand, knowing sources well and personally can be beneficial, as Rogahn points out: "The familiarity works the other way, too. People know me. They trust me. They tell me stories they wouldn't have told me on my first year on the beat. Some have even become whistle-blowers."[4] Reporters walk a tightwire in trying to maintain good relationships on their beats. Ideally, good reporters avoid the extremes—of the adversary or the ally.

Peer pressure also poses problems, particularly on highly competitive beats. Some reporters covering the statehouse, for example, may be reluctant to stray from what other members of the press corps consider the "news" in the governor's budget message. They might confer among themselves about what to emphasize or might fall back on a safe approach—going with a variation of a wire-service summary lead. This follow-the-crowd approach to reporting is called "pack journalism." Timothy Crouse describes a variation of the "pack journalism" phenomenon in his well-cited book— still read in journalism schools—about coverage of the 1972 presidential campaign, *The Boys on the Bus*. Reporters covering a debate during the campaign literally peered over the shoulder of Walter Mears, ace of the Associated Press staff, to see how he would begin his story. As Crouse explains:

> They wanted to avoid "call-backs"—phone calls from their editors asking them why they had deviated from the AP or UPI. If the editors were going to run a story that differed from the story in the nation's 1,700 other newspapers, they wanted a good reason for it. Most reporters dreaded call-backs. Thus the pack followed the wire service whenever possible. Nobody made a secret of running with the wires; it was an accepted practice.[5]

Pack journalism is a danger whenever reporters on beats compare stories or react to each other's signals. For example, a reporter new to the city hall beat discreetly watches veterans take notes during an aldermanic meeting. When they scribble furiously, the rookie figures the ordinance being discussed is significant. But when the old hands slouch listlessly in their seats as the treasurer's report is read, the rookie concludes—perhaps wrongly—that the report is of little news value. Even among the veterans, there is a reluctance to break away from the pack. As a result, news coverage on beats becomes standardized and reporters eventually lose confidence in their ability to judge news independently.

Computer technology puts another form of pressure on journalists. Years ago, beat reporters rarely wrote stories; they relayed information downtown, where the rewrite desk adroitly and speedily converted facts into stories. Once computers and modems allowed beat reporters to file stories directly to the newsroom, the days of "rewrite" were numbered. Today, rewrite persons are about as rare as pastepots and manual typewriters, a development that veteran journalists lament and not merely on sentimental grounds. News executive Michael Gartner remembers his initiation to journalism:

> In those days . . . the rewriteman would pepper the reporter with questions. In effect, the rewriteman was the reporter, and the reporter was the source. I knew that I couldn't turn in any story with holes because (they) would always spot them. So I decided stories I wrote had to be complete and fair and thorough and accurate—in those days, I was thinking more of saving my job than of helping the reader—and that's how I learned to report.[6]

Now beat reporters largely learn those lessons on their own, through trial and error, not under the tutelage of a skilled rewriteman.

REPORTER'S TIP FILE

Getting started on a beat

Orientation for new beat reporters usually involves tagging along for a day—a week at most—with an old hand. It is not a very systematic or effective way to learn a beat. In some cases, the new reporter simply acquires the same routines and sources the old hand relied on. Learning a beat cannot be reduced to a list of tips, but as a starting point, here is some advice:

Introduce yourself

Start with the top person on your beat. It might be the police chief or the chief circuit judge. Meet to explain your goals and perhaps go over some ideas for coverage of the beat. Ask for a tour, if that is appropriate. Some stories may come immediately to mind as you are shown around. Ask to be introduced to employees you encounter and remember their names—including custodians, clerks and secretaries. Introductions by the boss will open doors and loosen tongues. Ask the boss for access to people and records. Then you can say to a reluctant police department clerk, "Chief Jones said it was okay for me to check the incident log personally."

Make a good first impression

A simple way to quickly gain a positive reception on your beat is to do a "good news" story. Focus on awards, achievements and accomplishments. As long as the story is of legitimate news value, you will not blemish your journalistic integrity.

First impressions also influence editors. To start off positively and productively, send your editor a list describing stories you intend to pursue. A good source of ideas is the archive file of previously published stories; propose follow-ups for continuing issues and problems on your beat.

Reconnoiter and make acquaintances

Wander your beat; become familiar with the territory. If people seem willing to talk, "waste" some time in aimless conversation about the weather, ball games and today's teenagers. Remember birthdays; invest in a card. By doing so, you become a part of the place, not an intruder. Drop in on offices and collect directories, annual reports, budgets, in-house publications, organizational charts—anything that will help you get to know the beat. Find out where records are kept. Look about; a memo tacked to a bulletin board may yield a good story.

Educate yourself

Determine the key periodicals and publications on your beat. In colleges and universities, for example, many administrators and professors read or hear about articles in the *Chronicle of Higher Education*. Urge people on the beat to send you copies of important, interesting articles from their professional reading. Ask people what they do with old copies of publications; maybe they will give them to you. And encourage them to recommend books of relevance to your beat coverage. Then read the books and discuss them together.

Be available

Encourage people on your beat to call you. Give them a card with your home and business phone numbers and e-mail address. Investing in an answering machine pays off quickly. Try, as well, to maintain a schedule of when you will be on the premises of your beat. Some reporters establish a routine: coffee at the city manager's office at 9 a.m. on Mondays; a chat with the mayor at 3 on Wednesday afternoons. When people know your schedule, you make it easier and more likely for them to contact you.

Get organized

If you can, arrange a place to use as a home base, especially one with a telephone, an Internet connection and a drop-off point for mail and messages. On a big-city beat, there might be a press room.

Keep track of the whereabouts and agendas of key people on your beat. If you check the mayor's appointment book with a secretary, you may discover the mayor is lunching the next day with Mr. Yamashita and Ms. Osaki. Later the mayor confides, "They're from the Honda company. We're just starting to explore the possibility of Honda opening a plant here. We were hoping to hold off a story until next week, but since you've found out . . . ."

Another organizational tool is a personal file of experts or authorities. Whenever you seek information from someone, add his or her name, phone number, e-mail address, title and specialty to your file ("Jane Murray, grant coordinator, St. Clair County, 555-2323—authority on urban redevelopment"). Include several notations of the person's preferences and inter-ests ("Doesn't like phone interviews, big contributor to the Notre Dame alumni fund"). In fact, some reporters are as valued for their extensive "Rolodex" contacts (now more likely kept in a electronic address book) as for their writing or reporting talents.

Start other print or electronic files as well—a "futures" file to help you remember upcoming events and follow-up assignments; a clip file of published articles so you will not have to depend on the main office for background information; an anecdotal file of material from people on your beat that might be used later for a profile or an obituary; an idea file of material for features or depth stories. "Smart phones," like the BlackBerry system, and other electronic gizmos, such as Apple's iCal, a personalized calendar, help keep journalists connected, organized, up to date and on time.

Get out of the office

A beat is more than a building. Reporters who hang out at city hall or do their legwork by telephone or e-mail get stuck in ruts and miss important stories. Robert Jackson of the *Los Angeles Times* used the term *goyakod* to describe what beat reporters need to do more often: "The word is an acronym around our bureau for 'Go out, you all, and knock on doors.' The more you do that, the more you think you ought to throw away your telephone. . . . You get more out of somebody by seeing them in person. I kick myself every time I've given in out of weakness and simply called somebody on the phone."[7] Reporters who get out and about develop a broader spectrum of sources and different slants on news. Who knows more about traffic jams, dangerous intersections and poorly marked exit signs—a cab driver or a highway engineer? Reporters tethered to their beat are not likely to find out.

Methods of Reporting

Reporters learn about people and issues through *observation, interviews, data-document searches* and *social-science research*. Increasingly, they draw on all four methods. Interviewing, while still the mainstay of reporting methods, often yields what scientists call "impressionistic, anecdotal" evidence, and journalists who draw conclusions based solely on impressions and anecdotes flirt with error and distortion. Interviews remain important, especially for revealing personalities and reliving events, but human sources are fallible. Ideally, stories should be buttressed with multiple evi-dence—what researchers call *convergent validation* or *triangulation*. Convergent vali-dation, in simple terms, means using a combination of methodologies to examine the same phenomenon. A city hall reporter, for example, developing a story about the mayor's first-term effectiveness, might combine the methodologies of interviewing, observation and data analysis (studying the mayor's performance reviews) in seeking a comprehensive picture. One-dimensional, pencil-and-pad reporters may find some stories beyond their reach, particularly those requiring research and quantification.

Observation

Social science provides journalists with models for observation. Urban expert Jane Jacobs demonstrated how to observe city life in her book *The Death and Life of Great American Cities*, and sociologist Ulf Hannerz lived in a black neighborhood to produce his study *Soulside*.

Journalists continue to borrow social-science techniques and apply them to a variety of stories. Gloria Steinem established herself in journalism by landing a job as a Playboy bunny and writing about her experiences; reporter Ben Bagdikian posed as a convicted murderer to write about Cell Block A, his identity unknown to anyone at a Pennsylvania state prison. Hunter Thompson (1937–2005) risked life and limb to ride and party with the Hell's Angels. Tom French spent a year at a Florida high school, listening and observing to produce what he called a "portrait of the place where the battle for our future rages everyday." In *South of Heaven*, a book based upon his earlier newspaper series, French said: "I watched them fall in love, forge fierce alliances, escape death, get accepted to college, laugh their heads off, and dance as though there were no tomorrow."[8]

What does observational reporting yield? Sights-and-sounds reporting or what Gene Roberts, former editor of the *Philadelphia Inquirer*, calls *visual journalism*. Roberts' first boss, editor Henry Belk, was blind. When Roberts' stories lacked vividness and detail, Belk would admonish him, "You aren't making me see; make me see."[9] The idea is to put the reader at the scene, creating a you-are-there feeling. Drawing on an array of physical and emotional senses, observational reporters try to capture mood, symbolism, action, dialogue and characterization. The results can be powerful, as Hunter Thompson shows in the opening scene of his Hell's Angels story:

> California, Labor Day weekend . . . early, with ocean fog still in the streets, outlaw motorcyclists wearing chains, shades and greasy Levis roll out from damp garages, all-night diners and cast-off one-night pads in Frisco, Hollywood, Berdoo and East Oakland, heading for the Monterey peninsula, north of Big Sur. . . . The Menace is loose again, the Hell's Angels, the hundred-caret headline, running fast and loud on the early morning freeway, low in the saddle, nobody smiles, jamming crazy through traffic and ninety miles an hour down the center stripe, missing by inches, like Genghis Khan on an iron horse. . . .
>
> Little Jesus, the Gimp, Chocolate George, Buzzard, Zorro, Hambone, Clean Cut, Tiny, Terry the Tramp, Frenchy, Mouldy Marvin, Mother Miles, Dirty Ed, Chuck the Duck, Fat Freddy, Filthy Phil, Charger Charley the Child Molester, Crazy Cross, Puff, Magoo, Animal and at least a hundred more . . . tense for the action, long hair in the wind, beards and bandanas flapping, earrings, armpits, chain whips, swastikas and stripped-down Harleys flashing chrome as traffic on 101 moves over, nervous, to let the formation pass like a burst of dirty thunder.[10]

Beat reporters rarely enjoy Thompson's degree of literary freedom, but readers appreciate descriptive journalism, even in city council stories. Listen to the engaging

Gloria Steinem, journalist and feminist In the 1960s, Gloria Steinem reported on Hugh Hefner's publishing and entertainment empire by hiring on as a Playboy bunny in a notable example of participant-observation journalism. She later founded and served as publisher of *Ms.* magazine. She remains an influential advocate of women's rights. (Photo courtesy *U.S. News & World Report*.)

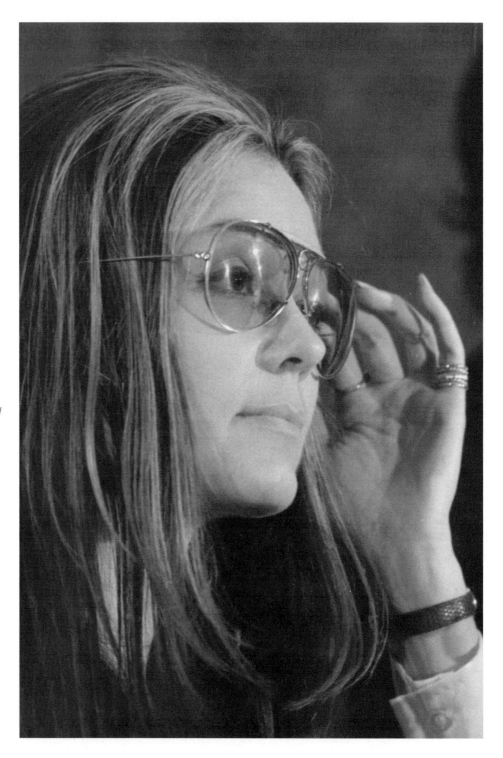

narrative style in *St. Petersburg Times* reporter Alicia Caldwell's opening for a short, simple story about a public forum on the city's proposed budget:

> Willard "Tiny" Weins had worked up a healthy sense of outrage by the time he took the microphone at the first public forum on the city's budget Monday night.
>
> He ranted at City Council members, calling them the "masters" and the residents "slaves." He denounced the city's downtown redevelopment projects. He said he is leaving the city as quickly as he can.
>
> "All the big projects we're building downtown, I know I won't live long enough and you won't live long enough to see them make a profit," said Weins. "This is really, truthfully disgusting. I can't get out of St. Petersburg fast enough."

Observational reporting also provides firsthand insight and experiential knowledge. As Ben Bagdikian explains:

> Prison experts agreed that perception of what it means to be imprisoned in America remains dim unless you are on the other side of the bars. They were right. Months of interviewing prisoners, former prisoners, corrections administrators and research scientists, as well as reading dozens of books and reports, had not prepared me for the emotional and intellectual impact of maximum-security incarceration.[11]

Can you write powerfully and perceptively about the dangers faced by coal miners without going deep into a coal mine? Can you write effectively about the homeless without at least sharing a meal and a park bench with a street person?

Observation not only allows you to describe places, study people and watch from multiple vantage points. Perhaps most important of all, it aids in the formulation of questions. When former *Miami Herald* police reporter Edna Buchanan went to crime scenes, she looked for details to add not only color but accuracy to her stories. The police report may say two bodies were found in a first-floor bedroom, but by visiting the scene, you observe that all the bedrooms are on the second floor. "What gives?" you ask. Some questions occur to you only by being there and seeing for yourself.

QUOTABLES

"In our field, journalism, I trust only those with scuffed shoes. The nicks in the polish, the ground-down heel, the mud and dust on the instep, all of these attest to the act of reporting. Scuffed shoes are evidence of enterprise. . . . There was history before Nexis, and there is research beyond Google. The very ease of online reporting makes it seductive and dangerous. In both the blogosphere and the ever-expanding field of media criticism, I see a version of reporting that eschews human contact and firsthand observation, two things that have an inconvenient way of complicating or contradicting one's preexisting opinions." (pp. 61, 63)

—Samuel G. Freedman, *Letters to a Young Journalist,* New York: Basic Books, 2006

Does observation ensure truth and accuracy? Not always. There may be truthful *versions* of the truth. Reporters must always observe carefully, aware of the potential for distortion, and they must approach the observations of others with similar care and skepticism.

Special caution is needed when it comes to *participant observation*, a method reporters occasionally use to gathering firsthand, intimate, experiential familiarity with the subjects of the story in their natural environment. Long used by anthropologists to study other cultures, journalists employ the technique to get an insider's view, which, presumably, would get them closer to reality—to the truth—than conventional reporting.

Steinem, Bagdikian and Thompson all used participant observation and with impressive results. But no reporting method is perfect, and participant observation has some inherent disadvantages and risks. First, journalists who engage in participant observation flirt with crossing the line that separates the *reporting* of news from the *making* of it. Becoming involved, even for a short time, also severely tests a journalist's ability to eliminate bias. Finally, reporters must decide whether their participation will be covert or overt. To participate covertly means assuming a hidden identity, which poses potential ethical and legal complications; to participate overtly means the reporter's presence is known, and the people under observation may deviate from their normal behavior.

Interviewing

Interviewing is as much an *attitude* as it is a *process*. As the word *inter*-view implies, it is not something one person *does* to another but rather something that is done *together*.[12] Reporters who adopt such an outlook naturally engage in empathic communication. They attempt to see the world of the other person, even if the person across from them is a convicted child molester.

Donald Murray (1923–2006), a journalist, educator and writing coach, encouraged this style of reporting. He offered a list of questions reporters should ask themselves before, sometimes during and even after an interview:

- How does the news source see the world? (Take a moment and view the world as the person you are interviewing sees it.)
- What does that person value?
- What does he or she fear?
- Why should the news source give you information? (And why is that person giving you information?)
- What are the news source's beliefs?[13]

Explaining why such questions are important, Murray said:

> It is one of the great failures of our profession that we assume that everyone inhabits our world. . . . We need to step behind our sources for a moment and imagine what we

would see from behind the mayor's desk, from a bed in the charity ward, from a conference table in the corporate lawyer's suite, from a seatless hopper in the prisoner's cell. If we can get out of ourselves and enter into the lives of those we interview then we may ask perceptive questions and may receive perceptive answers.[14]

Reporters who practice empathy usually operate from a position of strength, not weakness. Rarely do you have to "come on strong" to get answers. A key to empathic reporting is understanding why people are reluctant to talk. Rather than write off an apparently recalcitrant police chief as "a jerk," an empathic reporter tries to determine why the chief frequently says "No comment" or offers monosyllabic answers to questions. Among the internal questions the reporter might ask are these: "Is my method of questioning a turn-off?" "Is it the subject?" "Is the chief fearful of being burned by the press?" "Has he been burned before?" "Is he under pressure from the mayor or city manager to keep quiet?" "Is he, indeed, a jerk with something to hide?" Putting yourself in another person's skin also tends to hold biases in check: As a result you will listen more non-judgmentally and assess more objectively.

Interviewing need not be a selfish act of the reporter *taking* and the news source *giving*. Nor should it be seen as a contest, a test of wills or an interrogation. When reporters and news sources clash or play games with one another, can we expect a story that is fair, meaningful or complete? In many instances, the *amount* and *quality* of the "news" that emerges in an interview depend on how successful the reporter and interviewee are in a *mutual* quest to understand and be understood. Remember, however, that this approach assumes that the interviewee is not withholding information or lying. Occasionally, interviewees do not wish or intend to cooperate.

QUOTABLES

"It is possible, of course, for reporters to overdo their reliance on interviews—to believe that unless something is said during an interview it isn't real. . . . Still, 'interviewing' in the broadest sense involves a reporter's immersion in new information that will shape his views. Through the process of listening, learning, testing assumptions, and letting themselves be surprised by new evidence, reporters decide what they think is true enough to write (p. 58). . . . But the main work of reporting involves asking questions whose answers you don't know, simultaneously exposing your ignorance but opening up the possibility of learning something new." (p. 143)

—James Fallows, *Breaking the News,* New York: Pantheon Books, 1996

As a reporting method, interviewing allows journalists to probe for details, collect anecdotal material, verify conflicting information and capture the unique expressions of news sources. In combination with observational reporting, interviewing produces vivid, potent portraits of events and people. It is wrong, however, to assume that interviewing is simply a natural extension of talking—something intuitive for most of us. It is far more complex than that. Conversational ability certainly helps, but glibness is no guarantee for success. Successful interviewing depends on a reporter's attitude and communication literacy. Glibness cannot overcome self-centered attitudes or communication incompetence.

With time and experience, reporters learn lessons and mature as interviewers. But what happens while they are learning by experience? And what happens if they learn all the wrong lessons? Largely because interviewing is a personal process, advice is difficult to summarize. There is no one universal model for reporters to follow. An interview set in a professor's den may produce dynamics far different from one conducted in an inmate's cell. A style of questioning that works with a police officer may not work with a priest. Because a multitude of variables—personalities, time of day and type of story, to name a few—influence how an interview is conducted, any advice on interviewing must be qualified and generalized.

Like other reporting methods, interviewing is an imperfect process. When people communicate, no matter what their attitudes or how hard they try to mutually cooperate, messages go astray. (Chapter 3 offers guidance on how best to minimize the errors and distortions that occur during interviews.)

Obtaining interviews

For routine interviews, such as collecting eyewitness accounts of an accident, reporters usually identify themselves and start asking questions. Interviews demanding more time and involvement from the news source often warrant a formal request. Veteran reporters advise against seeking an "interview," a word that sounds imposing and intimidating to some people. It is often more useful to seek someone's "thoughts," "ideas" or "background."

Public affairs reporters on beats generally know sources well enough to dispense with the formalities and immediately get down to business. With strangers or "difficult" sources, though, patience and sensitivity may be needed. If someone is "too busy" to see you, be persistent and accommodating ("I really need to compare your perspective with Rep. Smith's, senator; maybe I can drive you to the airport for your flight back to Sacramento"). Remember that a "difficult" source might merely be anxious, insecure or inhibited. Practice empathy to gain a stranger's confidence and cooperation.

When arranging most interviews, state your purpose, review key questions you plan to ask and set a realistic time limit. Keeping an interviewee in the dark usually is counterproductive; being up front encourages openness and enables the interviewee to prepare. If you are calling the city attorney for reaction to a Supreme Court ruling, let her know what you intend to discuss; then she'll be able to do her homework and answer more authoritatively. There is a flip side to forewarning your news sources, however: Notice also gives them a chance to manufacture an artificial answer or concoct an alibi.

Preparation

Preparation enables reporters to ask perceptive, original questions; it also demonstrates to news sources that you are thorough and professional. People tend to trust a prepared reporter. With background information on nearly any subject available at a keystroke through database services and online search engines, there is seldom an excuse for not being prepared.

Greetings and rapport

When meeting news sources for the first time, consider first impressions—yours and theirs. Reporters cannot go wrong using a business-like greeting. Guard against letting first impressions affect your ability to assess and listen fairly. If a politician greets you with, "Well, well. A *lady* of the press," do not devalue what he later says because his seemingly condescending manner offends you. Remember, too, that some people are reluctant to talk to reporters. It may take time to build rapport. If you sense uneasiness, try some ice-breaking small talk to help others relax and feel comfortable talking with you.

Questions and probes

As the interview unfolds, additional questions naturally will surface. Be prepared to alter or abandon your original story focus along the way, if necessary. Guiding you should be this thought: Why is this story worth telling to others? Try to determine what questions readers would ask if they had the chance. If the assignment is to investigate the murky brown water coming out of faucets on the city's southeast side, the first question on the minds of readers will be, "Is it okay to drink?" A simple, "Yes, it's perfectly safe" from city officials will not suffice. Readers will want a fuller explanation and detailed reassurances.

Asking a question is not necessarily going to elicit a good answer—at least immediately. A variety of follow-up questions usually are needed. Some of these secondary questions are called *probes*, which serve to encourage fuller responses. Some probes are nonverbal, like the nod of the head or a smile, suggesting, "Go on; I'm with you." Others are more specific, seeking clarification or amplification: "Could you give me an example?" Above all, never be afraid to say, "I don't understand."

Questions are potent tools of communication whose effect on interview subjects needs to be considered. Some questions hurt, some soothe; some inspire, some bore. Rather than a volley of question-asking and question-answering, try to elevate interviews to the level of dialogue.

Studs Terkel, noted for his penetrating interviews with "non-celebrated" persons, said he gets others to speak so openly by engaging them in conversation. Being interviewed by Studs "is like having the intimacy of a therapist's office," says Sydney Lewis, a colleague of Terkel's and the author of three oral histories.

> You feel like you're cocooned by his interest. He listens really hard. He makes you feel wanted. . . . It's this gift he has. I think it comes from his immense respect for all human beings, and his incredible deep and genuine curiosity—a real hunger to know, a certain

nonjudgmentalness. And there's just something gleeful about him that makes you give him what he's asking for.[15]

Instead of following a strict question-answer format, Terkel talks and listens.

Listening

Hearing and listening are different. You can have perfect hearing and be a terrible listener. Listening, like interviewing, depends on cultivating an appropriate attitude. Good listeners concentrate, blocking out internal and external distractions. Empathy enhances your ability to listen; empathic reporters are receptive listeners. Lillian Ross, famed profiler for *The New Yorker* since 1949, says "*listening* is the quintessential word" for journalists. "I try to listen while I write, and if I can't do both simultaneously, my listening takes priority."[16]

Reporters ought to listen, too, with their eyes. Steady eye contact signals your involvement. Your eyes also help you "listen" for nonverbal communication. If the interviewee wrings his hands, what is the message? Anxiety? You may need to inquire or regulate your interviewing approach if you are making the person uncomfortable.

Indications that you are listening will be reassuring to the interviewee and rewarding for you. Simply leaning toward the speaker and nodding your head—not in agreement but to send the message "I'm with you"—reinforce your involvement. Knowing you are listening, the speaker is likely to reciprocate with greater energy and involvement.

Verification

Interviewing, even face to face, poses possibilities for garbled messages, misunderstandings and errors. Immediate feedback helps clear the air. A simple step to prevent mistakes is the *perception check*. It amounts to a restatement or paraphrase of previous communication. "Judge Owens, let me make sure I understand this *nolo contendere* plea. Correct me if I'm wrong, but it works this way. . . ." The perception check often reveals subtle yet significant shades of difference between what you understand and what the interviewee means.

There will be times when news sources lie, deceive or evade (see Chapter 3 for more examples). Detecting lies is not easy, but doing your homework helps. A well-prepared, well-informed reporter can often expose lies and evasion by pressing the speaker for details and particulars. Later, if necessary, you can seek corroboration through other sources or reinterview the original source to discuss contradictions and discrepancies. Try, though, to resist the urge to automatically question the motives of others. It is right to be alert for hidden agendas, but reporters who are on constant guard for lies or other forms of manipulation might not be able to judge messages objectively.

REPORTER'S TIP FILE

Ernest Hemingway's detection device

In today's world of political spin and doublespeak, reporters and writers also need what Ernest Hemingway described as a "built-in, shockproof, shit detector." Harry G. Frankfurt, a renowned moral philosopher, believes bullshit endangers the truth far more than lies do. "The bullshitter . . . does not reject the authority of truth, as the liar does, and oppose himself to it. He pays no attention to it at all," he says. Frankfurt's observations explain why reporters encounter bullshit so often:

> Bullshit is unavoidable whenever circumstances require someone to talk without knowing what he is talking about. Thus the production of bullshit is stimulated whenever a person's obligations or opportunities to speak about some topic exceed his knowledge of the facts that are relevant to that topic. This discrepancy is common in public life, where people are frequently impelled—whether by their own propensities or by the demands of others—to speak extensively about matters of which they are to some degree ignorant. Closely related instances arise from the widespread conviction that it is the responsibility of a citizen in a democracy to have opinions about everything, or at least everything that pertains to the conduct of his country's affairs.[17]

Do not, however, think of public figures and officials as B.S. artists in general and write off most of what they say. Reporters interviewing public officials should also consider ways they might inadvertently invite B.S., especially questions that do not press for details, context and evidence to support the speaker's statements.

Multitasking in interviews

Sometimes it is hard for reporters to multitask—to observe, interview and take notes at the same time. Walt Harrington, a proponent of "intimate journalism," uses a digital audio recorder to enhance his ability and opportunities to observe. With the audio recorder on, taking down long quotations, he uses his notebook to record facial expressions, body language and verbal clues, such as sighs and hesitations. "At various points in intimate reporting," he says, "it's valuable to just stop whatever you're doing and jot [pertinent] observations in your notes or dictate them into your tape recorder."[18]

Tight spots

From the reporter's perspective, the toughest interviews are those related to a tragedy. No advice will remove the discomfort of having to question the mother whose 6-year-old died in a hit-and-run accident. When those occasions arise, try to be composed, professional and sensitive. Do not be alarmed by tears; they are to be expected. For people in grief, talk about a loved one is a step toward healing the hurt. By asking questions about the tragedy, you may be helping the survivors learn *what* happened and *why* it happened, providing details and answers they have not received from the authorities. Nonetheless, reporters who cover stories of death and suffering must proceed cautiously and caringly. Resist probing grieving people too deeply about hurtful details of a tragedy; these are usually available from others less directly affected. When people do not want to talk, respect their wishes.

Pulitzer Prize-winner Rick Bragg says he takes particular care with so-called ordinary people "who found themselves, for so many reasons, in the path of the train. They were gracious enough to share with me their lives before, during, and after the extraordinary events that made them, for a time, news. I thank them for that."[19]

People in grief or "in the path of the train" are not the only interviewees who are vulnerable. Skilled reporters can reach deep within people, especially those unaccustomed to talking to the press. Journalist Elisa Bildner feels a responsibility when people confide in her. "They'll be holding my hands, pouring out their stories. As you spend hours and hours talking to someone they still know you're a reporter but they think of you as a friend."[20] At times, reporters are obligated to remind people that they are not simply talking to another person; they ultimately are talking to an audience of 100,000 or more.

REPORTER'S TIP FILE

Working the phones

The telephone is an indispensable reporting tool that saves time, beats deadlines and opens clogged avenues of communication.

Paul McLaughlin, author of *Asking Questions*, offers several good reasons for using the telephone to interview and gather information.

- The phone can neutralize power games. If a reporter faces an interviewee noted for intimidation or angry outbursts, the phone serves as a buffer zone. In some cases, it might save a reporter from a physical confrontation.
- The phone can cover an interviewer's insecurities; some reporters are less inhibited when communication isn't face to face. Conversely, some interviewees are more comfortable being interviewed by phone.
- The phone is familiar; North Americans are used to talking by phone and divulging information.[21]

The telephone, however, can be a crutch if reporters use it as an excuse to remain deskbound. Telephone interviews do not allow for observational reporting; they do not allow you to listen with your eyes; they are not conducive to establishing rapport.

On sensitive stories, especially ones containing damaging allegations, never let the telephone lead to irresponsible reporting, such as, "Mayor Thomas could not be reached for

---

comment" or "Mayor Thomas failed to return numerous phone messages left by a *Tribune* reporter." Even if readers do not question such behavior, libel lawyers will: "How many times did the reporter call?" "At what time of day?" "How many messages were left?" "Did the reporter explain the importance of the call?"

With certain stories, fairness demands an exhaustive effort, which includes going to the news source's home and office when phone calls are not successful or sending a certified letter to request an interview. Then if litigation results, the reporter at least can show she tried. No jury is going to be impressed by a reporter who says, "I called several times to get a comment, but I kept getting a busy signal."

Cyberspace interviews

Journalists now regularly conduct interviews by e-mail and other online communication venues, such as chat rooms and blog sites.[22] Some occur in real time, which approximates telephone interviewing but without the benefit (with most current technologies) of hearing actual voices. Online interviews can be like a long-distance chess match: I make a move; you respond and wait for my next move. Although spontaneity suffers, e-mail interviews do afford more time for reflection and consideration than face-to-face or phone interviews. Sometimes, in fact, it's possible to obtain an e-mail interview with a busy person who would otherwise turn you down.

New Yorker writer John Seabrook broke ground in electronic journalism when he based much of his portrait of Microsoft guru Bill Gates on e-mail interchanges. Seabrook thought that Gates, of all people, would be approachable through the so-called information highway. Seabrook sent a brief message identifying himself and explaining the story he was doing, ending with a question: "What do you think is unique about e-mail as a form of communication?" Eighteen minutes later, Gates responded. Their e-mail interview continued intermittently for a month.[23] A productive e-mail interview can also set the stage for an eventual face-to-face meeting.

Despite the advantages of online interviews, be wary of overusing them. Cyberspace interviewing allows a lazy or computer-dependent reporter to avoid legwork—getting outside the newsroom to meet, observe and talk with people in person. When conversation occurs online, you not only miss the body language, tone of voice, visual cues and natural dialogue of in-person interviews, but you can also risk falling victim to someone posing as a reliable source or someone he is not, resulting in the embarrassment, when exposed, of an invented story or hoax. Even when the disclosure online is honest and truthful, it is more likely to be monitored by government agencies or corporate watchdogs. Brant Huston, executive director of Investigative Reporters and Editors, particularly worries about journalists communicating online with confidential sources. "With e-mail," he says, "you're just laying a paper trail of what's supposed to be an anonymous source and an anonymous relationship."[24] (But a paper trail can be a benefit if a source later disputes the accuracy of an article based on an e-mail interview.)

Converged-media interviews

While reporting and news interviewing share common traits and practices across news platforms, in a converged-media operation, they require the special skills of journalists competent in coordinating the printed word with visual images and audiotape interviews. Although the merged-media environment comprises far more than interview-based information, interviewing for information that will be used across platforms complicates the work of reporters. Multimedia interviewers must not only get the facts right; they also must be aware of how facts will be best communicated in visual and auditory contexts.

Documents and Data

With an enormous amount of information now accessible online, reporters possess an incredibly powerful reference and research tool, to which today's journalism students might say, "So what's new?" But their boomer-age professors remember when it took a trip to the courthouse or county building to examine public records, provided they could be easily found and retrieved. The printed materials and stored data that reporters once laboriously searched for and scoured in person now are available at a keystroke from almost anywhere. The Internet, a virtual warehouse of information, includes both the public and private sectors. Even the smallest institutions or businesses use the Internet as a resource, knowing how people routinely seek information online through Google, Ask.com, Yahoo! or other search engines. Journalists still "work the phones" or do "legwork" as they pursue information for stories, but online reporting constitutes an invaluable shortcut, when used prudently and wisely.

Moreover, in digital format, records are organized and accessible by search commands. Not too long ago, reporters walked from their desks to visit the newspaper's "morgue," where they would retrieve previously published articles that had been clipped individually by newsroom clerks wielding long-tipped scissors. The clipped articles were then filed away in envelopes by subject and name headings, not by dates. The traditional newsroom morgues helped reporters acquire background material for stories on a particular topic rather than going through microfilmed, chronological reels of entire publications. Even now, editors often tell reporters to "check the clips," meaning to search digital archives for articles related to a story assignment. Increasingly, news organization allow open, often free, online access to their archives; search engines such as Ask.com help extend archival access to news organizations nationwide. Journalism has come a long way from its morgue days.

The explosive growth of information, together with advances in digital storage and retrieval, is both blessing and bane for journalists. Reporting in the Information Age can be overwhelming: Which materials should I use? How do I get at them? What can I trust as reliable? How much information is enough? Not all stories, of course, warrant extensive data-document searches. The importance and complexity of a story determine the extent of a reporter's search. But let computers do much of the legwork.

Today the enhanced ability of journalists to conduct data-document searches complements other methods of reporting. If the assignment is to produce an in-depth story on dangerous chemicals in drinking water, a thorough reporter might draw on background information from the published record of a congressional hearing, a cover story in *Newsweek*, a report by the state health department and a four-part series from the *Los Angeles Times*—all available online. This material is bricks and mortar for a story—dates, statistics, history and names of expert sources. For example, using databases years before the Internet explosion, reporters for the *Louisville Courier-Journal* developed a 1,600-item bibliography, the foundation of a 30-part series on toxic-waste dumps.[25]

REPORTER'S TIP FILE

Evaluating online sources

Librarian Susan E. Beck provides a guide for evaluating the trustworthiness and value of Web sites using five criteria—authority, accuracy, objectivity, currency and coverage.[26] A sampling of her evaluative methodology follows:

Authority. Is there a named author? Is the page signed? Is the author qualified? An expert? Is the sponsor of the page reputable?

Accuracy. Is the information reliable and error-free? Is there an editor or fact-checker?

Objectivity. Does the information show a minimum of bias? Is the page designed to sway opinion? Is there any advertising on the page?

Currency. Is the page dated? If so, when was the last update? How current are the links? Have some expired or moved?

Coverage. What topics are covered? What does this page offer that is not found elsewhere? What is its intrinsic value? How in-depth is the material?

Beck's guidelines especially help when judging the value of online sources of recent vintage. Reporters, however, wisely gravitate to sources they know well by reputations established long before creation of the Web.

By conducting an extensive background search, reporters also acquire expertise and insight. If you learn, for example, that not all cities put fluoride in drinking water, then you will know to ask whether your city's water is fluoridated. From your search, you become well informed about the various ways municipalities chemically treat water. Your new knowledge makes you a better observer, questioner and evaluator when inspecting the water plant with the public works director and at other points in your pursuit of the story.

Information is everywhere, but first journalists must be aware of what exists and where to find it. Here, in a nutshell, are the main sources:

Libraries

"Libraries must always be lumberyards to use, houses of building supplies," says columnist and grammarian James J. Kilpatrick. "There we go for the facts, dates, documentation that are the cinderblocks and cellar beams of our work. But we also go there for the columns and pediments and finials that add grace and adornment."[27] Libraries contain thousands of books, periodicals, government reports and reference works. Some material can be taken directly from the shelves. Of course, the ivy-covered, stone-columned library now includes a virtual "wing," which means more online visits by patrons.

Virtual libraries lack, of course, the warmth and comfort of bookcases and armchairs. They also suffer from the inherent shortcomings of searching through computer-stored information, often a hit-or-miss proposition. There are too many database services and too many variables in search techniques for electronic-information retrieval to be a snap. Even computer-savvy reporters might, at first, ask an experienced librarian or information specialist for instruction and assistance. The library—far from a relic of the print age—remains a vital hub of tactile, accessible information and human expertise.

The basic reference source for background information, especially for those who do not have access to electronic databases, remains old and reliable—the *Readers' Guide to Periodical Literature*. It provides indexing for approximately 200 magazines. Of the published guides to newspaper articles, the oldest and most complete is the *New York Times Index*, which indexes every article from the *Times'* late city edition by subject, geographic region, organization name and personal name, with ample cross-references. Under the heading "accidents and safety," for instance, are hundreds of "see also" entries, such as "baby carriages" and "skateboards." Abstracts of articles are included and often are detailed enough to save the user from having to examine the full story from the library's microfilmed back issues of the *Times* or conduct a needle-in-the-haystack search online.

Most newspaper reference rooms possess basic works, such as *Statistical Abstract of the United States,* a cornucopia of facts about American life compiled by the U.S. Census Bureau. It, too, now exists in digital form, available online. Among the tidbits of information found in the 2007 edition were these: 1.47 billion credit cards were in use in 2004, more than four cards for every man, woman and child in the United States; more than 415,000 Americans were living with AIDS in 2005; and the number of nuclear power plants has dropped from a high of 112 in 1990 to 104 in 2005. But many newspaper libraries do not possess lesser-known, valuable works like the *Encyclopedia of Southern Culture*, with entries ranging from Henry Aaron (major league home-run king) to zydeco (Cajun music played with an accordion); *What's What: A Visual Glossary of the Physical World*, a collection of illustrated definitions

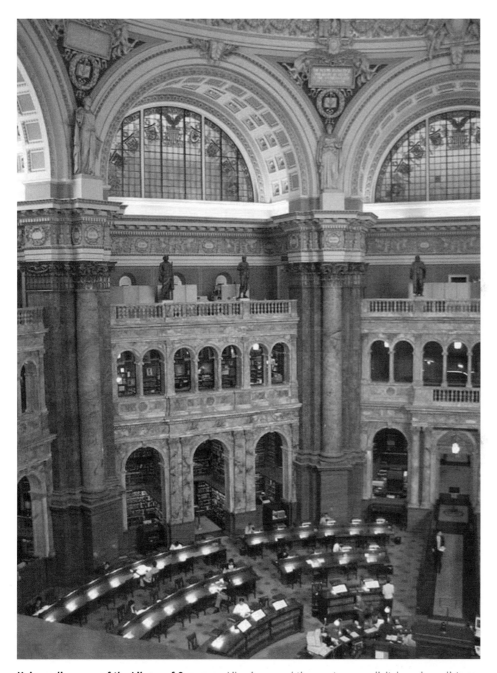

Main reading room of the Library of Congress   Libraries around the country serve digital-age journalists as places to go for answers, inspiration and expertise. In the film *All the President's Men,* reporters Bob Woodward and Carl Bernstein, portrayed by Robert Redford and Dustin Hoffman, pored over Library of Congress records, looking for books checked out by the White House, pursuing one of hundreds of leads in their famed Watergate investigation. (Photo courtesy of Soon Lee Teoh.)

of thousands of items, such as the nomenclature of a revolver; or *Maps on File*, which contains a vast assortment of maps, including, for example, one of the United States that highlights the states that suffered the greatest crop losses of drought years. A well-stocked library has an extensive reference section that detail-hungry reporters turn to regularly.

Other important, frequently used library sources include:

City and telephone directories

Until 1999, the R.L. Polk Co. of Detroit published directories for more than 1,400 U.S. cities. Each directory contains the name, address, telephone number, occupation and place of employment for adult residents of the city. Information is cross-listed by address. Polk directories also provide historical and statistical information about the city. Online people-search services rendered the Polk city directory obsolete, but libraries maintain past editions, dating as far back as 1893, partly for their historic value.

Phone books and city directories are basic tools with which reporters check names and addresses. Keep in mind, though, that any directory may contain dated, incomplete or erroneous information that should be double-checked. Online services enjoy no immunity to errors.

Biographical references

Who's Who in America provides sketches of more than 75,000 noteworthy living people. *Webster's Biographical Dictionary* briefly profiles 40,000 historically significant figures. Lengthier biographical profiles of famous living persons are found in *Current Biography*. There also are specialized biographical references for notable figures in art, journalism, medicine and science, for example.

Directories: The directory is a key to unlock warehouses of background material. Directories connect reporters with organizations and associations that function, in part, to provide services and information to the public. Five important sources are *The Foundation Directory, Consumer Sourcebook, Directory of Newsletters* (www.news-letteraccess.com), *Encyclopedia of Associations* and *Directory of Directories*. Using a directory as a guide, a reporter looking into U.S. Department of Transportation rules on wheelchair access to airlines might end up talking to a helpful spokesperson for the Paralyzed Veterans of America. Prior to referring to the directory, the reporter probably had no idea an organization of paralyzed veterans existed. Keyword searches online can also yield "beverages," under which you will find the Beer Institute and the International Bottled Water Association, and "metals," where you will find the Aluminum Association and the Institute of Scrap Recycling Industries.

Dictionaries

In newsrooms, the preferred source is *Webster's New World College Dictionary* (fourth edition), largely because it supports the Associated Press stylebook on questions of spelling and usage. For precision in the use of words, writers refer to sources such as the *Harper Dictionary of Contemporary Usage*, which will, for example, explain the difference between *continual* and *continuous* or provide the etymology of terms like *mickey finn*, or the *American Heritage Dictionary of the American Language*, which contains colloquial words such as *snarf*, presumably a combination of (sn)ort and sc(arf). Libraries stock dictionaries for nearly every field of knowledge, and generally these special collections will not be found stacked in a newsroom.

Encyclopedias

The printed, multivolume *Encyclopaedia Britannica* remains the *piece de resistance* of the reference world. Before the Internet and digital storage, America's families bought encyclopedias sold by door-to-door salespeople. To be without a set was not quite considered intellectual-educational child abuse—but close to it. At more than $2,000 for its complete "suite" of print and electronic materials, the 2007 *Encyclopaedia Britannica* is not something most 21st-century households will purchase, especially when online reference services, such as Wikipedia, are available for free. (Wikipedia, a collaborative collection of information written, edited and updated by its users, lacks the reputation for reliability and scholarship found in commercial publications.) The library houses a range of encyclopedic overviews of subjects, places and people. A reputable, well-researched encyclopedia is the recommended starting point for scholars, students and journalists to become familiar with a topic or individual before conducting a more focused search.

QUOTABLES

"Those of us who learned our journalism before the mid-1990s, . . . understand that not all of the world's accumulated knowledge exists on Web servers, and probably never will. . . . In the United States alone, more than three centuries' worth of records exist in non-digital form, and not every record generated today is computerized. . . . [S]earch-engine journalism won't allow us to dig deeply. While teaching the wonders of the Internet, we also must emphasize the importance of archives and libraries and human beings. Tomorrow's journalists must learn that the Internet hasn't made other research skills obsolete. It has made them more valuable—and necessary." (p. 74)

—John Lenger, "If a Tree Doesn't Fall on the Internet,
Does It Really Exist?" *CJR*, September-October, 2002

Government

A river of information, fed by dozens of tributaries, flows from government on the federal, state and local levels. Although government information is sometimes as murky and polluted as some river water, journalists cannot ignore or underestimate the studies, surveys and reports churned out daily by government offices. Reporters use government documents to produce important stories—on dangerous chemicals in fruits and vegetables, safety lapses at nuclear power plants, violent assaults on school teachers and near-collisions of passenger aircraft.

The single best guide to federal documents is the *Catalog of United States Government Publications*. Published by the U.S. Government Printing Office, it indexes material produced by federal agencies, departments and Congress. A reporter scanning the index for information about drug smuggling finds a hearings report by a Senate subcommittee investigating terrorism, narcotics and foreign policy. The hearings report is likely to be listed under several subject headings, such as "narcotics" or "foreign policy." If the report seems promising, the reporter can obtain a copy either from a library designated as a depository for government publications or directly from the agency or government branch that issued the report. A great deal of government information is available online.

Two other GPO publications are the *Congressional Record*, a daily, edited account of House and Senate proceedings, and the *Federal Register*, a daily compilation of rules and information issued by federal regulatory agencies. Not everything in the *Congressional Record* comes directly and verbatim from debate or discussion on the floor of the House or Senate. Members of Congress may edit remarks and insert assorted trivia and extraneous material, such as newspaper editorials, into the *Congressional Record*.

Remember that information produced by federal agencies and offices holds promise for local reporters as well as those assigned to Washington, D.C., bureaus. Congressional hearings, in particular, are valuable for background. Not only do they contain testimony by expert witnesses and their exchanges with congressional members and staff, but they also frequently include appendices of published material relevant to the subject of the hearings. Comparable indexes and government publications are also available on the state level.

Two other information sources used frequently by journalists are *blue books* and *statutes,* and they come in print and online versions.

Blue books

Blue books are directories of the executive, legislative and judicial branches of state government, although not all blue books are blue. For years, Missouri's blue book carried a green cover because the secretary of state was an Irishman. Most blue books contain profiles of state officials and information on agencies, departments and commissions and they generally are available to download online. At times, they yield newsworthy nuggets of information. The 2006 Illinois blue book, for example, describes the functions of the Division of Nuclear Safety, noting that its staff inspects and escorts every highway or rail shipment of spent nuclear material through the state. In an earlier report, the division said nearly half of the state's 5,000 X-ray machines checked the previous year failed to comply with safety standards after two inspections. The federal government's equivalent of the blue book is the *United States Government Manual*.

Statutes

Public affairs reporters often turn to bound collections of state or federal statutory law. In a digital age, most states now post their statutes online; for example, the state of Florida calls its Web site for legislative and statutory records "Online Sunshine." State statutes cover a broad, detailed range of laws passed by lawmakers. A dozen pages might be devoted to meat-packing regulations; another section might deal with procedures for drunk-driving arrests. Knowing the statutory law is essential in a society so entangled with legal issues. When the district attorney cracks down on adult book stores, an alert court reporter will study all applicable anti-obscenity laws. Annotated versions of statutes contain the legislative histories and legal interpretations of laws.

Government resources include compilations of reported court decisions at the state and federal levels. These sources will be discussed in Chapters 8 and 9.

Private sector

The pursuit of information may lead to dealings with lobby groups, special-interest organizations, business and trade associations, non-profit institutions and universities. Reporters are right to question information, especially from those trying to enhance images, sell products, shape public opinion or influence legislation. But do not automatically dismiss information from the private sector on grounds that it may be slanted. Be receptive but discriminating.

Companies and organizations usually have Web sites and free 800 telephone numbers, which help reporters obtain background information. During the brouhaha over the gambling troubles of baseball player and manager Pete Rose, two *Chicago Tribune* reporters called 1-800-GAMBLING, the phone number of the Illinois Council on Compulsive Gambling. Answering the phone was the organization's executive director, who provided quotable responses about compulsive gamblers. The organization is now called the Illinois Council on Problem and Compulsive Gambling, and it invites e-mail queries but still posts a phone number.

Often reporters must work through public relations representatives to obtain access to news sources or information in the private sector. To some reporters, public relations is practiced by unprincipled hacks; they are "hired guns." Actually, many people in public relations come from respectable careers in journalism. Normally, public relations people are as accommodating as their roles permit, provided the reporter is fair and decent in return.

Journalism sites

The near-astounding availablility of data and documents online encourages journalists everywhere to undertake investigative projects. Several helpful resources for journalists include JournalismNet.com, a rich reservoir of tips, links and resources for journalists doing Internet research and investigations, and the National Institute for Computer-Assisted Reporting (www.nicar.org).

Other professional organizations, such as the American Society of Newspaper Editors (www.asne.org), the Society of Professional Journalists (www.spj.org) and the American Press Institute (www.americanpressinstitute.org) offer tips and links to aid reporters. The Poynter Institute, a school for professional journalists, daily posts articles, links and studies helpful to journalists in their writing and investigations (www.poynter.org).

REPORTER'S TIP FILE

The cross-check game

Individual journalists often share their experiences and investigative techniques with their colleagues through seminars, workshops or Web postings. Joe Adams, a journalist and author of *The Florida Public Records Handbook*, encourages the use of public records to produce powerful stories through the method of cross-checking. For example, he suggests various comparisons as a starting point. Take, for example, data on fire station locations and compare it to flood-zone maps. Here are several other cross-checks even a beginning reporter could conduct with generally accessible public records:

- Sexual predator/offender database + school bus stop locations
- Teacher rosters + criminal background checks + sexual predator/offender database
- Elected constitutional officers + campaign contributions + employee raises/bonuses/promotions

In Adams' words, "Important life decisions hinge on what we know. From buying property and checking criminal backgrounds to selecting a school and researching a doctor, public records offer crucial insights for informed choices about our families, businesses, government and ourselves."[28] (A related Web site is www.idiganswers.com.)

The computer is a powerful ally for people engaged in gathering news, but, like the telephone, it can further tie reporters to the office when they should be out interviewing and observing. Reporters are advised not to use database services as a shortcut or excuse to bypass other methods of reporting. Nor should journalists accept everything from computers as gospel; all material from databases should be checked for accuracy.

Professional reading

Prepared, informed and enterprising reporters are eclectic readers. They do not subsist on a diet of big-city newspapers or *Time* and *Newsweek*. Instead, they seek insight and ideas from a diversity of sources, such as *Rolling Stone*, the *National Review, Mother Jones, Fortune, Money*, the *Village Voice, Cosmopolitan, Washington Monthly, Columbia Journalism Review*, the *New Yorker, Esquire* and *Wired,* to name but a few. They not only read; they clip or download articles for future use and story ideas.

Alert reporters also monitor the trade press, which often provides tips and background for their own reporting. John Gannon, a reporter for the *Daily Report of Executives*, focused on a obscure federal agency, the Chemical Safety and Hazard Investigation Board, and its investigations of several major accidents at industrial plants. Based on the board's findings, he reported that government officials were exercising little oversight over how diligently companies followed instructions for the safe handling of industrial chemicals. In another trade press scoop, the *Government Computer News* uncovered egregious resume padding by a top U.S. Department of Homeland Security official, which led federal agencies to tighten screening of job applicants.[29]

Social-Science Research

Communication theorist Alexis Tan describes the casual, non-scientific methods many people, including journalists, use to explain why things happen or conditions exist.[30] The methods are fraught with potential for error. One is the *method of tenacity*. Many beliefs are held simply because people always considered them to be true. How many children, for example, heard their mothers say, "If you play with frogs, you'll get warts"? Who has not used the expression, "Lightning never strikes the same spot twice"? By repetition, certain knowledge becomes engrained and feels unassailable. Tenacity, however, does not equal proof.

When evidence is conflicting or unclear, people turn to experts for proof—the *method of authority*. Seeking out experts is not inherently bad. Too many experts, though, are media ordained. In journalism circles, the method of authority involves "rounding up the usual suspects." The suspects are what media people call "quote-meisters" who traffic in opinion. They often become experts because of a job title they hold (or held) or a hot-selling book they have written. After being interviewed repeatedly by reporters and television hosts, they meet the basic criteria for authority status: availability and quotability. According to Marshall Wittmann, a senior fellow at the Democratic Leadership Council and a former GOP official, the quoting practices of journalism have become a self-validating process. "These people have been quoted so often that they've become the high priests of observerdom," he says.

Whether they are indeed knowledgeable and authoritative is another matter. Michael Abramowitz, national editor at the *Washington Post,* discourages his staff from recycling the pool of quoted experts. "Reporters should always be trying to challenge their assumptions about things," he says. "If we're talking to the same people all the time, we're not challenging our assumptions."[31]

Sometimes people let their gut feelings or common sense suffice as proof. Tan calls this the *method of intuition*. Intuition may be on target, but guard against being led astray by "gut feelings." A reporter whose intuition tells him "the mayor is a crook" may look for "evidence" that supports his intuitive sense and dismiss "evidence" that weakens his case.

Reporters who care about accuracy and fairness know the value of the *scientific method*. The scientific method takes various forms, but basically it involves a systematic, objective, vigorous search for answers. Scientific inquiry usually begins with a problem or question: "Why can't Johnny's father read?" Preliminary explanations are explored, and eventually a hypothesis is developed: "Johnny's father can't read because the educational system failed him and thousands like him." Next come careful study, observation and verification to confirm or refute the hypothesis. Finally, the findings and conclusions are presented in a report, which itself is subject to further scrutiny.

Although reporters may not follow the scientific method step by step, they should be guided by the spirit of scientific inquiry, particularly its emphasis on *doubt*. The scientific method demands that facts, theories, causes and effects be challenged and, if found suspect or wanting, rejected. Fallacies of reasoning and observation are considered; the potential for error is weighed; variables are explored; criteria are established and defined. A scientific-method reporter who wants to identify America's most dangerous city does not simply telephone a handful of quotable experts, plug in FBI crime statistics, relate some juicy anecdotes and call it a day. She questions the statistics, looking for variables; she pins down criteria to avoid loosely using the term *most dangerous;* and she asks a qualified social scientist to review her methods and conclusions. In journalism, the scientific method is most evident in political polls, opinion surveys, statistical interpretation and field experiments.

Surveys and polls

Opinion research is tricky business, but if done well, it reveals important and sometimes surprising findings. Opinion surveys challenge the conventional wisdom of experts and politicians who claim to know what the public thinks. According to conventional wisdom, let's say, Americans want to see drug-using pregnant women criminally punished for putting their unborn children at risk; an opinion poll reveals that 75 percent of the people polled believe society's proper response is counseling and medical assistance, not jail terms.

Care is needed in measuring opinions. Reporters, used to doing person-on-the-street polls, may assume that a random sample involves questioning people leaving a shopping center. There is randomness to such a method, but to be considered "random" in scientific terms, the sampling must be representative of the population defined in the study. Measuring opinion requires planning, pretesting and precision. Objectives are set; sample sizes determined; questionnaires constructed and reviewed; sample errors estimated; data collected, processed and interpreted. It is not a task for the uninitiated.

Do not, though, let the methodology of polling discourage you from doing opinion measurement. Some newspapers employ researchers to help conduct polls; a reporter with little experience in opinion polls can seek assistance from a social scientist, who probably is as nearby as the local university. Experiment in scientific polling on a small scale, asking a professional to critique your work. Remember, too, that legwork and door knocking remain valuable as informal, non-scientific ways of sampling how people feel about issues and events.

Even a well-constructed survey cannot be counted on to provide a perfect representation of the population studied. All sound surveys build in a *margin of sampling error*. The margin of error is based on several factors, among them the size of the sample population. Normally, the larger the sample, the smaller the margin of error. Let's say the margin of error is a plus or minus 5 percent. If a poll shows that 52 percent of the voters favor the incumbent, Sen. Thomas, that means Thomas' support could range from 57 to 47 percent. With such a wide margin of error, the reliability of polls to predict outcomes clearly is limited.

Whether reporters conduct opinion surveys themselves or report the results of surveys conducted by others, they must be wary of the power of polls, particularly voter surveys, to influence people and events. A common problem with campaign polls arises when they are used, like a scorecard, to keep tabs on who is leading and who is trailing or to predict, even before voting places close, winners and losers. A better use for campaign studies is to explain the bases and implications of voter behavior.

When relying on surveys conducted by outsiders, reporters are responsible for ensuring that polls do not manipulate or deceive. One safeguard is to include a "truth-in-polling" disclosure in all stories or broadcasts reporting the results of opinion surveys. The statement should disclose who sponsored the poll, how many people were sampled, what questions (with exact wording) were asked, who did the interviewing, how accurate the results are (the margin of error) and how the results were tabulated and analyzed. The *New York Times*/CBS News Poll includes a comparable disclosure statement.

Recently, political analysts spurred renewed fears that voters sometimes lie to pollsters, particularly over questions they are not willing to answer honestly, such as feelings about black candidates. In all instances, polls must account for the reliability of respondents. Surveys still involve a degree of guesswork, which is why political scientist Larry Sabato advises, "Let's pay a great deal less attention to polling. . . . You cannot precisely predict what human beings are going to do."[32]

Statistical analyses

Frequently, the grist for statistical analyses comes from readily available sources, like census data or court records. The term *statistics* refers both to a science and to the process of assembling, classifying and tabulating numerical data. Journalists long have used quantitative data in stories, shifting through piles of records and collecting numbers by hand.

Use of statistics is more common and meaningful now that "number crunching" by computer allows reporters to quickly test hypotheses and seek correlations. Suppose a court reporter decides to determine whether the state's new drunk-driving law is resulting in increased arrests and stiffer sentences, as its proponents claim. If driving-while-intoxicated cases are computerized, those claims can be put to a test quickly. *USA Today* uses computers to conduct nationwide statistical studies. A few years ago, the newspaper examined crime on college campuses, using a team of reporters to collect numerical data and conduct thousands of interviews. In one aspect of its computer analysis, *USA Today* identified and charted a campus "fear index" by region.

When public records, such as crime figures, are available on computer, a printout or tapes of raw data ought to be easy to obtain. Several software packages enable news organizations to take government records stored on tape drives and transfer them to personal computers for easier use and analysis. But raw data alone are not enough. A saying describes the problem of feeding questionable statistics into a computer: "Garbage in, garbage out." Reporters using statistical material must be sure data are sound and accurate.

REAL-LIFE LESSONS

The *Kansas City Star* spent more than four years researching the prevalence of AIDS in the priesthood and 18 months interviewing experts and priests and examining church documents and death certificates to ensure that its study was grounded in fact. In January 2000, the newspaper published an 11-article series based on surveys and statistics that concluded priests were dying of AIDS in the United States at a rate at least four times higher than the general population.

Controversy followed. A number of critics and colleagues felt that what the *Star* published was based on flawed research methodology and analysis. Among them was *Columbus Dispatch* reporter Jennifer Halperin, who interviewed a statistics expert who found the comparison between priests and the general public invalid. The expert pointed out the obvious: Priests are adult males. The general population includes women and children, who are much less likely to be infected with HIV. "By some calculations the AIDS death rate of adult males is about 4 per 10,000—about the same as the death rate among priests, and four times as high as the general population," the expert said.[33]

Critics also questioned the *Star*'s survey of 3,000 priests that yielded 801 anonymous responses. Was it too small a sampling and was it representative?

Still another critic asked: What if the editors compared priests to the most appropriate control group, other unmarried men? Would the headline then have read, "Celibacy saves lives"?

Star editor Mark Zieman was later quoted in *Editor & Publisher* magazine as saying, "We had the story reported at the time we decided to do the poll. But we felt the poll would lend more credibility. We believed we would be criticized for being too anecdotal, not scientific enough. We learned a big lesson. This has been a cautionary tale."[34]

The lesson: *Question the authority and validity of numbers, even those, at first glance, that seemed solid. In the* Star *episode, Philip Meyer, the author of the groundbreaking books* Precision Journalism *and the* New Precision Journalism, *said journalists tend to put scary information in the lead and then, buried deep in the story, add qualifying information. That is what the* Star *did; it provided a male-to-male comparison, but way too late, Meyer says.[35] Statistical controls and doublechecks would have spared the* Star *its embarrassment.*

Those preparing for careers in journalism ought to consider studying computer science, information systems and statistics. Some social-science methodology involves sophisticated computer-generated tabulation and manipulation of data that can only be conducted by highly trained researcher-reporters. Help is also available from several news organizations, among them the National Institute for Computer-Assisted Reporting.

Field experiments

Reporters should feel at home with field research that employs *controlled experiments*. Reporters have used field-experiment methods to determine whether ZIP codes get mail to destinations faster or whether small-town residents are more likely than urban residents to help a lost child. In controlled experiments, the researcher manipulates conditions or situations—the *independent variables*—to observe and measure effects. Independent variables are factors believed to cause or influence certain conditions. Suppose that real estate agents in the town of Pine River are rumored to discriminate against blacks. Since people are unlikely to admit they are breaking fair-housing laws, a field experiment might be the best way—perhaps the only way—to determine whether discrimination exists. So a black reporter and a white reporter separately visit all the town's real estate offices, posing as prospective home buyers. All field experiments, however, must be carefully designed, structured and controlled to ensure validity. Otherwise, there is a high probability that evidence will be flawed. For example, something other than race, such as differences in age, dress or manner, could influence how real estate agents treat the reporters.

As with other types of social-science research, problems arise in drawing conclusions based on field findings. In checking the honesty and competence of auto-repair shops, a reporter takes a car in perfect condition to several shops. Later, another car, with sparkplug wires intentionally crossed, is taken to a half-dozen other garages. When a shop charges $100 for an unnecessary tune-up, does that mean the owner cheats—or merely employs inept mechanics? Reporters have to be prepared to accept that the results of some field experiments may be inconclusive.

Field experiments can also be harmful, illegal or unethical. Several news organizations, including CBS News, have tested post–September 11 airline security by smuggling prohibited items, including knives, razors and pepper spray, through checkpoints at airports around the country.[36] When field experiments involve breaking the law or endangering people, they are difficult to justify.

The information this chapter provides on methods of reporting is not definitive. It is intended to point you in the right direction and to alert you to the reporting *problems* and *possibilities* ahead. Build on the fundamentals. Continue to learn and develop your research abilities. Ask for help when unsure of what to do. Never forget that the ultimate objective of all reporting methods is accuracy and *the best obtainable version of the truth*. All reporters stumble and err. Chapter 3 is intended to help you recognize and avoid the errors most common to reporting.

Exercises

1. Test the accuracy of your note-taking by watching "Meet the Press" or a presidential news conference and then comparing your handwritten notes to a transcript found at msnbc.com or another news Web site. Identify your mistakes and try to determine how or why they occurred.

2. Enlist the help of a documents librarian to track down congressional hearings or government reports on a subject of current interest, such as Medicare.

3. Attempt a field experiment to test a theory of your choice. You and other students might, for example, travel by various taxi companies to investigate suspicions that fares between downtown and the airport differ because some cab drivers charge higher fees for luggage or take roundabout routes.

Notes

1. Martin Mayer, *Making News* (Garden City, N.Y.: Doubleday, 1987), p. 9.
2. Quoted in Mayer, *Making News*, p. 2.
3. Jane Delano Brown, Carl R. Bybee, Stanley T. Wearden and Dulcie Murdock Straughan, "Invisible Power: Newspaper News Sources and the Limits of Diversity," *Journalism Quarterly*, Spring 1987, pp. 45–54. See, as well, Leon V. Sigal, *Reporters and Officials* (Lexington, Mass.: D.C. Heath, 1973).
4. Barbara Hipsman and Carl Schierhorn, "Sharpening the Eyes and Ears of Your Newspapers," *ASNE Bulletin*, January 1989, p. 14.
5. Timothy Crouse, *The Boys on the Bus* (New York: Random House, 1973), pp. 21, 22.
6. Quoted in "The Making of Journalists," *Gannet Center Journal*, Spring 1988, p. 38.
7. Quoted in Gary Atkins and William Rivers, *Reporting with Understanding* (Ames, Iowa: Iowa State University Press, 1987), p. 6.
8. Tom French, *South of Heaven* (New York: Doubleday, 1993), pp. xi, xii.
9. Gene Roberts, address before the American Society of Newspaper Editors, 1984.
10. Hunter S. Thompson, *Hell's Angels* (New York: Ballantine Books, 1967), p. 11.
11. Ben H. Bagdikian, *The Shame of the Prisons* (New York: Pocket Books, 1972), pp. 35, 36.
12. George M. Killenberg and Rob Anderson, *Before the Story* (New York: St. Martin's, 1989).
13. Donald M. Murray, "Writing on Writing," No. 3, *Boston Globe*, January 1988, p. 1.
14. Murray, "Writing on Writing," p. 2.
15. Ronald Kovach, "Studs Terkel on the Art of Interviewing," *The Writer*, May 2002, p. 26.
16. Lillian Ross, *Reporting Back: Notes on Journalism* (Washington, D.C.: Counterpoint Press, 2002), p. 8.
17. Harry G. Frankfurt, *On Bullshit* (Princeton, N.J.: Princeton University Press, 2005), pp. 61, 63–64.
18. Walt Harrington, *Intimate Journalism* (Thousand Oaks, Calif.: Sage Publications, 1997), p. xxx.
19. Rick Bragg, *Somebody Told Me* (New York: Vintage Books, 2000), p. 3.

20. Elisa Bildner, remarks at a seminar of the Poynter Institute for Media Studies, St. Petersburg, Fla., June 5, 1989.

21. Paul McLaughlin, *Asking Questions* (Vancouver: International Self-Counsel Press, 1986), pp. 37–42.

22. Adapted from Rob Anderson and George M. Killenberg, *Interviewing: Speaking, Listening, and Learning for Professional Life* (Mountain View, Calif.: Mayfield, 1999).

23. John Seabrook, "E-mail from Bill," *The New Yorker*, Jan. 10, 1994, p. 48.

24. Quoted in Kim Hart, "Inbox Journalism," *AJR*, December 2005–January 2006, p. 60.

25. John Ullmann, "Tapping the Electronic Library," *IRE Journal,* Summer 1983, p. 9.

26. Susan E. Beck, "Evaluation Criteria," *The Good, The Bad & The Ugly: Or, Why It's a Good Idea to Evaluate Web Sources*, 1997: http://lib.nmsu.edu/instruction/evalcrit.html.

27. James J. Kilpatrick, *The Writer's Art* (New York: Andrews, McMeel & Parker, 1984), p. 51.

28. Joe Adams, "Evidence Abounds; Public Records Are Public Treasures," *The Brechner Report*, April 2004, p. 4.

29. Robert Freedman and Steven Roll, eds., *Journalism That Matters: How Business-to-Business Editors Change the Industries They Cover* (Oak Park, Ill.: Marion Street Press, 2006).

30. Alexis S. Tan, *Mass Communication Theories and Research*, 2nd ed. (New York: Wiley, 1985), pp. 10, 11.

31. Mark Francis Cohen, "The Quote Machine," *AJR*, April–May 2005, pp. 54–59.

32. John Diamond, "Unexpected Outcomes Mean Voters May Be Lying to Pollsters," *St. Petersburg Times*, Sept. 24, 1990, p. 5a.

33. Tamara Slomka, "Why Too Many Journalists Get Crunched by Numbers—and Why Their Stories Often Don't Add Up," *Ryerson Review of Journalism,* Spring 2003.

34. Slomka, "Why too many. . . ."

35. Margaret Sullivan, "Some Doubts from a Founder," *CJR*, May–June 2001, p. 39.

36. Jane Kirtley, "Testing the System," *AJR,* November 2002, p. 70.

Striving for Accuracy 3

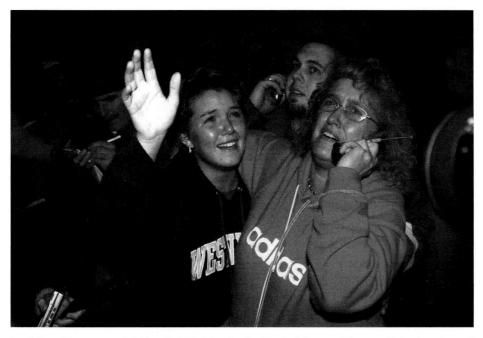

Joy followed by sorrow   Outside a West Virginia mine, families joyfully spread the news that a dozen trapped miners had been rescued. The news media conveyed the news to the world. Hours later, joy turned to sorrow when the true story emerged. (Photo by Todd Maisel, courtesy the *New York Daily News*.)

The news spread brushfire-quick at tiny Sago Baptist Church.

"They're alive," people shouted. Gathered in vigil for two days, the relatives of 13 workers trapped by an explosion deep in a West Virginia mine hugged one another and praised the Lord. Expecting bad news, their prayers seemed answered. The church bell tolled, and people ran along the road leading to the mine entrance to greet their loved ones once rescuers brought them to the surface. Swept up in the pandemonium, newspaper, radio, cable and television reporters stationed outside the church proclaimed the good news in breathless commentary and banner headlines. "Alive! Miners beat odds," *USA Today* trumpeted in its Jan. 4, 2006, edition. Other major news organizations, such as the *New York Times*, *Chicago Tribune* and *St. Petersburg Times*, joined the chorus.

Hours later the truth emerged. Only one miner survived. Joy turned to disbelief. Disbelief turned to anger. The families accused mine officials of lying to them and cursed news crews at the scene. Media organizations asked, "How could we get this so wrong?" In the end, answers remained unclear. Early news reports relied on attribution from relatives, giddy with joy. Did someone spread false information or did correct information get distorted through the filter of hopeful thinking? Regardless, the press committed a tragic error and people suffered needlessly as a result. In the rush to get the news out, reporters forgot a fundamental rule: Get solid attribution before releasing news publicly.

Errors happen daily in journalism. No one is perfect. At some point, all reporters err in print or on the air. Consider how confusing, complex and ambiguous stories can be. Consider, too, the fallibility of human communication, and then add deadline pressure. Columnist-commentator Andy Rooney, remembering his reporting days, understands how mistakes are made. "I am constantly amazed at how difficult it is to get accurate information about anything," he says. "No reporter sets out to print an inaccurate story but the truth is hard to come by."[1] Of course, Rooney himself inaccurately generalizes. Journalists, indeed, put inaccurate, false or fictitious stories into circulation. Chapter 3, however, focuses on the avoidable, innocent mistakes, not the mortal sins of plagiarism and fabrication of the news, which get needed attention in Chapter 11.

Despite the inevitability of errors, journalists must embark upon every assignment with Joseph Pulitzer's legendary refrain ringing in their ears—"Accuracy, accuracy, accuracy." More is at stake than professional pride or press credibility. When reporters err, lives can be affected. Although there is much talk about the power of the press to influence public policy and issues, that sort of power is abstract and difficult to measure. More concrete and measurable in human terms is the power of the press to confuse, inconvenience, embarrass or harm through erroneous reporting.

Grievous errors, like those that occurred during the West Virginia mine tragedy, are infrequent, thank goodness, but never underestimate the impact of so-called minor mistakes. Look at what happens, for example, when a reporter fails to double-check information about a public hearing on plans to reroute a state highway. Instead of confirming the time, date and place of the hearing, the reporter assumes the Department of Highway's press release is current and correct. It is not. The hearing is important to Tom and Tracy Gordon, whose home is in the path of the state's plans. So the Gordons and a dozen other homeowners, relying on information in the hometown newspaper, turn up on Thursday night at City Hall. They find the building dark and empty; a handwritten notice tacked to the door says, "Meeting postponed." Inconvenienced and miffed, the Gordons are reminded of other mistakes in the newspaper, like the time a family member's name was misspelled in an obituary. "You can't depend on them to get anything right," Tracy Gordon says. The next day, they call to cancel their subscription.

Another reporter, rushing through a stack of incident reports at the police station, takes sloppy notes, later misidentifying a woman in an auto accident as a shoplifting suspect. The woman, a respected, popular first-grade teacher, must face the embarrassment of repeatedly explaining the newspaper's error to friends and colleagues who inquire. A brief retraction, carried on page 12A, does little to ease the hurt or quiet wagging tongues.

Unfortunately, unless the error is serious and blatant, it probably will go undetected by editors or unreported by news subjects, who usually are not provoked enough to complain by letter, e-mail or phone call. In far too many instances, the offender moves on to other errors, unaware and unaffected by the mess left behind. If lessons are learned, they are apt to be learned the hard way—and at the expense of others. After the damage is done, says one observer, reporters react like people in shooting accidents who say, "I didn't know the gun was loaded."[2]

Warning: Potential Errors Ahead

Errors come in many forms and sizes. Some are products of haste, carelessness or inattention. A distracted reporter might scan his notebook and transpose the name "Davis Raymond" as "Raymond Davis." Other errors are barely detectable, rooted in the subconscious. A reporter's biases toward homosexuals, for example, may distort her ability to cover a gay rights march. Occasionally, a gullible reporter falls for a hoax story. Most mistakes, however, are as avoidable as they are intolerable, provided reporters know how to read warning signs and follow precautionary steps.

Recognizing Interviewing Errors

At the heart of many interviewing errors is the reporter's failure to make an accurate, thorough record. No reporter enjoys perfect recall; most take notes, but with varying degrees of precision. Reporters who are careless or casual about note-taking are bound to err. When they find that their disorganized, sloppy scribblings are difficult to translate later on, they may begin to assume—a dangerous, unacceptable practice.

Journalists who take a disciplined approach to note-taking neatly record interviews, usually in a reporter's spiral notebook that fits in a purse or coat pocket. At the outset, they record the date, time, place of the interview and the name, including middle initial, and the precise title of the interviewee. They take pains to produce legible, functional notes, which they save long after the story is published. Careful reporters often use a tape recorder to back up their notes. Transcribing takes time, but a tape recording is the reporter's best insurance policy against inaccuracy. A tape recording silences critics, reassures editors, guarantees accurate, precise quotes and forgives reporters for moments of distraction or lapses in concentration in an interview.

When reporters do misquote or err, the usual excuse begins, "I assumed" or "I guessed." *Reporters should never assume or guess; they should know.* They cannot engage in assumptions to fill in the gaps after an interview. "I am very concerned at how inaccurate reporting is," says Wendell Rawls Jr., a Pulitzer Prize-winning reporter who now heads the Center of Public Integrity. "[Reporters] don't take good notes. They are listening to only half the quote, then get back to the office and can't remember what the other half was and are embarrassed to call the person back to ask for a clarification."[3]

As soon as possible after an interview, review your notes to determine whether they are clear and complete. If questions surface, contact the interviewee, saying, "I just wanted to make sure that I have this right." Do not be embarrassed. Remember the editor's saying, "If you assume, you're likely to make an *ass* out of y*ou* and *me*." After all, what is more embarrassing: making a polite call to prevent an error or receiving an angry one after the error is published, posted or broadcast? Consider a *Rocky Mountain News* story that said James Dobson, founder and chairman of Focus on the Family, believed people who fail to practice what they preach should undergo an "exorcism." His quote, taken from a TV interview in the wake of the highly publicized firing of evangelical leader Ted Haggard for "sexual immorality," actually said: "Everybody gets *exercised* when something like this happens, and for good reason." The reporter, committing a "sonic" error—such as hearing "taught" when the word used was "taut"—assumed wrongly that Dobson's comment referred to expelling an evil spirit when he meant "getting worked up" over Haggard's problems.[4]

Veteran investigative reporter Steve Weinberg said that for the first 15 years of his journalism career he adhered to the profession's conventional wisdom: *Never show a story to a news source before publication.* Now he practices prepublication review—going over the draft with the subject and sources—and is convinced it results in more accurate, fair and thorough news reports.[5] Another veteran reporter, Richard M. Clurman (1924–1996), endorsed a "checkback" on important stories for a related benefit—clarity. "Rather than being a violation of journalists' rights or a threat to their independence, it can result in many appropriate instances . . . in new illuminations and nuances that otherwise would have escaped even careful reporting and checking."[6] Not every story requires review; some may simply need a recheck on the accuracy of a particular quotation or passage. But a checkback or prepublication review is often a step worth taking.

Even with the precautions of checkbacks, careful note-taking and tape-recorded interviews, errors can tiptoe past reporters, especially when they are lulled into a false sense of security by authoritative news sources. Reporters naturally gravitate to people they have come to expect to be accurate and articulate. But once reporters begin to anticipate the reliability of certain sources, they tend to become less demanding, less questioning and more receptive. If the superintendent of schools tells you, her voice brimming with certainty, "This is the first time we've ever had to close one of our schools," do not assume she is right. To be safe—and responsible—check it out.

The weight of authority works in other seductive ways. In the presence of a prominent, powerful figure, reporters may find the interview a heady, disorienting experience. If the governor grants you an exclusive interview, treats you like an honored guest, strokes your ego and whispers confidences in your ear, will your determination to ask hard questions melt away? Quite possibly. Try to maintain your resolve.

In another form of seduction, reporters sometimes uncritically lap up the words and opinions of notable, informative, quote-producing news sources. Consumer activist and former presidential candidate Ralph Nader, for example, enjoys special influence with reporters. As his biographer notes, "Nader [is] a reporter's dream because he not only had accurate, and sometimes sensational, information, but he knew how to present it to a newsman in a way that often saved the reporter from having to do much work."[7] No matter how reliable and quotable a news source has been in the past, reporters should never accept the latest information as gospel.

REPORTER'S TIP FILE

Accuracy checklist

As part of ASNE's Journalism Credibility Project, the *San Jose Mercury News* asked a group of editors and reporters to use a short checklist every time they put together a story. During an eight-month test in 1999–2000, the group had 10 percent fewer errors than a similar group not using the following checklist:

- Is the lead sufficiently supported?
- Have we double-checked, called or visited all the phone numbers, addresses or Web addresses in the story? Have we double-checked all names, titles and places mentioned in this story?
- Are the quotes accurate and properly attributed? Have we fully captured what the person meant?
- Is the story fair?
- Were all the stakeholders identified, called and given a chance to talk?
- Who will be annoyed/angry with this story tomorrow? Why? Are we OK with that?
- Did we pick sides? Did we make value judgments about outcomes we want? Will some people like this story more than they should?
- What's missing from the story?

Potential interviewing errors also lurk in the wording of questions. Guard, in particular, against ambiguity or murkiness in your questions. Interviewing expert Stanley L. Payne found that even common words could be misinterpreted. Several repairmen, for example, were separately asked, "How many radio sets did you repair last month?" Payne said the wording of the question seemed perfectly fine until one repairman said, "Who do you mean, me or the whole shop?" To the repairman, *you* had a collective meaning.[8]

In most cases, use simple, understandable, jargon-free language that is familiar to the average person. Avoid leading questions that suggest answers, such as: "Would you say the city was negligent in failing to put warning lights at the intersection?" Some news subjects may respond testily, "Don't put words in my mouth." Often, though, people try hard to please and will eagerly follow the reporter's lead: "Yeah. Somebody ought to be locked up. Any fool could see that an accident was bound to happen there." Reporters who use loaded, suggestive words may elicit juicy quotes, but do the "coached" quotes represent true feelings and opinions? Perhaps not.

With long, complicated questions, a simple, common-sense theorem applies: the longer the question, the longer the response. Thus, convoluted complex questions tend to produce convoluted, complex answers, compounding the chances of misunderstanding, misinterpretation and misquotation.

As an interview progresses, inwardly ask yourself, "Am I being clear; am I being understood?" Then, aloud, ask the interviewee, "Am I being clear? Am I understanding you clearly and correctly?" Far from alienating interviewees, your concern over the clarity of communication will be reassuring.

Less easy to recognize are errors resulting from the interviewer-interviewee relationship. A reporter who sends negative messages—indifference, boredom or hostility—can expect a less expansive, less cooperative interview partner than the reporter who sends positive messages. Biases, in particular, can poison interviews. A reporter assigned to interview a convicted rapist may lose emotional control and allow his feelings of contempt to show in his demeanor and questions. Those feelings also subvert his ability to listen and evaluate.

Besides keeping emotions in check, reporters must remain alert during an interview, assessing both speech and body language for meaning. Does sweat on an interviewee's forehead suggest she's lying? Does an obviously inappropriate response to your question indicate that the interviewee misunderstood you? If an answer is vague, is the interviewee being evasive? Do not jump to conclusions; consider and explore a full range of other possibilities. Perspiration may be a sign of nervousness, not lying. A disjointed answer might indicate a lack of knowledge or a poorly phrased question on your part, not misunderstanding. Instead of being evasive, an interviewee may simply be at a loss for a concrete example. Being sensitive and open-minded helps you anticipate communication problems and avert mistaken impressions that can lead to errors.

Above all, recognize the limitations of interviews. Have realistic expectations: How well can you get to know a person in a 45-minute interview? Remember, too, that the odds of an interviewing error decrease as the scope of your pursuit of truth and accuracy expands. Question and confirm; do not expect accuracy if you rely on one or two sources.

Seeing and Believing

No one's observational acuity is 20/20. One source of distortion involves a principle of physics known as Heisenberg's Rule of Indeterminacy. In simple terms, Heisenberg argued particles cannot be accurately studied because the light needed for examination alters the particles.[9] The rule applies, indirectly, to behavioral science as well. Reporters need to remember that their presence as observers can influence the behavior of others. Reporter Mary Lou Janson spent 80 days in a first-grade classroom, observing how children learn. At first she watched quietly from a first-grader-sized chair in the back of the room. She related her experience: "The first few weeks they would occasionally stare at me. But by mid-year they ignored me. Late in the school year, they would ask me how to spell words, or show me pictures they had drawn."[10] Janson's approach gave her—and her readers—an unusual exposure to education. But was it a *true* view? How did the students and teacher react to being watched? Did they really ignore her presence? Did they change as a result of Janson's presence?

Secretive observation and masquerades allow reporters to watch more discreetly, but such methods do not eliminate the possibility of distortion. In fact, a reporter posing as an abused wife risks affecting the dynamics of a therapy group at a women's shelter. Over time, the reporter might lose her objectivity as she begins to see the subjects as friends. She may become a leader in the group. Moreover, the reporter's perceptions change as she becomes immersed in the experience. Initially she felt a detached sympathy for battered women; now she fights to suppress feelings of outrage. Changes cut both ways: The reporter changes others as *she* herself is changed. Lillian Ross, known for her perceptive reporting for *The New Yorker*, described the inevitable *presence* of the journalist on assignment: "A reporter doing a story can't pretend to be invisible, let alone a fly [on the wall]; he or she is seen and heard and responded to by the people he or she is writing about; a reporter is always chemically involved in a story."[11]

Observation is affected by another form of distortion known as "the *Rashomon* effect." The term comes from a classic Japanese film (1950) that explores multiple accounts of the rape of a woman and the murder of her husband. In turn, each character in the film tells a markedly different story; ego and ulterior motives shape their versions. By the film's end, viewers find it impossible to know what really happened. Witnesses to news events react similarly. A bank guard describes how he kept his cool during an armed robbery; a teller, however, recalls seeing the guard cowering behind a post. Both versions are likely to be subjective. Although the *Rashomon* effect cannot be neutralized, obtaining and comparing as many accounts as possible help minimize its role. A thorough investigation can lead to dramatic results. In 1989, an acclaimed documentary, *The Thin Blue Line*, helped free a man wrongly convicted of murder by re-enacting and, in several instances, discrediting the conflicting stories of witnesses to the crime.

QUOTABLES

"Our unconscious is a powerful force. But it's fallible. It's not the case that our internal computer always shines through, instantly decoding the 'truth' of a situation. It can be thrown off, distracted and disabled (p. 15). . . . We don't know where our first impressions come from or precisely what they mean, so we don't always appreciate their fragility.

***Rashomon* holds lessons for journalists** Toshiro Mifune, who plays the bandit, and Machiko Kyo, who plays the wife, in a scene from the 1950 Japanese film that explores differing accounts of a rape and murder. Reporters face the challenge of determining the truth among conflicting viewpoints. (Image courtesy Wikipedia.)

Taking our powers of rapid cognition seriously means we have to acknowledge the subtle influences that can alter or undermine or bias the products of our unconscious." (p. 252)
—Malcolm Gladwell, *Blink: The Power of Thinking without Thinking*, New York: Little, Brown and Company, 2005

As *Rashomon* and *The Thin Blue Line* demonstrate, vantage points and emotional states contribute to observational distortions. Watching an anti-abortion rally from the speaker's platform yields one slice of reality; observing from the middle of the crowd offers another; standing with a contingent of police produces a third view. That is why reporters are encouraged to move about at news scenes, gathering and assessing various pieces of the picture, and to try to keep their own emotions in check.

REAL-LIFE LESSONS

The likelihood of observational distortion is high when a news event is chaotic or traumatizing. Witnesses, for example, to China's forced removal of student protestors from Tiananmen Square on June 4, 1989, described horrors previously unknown to them. "We expected tear gas and rubber bullets," said Huang Jing, a graduate student at Harvard, quoted in a *Newsweek* story. "But they used machine guns and drove over people with tanks. One line of students would stand up and then get shot down and then another line of students would stand and the same thing would happen. The soldiers were shooting everyone."[12] The account was powerful, emotional and authentic-sounding, but nearly a decade later, *Columbia Journalism Review* published an article entitled "The Myth of Tiananmen," written by Jay Mathews, who covered Tiananmen for the *Washington Post*. Mathews cast serious doubts on the *Newsweek* account and others news reports published or broadcast in June 1989. He wrote:

President Clinton's precedent-setting visit to China filled the front pages of American newspapers and led the evening television news for many days this summer. The stories focused on his controversial decision to attend a welcoming ceremony in Tiananmen Square, despite the stain of what reporters called the massacre of Chinese students there on June 4, 1989.

Over the last decade, many American reporters and editors have accepted a mythical version of that warm, bloody night. They repeated it often before and during Clinton's trip. On the day the president arrived in Beijing, a *Baltimore Sun* headline (June 27, page 1A) referred to "Tiananmen, where Chinese students died." A *USA Today* article (June 26, page 7A) called Tiananmen the place "where pro-democracy demonstrators were gunned down." The *Wall Street Journal* (June 26, page A10) described "the Tiananmen Square massacre" where armed troops ordered to clear demonstrators from the square killed "hundreds or more." The *New York Post* (June 25, page 22) said the square was "the site of the student slaughter."

The problem is this: as far as can be determined from the available evidence, no one died that night in Tiananmen Square.

A few people may have been killed by random shooting on streets near the square, but all verified eyewitness accounts say that the students who remained in the square when troops arrived were allowed to leave peacefully. Hundreds of people, most of them workers and passersby, did die that night, but in a different place and under different circumstances.[13]

The lesson: *Under trying, emotional conditions—through tears, outrage and pain—the vision of witnesses and journalists alike can become blurred.*

Reporters generally are sound observers, but they, too, are prone to perceptual errors. What you see is not necessarily what others see. Cultural differences, for instance, affect observation. To an Anglo observer, two older Hispanics haggling over the price of tomatoes appear so angry they may come to blows. In reality, the men are friends who re-enact the scene endlessly; it is part of a give-and-take heritage of bargaining.

A cognitive process called *selective perception* also influences the ability to observe. Selective perception affects reporters and news sources alike. People tend to see events and people through filters. Sometimes the process involves seeing what we *expect* to see, not actually what happened or what exists. A reporter who strongly believes career soldiers are hardened warriors may fail to see a general's peaceful, gentle side. Being aware of the power of selective perception can help reporters observe with greater care and remind them to seek out people and details to check the validity of their observations.

As with interviewing, reporters should have realistic expectations about the ability to observe. At best, observation yields an *approximation* of human experiences.

Counting on Numbers

To some people, there are lies, damned lies and statistics. Much public mistrust of statistics dates to Darrell Huff's 1954 widely read monograph, *How to Lie with Statistics*.[14] Actually, numbers do not lie until someone twists them or misreads them. A couple of relatively uncomplicated uses of statistics by reporters illustrate the potential for error.

Several years ago, a metropolitan daily in the Midwest published a story with the headline "Suicides Highest among the Elderly." Based on information from the reporter, a chart of suicides by age groups accompanied the story. The chart put the suicide rate for people age 65 and over at 21 percent per 100,000 people. The next day, with considerable embarrassment, the newspaper reported what should have been obvious to the reporter and editors handling the story: The suicide statistics were based on the *number* of persons per 100,000 people, not on a *percentage*. For every 100,000 people in the state over the age of 65, 21 committed suicide, not 21 percent.

The second example is a legendary case of statistical overstatement based on too small of a sampling. It dates to the New York City power failure of 1965, when about 30 million people went without electricity for up to 12 hours. Exactly nine months after the blackout, the *New York Times* tested a theory: With no television to watch, movies to attend or lights to read by, couples turned to each other for diversion. Surveying eight New York hospitals, the *Times* reported a dramatic increase in the birth rate. Later, though, an inclusive report from 100 local hospitals revealed that the number of births nine months from the blackout date was actually slightly lower than normal.[15]

Drawing conclusions from statistics is especially risky. Care must be taken to see that all variables—conditions that might affect conclusions—are considered. If the police department hires 50 additional officers and the number of home burglaries drops significantly the next month from the burglary rate of a year before, the statistics suggest a correlation: More police equals less crime. When the variables are considered, however—perhaps the new officers were sweating through training and not deterring burglars that month, perhaps changes in the weather, the economy or the unemployment rate were factors—it may not be possible to draw the obvious correlation.

Errors also occur when reporters confuse *percentages* with *percentage points*. In an election poll, for example, if 60 percent of the voters favor Candidate X in August, and her support wanes to 45 percent in October, she has not experienced a 15 percent drop in support. Her support dropped 15 percentage points; translated to percentages, she experienced a 25 percent loss of support.

REPORTER'S TIP FILE

Figuring out percentages

Web commentator Robert Niles, of RobertNiles.com, offers this simple formula:

> Simply subtract the old value from the new value, then divide by the old value. Multiply the result by 100 and slap a % sign on it. That's your percent change.
>
> Let's say Springfield had 50 murders last year, as did Capital City. So there's no difference in crime between these cities, right? Maybe, maybe not. Let's go back and look at the number of murders in those towns in previous years, so we can determine a percent change.
>
> Five years ago, Capital City had 42 murders while Springfield had just 29.
>
> Subtract the old value from the new one for each city and then divide by the old values. That will show you that, over a five year period, Capital City had a 19 percent increase in murders, while Springfield's increase was more than 72 percent.
>
> That's your lead.
>
> Or is it? There's something else to consider when computing percent change. Take a look at per capita to find out.[16]

John Allen Paulos, the author of *A Mathematician Reads the Newspaper*, says "'numbers stories' complement, deepen, and regularly undermine 'human stories.'" By "undermine," he means tools of quantification, such as mathematics, logic and statistics, often challenge the conventional "truth" found in purely anecdotal evidence. Paying attention to numbers, he says, tells us "which numbers, relations, and associations are to be trusted, which dismissed as coincidental or nonsensical, which [to be] further analyzed, supplemented, or alternatively interpreted." By way of example, he dissected a voting "analysis" that concluded blacks in New York City vote along racial lines more than whites do. But do they? he asked:

> The evidence cited was that 95 percent of blacks voted for (black) mayor David Dinkins, whereas only 75 percent of whites voted for (white) candidate (and victor) Rudolph Giuliani. This assertion failed to take into account, however, the preference of most black voters for any Democratic candidate. Assuming that 80 percent of blacks usually vote for Democrats and that only 50 percent of whites usually vote for Republicans, one can argue that only 15 percent of blacks voted for Democrat Dinkins based on race and that 25 percent of whites voted for Republican Giuliani based on race. There are, as usual at the politico-mathematical frontier, countless other interpretations.[17]

Numbers impress people. They carry the weight of authority. But whose authority? Question numbers; apply common sense when looking for errors; seek substantiation. (Chapter 9 addresses the problems of political polls.)

Out of Context

The story is familiar: Two old-school politicians are commiserating about the press. Sen. Blowhard, shaking a copy of the *Daily Bugle*, snorts, "There they go again, quoting me out of context verbatim." Reporters enjoy the story because, from their perspective, it rings true. In many instances, a newsmaker's complaint that "I've been quoted out of context" actually means, "I've been quoted correctly, but *now* I don't like the way my words read in print or sound on the air." But do not dismiss Sen. Blowhard's charges; people, indeed, are embarrassed and wronged by reporters who have quoted or paraphrased them accurately—but out of context.

REAL-LIFE LESSONS

All news organizations err, including the *New York Times*, which daily posts corrections in print and on its Web site. In October 2006, the newspaper posted this item:

> A front-page article on Sept. 14 (correction posted Oct. 2, 2006) reported that the inspector general of the Interior Department had accused top officials at the agency of tolerating widespread ethical failures. The article said that the inspector

general in a 2004 report had described J. Steven Griles, a deputy secretary accused of more than two dozen ethical lapses, as a "train wreck waiting to happen." That quotation was taken out of context. The quotation said in full: "Framed within the context of a train wreck waiting to happen, the Department of the Interior was presented with its most complex set of ethical issues with Mr. J. Steven Griles' appointment at a time that, following years of neglect, demise and compartmentalization, the ethics program was wholly incapable of addressing them."[18]

The lesson: *Quoting or paraphrasing people out of context is a serious problem for reporters. Rene J. Cappon, author of* The Word, *a book that focuses on newswriting problems, cautions about errors of context. "Next to getting the actual words right, the most important thing is to keep quotes in context. Failure usually arises from careless compression that makes a statement appear more emphatic than it is. A qualification may be dropped or buried, a speaker's elaboration of a point overlooked, or a remark intended as jocular reported deadpan."*[19]

Reporters frequently find themselves forced to condense and paraphrase, which sets the stage for another form of contextual error. Leo Della Betta, then ombudsman for the *Arizona Daily Star*, explained the problem. "There are times . . . when the editing philosophy of trim, trim, trim should be junked. Important details, supporting arguments and vital nuances can't always be subjected to telegraphic treatment."[20] That is particularly true of stories based on the ideas of expert news sources who need time and space to explain their views. Expert sources who find their words distorted by abridged treatment will be reluctant to share information the next time a reporter asks for an interview.

Be careful if a catchy quotation or an isolated remark becomes the central focus of your story or lead. As a safeguard, ask this important question: Do the words—without their context—fairly and accurately represent the speaker's *overall* views? If, for example, an interviewee spends 45 minutes saying positive things about the city's mayor, is it fair for a reporter to write a lead that highlights the one critical remark made during the interview?

Care also is needed with regard to two other contextual problems. One is juxtaposing remarks. When words spoken early in an interview or speech are placed next to words that came much later, reporters flirt with contextual problems. Let's say state Sen. Mary Bartlett comments to a reporter, "This is a rotten piece of legislation, and Sen. Davis knows it." She then spends 10 minutes explaining her point of view. Bartlett ends by saying, "He really sold out on this one." The reporter splices the two quotations, leaving the impression that Sen. Davis acted improperly or illegally. But the full context of the interview clearly indicates that Bartlett believes Davis "sold out" in the sense that he reneged on an earlier pledge to Bartlett to vote against the legislation. Is this sloppy reporting? Is it unethical? By juxtaposing the comments, the reporter, at the very least, distorted Sen. Bartlett's position.

Cappon underscores the other contextual problem: "You can . . . skewer a quote by converting a long, involved question into the subject's answer." He offers this example:

> *Reporter:* "Do you feel the verdict was wrong, that it was a gross miscarriage of justice?"
>
> *News subject:* "Well, yes."
>
> *Copy:* He said "he felt that the verdict was wrong and a gross miscarriage of justice."[21]

Unfairly and inaccurately, a brief, qualified response, "Well, yes" is converted into a full-blown, unequivocal statement.

Whenever there is doubt about misrepresenting someone's comments or views, consider consulting with news subjects and allowing them to hear what you have written. Remember, you are not asking them to edit or censor your story; you are merely trying to ensure that justice is done for everyone concerned—you, the news subject and the audience.

Not Getting Fooled

Be prepared. People will to try to fool you. Gullible, careless, naive, arrogant or mean-spirited reporters are especially tempting targets for someone's hoax, setup or revenge.

In particular, watch out for pranks. Some are intended to embarrass an unpopular reporter; others amount to an initiation for a newcomer to a beat. A detective, for example, baits a hook, not really expecting the cub reporter to bite. "Hey, Joe, we've got a lead on a guy who steals steaks, chops and ribs right off people's grills. We call him the 'barbecue bandit.'" The reporter, pleased the detective is helping him on a story, dutifully asks questions and takes notes. The detective, grinning throughout, says to himself, "Who'd swallow such a story?" He is shocked when a brief story about the "investigation" appears in the newspaper. When practical jokes go this far, everyone gets in trouble. Admittedly, even a veteran journalist initially might believe the detective's story; it promises to be a decent "brite" (a light, humor-oriented story) on an otherwise dull news day. But few reporters would publish without asking for details and talking to victims, steps that would expose most pranks.

Occasionally, people orchestrate elaborate hoaxes, holding media events, issuing press releases, publishing studies and constructing identities to entrap the press. Over the years, Joseph Skaggs, a New York artist and journalism teacher, staged events and issued news releases to prove his contention that the press is easy to dupe. For one skit, he posed as Dr. Josef Gregor, a fictitious scientist from South America. Skaggs held a news conference to discuss Gregor's group, Metamorphosis, and his experiences with the curative powers of cockroach pills. The hoax was inspired by Franz Kafka's story in which Gregor Samsa awakens to discover he has changed into a cockroach-like creature. United Press International covered the news conference, and dozens of newspapers carried the story of Gregor and his cockroach pills. Skaggs believes it is easy to fool the media, especially with sensational, sexy or funny stories, because reporters fail to check the facts.[22]

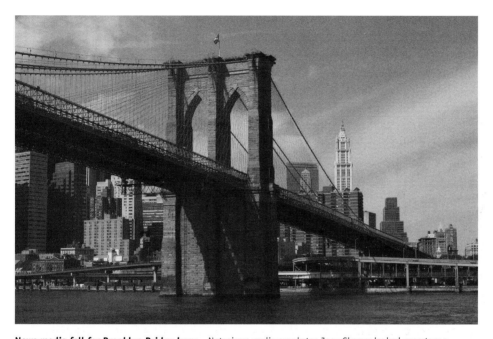

News media fall for Brooklyn Bridge hoax   Notorious media prankster Joey Skaggs leaked reporters a fake inter-office memorandum purportedly from then New York City Mayor David Dinkins. To sweeten the bait, Skaggs attached a handwritten Post-it note that read: "Thought you might be interested in seeing what the Mayor's up to! 'Mayor to Sell the Brooklyn Bridge!' Think this will fly?? I love New York!!!" The AP, WABC and WPIX fell for the hoax, thinking it came from a mole inside city hall. They reported that the Dinkins administration, wrestling with a way to raise funds to repair the city's decaying infrastructure, was about to institute a lottery with renaming rights to the landmark as the first-place prize. (Photo courtesy of iStockphoto, McSilvey, Image # 885355.)

Today, the Internet appears to be the instrument of choice for pranksters. *USA Today*, the *Associated Press* and the *Wall Street Journal* were among news organizations initially fooled by Alek Komarnitsky's Christmas hoax. Komarnitsky, a real person, set up an elaborate Web site that purported visitors could use interactive technology to view and operate his holiday light display online. When a Denver TV station helicopter hovered over his home for a live report, Komarnitsky's wife was inside, flipping the lights off and on to maintain the ruse. After the hoax was exposed, a *USA Today* story said reporters failed to investigate closely enough to detect the hoax. The AP, for example, picked up a story from a local newspaper and checked out the Web site but never visited the house; a USATODAY.com writer corresponded with Komarnitsky and visited the site but also never saw the house in person.[23]

The hardest hoaxes to detect and combat are those perpetrated either deliberately or accidentally by flesh-and-blood news subjects who appear truthful and sincere. In late 2003, 12-year-old Emily Streight of Carlton, Ore., slipped a note into a plastic water bottle, sealed it with duct tape and tossed the bottle into a creek that fed to the Pacific Ocean. She never expected it to get far, much less to the shores of Hawaii. But in 2006, she received a note from 16-year-old "Keoni," saying he found the bottle on a Honolulu beach; he returned the girl's handwritten note as proof. The McMinnvile *News-Register* interviewed Streight for a feel-good story; within a few days the truth emerged. It turned out a visitor from Hawaii found the bottle while clearing brush near his fiancé's Oregon home, took the bottle back to Hawaii and concocted the tale about Keoni, using his correct return address on the letter to Streight. A Honolulu TV reporter tracked him down and he admitted his prank.[24]

How do you expose Joey Skaggs and his imitators and avoid getting burned by news sources? Skepticism and digging remain the best weapons against a hoax. Verify credentials and claims. Ask for documentation. Unless there is no doubt about the newsmaker's authenticity, routinely check the background of everyone you cover. Certain stories are, indeed, too good—or too bizarre—to be true; some, however, despite straining credulity, are true. It is up to you to uncover the bogus stories without blithely dismissing legitimate ones. Several Web sites help track urban legends and hoaxes, among them Snopes.com. Reporters who seek multiple confirmations rarely fall victim to pranks.

A close relative of the hoax is the media event, staged to attract press coverage. Media events may generate bonafide news, such as a politician's tour of a flooded town or an NAACP march in front of the mayor's house. In fact, groups and individuals outside normal news channels resort to media events simply to gain a hearing. Although their methods may be contrived, remember that their message might have merit.

Most efforts to fool or manipulate reporters are not malicious. There are exceptions, however, like this one:

> A man posing as a well-known assistant district attorney calls the newspaper's courthouse bureau 20 minutes before deadline to report the out-of-town arrest of a local business executive. The news is not unexpected; the executive has been in legal trouble previously. Moreover, the assistant DA is quite convincing; although the reporter has not met him, she recognizes the name and knows the assistant DA's reputation for being a straightshooter. Her cell phone caller ID shows "unknown caller," but that's a heading she sees on a lot of incoming calls she gets. The attorney even leaves an off-duty number. "You can reach me there in an hour or so, in case you have other questions," he says.

The trap snaps shut, and a fake story is published. Later, the business executive threatens to sue for libel. Was the newspaper set up so the executive could have grounds for a libel suit? Did an enemy of the executive use the newspaper to get even? Did someone in the district attorney's office play an irresponsible joke on the reporter? In any case, the antidote is the same: Planted stories quickly unravel when reporters take a few minutes to verify the identity of news subjects and the authenticity of information.

Finally, there are stories so captivating or plausible they gain news legitimacy by being retold and embellished repeatedly. Jan Harold Brunvand calls these accounts "urban legends." They usually begin as orally transmitted folklore. In his books *The Vanishing Hitchhiker* (1982), *The Choking Doberman* (1986) and *Too Good to Be True* (2001), Brunvand relates the history and meaning of such stories, which include, he says, pets accidentally cooked in microwave ovens, alligators lurking in New York City sewers and convertibles filled with cement by jealous husbands. Most often, reporters recognize the stories as rumors and try to dispel them. Now and then, though, over-eager, imprudent journalists fall prey.

One seemingly irresistible urban legend centers on drug dealers who try to entice children by lacing Mickey Mouse lick-and-stick tattoo transfers with LSD. The story achieved credibility because of a 1980 bulletin issued by the narcotics bureau of the New Jersey state police, warning that some drug-laced "blotter sheets" were imprinted with cartoon-like figures that children might find attractive. The bulletin carried an illustration of a "sorcerer's apprentice" that vaguely resembled Mickey Mouse. A year later, the superintendent of the Ohio Bureau of Criminal Investigation inadvertently lent further credibility to the legend by being identified as the source in several stories recounting the arrest of a drug dealer caught with 5,000 tabs of blotter acid in his car. Reporters covering the case asked about the rumored Mickey Mouse connection. Patiently and repeatedly, says Brunvand, the superintendent denied the existence of Mickey Mouse-inspired acid stickers, but the rumor persisted, thanks, in part, to press hype.[25]

Exaggeration

Be wary of overstating the importance of events, such as court rulings, election outcomes or scientific discoveries. Certain words—*landmark*, *unprecedented* and *breakthrough*—should sound an alarm. Ask yourself whether you are inflating or overestimating the story. Ask, too, if the source of the news is exaggerating the importance. To avoid errors of exaggeration, check with other knowledgeable news sources to see whether they see the event or development similarly. In the summer of 2001, several shark attacks on humans resulted in sensational headlines suggesting a heightened threat to surfers and swimmers. The *Los Angeles Times* contacted researchers at the University of Florida who reported 76 unprovoked attacks by sharks on humans worldwide, *down* from 85 recorded the previous year.[26]

Contributing to errors of exaggeration is the pressure to produce stories that prompt editors to tell the reporter, "Good stuff." Historian David Hackett Fischer used the term *prodigious fallacy* to describe accounts that attempt to equate sensation with significance. Prodigious fallacies, he says, are widely disseminated by journalists, who freely use terms like *historic* for anything from state funerals to transatlantic canoe trips.[27]

People depend on journalists to help them measure the importance of events. Cancer patients, for example, eagerly read stories about new drugs or treatments. Reporters should not raise false hopes by producing overblown accounts, nor should they unduly cause alarm. Has sensationalized press coverage created a generation of hypochondriacs? Sensationalism remains a problem of journalism, which is why in some newsrooms, reporters are told to be mindful of a simple rule: If you err, err on the side of restraint. There is always tomorrow's—or next week's—newscast, podcast or newspaper.

Misshaping the News?

Few stories are outright fabrications, premeditated and calculated. More often, reporters produce pseudo-stories, creations inspired by a personal agenda or moral indignation. Media observer Bob Kohn criticizes the *New York Times* for intentionally overplaying coverage about Augusta (Ga.) National Golf Club, host of the Masters tournament, over the club's refusal to accept female members.[28] In 2002–2003, the *Times* published more than 30 articles about the club's membership policy and its dispute with Martha Burk and the National Council of Women's Organizations. The *Times'* heavy coverage of Burk and her cause seemed incongruous when fewer than 40 supporters showed up for Burk's highly publicized protest in Augusta as the 2003 Masters tournament opened. The next day the *Times* reported: "With this year's Masters concluded and Burk's one-hour rally Saturday leaving little more than a few muddy footprints in an Augusta field, the question becomes: What next?"[29] The climax of Burk's efforts fizzled as a media event, which raises a question in itself: Did the newspaper err when it defined the Burk assault on Augusta National as a major, significant fight for the rights of women?

Innocent shaping of the news occurs daily in journalism, largely in the form of "reaction" stories. Countless news stories follow a similar pattern. A congressman, for example, is arrested for soliciting a prostitute; reporters rush to seek reaction from his friends and foes. The reporters probe in leading ways: "Shouldn't the congressman resign?" "Isn't his credibility so seriously damaged that he can no longer be effective in the House?" "Isn't this going to kill his chances for re-election?" The answers generate a story that says: "Friends and foes of Congressman X, saying he has lost his credibility to be effective in the House, believe he ought to either resign or not seek re-election." In another instance, a judge, prodded by a reporter's line of questioning, criticizes police for sloppy arrest procedures in a rape case; the reporter conveys the judge's remarks to police officers, who respond in kind. The story that emerges begins: "Judge X and police officers are feuding over the handling of a rape arrest earlier this month." Can you say such stories "existed" before reporters entered the picture? To be sure, the press plays an important catalytic role in bringing society's issues and problems to public attention and reaction stories certainly are needed. Moreover, reporters are right to ask tough questions and, at times, even leading questions. But whenever journalists cross the line from reporter to *agent provocateur*, they tamper with reality.

Haste and Waste

News consumers expect news quickly, but they dislike reports containing contradictory information. Reporters are caught in the middle: If they move too quickly, they risk error; if they move too slowly, they risk being scooped.

Television, cable and Internet news organizations are particularly vulnerable to haste-induced errors. In 2005, an independent review commissioned by CBS criticized network news executives for their "myopic zeal" to rush an investigation of President Bush's military record. A "60 Minutes" report used dubious documents and sources, the review concluded, in reporting that Bush skirted duty obligations, including missing a mandatory medical exam, while serving in the Texas Air National Guard.[30]

The danger heightens with breaking news, during live, on-the-scene news reports, as news outlets scramble to air or post the news first. Channel 5's reporter rushes to report the kidnapping of a 16-year-old girl by two black men. In a live broadcast, the girl's sister describes how the teenager was grabbed off the street. The teenager's tearful father holds a picture of his daughter, pleading with the abductors to release her unharmed. It is a powerful, potentially inflammatory story. The police, however, are noncommittal, with reason. The following morning, the sisters admit to inventing the story so the teenager could spend the night with her boyfriend.

Official sources, confused by events and pressured to deliver facts to reporters, err, too. A dramatic example of hasty, faulty reportage occurred in 1971 when inmates at New York's notorious Attica prison revolted and seized guards as hostages. In a bloody counterattack, police and state troopers reclaimed the prison. With tear gas and gunsmoke still in the air, shaken law enforcement officials met the press, describing how inmates slashed the throats of the hostages. One hostage was castrated, the *Washington Post* reported. The next day, however, autopsy reports revealed that all hostages died of gunshot wounds and none was castrated. Furthermore, prison officials acknowledged that no guns were found among the inmates' collection of handmade weapons. Apparently, the hostages were killed by police bullets.

What happened? One reporter on the scene believes journalists were mentally conditioned to believe the official account even prior to the attack. "Before they went in," he said, "everybody was telling us about knives pointed at throats, that these guys weren't joking, and so on. Your mind was prepared for the idea that the prisoners were going to be violent. Then when the troopers and prison people came out with stories of throats cut, everything seemed to dovetail."[31] No reporters actually saw any of the Attica killings. They were kept outside the prison, piecing together stories from an assortment of available witnesses and participants. Had reporters and officials questioned accounts more carefully or waited for autopsy results, serious mistakes could have been avoided. Of course, with breaking stories of such magnitude, reporters sometimes have little choice but to rely on information provided by officials. But always question official accounts, insisting on as many details and particulars as possible.

With certain stories it is difficult to know just when to go public. Rumors and innuendo fall into this category. In 1989, premature media reports, fed by unnamed Navy sources, implicated a young gunner's mate, Kendall Truitt, in an explosion on the battleship *Iowa* that killed 47 sailors. According to published rumors, Truitt and a shipmate who died in the blast were in a homosexual relationship that soured. Adding fuel to the rumors was a single fact: Truitt was the beneficiary of the dead shipmate's life insurance.

For weeks, Truitt denied the rumors and proclaimed his innocence. Finally, the Navy officially cleared Truitt of any involvement in the explosion. By then, though, Truitt said, the Navy and news media had ruined his life. Were reporters too hasty in covering the Truitt story? Once the Truitt story surfaced in one newspaper, did other reporters rush like lemmings after a titillating rumor? Was it too much to ask the news media to wait for concrete, on-the-record evidence of Truitt's guilt or innocence?

Jean Otto, at the time associate editor of the *Rocky Mountain News*, urged reporters to be particularly skeptical about the motives of government sources. In her view, the press often reacts too quickly—and without regard for errors of haste.

> Why do we grab it and go with it? It's partly competition. "Get it first and correct it later" is still an operating principle, if not a motto. Having to correct it later can be devastating to some individuals' lives. And we frequently, in pursuit of a story, don't think about the target of that story. . . . After the fact is terrific, but after the fact doesn't save the destruction of somebody's reputation.[32]

Reports from the police beat also force reporters to make tough decisions. Because allegations by victims may turn out to be concoctions, police carefully challenge all serious accusations. How long do you wait, for example, before identifying a minister accused of indecent exposure? And what about possible false alarms? If a teenager is reported missing by her parents, do you wait to see whether she is an overnight runaway and not a victim of foul play? With other stories, procedures are clear. For example, you do not report the names of accident victims prematurely; reporters wait until identities are confirmed and relatives are notified and cared for by family or friends.

Although we live in a fast-paced, media-intensive world, certain stories and situations call for deliberation and restraint. Reporters should not let deadlines, peer pressure or competition for a scoop force them into filing a hasty, ill-advised story.

REPORTER'S TIP FILE

A question of taste

A story can be factually correct and still wrong in the sense of inappropriate language or bad taste. Although reporters strive for vivid writing, some details are too gruesome for the sensibilities of most readers and viewers. Accounts of sex crimes and traffic accidents often are sanitized.

But deciding where to draw the line can be difficult. A reporter obtains a dramatic, wrenching transcript of a taped 911 call. It contains the sobbing pleas of a 10-year-old who accidentally shot and killed his little sister: "I shot her. I didn't mean to. Please don't die. Please, God, please, don't be dead. Oh, please help me." In print the words are disturbing; an audio replay might be extremely distressing for audiences. Yet put in the context of a significant increase in accidental shootings, perhaps people need to feel the full impact of a tragedy to prevent further tragedies.

Around newsrooms people talk about the breakfast test: Could you read or view the story over a bowl of cereal without your stomach turning? This subjective test would kill some stories that should be told regardless of how they affect someone's appetite, but as a general rule, if details or words would disturb a sensitive person you know, soften or withhold them.

Failure to Admit Ignorance

Nearly all errors by journalists are embarrassing in one way or another. But errors of ignorance are among the most embarrassing of all.

Surprisingly, some reporters stumble over language usage. They mix metaphors, such as "He's been keeping his ear to the grindstone" or "It's time the project be sent back to the cutting board." They translate unfamiliar words to familiar ones, spelling "microfiche" as "microfish" or "taut" as "taught." Writer Bob Swift collects hybrid abominations, calling them "malaphors"—the fusion of mixed metaphors and malapropisms. "They almost make sense, then you do a double take," he says. A friend of Swift's puts malaphors in the realm of "fruitworthy English," named for Chicago Mayor Jane Byrne, who once said she hoped an investigation would "prove fruitworthy." Among Swift's favorite malaphors are "He's a ragged individualist"; "I was up at the crank of dawn"; and "He's a fly in the oatmeal."[33] Cliches and careless use of figurative language reveal a common flaw in journalistic writing.

QUOTABLES

"A journalist friend asked me if I had noticed that the verb *roil* was becoming more common in newspapers. Not surprisingly, as soon as she pointed it out I started noticing it all over the place. . . . There's nothing new about *roil*—it has been around since Shakespeare's time as a slightly recondite synonym for 'churn up' or 'perturb.' . . . You don't hear *roil* a lot in everyday conversation. It isn't really a word of American English at all—it belongs to the patois of that exotic alter-America that we read about in the newspapers, a world populated by strongmen, fugitive financiers, and troubled teens, where ire is always being fueled until violence flares, spawning hatred and stirring fears until hopes are dashed. . . . Editors are always deploring the excesses of journalese, but for every embellishment they manage to discourage, three new ones spring up in its place. . . . Saying that the mayor's decision roiled voters feels more vivid than merely saying that the decision troubled them—it makes it sound as if something has actually taken place since the last edition went to press." (pp. 192–194)

—Geoffrey Nunberg, *Going Nucular*, New York: PublicAffairs, 2004

Journalists with deficiencies in basic knowledge also make mortifying mistakes. What constitutes basic knowledge? Conversational familiarity with a variety of subjects is one measurement. A knowledge of history and culture is another. In Chapter 2, reporters were encouraged to read extensively. Reading the *New York Times* or *Newsweek* regularly is a step in the right direction, but it is not enough. Well-read journalists accumulate story ideas, expand their vocabulary, sample new experiences and stay abreast of current affairs.

Familiarity with important moments in history is particularly important. What do you know about Franklin Delano Roosevelt's court-packing scheme? What's the historical significance of *Lebensraum*? History provides perspective and context for today's news. Unschooled reporters, for example, might assume that Ronald Reagan was the first American president to send Marines to Lebanon, not knowing that Dwight Eisenhower dispatched troops there in 1958. Knowledge of local history is just as important.

Columnist Meg Greenfield, however, warns us not to mistake a mountain of information for actual understanding. As she explains:

> It is one of the ironies of the current well-documented information explosion with all its instantaneous transmission of news and data around the globe and right into your car radio that we get the impression that we know more than we do. . . . Our heads are stuffed full of snippets of lore that give us the false impression that we know something when we don't or when what we do know is only the most superficial skimming of the pond.[34]

Her warning is particularly applicable as reporters attempt to understand people and events foreign to them. Instead of accounting for cultural and political differences, underinformed journalists tend to superimpose an American template on developments elsewhere. One way to avoid errors of ignorance is to be smart enough to ask questions whenever you do not *know* or are not *sure*.

Evaluating and Selecting Information

It is time to write. Before you are notes, observations, documents, figures—the raw material for your story. Reporters should evaluate material throughout the reporting process to determine whether it is logical, accurate, valid and fair. Now, though, you must evaluate yourself—your decision making—as you put together the story.

Do not expect to be absolutely sure of doing the right thing. In fact, uncertainty will keep you vigilant. Each story poses its own set of problems, questions and uncertainties. But evaluative errors frequently creep into journalistic writing, and reporters should be especially alert for them.

One involves what David Hackett Fischer calls the *lonely fact*.[35] The lonely fact follows a sweeping generalization. Often the lonely fact is prefaced by the telltale phrase "for example" or "for instance." Generalizations in news stories follow a familiar form:

> Feminists are up in arms over the president's failure to appoint a woman to the cabinet.

On the heels of the generalization is an authoritative quote or two:

> "It's a slap in the face to all women," says Sally Porter, spokesperson for Women for Women.

There is nothing wrong about using a single supporting example, as long as it is representative of a convincing stack of uncited evidence. Are "all" or even most feminists *really* "up in arms," or is it just a few? Never use a single fact to prop up a dubious generalization.

Journalists readily reach for words that appear to convey authority and significance, such as *many*, *most* and *widespread*. These, too, are generalizations, and without the support of numbers and evidence, they are weak, meaningless words. Reporters who casually use such words without being sure they rest on a solid foundation of facts are imprecise at best and misleading at worst.

Other words carry a connotative power that should never be underestimated. In evaluating the tone or emphasis of your story, ask whether you are using what semanticist S. I. Hayakawa calls "snarl words" or "purr words."[36] These words suggest approval or disapproval or promote negative or positive images. In describing a civil rights activist, a reporter could call her "committed," "intense" or "obsessed." A story about a first-year legislator might describe him as "timid" instead of "cautious." When a police chief will not answer questions about a murder, does he "decline" or "refuse" to comment? Reporters must recognize whether they are using words that snarl or purr, check their biases and, at times, substitute less judgmental language.

Historian Fischer's observations also apply to another journalistic tendency—the *fallacy of responsibility*. The fallacy, he says, is most likely to arise when people try to explain bad news.[37] A bridge collapses, a space shuttle explodes, a riot erupts. At first, reporters ask, "What happened?" and "What caused it?" Soon, though, the question becomes, "Who is to blame?" and the focus, he says, usually turns to finding a human agent. Reporters are supposed to ask questions to determine cause and to fix accountability, but they cannot assume that a culprit exists. In fact, they must consider the possibility that no one is to blame.

REPORTER'S TIP FILE

What's in a name?

What is signaled by a mistake in a name?

Name errors quickly and decisively reduce the credibility of journalism and journalists. Can you expect people to have much confidence in other details of a story if they know a name is not reported accurately?

Reporters should unfailingly check every name and title in a story—double-check, in fact. Always ask people to spell their names—first, middle initial and last. Ask how they prefer to be named and identified. Some reporters even hand their notebook to their sources and ask them to write their names.

Never assume you know how a name is spelled. Years ago, you could expect common spellings and common names—*Tom, Mary, Robert*. Now you can count on fanciful, unusual names and spellings. You cannot even assume that family members spell their last names the same. In an Associated Press story, an alert reporter learned that one news subject spelled his name Marasciullo, but a sister, also quoted, had dropped an *l* from her name years before.

Foreign names present special problems. Is Libya's leader *Muammar Khadafi* or *Moammar Qaddafi* or *Muammer al-Gadafy*? News organizations spell his name different ways because there is no correct English spelling. Each version is an attempt to capture the correct phonetic transliteration of his Arabic name. Korean names generally consist of a family name followed by a two-element personal name, but not always. While the current president, Roh Moo-hyum, is referred to as *Roh* on second reference, Syngman Rhee, South Korea's first president, was *Rhee* on second reference.

Do not count on directories, nameplates or business cards to be correct or up-to-date; whenever possible, ask the person directly.

Continue to check and be exact in using the names of organizations and businesses. Is it *K-mart, Kmart, K-Mart* or *K mart*? Does *Corp., Inc.,* or *Ltd.* follow a company name? Is it the *Sunshine Foundation*—or the *Sonshine Foundation*? Be sure.

Roy Peter Clark, senior scholar at the Poynter Institute, a school for professional journalists, relates an experience with incorrect names. It involved a story about a young man who drove a truck through the window of a donut shop. The young man was identified as a student from Sunnybrook College in New York. "Since I spent four years there, I know that's not the name of the school," Clark said. The next day the paper corrected the error: The school was the State University of New York at Stonybrook Long Island. "That's closer," Clark said, "but the correct spelling is Stony Brook."

Clark suggests this antidote for errors: "The best lesson on the need for accuracy is to have a story written about you."[38]

Telling the Whole Story

"Woman jumps from bridge," a headline says. At first glance, the story that follows is a precise account—accurate and complete. It includes details about the search for the woman's body, a description of how she was dressed, comments from a state trooper who saw the woman jump. Still, there is an error. It could be called an error of omission. An important detail is missing: How high is the bridge? The answer to that question raises another: Could someone survive a jump from that height?

Another story tells how a 24-year-old mentally impaired woman killed a motorist in a traffic accident. The woman, police say, has never had a driver's license and cannot read or write. Details about the accident are included, but unanswered is a series of questions that seem so apparent: How did she get a car? Who owns the car? How did she learn to drive?

Police officers interrupt an attack on two women in the parking lot of a fast-food restaurant. They heard the women scream, the newspaper reports, and they chased the man, arresting him after he circled back to the parking lot. No other details were provided. But questions remain: Where were the officers when they heard the screams? In a patrol car? On foot? Coming out of the restaurant? How did they chase the suspect? On foot? By car? Both? How long did the chase go on? How did they capture the man? At gunpoint? Did he resist? Did he say anything? Space is not an excuse; the story is 14 paragraphs long.

A high school student dies early in the morning after his sports car hits a horse wandering on a lonely stretch of road. The story is a sparse, mechanical account, like too many traffic-accident stories. There are no details about the boy or explanations about what he was doing out at that hour. Was he an honor student? Was he working as a bus boy to earn money for college? How did he die—thrown from the car? Who found him? Where did the horse come from? And what happened to the animal?[39]

Police arrest three people suspected of wounding a guard, shooting open display cases and fleeing with $250,000 in jewelry in a daring mid-day holdup of Tiffany & Co., a jewelry store. The story simply says the three were arrested at 11th and Market streets. Could it be so simple? How did police find the suspects? Were they armed? Did they resist? What's at the intersection of 11th and Market? A church? Tavern? Were the suspects standing on the corner, sitting in a car or sleeping inside an apartment building? Given the nature of the crime, the arrest seems anticlimactic. Was it? Readers never find out.

Some might quarrel that these missing details are not errors. But if you define error as "something incorrectly done through ignorance or carelessness," then their carelessness makes them errors. They certainly are every bit as damaging to press credibility as misspelled names or incorrect facts. Broadcast journalist Paul Davis, speaking for many viewers and readers, expresses the feelings of frustration caused by errors of omission. His remarks, aimed at radio news, apply to all fields of reporting. "At times," he says, "so much basic information is missing that I yell at the radio. Having a cellular phone in my car has become a burden because I want to immediately call the station and register my objections to the short-sheeted story I have just heard. Missing locators, missing names, missing details. Aaargh!"[40]

When readers and viewers get a steady diet of underdeveloped stories and unanswered questions, they rarely write letters to the editor or call the station. They do not even let out an "Aaargh!" Passively, many readers and viewers expect to be left guessing. Those who are especially frustrated and dissatisfied finally turn away from the newscast or newspaper to watch a game-show rerun or read a book.

Davis offers advice to curb errors of omission. "Writers who can distance themselves enough to check their copy as if they were a casual reader will probably spot the copy's weaknesses, the contextual assumption or missing detail."[41] His point is vividly evident in the following story taken from a metropolitan newspaper. It reports the apparent suicide of a doctor. As you read it, look for questions the average person might ask.

MIDDLETOWN—The body of a 27-year-old woman physician, missing since Oct. 30, was found near some railroad tracks in Middletown Sunday, police reported.

The woman was identified as Dr. Linda Kline, of 1952 Greenpoint Drive, in Greenbriar Apartments, at Central Avenue and Interstate 120.

Lt. James Gregory of Middletown Police said he was told Saturday that the woman had been depressed and had told her husband that she had taken an overdose of an antidepressant drug.

Her fully clothed body was found about 3:30 p.m. Sunday about 300 yards northeast of the Reading Railroad tracks at Baylor Road just north of Pinewood Avenue by a helicopter hired by her father, police said.

Police said there was no reason to suspect foul play. Gregory said he was told that the woman telephoned her husband, Dr. Larry Kline, about 11:45 a.m., Oct. 30, and told him she had taken an overdose.

Gregory said Dr. Larry Kline told his wife to induce vomiting and rushed home. When he arrived, his wife was missing, Dr. Larry Kline told police.

Police said the woman's purse was still at her home and nothing was missing from the house.

The story is sterile and cold. It sounds as though a computer wrote it. Moreover, the reporting is lazy and insensitive. Lack of effort, lack of empathy and lack of imagination combine to result in a story riddled with holes. Among them:

- Who are the Klines? Where are they from? If they both held jobs, where did they work? What branch of medicine? What kind of people are they? Friendly? Reclusive? Driven?
- What made Linda Kline depressed? Was she having problems at work or at home? Was she ill?
- Was an empty bottle of an antidepressant drug found at the apartment? Was she taking drugs? If so, what kind and who prescribed them?
- Who is the father? Would men of normal means hire a helicopter to search for a missing daughter? He sounds extraordinary. But his story is untold.

- What about where her body was found? What's there? An empty lot? Brush? Where is the site in relation to the Klines' apartment? Could she have walked there? If it is miles away, how did she get there?
- Why didn't the husband first call the police or an ambulance when his wife said she had taken an overdose? How far is the apartment from his work? How long did it take him to get home? What did he do once he got there? His is another untold story.

At the core of the story's many problems is poor journalism. It appears the reporter relied on police records and one live source, Lt. Gregory. And Lt. Gregory, it seems, is either a secondhand or third-hand source. There's no indication that Gregory talked to Larry Kline or went to the scene. The reporting—or what passes for reporting—probably was conducted via telephone, perhaps by a single call to Gregory.

Most stories are not this glaringly devoid of detail and life, but nearly every day nearly every newspaper, newscast or Internet news service contains nagging errors of omission. Some errors of omission are attributable to sloppy reporting, but many more are the result of unimaginative, one-dimensional reporting. Unimaginative journalists are not very curious. They fail to ask enough "How?" "Why?" and "Why not?" questions. Certain questions never occur to them. Of course, no two reporters handling the same assignment are going to ask identical questions. But some questions are so compelling they beg to be asked no matter who is covering the story. And these are the questions that will occur to discerning news consumers.

Consider another example. A man, 77, and his wife, 74, set out in their pickup truck to visit a daughter 40 miles away. When they fail to show up, the family calls the police. After a nine-day search that includes use of a divining rod and a psychic, police find the two at a motel 150 miles from their home. Motel receipts, canceled checks and witness accounts indicate they crisscrossed several states in their unexplained odyssey. But only one news account of their travels answered what should have been an obvious question: "How far did they travel?" The sharp reporter who asked the question got an answer from the couple's nephew—"4,000 miles." How did the nephew know? It turns out that shortly before the couple disappeared, he changed the oil on the truck, noting the mileage on the odometer. When he later retrieved the truck, he checked the odometer again.

How do you know what to ask? It helps to try to put yourself into the story. Close your eyes and visualize what happened and why. Speculate if necessary. Your picture of what unfolded may conflict with official accounts. Witnesses, for example, describe how a handcuffed burglary suspect manages to escape in a police car and later, after a standoff, kills himself with an officer's gun. Puzzled, you might ask, "Why did the officer leave his gun in his car? Doesn't he carry it in a holster strapped to his waist?" By asking those questions, you learn the gun used in the shooting was a spare the officer kept under the seat of his patrol car. That twist in the story sets off another round of questions: "Do officers generally keep a spare gun in a patrol car?" "What's department policy on spare firearms?"

Sometimes reporters avoid errors by simply applying common sense. If the coroner says a duck hunter drowned when his johnboat, a small, flat-bottomed craft used in shallow waters, went through the lock, common sense tells you that the mechanics of going through a lock are not going to cause a fatal accident. A lock is an enclosed section of waterway, equipped with gates, to raise or lower boats from one level to another. The process of going through a lock is slow and usually routine. "Hmmm," you say to yourself. "This doesn't sound right. Something's missing." Checking, you discover the boat went *over the dam*, not *through the lock*.

One of the benefits of the computer revolution in journalism is the increased use of diagrams and illustrations. In turn, the emphasis on graphics is sharpening the reporting and observational skills of reporters. They are now expected to help artists recreate scenes and events by providing a detailed, step-by-step chronology.

Reconstructing an event can begin with a simple request: "Show me what happened." For particularly complicated happenings, offer witnesses and officials pencil and paper and encourage them to tell the story through drawings and diagrams. Ask questions that help elicit details. "What's the approximate size of the room?" "What happened next?" "Where was the suspect when he opened fire?" Reporters who attempt to graphically recreate news events will be less likely to leave key questions unanswered. They will be more likely to catch the mistakes of others and less likely to introduce mistakes of their own.

Reporters do not ask questions merely to satisfy the curiosity of readers, listeners or viewers. Much more is at stake. As the public's surrogates, reporters are obligated to tell the whole story so officials and newsmakers can be held accountable for their actions and decisions. When the prosecuting attorney drops a case, reporters are obligated to ask *why*. When the highway commission votes to relocate a neighborhood so a road leading to a shopping center can be widened, reporters are obligated to name the commissioners and ask them to explain their vote. If a court of appeals votes to overturn a murder conviction, reporters are obligated to name the judges and how they stood on the issue.

Occasionally, journalists can be excused for not telling the whole story. One of those times is when a story is too difficult, hidden or complicated to be told in a single account. Watergate is the classic example. *Washington Post* reporters Carl Bernstein and Bob Woodward never dreamed that what began as coverage of a burglary report would put them on a tortuous trail that ultimately led to the Oval Office. By necessity, the Watergate saga emerged story by story. Publishing pieces of an incomplete puzzle, Bernstein and Woodward kept the Watergate investigation alive so that additional facts could be discovered.

After a long-running story is told in bits and pieces, some journalists need to climb to a high vantage point for a panoramic, retrospective view. The result may be a comprehensive piece that weaves the threads from dozens of stories into a tapestry. Readers who have followed the piecemeal coverage appreciate the big picture.

Reporters can expect frustrations as they attempt to tell stories fully and accurately. Some find the task too frustrating. That is why Russell Baker of the *New York Times* turned to column writing. Reflecting on his reporting days, Baker said: "It's almost impossible to get it right. The deadlines are too quick, and you don't have time to go into the background. It's *Rashomon*; you interview four different people, you get four different answers."[42] Conscientious reporters share Baker's feelings. But rather than surrender to the uncertainty and frustration of reporting, they persevere. Let the uncertainty and frustration motivate and energize you to do your very best to get it right.

Exercises

1. Interview a classmate and ask the classmate to interview you. Then each of you should write a miniprofile of the other. Together, go over the stories to check for accuracy. If you find mistakes, try to determine how they occurred.

2. Test the reliability of witness accounts. With your teacher's permission and assistance, stage a fast-moving, unexpected happening in your classroom. You might ask two theater students to pose as an odd-looking couple who disrupts class, going from student to student asking for a handout. (A more effective test might be one that is shocking, such as a staged holdup. But give the class warning before any enactment that could be frightening.) Afterward, interview students separately, asking them to recount what happened and to describe the participants. Later, as a class, discuss the differences in accounts.

3. Look for a news story that catches your attention but fails to deliver with enough detail or explanation. Study the story carefully, and then develop a list of questions you believe *should* have been asked and answered.

Notes

1. Andy Rooney, "Thinking It Over," undated column.
2. Herbert Strentz, *News Reporters and News Sources*, 2nd ed. (Ames, Iowa: Iowa State University Press, 1989), p. 3.
3 Quoted in Martin Gottlieb, "Dangerous Liaisons," *Columbia Journalism Review*, July–August 1989, p. 26.

4. "Correction," http://www.rockymountainnews.com/drmn/local/article/0,1299,DRMN_15_5166907,00.html.

5. Steve Weinberg, "So What's Wrong with Pre-publication Review?" *The Quill*, May 1990, p. 26.

6. Richard M. Clurman, *Beyond Malice* (New York: New American Library, 1990), p. 11.

7. Quoted in David Bollier, "Ralph Nader: News Creator," *Columbia Journalism Review*, May–June 1990, p. 52.

8. Stanley L. Payne, *The Art of Asking Questions* (Princeton, N.J.: Princeton University Press, 1951), pp. 158–176.

9. "The Uncertainty Principle," *Stanford Encyclopedia of Philosophy*, http://plato.stanford.edu/entries/qt-uncertainty/.

10. Mary Lou Janson, "Mrs. DeBoe's First Grade," reprint, *Tampa Tribune*, 1983.

11. Lillian Ross, *Reporting Back: Notes on Journalism* (Washington, D.C.: Counterpoint, 2002), pp. 5, 6.

12. "What I Saw Is Bodies, Bodies, Bodies," *Newsweek*, June 19, 1989, p. 22.

13. Jay Mathews, "The Myth of Tiananmen and the Price of a Passive Press," *Columbia Journalism Review*, September–October 1998, p. xx.

14. Darrell Huff, *How to Lie with Statistics* (New York: W.W. Norton & Company, 1954).

15. "From Here to Maternity," http://www.snopes.com/pregnant/blackout.asp.

16. "Percent Change," http://www.robertniles.com/stats/percent.shtml.

17. John Allen Paulos, *A Mathematician Reads the Newspaper* (New York: BasicBooks, 1995), pp. 3, 5–6.

18. "Editor's Note," http://www.regrettheerror.com/2006/10/index.html.

19. Rene J. Cappon, *Associated Press Guide to News Writing* (New York: Macmillan, 1991), p. 87.

20. Quoted in Richard P. Cunningham, "Distortion through Brevity," *The Quill*, July–August 1986, p. 9.

21. Cappon, *News Writing*, p. 88.

22. Chris Berkik, "DUPED! When Journalists Fall for Fake News," *The Quill*, May 2002, pp. 22–26.

23. Angela Gunn, "Lights? Not Quite: 'Interactive' Setup a Happy Hoax," USATODAY.com, http://www.usatoday.com/tech/news/2004-12-28-xmaslights_x.htm.

24. Paul Daquilante, "Hawaiian Bottle Find Turns Out a Hoax," McMinnville (Ore.) *News-Register*, Oct. 31, 2006, http://www.newsregister.com/news/results.cfm?story_no=214411.

25. "Despite Headlines, '01 Saw Fewer Shark Attacks," *Los Angeles Times*, Feb. 20, 2002, p. A6.

26. Jan Harold Brunvand, *The Choking Doberman* (New York: Norton, 1984), pp. 162–169.

27. David Hackett Fischer, *Historians' Fallacies* (New York: Harper Torchbooks, 1970), p. 71.

28. Bob Kohn, *Journalistic Fraud* (Nashville, Tenn.: WND Books, 2003), p. 13.

29. Bill Pennington, "She Did Not Prevail This Year, but Burk Has Time on Her Side," *New York Times*, April 14, 2003, p. D1.

30. Jacques Steinberg and Bill Carter, "CBS Dismisses 4 Over Broadcast on Bush Service," *New York Times*, Jan. 11, 2005, p. 1A.

31. Brian Donovan, "The Attica Errors," *The Quill*, October 1971, p. 38.

32. "Get It First, Correct It Later," *The Quill*, December–January 1990, p. 16.

33. Bob Swift, "You'll Need an Eagle Eye to Spot Best 'Malaphors,'" *Miami Herald*, May 2, 1989, p. 2C.

34. Meg Greenfield, "Misled by the 'Facts,'" *Newsweek*, June 26, 1989, p. 76.

35. Fischer, *Historians' Fallacies*, p. 109.

36. S. I. Hayakawa, *Language in Thought and Action* (New York: Harcourt Brace Jovanovich, 1978), pp. 38–40.

37. Fischer, *Historians' Fallacies*, pp. 182, 183.

38. Roy Peter Clark, "Diary of a Newswriting Guru," *ASNE Bulletin*, April 1981, p. 15.

39. This example comes from Carl Riblet Jr., *The Solid Gold Copy Editor* (Washington, D.C.: Falcon Press, 1972), p. 374; other examples come from published stories.

40. Paul M. Davis, "Simplicity Not Always the Answer; Add a Graph," *The Quill*, February 1989, p. 40.

41. Davis, "Simplicity," p. 39.

42. Quoted in "It's Almost Impossible to Get It Right," *Newsweek*, June 12, 1989, p. 65.

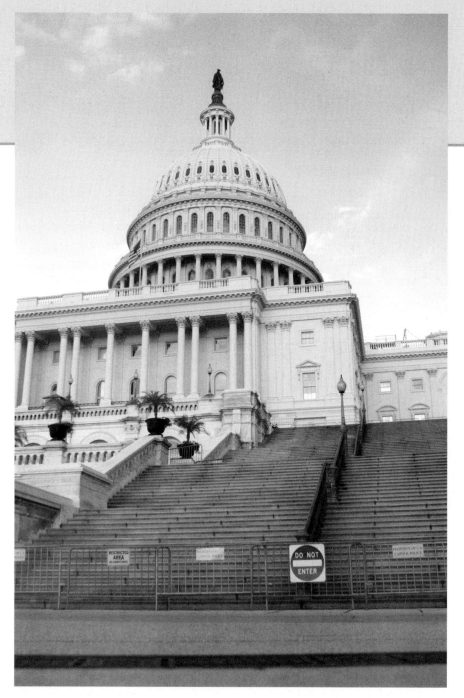

Restricted area of the U.S. Capitol A barricade and the signs "Restricted area: no admittance" and "Do not enter" seem incompatible for the U.S. Capitol, the world-famous symbol of democracy. But as a result of both security measures and construction projects, the public must abide by stricter rules governing access. To critics of government secrecy, the photograph also represents barricades limiting press and public access to government documents and operations. (Photo courtesy of iStockphoto, gingwa, Image # 2182495.)

Closed Meetings, Sealed Records and "Off-Limits" Signs 4

Not all watchdogs carry press credentials.

Mike and Linda Raymond of Woburn, Mass., took a stroll down a wooded path near their home one day and saw, to their dismay, huge trucks loaded with debris rumbling up to the city landfill, long dormant. They began to ask questions: When did the landfill reopen? What was being dumped there? Why weren't people in the neighborhood told? The name Woburn may sound familiar because a best-selling book and popular movie, *A Civil Action*, recounted the protracted, costly and emotional lawsuit by residents against local industries they accused of polluting the community's drinking water and causing an increase in leukemia deaths. The Raymonds felt they were right to worry about the landfill. City officials would not answer their questions and requests for additional information, they said.

So the Raymonds drew upon open meetings and records laws to pry information from state and local officials. They learned, among other things, that a contract between the city and the waste hauler called for disposal of 300,000 tons of debris, but the town, they were stunned to discover, was considering *expanding* the landfill by another million tons. As the news spread through a series of town meetings and news coverage, the city shelved its plans.[1]

The Raymonds represent the experiences of citizens and journalists as they encounter closed doors, sealed records and off-limits signs, which happens far too often. Consider these scenarios:

- Reporters are denied records of an FBI investigation into the mysterious death of a worker who uncovered safety violations at a nuclear plant.
- With incident reports screened and police officers under orders not to talk to the press, a half-dozen brutal home invasions are hidden from public attention.
- Just 25 minutes into its meeting on teachers' contract demands, the school board goes into a closed-door session to weigh strategy in the event of a strike.
- A judge closes a potentially explosive rape trial involving four youths while the victim, a minor, testifies.
- Terrorist suspects are held incommunicado in federal prisons, and the press cannot get access to their names.

Acting as watchdogs, journalists, joined by citizens like the Raymonds, serve the public's right to know about government activities and behavior.

QUOTABLES

"If you want a watchdog to warn you of intruders, you must put up with a certain amount of mistakened barking. Now and then he will sound off because a stray dog seems to be invading his territory . . . or because he is outraged by a postman, and that kind of barking can, of course, be a nuisance.

"But if you muzzle him and leash him and teach him decorum, you will find that he doesn't do the job for which you got him in the first place. Some extraneous barking is the price you must pay for his service as a watchdog.

"A free press is the watchdog of a free society. And only a press free enough to be somewhat irresponsible can possibly fulfill this vital function."

—Alan Barth, *Speaking of a Free Press*, American Newspaper Association Foundation, 2005

Another analogy, based on the benefits of sunshine, applies to access to government information and activities. Sunshine illuminates what is dark and hidden from view. In fact, many open-meetings and open-records statutes are known popularly as "sunshine laws." To promote public awareness and support for transparency in government, in 2005 the American Society of Newspaper Editors (ASNE) launched a nationwide "Sunshine Week," held in mid-March. The ASNE, in alliance with other open-government advocates, asks news organizations to dedicate themselves to educate the public and combat open-records and -meetings abuses in their communities throughout the year but especially during Sunshine Week.

Increasingly, however, shadows are falling on areas once exposed to sunshine. Important stories are becoming difficult to tell because public officials are denying reporters access to information and imposing restrictions on newsgathering. Despite the profession's emphasis on freedom of information, journalists have continued to lose crucial contests over the past several decades.

In March 2004, for example, the U.S. Supreme Court turned down an FOIA request for postmortem photographs of Vincent Foster, a former White House aide found dead in a federal park. Attorney Allan Favish sought the photographs to investigate whether Foster died from a self-inflicted gunshot or was murdered. The Court, however, sided with Foster's surviving family members, saying their privacy rights outweighed public interest in disclosure. The decision also carried an ominous warning for anyone seeking by FIOA information deemed of a "private nature" on alleged grounds of government negligence or impropriety: "The requester must establish more than a bare suspicion to obtain disclosure," Justice Kennedy wrote in the opinion of the Court.[2]

The decision expanded the "privacy exemption" of the FOIA to include the surviving family. Moreover, the case, *National Archives and Records Administration v. Favish*, follows a pattern by the Supreme Court of narrowly interpreting the FOIA in favor of non-disclosure of public records. The Favish decision prompted two Florida newspapers to drop their legal challenges to a Florida law barring public access to autopsy photographs. Lawmakers enacted the law to protect the privacy of the family of NASCAR driver Dale Earnhardt, killed in 2001 in a crash at the Daytona 500.

September 11, 2001, brought the nation into a war on terror that has further hampered the ability of the press and public to monitor government. The White House, setting an example emulated by the legislative and judicial branches as well, actively expanded the classification of information as "secret." In testimony before Congress in 2005, J. William Leonard, director of the Information Security Oversight Office, an agency created by President George W. Bush, said secrecy in the name of national security came at a price. "It is my view that the government classifies too much information," he said, adding that "classification often becomes an automatic rather than an informed, deliberate decision."[3] As evidence, he said his office, which oversees the classification system, recorded a rise from 9 million classification actions in 2001 to 16 million in 2004.

Reacting to Leonard's statistics, open-government advocate Steven Aftergood said an even more aggressive form of government information control had gone unenumerated and often unrecognized in the Bush era, as government agencies have restricted access to *unclassified* information in libraries, archives, Web sites and official databases. "Once freely available, a growing number of these sources are now barred to the public as 'sensitive but unclassified' or 'for official use only.' Information is the oxygen of democracy. Day by day, the Bush administration is cutting off the supply."[4]

Despite the spread of secrecy, public officials do champion open government. Florida Gov.-elect Charlie Crist, for example, announced in late 2006 a plan to create a state Office of Open Government to train public employees on open-records and -meetings requirements and ensure compliance with those laws. Barbara Petersen, president of the Florida First Amendment Foundation, said she was ecstatic. "This is his first act as a new governor—he hasn't taken office yet," she said. "It shows his priorities. I was hoping he would mention open government in his inaugural address."[5] Indeed, Crist did, saying, ". . . We must continue to strive to put government in the service of the people. Of the people, by the people and for the people—powerful words of Abraham Lincoln. Our Constitution requires that our government be open and transparent, and under my administration it will be like never before."

Good intentions, however, sometimes get garbled in translation or diluted as they trickle down the chain of command in federal, state or local government. As a result, journalists and others requesting access to records or meetings encounter a general reluctance to comply in passive-resistance manner—bureaucratic footdragging, nitpicking over specifics, delays in release of information and unrealistic charges to reproduce or copy material. The Coalition of Journalists for Open Government (www.cjog.org) keeps tabs on threats to access, and its Web site shows the type, manner and implications of government actions that reflect widespread *de facto* "non-compliance" with the FOIA and comparable laws at the state and local levels.

If officials deny requests for information outright and news organizations are forced to sue for access, the cost in time and money mounts. Waging a court battle may take years and thousands of dollars in legal fees. Determination goes far to unlock records and open doors, but when the only option remaining is legal action, journalists must be prepared to pay the price. As Clarence Pennington, editor of the *Review Times*, a 7,500-circulation newspaper in Fostoria, Ohio, sees it, "It's part of the cost of doing business, and if we don't do it, we ought to just quit the [journalism] business and run pickle factories or something."[6]

Access to information is at the heart of the news enterprise. If journalists cannot get to the people, places and information that make up the news, other legal questions become moot. Access is treated separately in this chapter rather than in Chapter 11, which explores libel, privacy and journalists' privilege.

Access and the Right to Gather News

Freedom of information is a democratic principle rooted deeply in the American experience. "We the people" begins the preamble to the Constitution. In our self-governing society we delegate authority to legislators, judges and political leaders, and we depend on a free flow of information to help us understand, debate and decide public issues, including who will be our governors. As James Madison said 200 years ago, "A popular government without popular information or the means of acquiring it is but a prologue to a farce or a tragedy; or, perhaps both. Knowledge will forever govern ignorance: and a people who mean to be their own governors must arm themselves with the power which knowledge gives."[7]

To develop and sustain Madison's ideal of self-governing, informed citizenry, a controversial principle—the "public's right to know"—has evolved. Most Americans lack the means and time to stay fully informed, so the press has assumed the role of surrogate, exercising and defending the public's right to know.

QUOTABLES

"The press was to serve the governed, not the governors. The Government's power to censor the press was abolished so that the press would remain forever free to censure the Government. The press was protected so that it could bare the secrets of government and inform the people. Only a free and unrestrained press can effectively expose deception in government."

—Justice Hugo Black, *New York Times v. U.S.*, 403 U.S. 713 (1971)

The right to know, however, is not guaranteed under the Constitution. Members of the Constitutional Convention met in secrecy, and they produced a document that says little about openness and access to information. Nowhere does the Constitution mention the public's right to know or the press's right to gather information on the public's behalf. Moreover, the U.S. Supreme Court, although repeatedly acknowledging the importance of a well-informed citizenry, has never expressly recognized a constitutional right to know.

On the other hand, newsgathering enjoys a degree of constitutional legitimacy as a result of Supreme Court rulings. But any right to gather news apparently excludes a broad *right to access* to government and its information sought by the press. In a

1977 case involving press access to a jail, Chief Justice Warren Burger said this about freedom of information: "This Court has never intimated a First Amendment guarantee of right of access to all sources of information within government control."[8] In more forceful words, William Rehnquist, later to become chief justice, concluded in another decision: "This Court emphatically has rejected the proposition . . . that the First Amendment is some sort of constitutional 'sunshine law.'"[9]

The First Amendment may not be a sunshine law, but it does give reporters considerable latitude to pursue the news, provided they are ready to expend the effort. In 1974, Supreme Court Justice Potter Stewart aptly described the issue of press and access in these words:

> The press is free to do battle against secrecy and deception in government. But the press cannot expect from the Constitution any guarantee that it will succeed. There is no constitutional right to have access to particular government information, or to require openness from the bureaucracy. The public's interest in knowing about its government is protected by the guarantee of a free press, but the protection is indirect. The Constitution itself is neither a Freedom of Information Act nor an Official Secrets Act. The Constitution, in other words, establishes the contest, not its resolution.[10]

Indeed, some reporters welcome the challenges of a contest. Reporter Steve McGonigle, recipient of the Brechner Award for Freedom of Information Reporting, lightheartedly says, "I love secrecy. It enables me to write stories nobody can get. I don't know what I'd do without it."[11]

Access to Governmental Meetings

In the 1950s and 1960s, before sunshine laws became common-place, public bodies occasionally made a mockery of the democratic process of government by meeting at odd hours, without notice and in out-of-the-way places, such as gathering on Christmas Eve in the back room of the Kozy Korner café. Today, with statutes in force, officials sometimes resort to novel tactics to stay technically within the law. In Walla Walla, Wash., for example, the county commission adopted an annual schedule, as law required, setting regular meetings on "each workday of every week of the year." Rick Doyle, managing editor of the *Walla Walla Union-Bulletin*, saw the schedule as a ploy to discourage the press and public from attending meetings. "This means they can meet at any time any day of the week," he said. The newspaper countered by suing the commission and stationing a reporter in the council chambers eight hours a day throughout the week.[12]

On occasion, secret meetings cover misdeeds and corruption. Most often, though, public officials sincerely believe they can work more effectively if the process of government is not complicated by the presence of nosy reporters and meddlesome citizens. Officials still meet in private to debate and discuss sensitive matters and arrive at conclusions—no fish bowl for them. Later, when these same officials go through the motions of a public meeting, they vote in apparent harmony, without debate or discussion. Reporters ought to look suspiciously on a pattern of no debate and unanimous votes by a public body.

William Small, author of *Political Power and the Press*, explains the mentality that leads to closed meetings and closed records:

> If there is a law in press-government relations it is that information is provided in reverse proportion to the amount of controversy involved. Cooperation decreases in direct relationship to the sensitiveness of the subject matter. What the politician does not share willingly is that material which either reflects unfavorably on his administration or that which he judges must be kept from the public for its own good. It is the arrogance of political power that those who have it always know best when the public should know least.[13]

Not all public officials are infected by the arrogance of power Small describes. Nevertheless, the tendency in government circles is to interpret sunshine laws narrowly and negatively, not affirmatively, as the term *open meetings* implies. From that perspective, the statutory *exceptions to openness* are twisted to become *imperatives for closure*. No law gives the press and public absolute, unconditional rights of access. But with all open-meetings laws, there is an underlying *presumption* of openness, and that presumption gives the press leverage to pry open shut doors.

Although every state has an open-meetings law, they vary dramatically in scope, strength and specificity. Journalists need to possess an intimate knowledge of what the law permits and prohibits if they hope to gain access. That knowledge includes how the law has been interpreted in court decisions and in legal opinions by the state attorney general's office. Such information is available from several sources. In some states, the attorney general's office publishes an annotated version of the law, including legal interpretations. As a public service, various state bar associations provide detailed handbooks for reporters. To date, the best comprehensive reference work is the *Open Government Guide* (previously called *Tapping Officials' Secrets*), a state-by-state compendium of information on every state's open-meetings and open-records statutes. It is published by a Washington, D.C.-based organization, the Reporters Committee for Freedom of the Press, and can be viewed online at www.rcfp.org.

The laws generally do not apply to the legislature or the judiciary, which operate under their own rules and policies. State legislatures almost always meet in open, public sessions, so it is rare when the press finds the lawmakers skirting the law, as happened when Lucy Morgan caught GOP senators meeting at a fancy private restaurant (see "Real-Life Lessons").

Your knowledge of the open-meetings laws should include these points:

What public bodies are covered?
Usually the law applies to any agency or body that receives or expends public money. Still, there are many gray areas. Is the faculty senate at the state university covered?

What about the board of directors of a non-profit organization contracted to run a city-owned hospital? It may take a time-consuming, costly court fight to find out.

Some bodies are specifically excluded—and with good reason. An example is a state investment board; premature disclosure of its deliberations could lead to improper speculation in securities. But other bodies, like parole boards, may be excluded for no better reason than tradition or political expediency. Parole boards, entrusted to decide when convicted criminals can safely re-enter society, ought to be subjected to scrutiny; too often they operate in secret, fueling suspicions of payoffs and favoritism.

What constitutes a meeting?

Florida is noted for a strong record on access, but its open-meetings statute is brief and general; it does not precisely define *meeting*. When Florida officials discuss public business at a cocktail party or golf club, is that a "meeting"? Fortunately, court rulings in Florida have established that a meeting occurs whenever two or more members of the public body meet to discuss official business. In Illinois, by contrast, the law is more definite but not necessarily stronger. A "meeting," the law states, "means any gathering of a majority of quorum of a public body held for the purpose of discussing public business."

REAL-LIFE LESSONS

Tallahassee state capital bureau chief Lucy Morgan earned a reputation with legislators and state leaders—from the governor to the commander of the state police—for her doggedness about stories she pursued. When she retired from the *St. Petersburg Times* in 2005, her former boss, Andrew Barnes, said: ". . . [S]he scared the pants off politicians with something to hide. I have never known a reporter who was better at ferreting out facts."[14] In 1985, she and fellow *Times* staffer, Jack Reed, shared the Pulitzer Prize for investigative reporting that exposed corruption in the Pasco County Sheriff's Office.

Morgan hated it when officials tried to keep secrets and hide their business from public view. Here's how she used the power of publicity to shame lawmakers she caught meeting behind closed doors:

> Just hours before their most important debate of the 1999 legislative session, 20 of the 25 Republican senators gathered at a gourmet restaurant Monday night in an apparent violation of Senate rules that require public notice of their meetings.
>
> Over grouper, amaretto, steaks and dessert, the lawmakers discussed the controversial education bill being pushed by Gov. Jeb Bush, legislation to rein in big jury awards and the spending projects sought by individual legislators for their hometowns.
>
> The senators invited Ken Plante, chief lobbyist for the governor, to discuss a number of issues, including rumors that Bush has threatened to veto some of their pet projects. Plante brought some reassuring words about Bush's intentions.

> "Unless you hear that word from the tall, lanky one himself, it has not been said," he told the senators.
>
> Their meeting took place in the back room of Georgio's Restaurant, about 8 miles north of the Capitol. When a *Times* reporter appeared at the meeting, the senators let her in without complaint. . . .[15]
>
> Morgan tried her best to keep government open and above ground. Her efforts did not always endear her to public officials, but she earned their respect. In 2005, at the end of Morgan's last legislative session in Tallahassee as an active reporter, the senate honored her by renaming the press gallery, the Lucy Morgan Senate Press Gallery.

When laws are vague in defining a meeting, reporters can expect public officials to wiggle through the loopholes. In Minnesota, for example, three members of a seven-member school board met at the home of one of the board members to discuss the superintendent's performance. Meanwhile, three other members of the board met at a bank for the same purpose. Later, notes were compared in a telephone conference between an attendee of each meeting. A court, asked to determine whether a meeting occurred, decided that the law did not apply to groups too small to officially make a decision.[16] The school board followed the letter of the law but violated its spirit.

What does it take to close a meeting?

Must a motion be made? Is a vote taken? Is a majority needed? Two-thirds? Must officials cite a statutory exemption to the open-meetings law? A strong law puts officials on record, requiring a voice vote and a specific, declared, legal reason for meeting in secret.

What subjects or topics are exempt under the law?

Not all exemptions are found within the text of the open-meetings law. Some are provided for in separate statutes. Often, open-meetings laws include a catchall disclaimer: "All meetings are open except those involving matters specifically exempted from disclosure by federal or state law." The disclaimer might cover hundreds of subjects.

You will find that the language of sunshine laws can be misleading. The law might sound sweeping and unconditional—"All meetings of public bodies shall be open"—but several paragraphs later may list a half-dozen exceptions. These exceptions allow customarily open public bodies, like school boards and city councils, to go into "executive session," a euphemism for a secret or closed-door meeting.

"Personnel matters" and "litigation" are the two most frequently cited reasons for holding an executive session. Other areas often exempted are discussions of disciplinary cases, collective-bargaining negotiations, real estate transactions, employment and dismissal of public employees and litigation involving the public body. In almost all instances, votes on matters discussed in closed session must be conducted in an open session.

Be sure to know the parameters of general categories such as "personnel" or "litigation." Usually, laws that exclude discussion of personnel matters apply to individual cases, most commonly the hiring and firing of a particular employee. But some public officials will stretch the meaning of *personnel* to cover nearly every subject dealing with employees. Comparable problems apply to use of the term *litigation*. Does the open-meetings law distinguish between imminent litigation or cases presently being adjudicated? Discussion of an *existing* lawsuit against the city might be exempt; discussion of a *threatened* lawsuit might not, a distinction city officials could try to blur.

What notice is required to postpone, reschedule or move meetings?
Notice provisions were enacted because unscrupulous public officials in many states manipulated the law by changing meeting sites and dates without informing the press or public. Nearly all state laws require public bodies to post an annual schedule of meeting dates, times and places. Of course, emergencies may force officials to make changes, but a strong law requires at least a 48-hour notice of changes to the regular, posted schedule. In some cases, though, reporters must annually request in writing that the agency notify them of changes. Online calendars posted by government offices allow reporters to more easily keep track of scheduled meetings.

When a meeting is closed, what record is required?
Most states require a record of meetings, although it may amount only to a "general description" of the matters discussed, not a verbatim audio or video recording. The record also may be hard to obtain. Although many laws set a time limit for release of minutes, there sometimes is a potentially restrictive condition: Minutes are to be made available only after the public body determines that it is no longer necessary to protect a public interest or the privacy of individuals. Such a caveat puts reporters at the mercy of officials who can, by inaction or refusal, set an indefinite time limit on release of minutes. Legal action may be the only way to wrest the minutes away from them.

What legal relief is available to contest closure or non-compliance?
Legal action often is not practical when reporters are locked out of a meeting. By the time a complaint can be heard in court, the news may be stale. If, for example, the city council is considering disciplinary action against the police chief, the news value is in being there to report what was said and done.

Still, when a legal challenge is needed to prevent future abuses of the law or to send a message to public officials, the press will not get far without the cooperation of law enforcement officials. Often, a key figure is the local state's attorney, who may be empowered to bring civil action for non-compliance. Among the legal tools available are the *injunction*, a court order that prohibits officials from further violations, or a *writ of mandamus*, another form of court order that requires officials to fulfill their duties under the law.

Proving non-compliance is not easy if public officials, in a united front, proclaim they acted properly and leave no evidence that they acted improperly. Who is to know? The law may require a judge to examine the minutes of a closed meeting privately, but nothing keeps dishonest public officials from editing or falsifying that record. If there is a will to deceive, usually there is a way.

What are the penalties for violating an open-meetings law?

Do not expect violations of sunshine laws to be accompanied by thunder and lightning. Although some open-meetings statutes include criminal penalties, they are misdemeanor offenses that seldom include jail time. In 2003, a suspended Escambia (Fla.) County commissioner began a 60-day jail sentence, becoming the first elected official to be jailed for violating the open-meetings section of the Sunshine Law.[17] A jury convicted the commissioner of improperly discussing redistricting in a telephone call with the county election supervisor while another commissioner listened on a speakerphone. More serious violations, however, go unpunished in states without jail terms or where the punishment amounts to fines, usually ranging from $500 to $1,000. The penalties, civil or criminal, may not be enough to deter lawbreakers; some consequences are so slight that officials feel free to flout the law.

REPORTER'S TIP FILE

What do you do when a meeting is closed?

You are covering a meeting of the Pottsville City Council. After about a half-hour of routine business, a council member says, "Mayor Davis, I move that we go into executive session to discuss this next matter." The motion is seconded, a quick vote taken and the council members rise and move to the mayor's private meeting room. What should you do? Here are some suggestions:

Know the law. Remember, your best defense against evasive tactics is to be an authority on your state's open-meetings statute. Make sure officials know the law, too. Usually, an attorney retained by the public body attends meetings and offers guidance when officials propose to go into executive session. But the attorney, despite an air of assuredness, may have only a casual knowledge of the law. By establishing that you know the law and are determined to see it properly applied, you might convince officials to yield to its authority. Or you might raise enough doubt in the attorney's mind that he or she will recommend against closure.

Speak up. Do not be timid about your rights. The First Amendment Foundation, among other open-government organizations, suggests that when public officials try to close a meeting, reporters read a statement modeled after this one:

Florida Statute 286.011, the government-in-sunshine law, requires that all meetings of state or local governmental boards or commissions be open to the public unless there

---

is a specific statutory exemption. If I am ordered to leave (or forbidden to enter) this meeting, I ask that you advise me of the statutory authority for your action. Otherwise, my editors have instructed me to insist on my right to attend this meeting.

Get it on record. Insist that public officials specifically identify the exemption being cited to close a meeting. A reference to "personnel matters" is inadequate. Ask the presiding officer to identify exactly what personnel matters are involved—the hiring of a new city manager, disciplinary action against a housing inspector, labor negotiations? Be persistent, although you still may not get a satisfactory answer.

Stay under control. To physically resist expulsion from a closed meeting is counterproductive and may lead to your arrest. Instead, state your objections, then retire to fight again with the help of your editor and attorney.

Publicize closed meetings. Let people know whenever a public body meets in private. Negative publicity has a way of making officials reconsider past ways.

What do you do when officials invite you into a closed meeting—but with strings attached? You may be told you can stay if you agree not to publish what transpires. Do you accede to conditions that gag you? Taking a vow of silence might be preferable to being left in the dark. Then again, it may be best to fight for openness or seek information by other means. Before accepting any conditions, consult with your editor.

Access to Government Records

John Walsh fumed. As executive director of St. Louis' Visitors Bureau, he had been ordered by the chairperson of the board—his boss—to surrender records to a *St. Louis Globe-Democrat* reporter investigating the use of public money to host the Miss Universe Pageant. Since hotel and restaurant taxes heavily financed the Visitors Bureau, the *Globe-Democrat* argued that expense figures should be open for public inspection. The newspaper won its point.

The records revealed that the pageant, which cost $1,479,000 to put on, earned $694,000, leaving $784,000 to be paid by tax money. Among the expenses were $300,000 for scenery, $30,000 for local transportation and $122,000 in local hotel bills. Walsh's comment: "You [reporters] have this fascination with nit-picking details like why we spent $143 on a luncheon somewhere." His parting shot: "If I had my way, I wouldn't talk to you at all."[18]

A sure way for public officials to stir journalists is to say, "You can't have it." As one observer put it, "In some ways, journalists are like children. The more they're told to stay away from something, the more interested in it they become. Their motive is more than childish curiosity. They know that the person or group warning the media away must consider the information important, and if it's important, it's probably something the public should know."[19] Here is what to expect when you seek government records:

Loopholes and Exemptions

Like miners panning for gold, reporters routinely inspect records to see what is happening on their beat. They review travel vouchers, purchase requisitions and real estate assessments, for example, as part of their watchdog role. Perhaps the odds are against it, but one day their panning could turn up irregularities that warrant coverage. It took a freedom-of-information request, but *Detroit News* reporter Angie Cannon gained access to the city's employee overtime records. She discovered that annual overtime amounted to $40 million, half of Detroit's deficit.[20]

By custom and practice, access to certain records, such as land deeds and tax rolls, is almost taken for granted. But statutory law now encompasses and codifies much of what was covered by common law. Ironically, in some instances, the passage of state sunshine laws gave legislators the opportunity to enumerate a long list of records and materials *exempt* from public disclosure.

Illinois provides an example of how exemptions weaken open-records laws. For years, Illinois operated under a narrow law that vaguely covered fiscal records of "obligation, receipt or use of public funds." No one was quite sure what the law covered. Were invoices and payrolls, for example, subject to the law? A haze hung over other records of government, such as police reports.

Beyond the law's lack of specificity and scope, it contained three conditions that encouraged public officials to deny requests: At their discretion, officials could require 24-hour written notice before allowing inspection of records, insist that those seeking information precisely specify the records they intended to examine and refuse to release the material requested if it was "in use" by "authorized" personnel.

In 1984, however, Illinois enacted its first comprehensive open-records statute—the Freedom of Information Act. It listed 14 types of information that fall under the statute's definition of "public record." Yet more than one-half of the text of the law was devoted to describing the types of records *exempt* from disclosure requirements—26 exemptions in all. Since then, lawmakers have expanded the number of exemptions, particularly to protect individual privacy or homeland security.

The largest group of exceptions pertains to invasion of privacy, such as a ban on release of the names of individuals receiving public aid. Another set pertains to law enforcement records. Nearly all investigative records are closed; arrest logs are open but only to the extent that the information they contain does not constitute an "unwarranted" invasion of an individual's privacy. The names of persons filing criminal complaints are not public. A third category covers documents related to internal operations of public bodies, such as "preliminary drafts of memoranda in which opinions or policies are formulated." The fourth category of exemptions is designed to protect business or financial interests of both private persons and public bodies. Among the exemptions in this category are bids for contracts that, if disclosed, would frustrate procurement or give an advantage to anyone proposing to enter into a contract with a public body.

Important public interests are evident in several of Illinois' exemptions—for example, non-disclosure of engineering and architectural plans for public buildings, which would jeopardize security if they fell into the hands of terrorists or criminals. There is usually, though, a reverse side to this type of non-disclosure. If a walkway in a public building collapses, killing dozens of people, the engineering plans might reveal a structural defect attributable to negligence on the part of public officials responsible for overseeing construction. When a statute like Illinois' is riddled with escape clauses, those wishing to withhold information can readily find an exemption to apply.

With customarily open records, such as court documents, access rarely is a problem. It is the nebulous, fringe areas of the law that most often are troublesome. One recent legal debate centers on private developers who receive low-interest, tax-free *industrial-revenue bonds* to finance construction of hotels, factories and shopping malls. Are those developers agents of the municipalities that arranged for the industrial-revenue bonds and therefore subject to provisions of the state open-records law? This type of access debate usually requires a court challenge to settle.

Inconsistent application is another problem. The police chief in Jonesboro gives reporters unlimited access to arrest reports; 15 miles away in Smithville, the chief, fearful of invasion-of-privacy lawsuits, filters all arrest reports through shift commanders, who are instructed to remove any information that might embarrass victims or expose witnesses. The police chief of Smithville cautiously puts privacy interests ahead of the press's interest in informing the public. Perhaps he is overly sensitive, but you cannot say he is corrupt or, for that matter, wrong. He has his perspective; the reporter has another.

Strategies for Obtaining Information

Before going to the trouble of filing a written request for information, try an informal approach. A polite, persuasive request made in person is likely to raise fewer objections than a stiff, formal statement received in the mail or online. In person, you can state your reasons for requesting the information, counter reservations officials might have about releasing records and negotiate conditions for inspecting and copying the records. Investigative reporter Jim Steele of the *Philadelphia Inquirer* offers additional advice: Do not be stymied by clerks. He suggests carrying copies of the open-records law and politely reading them aloud. If that fails, speak with a supervisor or stand around until the clerks relent.[21]

Public records, filed away In a digital age, paper records still exist, and on public affairs beats, reporters need to know where they are stored, what they contain and how to gain access. (Photo by Robbie Arkovich.)

When informal methods prove to be futile, consult statutes on access to government information. They contain procedures detailing how written requests are to be handled. Usually, officials must act on requests for records within seven to 10 working days, but time limits tend to expand, especially if the request involves large amounts of information scattered among several offices. The law generally permits public bodies to charge a fee for copying records, but a number of states allow fees to be waived if it is established that release of the information benefits the public.

Some laws explain how to make a request for government documents. Several news organizations also provide sample letters of request, among them the Reporters Committee for Freedom of the Press. Its Web site (www.rcfp.org) features a software program to individualize letters requesting records.

If a request is denied, the laws also contain appeal procedures. Typically, an open-records statute gives state courts jurisdiction to conduct *in camera* (private) examination of the documents in question. The burden of proof usually is with the public body, which must establish that its actions comply with the law. If the appeal determines that public officials withheld the information without a basis in law, then some states allow courts to order the public body to pay attorney fees connected with the appeal.

Sample Letter of Request

Agency head [or *Freedom of Information officer*]
Name of agency
City, state, zip code
Re: Freedom of Information Act request
Dear [*FOI officer*]:

I request that a copy of the following documents [*or documents containing the following information*] be provided to me: [*identify as specifically as possible*].

In order to help to determine my status to assess fees, you should know that I am [*insert description of requester and purposes of request such as "a representative of the (name of newspaper, broadcast station, etc.)"*], and this request is made as part of newsgathering and not for commercial use.

[*You may also offer to pay fees up to a certain amount or request a fee waiver.*]

Thank you for your consideration of this request.

Sincerely,

In truth, though, open-records laws are only as good as the willingness of public officials to honor them. Even when records are clearly public under the law, it still may take repeated requests followed by lengthy litigation before files are made available for inspection and copying. Key passages may be blackened out, leading to another legal tug of war. Before long, the story is likely to be old news, and the reporter who made the request may be at a new job, thousands of miles away and hundreds of assignments beyond the original assignment. If records are the path to an investigative story, reporters are likely to find tracks covered and the trail cold by the time the information is handed over.

Access to records is difficult. Do not, however, let discouraging complaints from reporters deter you from seeking records; do not assume the answer will be no. Many public employees are committed to the principle of open government. They help and cooperate with information seekers. Remember, too, the importance of good relations with news sources. The front door to records may be barred, but files may be slipped out the back door to a conscientious, trustworthy reporter. Lauren Cowen of the *Oregonian* reinforces the importance of good sources: "Even if the FOIA were perfect and acted the way it was supposed to, and we got all of the information we were asking for within 10 days, I would never substitute the use of personal contacts within the agency and strictly use the act. You still need those officials within the agency to explain the documents. I would do both."[22]

Online Access to Records

Nearly all government entities provide some degree of online access to information, but a general wariness exists among public officials that the Internet constitutes an unlocked and unguarded door for identity thieves and other unwelcomed intruders. When someone appears in person at the county building to request, say, a death certificate or property tax records, there is, potentially, the ability to screen the request and identify the person making it. Information retrieved online is often done anonymously, without witnesses. To protect personal privacy and guard against criminal use of information, most government and court entities withhold from public view records that contain social security numbers, addresses or personal details about individuals or families, such as adoption proceedings.

Online access, of course, serves the cause of open government, so, despite concerns about abuse, public officials at the federal, state and local levels feel obligated to use the Web as a portal for citizens to tap an array of services, information and records. For example, many city governments put official forms, such as building permits, for download online and post the municipal budget and minutes of the city council. County governments usually put their records online, such as tax appraisals, court dockets and vital statistics. Many states provide online access to legislation, statutes and constitutions. Privacy and personal safety issues continue to pressure officials to find the proper balance between open and closed online records.

Access to public records via the Internet varies dramatically. In some cases, nearly everything traditionally considered "public" is available for free online through government-supported Web sites. Smaller cities, in particular, limited in resources, simply offer a token Internet presence. Access through commercial Internet services, under government contract, usually is fee-based, and the fees, too, vary—from nominal to exorbitant.

Reporters often take advantage of online services, but going in person remains the best approach when seeking public records.

Access to Federal Records and Meetings

Since July 4, 1966, records of the federal government have been open under the Freedom of Information Act. The father of the law, Rep. John E. Moss of California, began his quest for open records in 1953. Moss, then a freshman in Congress, found he could not obtain information about Sen. Joseph McCarthy's allegations of disloyalty among federal employees even though Moss was a member of the Post Office and Civil Service Committee. Recalling those days, Moss said, "I thought if the committee couldn't get any information who the hell can?"[23] It took 13 years, but Moss eventually helped open the records of government to the public and press. In 1989, Moss (1915–1997) said the FOIA had met his "minimal expectations, but not my highest hopes," adding that the law has suffered "widespread abuse."[24]

In 1977, the Government in Sunshine Act, which requires open meetings by a range of federal agencies, commissions, boards and departments, became law. It covers public bodies whose members are appointed by the president and that have some independent authority, such as the Federal Trade Commission and the Federal Reserve Board.

Together the two acts constitute a commitment to openness in government, but, by no means, are the laws perfect. Reporters find themselves fettered and frustrated by a spate of exemptions, uncooperative officials, restrictive amendments and narrow interpretations by the courts.

The federal FOIA marked its 40th anniversary in 2006, and law professor Martin E. Halstuk acknowledged its past and present conditions. "Over the decades, the FOIA has helped expose waste and fraud in the federal government, and uncover a wide variety of unsafe consumer products, dangerous drugs, and health hazards," he said. "But more recently there has been a steady erosion of the freedoms enshrined in both the letter and spirit of the law." He cited the costly, lengthy litigation necessary to get the government to hand over "indisputably" public records and a judiciary that broadly interpreted the FOIA exemptions.[25]

Many exemptions under the FOIA parallel those found in state open-records laws. That's not surprising; the federal FOIA served as a model for laws in a number of states. In brief, the act's nine exemptions cover:

- national security
- internal agency personnel rules
- information specifically exempted by other federal statutes
- trade secrets
- internal agency memoranda and policy discussions
- personal privacy
- law enforcement investigations
- federally regulated banks and financial records
- geological information

Note that government officials are permitted, but not required, to suppress information under the FOIA exemptions.

Exemptions to the federal open-meetings law cover many of the sensitive areas exempted under the FOIA. They include matters of national security, law enforcement investigations and trade secrets. Like state open-meetings laws, the exemptions offer numerous excuses for closing doors. Moreover, the federal law does not apply to cabinet-level departments or advisory bodies closest to the president, such as the National Security Council.

In short, the law leaves much to be desired. Bodies that make some of the most important decisions affecting the public are not covered. But the Government in

Sunshine Act is a first step toward making the sprawling federal bureaucracy open and more accountable to the public. The act helped open the door for the cable network C-SPAN to air virtually all significant hearings in Congress, as well as a great number of federal agency meetings.

Access to the Judicial System

At the heart of many access disputes involving the courts and the press are the sometimes competing interests of the First and Sixth amendments. Reckless news coverage can threaten a defendant's Sixth Amendment rights to a fair trial by an impartial jury. On the other hand, aggressive yet responsible reporting can help ensure that justice is done. Today's reporters generally are sensitive to the issues of *free press versus fair trial*. Where to draw the line, though, poses problems. Reporters must ask themselves which interests are paramount—those of society or of the accused?

Much of today's friction between the press and courts dates to a series of developments that occurred in the 1960s. In 1964, the Warren Commission, formed to investigate the assassination of President John F. Kennedy, criticized the police and press for releasing incriminating information and statements about Lee Harvey Oswald, the accused assassin. Two years later, in the case of *Sheppard v. Maxwell*, the U.S. Supreme Court overturned a murder conviction of a prominent doctor on the grounds of prejudicial pretrial publicity. In doing so, the Court chastised the judge for failing to maintain order in the courtroom and control over the release of non-admissible *extrajudicial* information.

Finally, in 1968, the American Bar Association released the report of its Advisory Committee on Fair Trial and Free Press, better known as the Reardon Report. Inspired, in part, by the Warren Commission's findings and influenced by the *Sheppard* case, the Reardon Report urged judges to use their powers to guard against prejudicial publicity. The committee's recommendations to judges included closing pretrial hearings if a fair trial appeared to be in jeopardy, ordering participants in the case and reporters covering it to adhere to gag orders governing release of information and punishing violators of court orders by issuing contempt citations.

In the wake of these developments, some judges overreacted to the possibilities of "trial by mass media." Rather than risk the embarrassment of having a ruling overturned or a case retried because they failed to maintain control, judges began to get tough—issuing gag orders, closing pretrial hearings, sealing records and even closing trials. Clashes between the courts and the press increased, forcing the Supreme Court to intervene. In a string of cases, the Court reminded lower courts to impose restrictions on press coverage only under serious circumstances.

Helping ease tension between the press and courts are voluntary press-bench-bar guidelines that protect the rights of individuals while also recognizing the important watchdog role of the press. Not all journalists think such guidelines are a good idea, because they tend to curtail aggressive, independent news coverage of the courts.

Understandably, skirmishes continue to occur. The following overview outlines what reporters can expect regarding access to the courts:

Grand Juries

The principal role of the grand jury is to determine whether evidence against an individual accused of a crime is strong enough to send the case to trial. Grand jury proceedings are one-sided presentations by the prosecution; normally, the accused cannot contest the evidence presented or mount a defense. In addition, the rules of evidence are not as strict as those governing trials. Grand jurors themselves occasionally are free to question witnesses. Secrecy is needed, court authorities contend, to safeguard the Sixth Amendment rights of accused persons, to encourage witnesses to come forward and give frank testimony without fear of retaliation and to protect the good reputations of those who are investigated and cleared.

As a result, grand jury proceedings are closed to the public and press, and grand jurors and court officials who work with the grand jury are bound by an oath of secrecy, at least as long as the grand jury is in session. Reporters can cover grand jury proceedings indirectly by questioning people before and after they testify, provided the court system's rules of procedure allow witnesses to discuss what they said or heard inside the grand jury room. Not all do. In some jurisdictions, secrecy obligations continue even after a grand jury investigation has concluded. Reporters who aid or abet grand jurors or court officials in breaking their oaths venture into a legal and ethical morass. Fortunately, in 1990, the U.S. Supreme Court ruled that once a grand jury is discharged, a state's interest in preserving secrecy is not sufficient to warrant a ban on speech by witnesses.[26]

Reporters are entitled to reports and documents coming from the grand jury at the conclusion of its deliberations. One exception is a sealed indictment. When a grand jury decides that evidence warrants a trial, it issues an *indictment*, which becomes the basis for an *arrest warrant* to apprehend an accused person who is not already in police custody. If the press reports the indictment before police can serve a warrant, the suspect named in the indictment might flee. When an indictment is sealed, its contents are kept from the press until an accused individual is confronted in open court with the allegations in the warrant's charges.

Juvenile Cases

Juveniles receive special treatment from the courts. Hearings and records often are kept confidential to shield minors from potentially injurious publicity. There is a tendency to think of juvenile court as a place for trying young offenders, but other legal issues, such as child abuse, adoptions and parental rights and duties, also are heard in juvenile court. The juvenile court system generally is committed to aiding, educating and protecting young people.

Access to proceedings and records involving juveniles is not impossible, however. High-profile shootings by minors at schools in Arkansas and Colorado brought changed attitudes about the juvenile justice system and the privacy rights of youthful offenders. A number of states give judges discretion over access, although as a condition for access, reporters might be asked to keep the identity of juveniles confidential. There are signs that the press's rights to cover juvenile courts are increasing. Recently, several state supreme courts, for example, affirmed the right of reporters to attend proceedings—called *transfer hearings*—held to determine whether juvenile murder suspects should be tried as adults (transferred to adult courts). Regardless of improved access, the tendency by officials to protect juveniles from press scrutiny remains strong and widespread, which means reporters must be prepared to be persistent.

In many states, statutes prohibit public officials from releasing the names of juvenile offenders. Despite such prohibitions, it is not unusual for reporters to learn identities by standard newsgathering means, such as tips from sources or interviews with witnesses. Law enforcement agencies typically withhold—or at least expect reporters to withhold—the names of juveniles identified in police reports. Although reporters often comply voluntarily, they cannot be prohibited by statute from publishing names. In 1979, the U.S. Supreme Court struck down a West Virginia law that made it a crime to identify juvenile offenders without a written order of the court.[27] A related problem is less clear: What if a *judge* orders a reporter not to publish the name of a juvenile? Violating a judge's direct order could lead to punishment by a contempt-of-court citation. If faced with a judicial order, seek legal advice.

Pretrial Proceedings

Reporters are most likely to confront closed doors at pretrial hearings or proceedings, which are conducted under a less formal set of judicial rules than trials. An example is the *preliminary hearing*, also known as a *probable cause hearing*. It is used to determine whether sufficient evidence exists to prosecute an individual. Secondhand information called *hearsay evidence* is usually permitted. For instance, when an arresting officer cannot be present for the hearing, his account may be read by a detective handling the investigation. Some incriminating evidence presented at a preliminary hearing may not be admissible at the trial.

Another pretrial proceeding is called a *suppression hearing*, which is held in advance of the trial to determine whether evidence or statements should be withheld from the jury. If a judge, for example, accepts a murder suspect's argument that the police forced him to confess, the confession will be suppressed and cannot be used in the trial. Problems arise, though, when evidence the court decides to suppress is nevertheless revealed to prospective jurors through news reports of the hearing.

To guard against a mistrial or an overturned conviction due to prejudicial pretrial publicity, some judges take the safest course and close a hearing at the defendant's request. In the 1979 case of *Gannett v. DePasquale*, the U.S. Supreme Court gave judges even greater latitude to decide whether closure serves the rights of the accused. In an opinion that evoked severe criticism, the Court said the Sixth Amendment guarantee of a public trial pertains directly to defendants and did not entitle the press and public access to courtrooms. Since then several judges have referred interchangeably to pretrial hearings and trials, and, at first, the *Gannett* case left the impression there were no First Amendment rights of access to any criminal proceedings, including trials.[28]

Certainly, there is much more at stake than defendants' rights if trials can be conducted in secrecy. But even closure of hearings is a serious matter largely because so many criminal cases—up to 90 percent in some jurisdictions—never go to trial. For example, in New York's Seneca County, origin of *Gannett v. DePasquale*, not one felony case went to trial in 1976, the year the *Gannett* case arose. In those cases, the hearing is the trial. Because many criminal cases end in *plea bargains*, or what court officials prefer to call *negotiated settlements*, it is important for the press to monitor hearings.

An open system allows the public and press to evaluate the performance of police, prosecutors and judges. If reporters are present, judges are not likely to reduce a DWI charge against a political bigwig to reckless driving; prosecutors are not likely to pad their conviction ratio by allowing an accused rapist to bargain for a reduced charge of assault; and police are not likely to go to court with a weak case built on a questionable confession.

Trials

Access to trials is less of a problem for reporters since the Supreme Court's 1980 decision in *Richmond Newspapers v. Virginia*, which came in the wake of the *Gannett v. DePasquale* storm. Despite its confusing position on access to courtrooms a year before, in the *Richmond* case the Court recognized a First Amendment right for the public and press to attend trials. Chief Justice Warren Burger, writing for the majority, did not, however, rule out closure of trials, but he did make it clear that only under extreme circumstances could a judge justify such action. Still unclear, though, is whether Burger's opinion about the First Amendment applies to pretrial hearings. Nonetheless, lower courts are bound to be influenced by the strong endorsement of open trials contained in *Richmond Newspapers v. Virginia*.[29]

REPORTER'S TIP FILE

What to do when a courtroom is closed

Reporters, unaccustomed to speaking out in a courtroom, might be reluctant to protest a closure motion. But if they hear no objections, judges may conclude that closing the courtroom is the path of least resistance. Reporters must be prepared to object. Some news organizations provide a sample statement to be read in court, such as this one:

Your honor, I am _____, a reporter for _____ _____, and I would like to object on behalf of my employer and the public to this proposed closing. Our attorney is prepared to make a number of arguments against closings such as this one, and I respectfully ask the court for a hearing on those issues. I believe our attorney can be here relatively quickly for the court's convenience, and he will be able to demonstrate that closure in this case will violate the First Amendment, and possibly state statutory and constitutional provisions as well. I cannot make the arguments myself, but our attorney can point out several issues for your consideration. If it pleases the court, we request this opportunity to be heard through counsel.

If the judge refuses to grant a hearing, legal experts advise reporters to then ask the judge to *stay*, or postpone, the proceeding that is about to be closed. You still may fail and be ordered to leave. Resisting ejection is asking for trouble; it is better to retreat and seek legal counsel. In emergencies, the Reporters Committee for Freedom of the Press offers free legal advice at a toll-free "hotline" number: 800-336-4243. (The Student Press Law Center provides help for students encountering legal obstacles (www.splc.org).)

Restrictive Orders

Judges use *restrictive orders* to keep a lid on potentially prejudicial information. *Gag orders*, as the press prefers to call them, come in a variety of forms. Some cover testimony, while others apply to records and evidence. A judge in Baton Rouge, La., for example, conducting a preliminary hearing for a civil rights activist accused of conspiring to kill the city's mayor, announced from the bench: "It is ordered that no report of the testimony taken in this case today shall be made in any newspaper or by radio or television, or by any other news media."[30] Judges can gag both reporters and trial participants. But gagging the press puts judges squarely on a collision path with the First Amendment. The U.S. Supreme Court, addressing the problem in a 1976 decision, said gag orders are prior restraints on the press and therefore presumptively unconstitutional. Gag orders against the press are justifiable, the Court said, only when there is no other way to ensure a fair trial.[31]

A gag order against trial participants is another matter; their free speech rights are less clear. Reporters who elicit information from people who have been placed under a gag order are likely to cause them trouble. The reporters involved might even be viewed by the court as accomplices to an illegal act. Reporters who plan to circumvent a gag order on participants ought first to ask an editor for advice and legal counsel.

The Supreme Court helped curb but not eliminate the use of gag orders against the press. Under normal conditions, reporters are free to report anything they see or hear in an open courtroom. A gag order changes the rules. The reporters may rightly conclude that the judge acted without legal justification, but anyone who ignores a gag order, even one that appears to be patently unconstitutional, risks being cited for contempt and jailed. In the Baton Rouge case, reporters ignored the judge's order, and although an appellate court eventually ruled the gag order invalid, the court *also* upheld the contempt-of-court citation against the reporters, saying, "[Journalists] may not now escape the inescapable legal consequence for their flagrant intentional disregard of the mandate of a court."[32]

Court Records and Documents

FOIA and state open-records laws do not apply to the federal or state judiciary, which operate under separate rules and policies regarding records under their jurisdiction. Generally, however, there is ample access to a broad range of legal documents held by the clerks and administrators of the court systems. But not all court records are considered fully "public." More courts are sealing records, some permanently, to protect a variety of public interests, usually those centering on the privacy rights of individuals. A judge, for instance, handling the case of a big-league pitcher, decides to seal all records of the ballplayer's arrest for scuffling with police officers at a bar. The judge says he was influenced by the exemplary way in which the ballplayer carried out the terms of his three-year probation. Another judge decides to seal videotapes of police sting operations that show a prominent lawmaker accepting a bribe. The judge fears broadcast of the tapes might make it difficult to find an impartial jury if the lawmaker, on appeal, is retried.

Judges sometimes seal the names and addresses of jurors to protect them from outside pressure, including, at times, inquiries from reporters. Details of divorce actions, such as testimony about peculiar sexual behavior, may be put off limits to prevent damage to reputations and to shield the parties' children from embarrassment. Frequently, courts recognize a need to protect the identity of informants or undercover police officers whose names appear in court records.

Gaining access to sealed records may prove to be difficult without a court challenge. As with other questions of access, consult your editor and media attorney. A written request to the judge who sealed the records is a first step and should include a diplomatic reminder about the presumption of open records. If the judge denies the request, ask for the denial in writing. Even going to court to challenge the sealing of records may not help. The law is much clearer and stronger on reporters' rights to attend court proceedings and listen to testimony than it is on access to records.

Actually, many so-called sealed records are not physically sealed or locked away. Sometimes they are kept with other open records of the case. Veteran reporters with ready access to offices and records in the courthouse may be able to inspect sealed materials. The important point to remember is that publication or broadcast of sealed records might hurt innocent people or jeopardize someone's rights. There are often good reasons why the press and public are denied access. Nevertheless, if it can be shown that a judge has sealed records for improper motives, reporters are right to publish what they are able to obtain. However, they must be prepared to face the consequences if a judge finds they acted improperly or committed a contempt of court.

Civil Law and Access

Reporters and courts clash most often over access to criminal records and proceedings. But problems arise, as well, in civil law. Of concern lately is the increasing number of secret out-of-court *settlements* in civil lawsuits, especially in product-liability actions, such as a string of cases against General Motors Corp. by crash victims who accused GM of negligence in the design of its gas tanks. GM, the *Washington Post* reported, paid millions of dollars to settle cases before trial. The settlements typically included agreements barring the parties and lawyers in the case from revealing records in the case or talking about the design of GM fuel tanks. The reporters said they learned from documents that GM officials were warned that the gas tanks were vulnerable to punctures in high-speed crashes.[33] Companies usually argue for secrecy to prevent disclosure of the size of the monetary settlement or to protect trade information from competitors. But reporters covering sealed cases around the country, some of which are identified in court files only as *Sealed vs. Sealed*, contend secrecy keeps important information about dangerous products and practices hidden from the public.

In response to abuses, the Florida legislature passed a "Sunshine in Litigation" statute in 1998 that prohibits settlements and agreements that conceal a public hazard or hazardous product. By and large, though, settlements, even when the public interest in disclosure is high, stay under wraps.[34]

Unfortunately for reporters, access rights in civil courts are not as well defined as those in criminal courts. The Supreme Court, for example, has yet to clarify whether the public and the press have a First Amendment right to attend civil proceedings. Additionally, arguments for access are less convincing in civil litigation because many cases involve primarily private matters. Nonetheless, reporters ought to challenge closed civil courtrooms and records, particularly in matters that extend beyond merely private litigation to encompass important societal questions. Recent examples include disputes over the right to die and surrogate motherhood. In both instances, litigation focused intense media attention on private individuals in painful situations. But the cases could not be ignored, because they involved moral and legal questions of great magnitude.

Contempt Power

Complicating access to the courts is the contempt power. Judges can back up their orders and actions by subjecting violators to swift and serious consequences. Melody Perkins, a reporter for the *Great Falls* (Mont.) *Tribune*, found out how thin-skinned some judges can be if they perceive that their authority is being challenged. When

Perkins, following instructions from her editor, asked the judge to delay his decision to close a hearing until the newspaper's attorney could be consulted, the judge called her "insolent," cited her for contempt and fined her $300.[35]

Judges are most likely to react when reporters directly violate judicial orders or encourage others to break the rules. Bob Woodward and Carl Bernstein were scolded for tampering with justice during the Watergate investigation of the Nixon administration. Woodward and Bernstein contacted several grand jurors, hoping some of them would talk about their Watergate deliberations.

When John Sirica, the judge overseeing the grand jury, learned about the reporters' inquiries, he sent a message to Woodward and Bernstein through *Washington Post* lawyer Edward Bennett Williams. Woodward and Bernstein described the scene in their book, *All the President's Men*. Williams sternly told them Sirica, known as "Maximum John" for his tough sentences, meant business. "Judge Sirica is some kind of pissed at you fellas," Williams said. "We had to do a lot of convincing to keep your asses out of jail." Williams offered some parting advice: "Keep your noses clean."[36]

Dealing with "Off-Limits" Signs

What began as a protest against construction of a nuclear power plant near Tulsa, Okla., ended in a setback for journalists' rights to report breaking news events on private property. Reporters covering the 1979 demonstration followed several hundred protestors onto the power company's property. Not only were the protestors arrested and charged with trespassing, but so were nine journalists.[37]

In appealing their convictions, the reporters raised a number of important arguments in support of access. To begin with, the reporters accused the power company and county authorities of conspiring to minimize publicity about the protest. The power company tried to restrict the reporters to a viewing area a mile away from where the protestors planned to enter the property. The sheriff stationed officers on the site to begin making arrests as soon as the demonstration began.

The public, the reporters argued, needs to be informed about developments in the national debate over nuclear power, even when the debate spills onto private land. They asked for the right of reasonable, unimpeded access to private property to observe peacefully and report on a newsworthy event in progress. Their arguments applied to any number of "hot news" situations, such as an explosion at an oil refinery or a fire at a condominium complex.

The reporters argued to no avail. The U.S. Supreme Court declined to hear the case and let stand the criminal trespass convictions against them. Their experiences reflect the difficulties journalists face in gaining access to newsworthy events and places. Not surprisingly, few judges would interpret the First Amendment as a license to trespass or break the law in pursuit of news. There is little help from the Supreme Court; on several occasions the justices have said the Constitution does not entitle the press to special rights of access to information or places beyond those afforded to the general public. Many journalists feel that the Court could be more sensitive to the press's role as a watchdog and guardian of the public's right to know.

The power plant protest also illustrates the problems of access to private places when reporters are unwelcome or uninvited. By customary practice, reporters enter private property to cover accidents or disasters. But police and other public authorities are not necessarily empowered, for example, to invite reporters to accompany them on a drug raid of a private home. In 1999, the U.S. Supreme Court unanimously ruled that when law enforcement officers permit reporters to follow them as they enter private property to make arrests or conduct searches, they violate Fourth Amendment rights of residential privacy.[38] At the very least, reporters who enter private property without permission risk an invasion-of-privacy suit.

Covering news occurring on public land or government-owned property usually presents fewer problems, but there are always exceptions. Police officials, in particular, may bar reporters from crime scenes or accidents in the name of maintaining order and protecting lives and property. Although police officers usually are cooperative when dealing with reporters they know and respect, their behavior may alter under pressure or trying conditions. They might, for example, banish reporters from otherwise public places, like sidewalks, parks or government buildings. Reporters who resist flirt with arrest for criminal trespass, disorderly conduct or interference with a police officer.

Although police can be obstinate about press access, sometimes their demands are reasonable. At crime scenes, police and firefighters must be sure that evidence is preserved and untouched by outsiders. During an emergency, reporters cannot expect to peer over the shoulders of police as a negotiator tries to talk a gunman into releasing hostages. In many circumstances, a solid professional relationship with police and emergency crews will be a surer means of access than a First Amendment demand.

Reporters can also expect to encounter restricted access to penal institutions, partly because of several U.S. Supreme Court opinions on the subject, including one in 1978. The case involved a California sheriff who limited press access to the county jail to once-a-month guided group tours for the public. A San Francisco television station sought permission to inspect and videotape the jail after an inmate committed suicide. The tours did not permit use of cameras or tape recorders and did not include disciplinary cells or the section of the jail where the suicide occurred.

Chief Justice Warren Burger, delivering the majority opinion, rejected the role of the press in serving the public's right to know. As he put it: "Unarticulated but implicit in the assertion that media access to the jail is essential for informed public debate on jail conditions is the assumption that media personnel are the best qualified persons for the task of discovering malfeasance in public institutions. But that assumption finds no support in the decisions of this Court or the First Amendment."[39] Burger said the sheriff's rules did not prevent the press from learning about jail conditions, albeit "not as conveniently as they might prefer." Reporters could receive letters from inmates that criticize and report conditions, interview their lawyers, talk to prison employees and public officials and seek out former inmates and jail visitors, Burger advised. Success at following his advice, of course, depends on whether inmates and people connected with the jail speak freely without fear of retaliation. Despite the Supreme Court's stance on prison access, not all prison or jail officials turn away reporters. In fact, some jail superintendents welcome the press and proudly show off their facilities.

Access to voting places presents another problem for reporters. A number of states attempted to limit reporters from conducting *exit polls*, which involve interviewing voters immediately after they cast their ballots. Washington, for example, banned exit polling within 300 feet of voting places. The limits came partly as a result of intense criticism over the networks' use of exit polls to predict election results while people were still voting. Exit polls, however, also yield important information used to interpret voter patterns and behavior. Several court challenges suggest that limits on exit polling are unconstitutional, but reporters can anticipate continued resistance from public officials who say the privacy rights of voters take precedence over the newsgathering rights of reporters. In 2006, news organizations in Ohio, Florida and Nevada were battling 100-foot limits on exit polling, alleging a violation of First Amendment rights.

Legislative chambers, municipal buildings and courthouses are among the most public of buildings; still, unlimited access to any government facility is rare. Reporters, for example, may be restricted to a press gallery when the legislature is conducting business. Occasionally, a mayor will ban "unfriendly" reporters from her office or press conferences. Obviously, during emergencies, any public building might be put off limits to the press.

New Battlegrounds over Access

New access battles continue to erupt. Among the latest issues pitting journalists against public officials are access to military operations, electronic records, videotapes, medical information and details about prisoners held as terror suspects.

Military Operations

The Grenada invasion of 1983 broke with a tradition of reporters following American troops into action. The military has long engaged in various forms of news management—VIP treatment, denial of travel to "restricted" areas, staged news events and separation of reporters from fighting troops. But Grenada set a new standard for government control and manipulation of the news media.

In mid-October of 1983, reports circulated about U.S. plans to invade the Caribbean island of Grenada after a violent coup by a Marxist military leader who imposed a 24-hour-a-day, shoot-on-sight curfew. On Oct. 24, White House press spokesperson Larry Speakes told reporters that the invasion rumors were "preposterous." The next day, American troops landed on the island. Later, officials said they invaded Grenada to protect and evacuate about 1,000 Americans on the island, most of them students at a medical school. Secretary of State Caspar Weinberger said secrecy was necessary to ensure the mission's success.

A few journalists tried to slip onto the island by boat or plane, but the military turned them back, in several cases at gunpoint. When enterprising reporters used ham radio operators to seek information from islanders, the Federal Communications Commission issued a warning, saying regulations prohibited use of amateur radio for newsgathering. Two days after the invasion, a 15-reporter pool, escorted by military personnel, arrived on Grenada. Finally, on Oct. 30, the military gave reporters unlimited access. But the initial reports, photographs and videotapes Americans received came from the Pentagon, not the press.[38] Left behind, reporters could not judge for themselves the dangers posed to American citizens, the strength of Cuban troops on the island or the conduct of American forces.

Complaints by the press led to the formation of a commission that recommended a rotating pool of reporters to cover future military operations. Under the rules, reporters would accompany troops, but not necessarily the first wave; moreover, they would be sworn to secrecy until the military lifted any news embargo. Early non-combat tests of the pool concept went smoothly, but under battle conditions or during secret missions, the press found itself behind the lines or kept at bay by tight restrictions on travel and access to troops. That was the pattern for the post-Grenada military operations in Panama and Saudi Arabia. In 1990, the first press pool was not taken to Saudi Arabia until five days after the U.S. deployment began. *Time* reported that American journalists suspect the unstated purpose of the press pool is to prevent serious coverage during the early stages of military actions.[40] With operations in isolated areas under strict military control, there may be little choice but to follow rules, as journalists covering the first Persian Gulf war and the U.S. invasion of Afghanistan discovered.

During the 2003 invasion of Iraq, the Pentagon and White House tried what critics called a clever, new tactic to control reporting through "embedding" journalists with military units. The military offered journalists the chance to go into combat after undergoing boot camp-like training. The quip "inbedded" reporters surfaced to suggest that the press and military were getting too cozy and interdependent. Nonetheless, the embedded operation gave journalists and the public real-time access to breaking news in the field.

Does the Iraq experience signal an improved press-military relationship? Remember that journalists and the military represent two distinct ways of thinking and acting. The military accentuate conformity, control, discipline and loyalty. The press culture generally values independence, spontaneity, enterprise and advocacy. In World War II, Prime Minister Winston Churchill said, "In time of war, the truth is so precious, it must be attended by a bodyguard of lies." The military has its mission, and its first obligation is not to help reporters do their jobs.

An access problem related to the War on Terror—encompassing military and intelligence-gathering operations around the world—has been the literal wall of secrecy surrounding detention centers that hold, incommunicado, U.S. and foreign prisoners

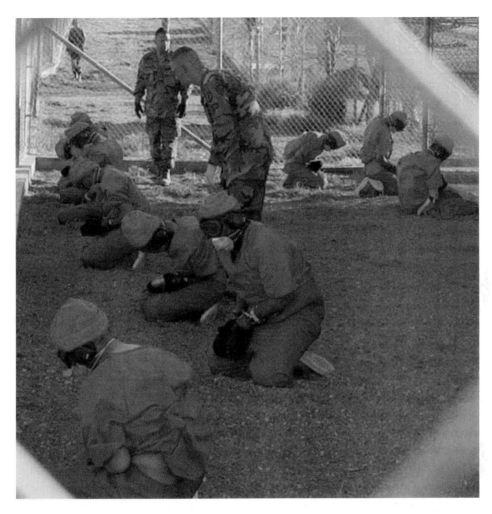

Guarded by a wall of secrecy   With their eyes, ears, mouth and hands covered and wearing orange jumpsuits, detainees from the war on terror kneel in a holding area at Camp X-Ray inside the naval base at Guantanamo Bay, Cuba, during processing in January 2002. Journalists have battled for access to and information about the detention camp, particularly regarding allegations of torture. (Department of Defense photo.)

suspected of or charged with terror-related crimes. Associated Press writer Paisley Dodds overcame obstacles to produce a series that examined the treatment and prosecution of detainees at Guantanamo Bay. She received the 2006 Joseph L. Brechner Center for Freedom of Information Award for her efforts.

Access to Electronic Records

Access to electronic records poses an array of legal, logistical and policy problems unanticipated when most open-records laws originally were enacted. Public documents stored in computer databases present a tempting opportunity for officials to keep electronic records away from public scrutiny. With government agencies at all levels moving toward "paperless" operation—electronic storage of vast amounts of information—the press has good reason to fear more access difficulties.

Various states and the federal government responded in the 1990s with amendments or new laws to cover electronic records. The federal Electronic Freedom of Information Act (e-FOIA), which became law in 1996, does not define "electronic records," leaving that job to federal agencies or courts asked to intervene in a dispute over access. The law, despite its flaws, makes it clear that electronic records fall under the same standards of disclosure that apply to paper documents.

The battle lines are still being drawn. Some public officials, for example, believe that an electronic search for data an agency does not ordinarily compile creates a *new* document; public-records laws, they say, cover only *existing* documents. Of course, with computer security an understandable consideration, it is not likely that reporters will be given passwords and clearance to search randomly for information in government databases. The bottom line: Implementation and interpretation of rules covering electronic access will continue to develop over time and undoubtedly lead to more legal challenges.

The electronic debate includes whether goverment e-mail constitutes a public record. According to a study in 2003, eight states make no reference to e-mail in their open-records laws. In other states with e-mail provisions, confusion and disagreement mark interpretation of when and what type of e-mail should be disclosed. In Washington and Florida, for example, courts have ruled that the private, personal e-mail of government employees is not covered under the state open-records law. "Without more specific laws, officials frequently conduct official business via e-mail outside public meetings or delete important e-mails without following state archiving policies," said Bill Chamberlain, who directed the study.[41]

Another development in government record keeping promises to further complicate access. To reduce costs and waste in government, some agencies have transferred data collection and storage to private, profit-making companies, which, in turn, sell the data to their subscribers. Communications lawyer Donna Demac is alarmed by this trend, which has been referred to as *privatization* of government information. "Since these private entities are not subject to federal rules regarding public access and are able to charge whatever the market will bear, privatization has the effect of further promoting government secrecy."[42] Other critics of privatization fear that the high fees private companies are expected to impose for retrieval of electronically stored information will prohibit reporters, especially those with limited budgets, from investigative journalism.

Access to Visual Records

Videotape (and digital video) is fast becoming a contested "visual record." Police are making wider use of video for statements and evidence, such as filming drivers suspected of driving while intoxicated. In some crime-infested cities, citizens are using camcorders and digital cameras to discourage criminals and collect evidence of drug

deals, theft and prostitution. With video equipment inexpensive, compact and ubiq-
uitous, nearly every news event is apt to include someone's videotaped record. In Los
Angeles, for example, an amateur videographer captured police repeatedly beating a
helpless suspect named Rodney King. Airing of the tape on newscasts spurred charges
of police brutality. Four officers subsequently were tried for the King beating; when
they were acquitted in 1992, Los Angeles erupted in violent riots.

Inspired by the King episode, law enforcement and correctional agencies now use
digital video cameras not only as a visual record; they also know video helps defend
against complaints of improper behavior in the arrest and incarceration of criminal
suspects. Do not expect ready access to audio or video recordings. The standard arguments for withholding print records—privacy, security and fair trial rights—are being
applied to visual records.

Because this is an emerging area, legal precedent is limited. A California appellate
court ruling, however, indicates what journalists might anticipate when requesting
videotape from public officials. The case involved a police videotape of the execution of a search warrant at the home of a psychotherapist who allegedly possessed
evidence needed in a murder investigation. The videotape covered several sections
of the home, including bedrooms, and showed the therapist's wife dressed in a robe.
In arguing for release of the videotape, CBS and ABC cited the watchdog role of the
press to monitor how police and court officials carry out their duties. The appellate
court decided the videotapes were not subject to the state's public records law unless
the tapes were admitted into evidence. Historically, the court said, the public has not
had pretrial access to items seized under a search warrant. The court also raised the
issue of privacy, concluding that examination of the videotapes constituted an inva-
sive search of the therapist's home by the media.[43]

Access to Medical Information

When government officials refuse to disclose information, they often cite "privacy
rights." The scope of privacy rights expands daily, and for good reason; not much
of our lives remains private. Nonetheless, the press, in its watchdog role, sometimes
pursues a higher public interest in disclosing private information. As concern over
privacy invasion has grown, so has the number of laws at the state and federal levels
precluding access to government-held information.

A relatively new federal policy covers health and medical records. Called HIPAA
(Health Insurance Portability and Accountability Act) rules—and pronounced hip-a—
it limits press access to information about hospital patients and medical files in
the custody of health-care providers. Like federal rules covering release of student
records, HIPAA, on occasion, has been applied more broadly than intended. For example, a Pennsylvania hospital cited HIPAA in withholding information about a hepatitis
outbreak, and police and emergency services often refer to HIPAA to deny access to
records, even though the rules do not apply to their agencies.

Fear of Talking

In a post–September 11 world of heightened security, surveillance and scare tactics, critics contend a fear factor hovers over us. To raise your voice against authority— even to question a rude airport screener—puts you in jeopardy of retaliation, even arrest. Don't dare step out of line; don't dare sympathize with the other side; don't dare step, figuratively, on the flag. Big Brother is not only watching but also ready to add you to his data bank. In such a climate, whether the threats are more imagined than real, most of us lack the fortitude to stand out or to stand up. The cumulative effect is a spiral of public silence.

Most troubling of all access problems is the real or implied threat of retaliation against public employees who, without authorization, provide information to reporters. Increasingly, rules and penalties governing release of government information are making it difficult and dangerous for employees at all levels of public service to talk to the press. Police departments, for example, often invoke a "spokesperson-only" policy to centralize and control release of news. The policies usually forbid officers on beats or at crime scenes from answering reporters' questions.

Some institutions and government agencies take an indirect approach to control communication, but the message usually is clear. A state university in the Midwest, for example, operates under a five-page set of procedures for "media relations and information dissemination." Employees are "urged" to go through the university's director of news services whenever a reporter calls for an interview or information. Throughout the document are strong hints that employees are duty-bound to avoid answering inquiries that might "embarrass" or "hurt" the university. And there are the direct approaches, such as one that dates to 1989, when U.S. Attorney General Richard Thornburgh announced that the Justice Department would criminally prosecute federal employees who leaked information about government investigations to the press.

In response to the Justice Department's policy, media attorney Bruce Sanford remarked, "The good ship of government is probably the only ship that operates best with leaks."[44] Sanford alluded, in part, to leaks by "whistleblowers"—people who follow their conscience to expose wrongdoing in government or the private sector. From aerospace companies to the State Department there are examples of recriminations, dismissal or prosecution against whistleblowers. Employees who violate policies or go against the wishes of their superiors also face hidden acts of punishment, such as being passed over for promotion or denied a merit raise. In some government offices, workers are so concerned they fear even being seen with a reporter.

A few safeguards for whistleblowers exist. Federal and state laws protect some private-sector employees, such as miners or workers at nuclear plants, who disclose safety hazards at work. Whistleblower laws generally protect workers from being fired, threatened or discriminated against. But protection is not universal, and where laws exist, whistleblowers still face forms of retaliation and censure for speaking out.

Newsgathering in the digital age is increasingly difficult and complicated. Gaining access to people, places and records involves more than knowing what information is available, where it can be found and who holds the keys to its release. Journalists must aggressively seek information and access. Those who resignedly settle for news releases and tamely submit to agency rules on access to records and meetings only encourage public officials to keep the people's business private.

Computers and information-retrieval systems have opened vast, unexplored territories of news and analysis to reporters. But conversely, as more information is converted to electronic form, technology poses serious threats to freedom of information if reporters fail to lay claim to those new territories. The sheer volume of information and the speed with which it is generated and disseminated call for journalists with the ability and determination to keep a self-governing people informed and their leaders accountable.

Exercises

1   Carefully read your state's open-records law. Then make a freedom-of-information request for public records at your school. Do not pursue records that are clearly unobtainable under the law. Seek those on which you can build a story. For example, you could ask for parking-ticket receipts to see how much money the school collects each semester. Is your school about to hire a new dean or administrator? As part of your coverage, ask to examine the applications. If you attend a private school, you cannot count on support from the state's open-records law; it applies only to public institutions. But you still might consider making a request for similar information and writing about the experience—as long as it does not get you into trouble with school officials.

2   Interview several local journalists who cover public boards or agencies. Ask them to assess how true public officials are to the spirit and the letter of the state's open-meetings law. Next, obtain the perspective of the public officials involved. In a story, compare and contrast the different positions.

3   Talk to the manager (or public relations spokesperson) of a nearby factory, power plant or refinery about policies on press access to their facilities in the event of an emergency. Some companies have detailed procedures for handling journalists, but officials may not want to reveal those procedures or speak openly about press relations. Try your best to find out why companies often see a need to manage news coverage in an emergency.

Notes

1. Micah Morrison, "How They Uncovered the Truth," *Parade*, Jan. 25, 2004, p. 4.
2. *National Archives and Records Administration v. Favish*, 541 U.S. 157 (2004).
3. J. William Leonard, formal statement, Subcommittee on National Security, Emerging Threats, and International Relations, U.S. House of Representatives, March 2, 2005.
4. Steven Aftergood, "The Age of Missing Information," Slate.com, posted March 7, 2005.
5. "Governor-elect plans Office of Open Government," www.rcfp.org, posted Dec. 14, 2006.
6. Guy Munger, "FOI Court Battles Can Be Expensive," report of the Freedom of Information Committee, Associated Press Managing Editors, October 1988, p. 25.
7. Gaillard Hunt, ed., *Writings of James Madison* (New York: Putnams, 1900–1910), 9:103, letter to W. T. Barry, Aug 4, 1822.
8. *Houchins v. KQED*, 438 U.S. 1 (1978).
9. *Gannett v. DePasquale*, 443 U.S. 368 (1979).
10. *New York Times*, Nov. 3, 1974, p. 37A.
11. Steve McGonigle, "Media Access to Government: An Open or Shut Case?" Fifteenth Annual Media Law Conference, Florida Bar, Orlando, Fla., Feb. 25, 1989.
12. Quoted in M. L. Stein, "Reporter Stationed in Council Chambers Eight Hours a Day," *Editor & Publisher*, Jan. 21, 1989, p. 18.
13. William J. Small, *Political Power and the Press* (New York: W.W. Norton, 1972), p. 382.
14. "Veteran Times Staffer, Pulitzer-Prize Winner & Tallahassee Bureau Chief, Lucy Morgan to Retire," press release, *St. Petersburg Times*, http://sptimes.com/connect/pressroom/.
15. Lucy Morgan, "Senators Meet Without Notice," *St. Petersburg Times*, April 14, 1999, p. 1A.
16. "The Open Door to Government in Minnesota" in *Tapping Officials' Secrets* (Washington, D.C.: Reporters Committee for Freedom of the Press, 1989), p. 9.
17. "County Commission Chairman Jailed for Violating Sunshine Law," www.rcfp.org, posted May 16, 2003.
18. Les Pearson and Bill Smith, "'Nit-Picking Details' of Pageant Add Up," *St. Louis Globe-Democrat*, Oct. 25, 1985, p. 1.
19. Jane T. Harrigan, *Read All About It!* (Chester, Conn.: Globe Pequot Press, 1987), pp. 14, 15.
20. Angie Cannon, "How Much Overtime Does Your City Pay," *Editors' Exchange*, July 1990, p. 2.
21. Jim Steele, "Tips on Investigative Reporting," *Editors' Exchange*, September 1990, p. 4.
22. Quoted in Richard P. Kleeman, "Life on the FOIA Front," *The Quill*, December–January 1990, p. 19.
23. Laird B. Anderson, "FOIA Founder Looks at Law Today," *1988–1989 FOI Report*, Society of Professional Journalists, p. 13.
24. Anderson, "FOIA Founder Looks at Law Today," p. 13.
25. Martin E. Halstuk, "The Law Still Works, but It Needs a Tune-up," *CJR*, September–October 2005, p. 45.
26. *Butterworth v. Smith*, 494 U.S. 624 (1990).
27. *Smith v. Daily Mail Publishing Co.*, 443 U.S. 97 (1979).
28. *Gannett v. DePasquale*, 443 U.S. 368 (1979).
29. *Richmond Newspapers v. Virginia*, 448 U.S. 555 (1980).
30. *United States v. Dickinson*, 465 F.2d (5th Cir. 1972).
31. *Nebraska Press Association v. Stuart*, 427 U.S. 539 (1976).
32. *United States v. Dickinson*, 465 F.2d 496 (5th Cir. 1972).

33. Elsa Walsh and Benjamin Weiser, "Public Court, Private Justice," *Washington Post National Weekly Edition*, Nov. 28–Dec. 4, 1988, p. 6.

34. Ray Shaw, "Sunshine in Litigation," *Florida Bar Journal*, January 2000, p. 63.

35. "Judge Fines Reporter $300 for 'Insolence,'" *Editor & Publisher*, May 20, 1989, p. 24.

36. Carl Bernstein and Bob Woodward, *All the President's Men* (New York: Warner, 1975), pp. 236, 237.

37. *Stahl v. State*, 665 p. 2 of 839 (Okla., 1983); see also "Justices Allow Reporters' Convictions for Trespass," *News Media & the Law*, January–February 1984, p. 7.

38. *Houchins v. KQED*, 438 U.S. 1 (1978).

39. "Coverage Efforts Thwarted," *News Media & the Law*, January–February 1984, p. 6.

40. Stanley W. Cloud, "The First Casualty," *Time*, Sept. 10, 1990, p. 69.

41. "Study Suggests States' Records Laws for E-Mail Inadequate," press release, University of Florida College of Journalism and Communications, May 19, 2003.

42. Donna A. Demac, *Liberty Denied* (New Brunswick, N.J.: Rutgers University Press, 1990), p. 119.

43. *Oziel v. Los Angeles*, 18 Med. L. Rptr. 1113 (1990).

44. George Garneau, "Clampdown on Sources," *Editor & Publisher*, Aug. 12, 1989, p. 11.

The Neighborhood Approach 5

Divergent cultures commingle in an urban neighborhood A woman waits for a bus where neighborhood schoolchildren park their bikes for the day. A building's stone facade serves as a canvas for graffiti, considered by its practitioners an urban art form. The scene evokes layers of cultural diversity. (Photo by Robbie Arkovich.)

Step into a neighborhood like The Hill in St. Louis. Behind a tavern, a bocce ball game—the Italian version of lawn bowling—draws a group of kibitzers. Nearby, the aroma of focaccia wafts from a storefront bakery. Narrow, tidy homes called shotgun houses, built at the end of the 19th century for workers at the local clay mines, abut the sidewalks. People sit outside, on the stoop, to greet passersby. The Hill pulses with activity and civic pride.[1]

In Tampa, Fla., another neighborhood struggles to retain its cohesiveness and identity. Called Progress Village, its residents, too, share a pride of ownership and heritage. In 1959, Progress Village arose from a cow pasture in western Tampa, about

11 miles from downtown. A non-profit group used private donations and federal aid to develop decent, low-cost housing as a way to improve the city's race relations. For $200 down and a mortgage of about $50 a month, anyone could own a one-story, cement-block house.

Eventually, 800 residences were built, and a community center, churches and businesses followed. As Progress Village approaches its 50th anniversary, long-time residents hope they can stave off blight and crime encroaching upon the neighborhood and deter the real estate speculators they see as preying on a weakened community. The president of the civic council told a reporter in late 2006, "If we can make this a historical community, it will not be gobbled up or eaten."[2]

Jane Jacobs, author of the influential book *The Death and Life of Great American Cities*, championed the vibrant neighborhood as the salvation of cities in decline.[3] Her philosophy, criticized by some as naïve and idealistic, nonetheless inspired the preservation and resurgence of neighborhoods across the country.

The neighborhood—in its present and past forms—remains a constant in American communities. Before the Internet, shopping malls and Interstate highways—when a family considered itself lucky to own one car—people identified themselves with neighborhoods. In a typical neighborhood, apartments, single-family homes, schools, churches, fraternal halls and public parks commingled, all within a short walk from your front door.

A neighborhood often found itself associated with a business district, where every need and necessity could be served: the corner grocery, confectionary, bakery, barbershop, hardware store, movie theater, haberdashery and funeral home. The people who ran these businesses sometimes lived in an upstairs apartment or a few blocks away, with their families, who pitched in at home and work. A sense of pride and unity marked neighborhoods of old.

People born prior to the mid-1950s relate to neighborhoods where they grew up and discovered the world outside their parlors. Now, in some cases, they can only reminisce, savoring the memories of Cherry Cokes at the corner confectionary and dancing under the stars at the local biergarten (beer garden). Their neighborhoods disappeared in a wave of urban renewal that broke the pattern of being reared, settled and dying in the community of one's birth. People moved to suburbs and their sprawling residential communities. Despite homey names and instant landscaping, the suburbs lacked the history, distinctiveness and cohesiveness of the city neighborhood that developers tried to replicate.

Today, the neighborhood can still be considered the cement of urban life, despite its once lost and now rediscovered status. From Seattle to Kansas City to Tampa, neighborhoods have gained economic, political and cultural muscle. Moreover, as the housing developments of the post-World War II boom have matured socially and physically, they, too, have evolved into neighborhoods.

The rise of neighborhoods in city planning and management demonstrates the importance of *sense of place*—a sense of belonging and a sense of control over our lives. A sense of place can include such variables as emotional attachments, moral, ethical stewardship, economic pragmatics and familial ties. People love, protect and nourish their neighborhoods. As a result, neighborhoods encourage civic life as residents tackle problems and take steps for the benefit of all—reopening a shuttered theater as an arts center; petitioning for speed bumps to control speeding; marching with bullhorns to shout down drug dealers; protesting the city council to deny a developer's plans for a megamall.

The neighborhood is not the only means people use to fulfill the need to belong and connect with others. We see communities built around common pursuits and interests. Associational communities include Little League boosters, a bingo hall, hospice volunteers, a gun club or an online investment group. The neighborhood, however, brings together people on the basis of the physical place and the daily details of life they share. The neighborhood's presence and role in civic life cannot be ignored or underestimated by politicians and journalists alike.

The Fall and Rise of Neighborhoods

Not all neighborhoods of that simpler time were idyllic, even those that seemed that way. Not everyone got along, and neighborhoods varied dramatically in terms of social stability and economic health. By and large, neighborhoods developed along ethnic or racial lines, some by preference, others by circumstance. Racial divides, of course, existed in nearly every community. African-Americans, in particular, found themselves forced into corners of the larger community. Segregation, however, enabled African-American communities to thrive as distinct, self-reliant neighborhoods.

Ironically, in the 1960s, a period of intense social upheaval, neighborhoods declined as hubs of community life. The barriers that divided communities by race gradually came down. But the consequences were not always positive. For example, the integration of schools—often under court order—led to busing to achieve racial balance. Students no longer walked to a nearby school; they boarded buses in the pre-dawn to attend schools remote in distance and demographics from their own. As a result, local schools began to decline, as did whole neighborhoods.

On the outskirts of communities, the rise of fancifully named suburbs like Oak Park and Greenbrier beckoned as an alluring alternative to city life. Families, both white and black, moved from historic neighborhoods to mass-produced homes. Hastily assembled shopping centers, occupied by big chains, swallowed up the ma-and-pa businesses that were the anchors of city neighborhoods.

As people and businesses moved out, blight began to settle in, marked by boarded-up storefronts, abandoned homes and empty streets. City planners decided that to save communities, the areas experiencing the worst decay had to be eradicated. So across the country, so-called urban renewal projects bulldozed entire sections of towns and cities. Displaced residents, unable to afford a home elsewhere, ended up in nondescript public housing. Neighborhoods that escaped being targets of urban renewal were often left to languish.

Neighborhood Perspectives

Today historic neighborhoods are undergoing a resurrection. Churches, banks, non-profit groups, local government and private entrepreneurs have provided the capital and resources. Communities still struggle to restore or recreate the idealized neighborhood, but there is abundant evidence that a decentralized, neighborhood-oriented approach to community building and local decision making has taken root. Cities and towns have established special departments to work with neighborhood associations and other local groups.

The city of Seattle, for example, created a Department of Neighborhoods with a stated mission "to bring government closer to the residents of Seattle by engaging them in civic participation; helping them become empowered to make positive contributions to their communities; and by involving more of Seattle's underrepresented residents, including communities of color and immigrants, in civic discourse, processes, and opportunities." Its projects include P-Pockets, community gardens, for residents of 44 Seattle neighborhoods who grow organic vegetables on more than 1,900 plots.

The focus on neighborhoods includes delivery of city services. In Waynesboro, Va., the police department created a program, CLEAN (City, Citizens and Law Enforcement Adopting Neighborhoods) to identify, address and enhance the quality-of-life issues. Teams comprised of police officers, city officials and residents walk streets and alleys, looking for code violations, abandoned cars, shut-in elderly or disabled residents, gang graffiti—anything that needs attention from the city.

The neighborhood theme can also be seen in newly created cities, such as Celebration, Fla., built by the Disney Company in the 1990s. Celebration and planned communities modeled on it attempt to reproduce neighborhood life and illustrate a concept sometimes called *New Urbanism*. New Urbanism encourages developers to increase the density of residential areas and build schools, stores, offices, and recreation within walking distance. The influence of Jane Jacobs can be seen in the attempts of these developments to encourage neighborly interaction through front porches, stoops and balconies and, in some cases, by mixing housing for different levels of income.

An influx of immigrants from Cambodia, Lithuania, Somalia, Haiti, Russia and a score of other countries contributed to the growth of neighborhoods united in ethnicity, culture and common goals. In the University Avenue neighborhood of St. Paul, Minn., for example, a Hmong enclave thrives. The Hmongs, who allied with America during the Vietnam War, began to immigrate here after the Communist takeover. Many settled in St. Paul, where an estimated 250 Hmong-owned businesses—markets, clinics, day-care centers, financial firms, restaurants—have helped revitalize the neighborhood, and the Hmong Cultural and Resource Center presents exhibitions about Hmong history and culture.[4]

As cities and towns promote neighborhood development, the neighborhoods themselves have organized into associations and discovered that their elevated status in the eyes of public officials gave them the economic and political clout to seek grants, promote legislation and achieve policy changes at city hall. In St. Petersburg, Fla., a coalition of neighborhood associations called the Council of Neighborhood Associations of South Pinellas County (CONA) addresses communitywide concerns and gives its member organizations the power of a unified voice.

Not all communities have experienced a resurrection of neighborhood life—even when the concept has been enthusiastically embraced and promoted by public officials. When it does take hold and flourishes, few people consider the neighborhood philosophy a panacea for all the ills of a community.

We need a realistic, objective view of neighborhoods. Neighborhoods can exist in name only, with civic life dormant or non-existent. Neighborhoods certainly are not perfect; they can be unfriendly and uninviting. Another realistic view tells us people living in a city or town can choose isolation and spurn connections. Isolation can come from living behind the walls of a gated community or the doubled-locked doors of an apartment complex. It can be physical or emotional.

Still, humans typically yearn for a real sense of belonging. Belonging begins where people live, raise families, make friends and take a stand. A sense of community, a concept embraced and ballyhooed, often begins and ends within a segment of the larger community—a neighborhood.

Neighborhoods and News Organizations

News organizations, as well, have adopted the neighborhood view, motivated by the *public* or *civic journalism* movement that evolved in the 1990s. Public journalism, in part, arose in response to a perceived estrangement between news organizations and the communities they serve. Defined and practiced in dozens of different ways at broadcast and print news organizations around the country, public journalism seems best understood as a philosophy that challenges journalism's traditional role as a detached conduit of news—a mirror of society. Commonly cited tenets of public journalism include a proactive role in identifying and addressing the problems of a community through deliberative dialogue and a rekindled emphasis on the lives of ordinary people who are seen as citizens, not as bystanders or consumers of the news.[5]

Not all journalists endorse or practice public journalism. They fear it undermines journalistic objectivity and smacks of community "boosterism." But no matter where journalists stand on public journalism, the neighborhood movement challenges *all* of them to ask: "Where do we stand? What role do we play? Where do we fit in?"

Several news organizations, in response to questions like these, have employed innovative ways to cover neighborhoods. In Savannah, Ga., the *Morning News* trained residents as neighborhood correspondents. One of them, grandmother and retired pipe fitter Margaret Bailey, covers Liberty City, where she's lived for 15 years. Bailey said she's trying to fill a gap in the *Morning News*. "Story ideas come from my surroundings, whatever is happening in my neighborhood or something that we're interested in my neighborhood," Bailey said. "I receive the paper, but a lot of things I skip over because I don't think it pertains to me. That's the part I'm trying to add, not only for the paper but for the black community."[6]

Another concept—mobile journalists, called "mojos"—capitalizes on the space available on news Web sites to expand neighborhood coverage. The mojos—outfitted with ThinkPads, digital audio recorders, digital still and video cameras—operate on the road, without an office, desk or land line. At *The News-Press* in Fort Myers, Fla., mojos prowl for stories. "We kept hearing from our readers that they wanted really local news, hyper-neighborhood stuff," says executive editor Kate Marymont. "They want to know what's going on in their backyards. If we were to put all that stuff in the print edition, we'd have to deliver it in a wheelbarrow." The mojos also help train citizen journalists to post their own reports online. Marymont adds: "It's a way to get the communities involved."[7]

These adventures in neighborhood initiatives reflect the spreading realization within the profession that people still yearn for local news—provided it connects.

Local News as Community Connector

The red and white signs sprouted in the Garden Manor neighborhood of St. Petersburg, Fla.: "Save Our Neighborhood: Say 'No' to Commercial Rezoning." The people who live in Garden Manor and five other neighborhoods rallied to fight a developer's plans to build multifamily housing, professional offices and a shopping center on vacant land owned by the Catholic diocese, contingent on rezoning from "institutional" to "commercial."

When the city council considered the Sembler Co.'s request to rezone the 18-acre site—once the home to Notre Dame Academy, a girl's high school—hundreds of people filled the council chamber, spilling out to other rooms in city hall. In solidarity, they wore red shirts reading: "Commercial rezoning. I don't want it. I don't need it. Just say no!"[8]

The neighborhoods would turn out in force whenever a hearing or vote on the rezoning proposal came up. They passed the hat to collect donations to hire an attorney. They stood up to Mel Sembler, a former U.S. ambassador, a Republican fundraiser and founder of the development company. Lance Lubin, the president of a neighborhood association, framed the dispute as residents united against a common foe. "That's been a blessing in this whole thing," said homeowner Ed Carlson in agreement. "This is the first thing in West St. Petersburg that's ever drawn this much attention from so many neighborhood associations together. This is huge."[9]

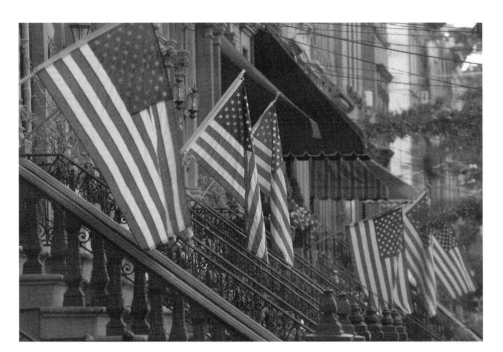

A neighborhood projects its identity in stars and stripes   Flags jut from the front stoops of row houses in a patriotic salute. When a neighborhood rallies around a cause or event, past differences often are put aside for the sake of unity. In particular, if threatened by, say, crime or city hall, neighborhoods pull together in self-defense. (Photo by Robbie Arkovich.)

QUOTABLES

"One of the things I think is still true but has been totally forgotten by the people who have been buying, trading and owning newspapers as assets in a portfolio is that news-papers are one of the four or five institutions in a community that help the community define itself. We're part of the civic glue. We're the place where the community thinks out loud." (p. 26)

—Chris Satullo, editorial page editor of the *Philadelphia Inquirer*, quoted in Rob Gurwitt, "Blackout," *Governing*, December 2006

News is local. It is not simply the notion that proximity equates news—that the closer news occurs to home, the more likely it is something we want to know about. More than anything, local news gives us grounding, reinforcing and expanding our connections with a place we know as home.

If local news constitutes a connection with home, what, then, is considered "news"? In conventional practice, newscasts and publications highlight violent crime, spectacular accidents, sexual escapades of all varieties, political scandals in general and almost anything that pits one group against another. Conflict dominates as a frame for many stories—race-related protests outside police headquarters; clashes between pro-life and pro-choice zealots outside an abortion clinic; lawsuits by homeowners against shoddy builders.

A neighborhood approach does not require journalists to abandon conflict and other norms of journalism coverage altogether. A neighborhood approach does, however, require that journalists see news value in the ordinary.

The stories emerge where people live, work, pray and relax. The stories are found on city buses, at beauty parlors, church halls, social clubs and playgrounds. The stories acquired at such venues often raise issues every reporter can find at city hall or the courthouse, such as crime prevention, disbursement of tax money, economic development and race relations. But the perspectives are different. Even when they are not that different from official viewpoints, the words of citizens ring true and genuine because they come out in unrehearsed, natural and refreshing ways. No one at the corner market speaks in sound bites.

When reporters delve into a neighborhood, they find details and insights that add dimension and context to conventional articles that originate from the mayor's office or police headquarters. In neighborhoods, homes and shops, people strain to comprehend and, if possible, resolve the problems and frustrations that loom large in their lives. Neighborhood journalism puts people first; it listens carefully and responds appropriately. We read news about people in Bangladesh or Peru, and we do not feel an attachment. That can happen at home, too, in Chicago or Toledo, Ohio, if journalists fail to connect with people on their terms and turf.

A cautionary word about defining news through the prism of the "ordinary" comes from former *St. Louis Post-Dispatch* editor William Woo. "I am cautious about an assumption that holds that the opinions of the man or woman in the street shed as much or more light on a complicated issue as those of a politician, a college professor or, heaven forbid, a bureaucrat—people, in short, who have spent a career focused on an issue. . . . The profoundly ordinary is noncontroversial and mediocre in content. It takes no courage to reflect the profoundly ordinary."[10]

On the other hand, Woo, a few years earlier, spoke by invitation at a prayer breakfast of a suburban Kiwanis Club on the subject of ethics and journalism. He had this to say afterward:

> Like most big-city papers, we do not regularly cover such events. In fact, I suspect that many journalists, like myself, have little personal experience with them. Yet here at 7 a.m. were 300 people, paying $5 a ticket, listening to a 25-minute speech without a single joke—and not a cough or a scraping chair in the audience. Here, in short, was a piece of community fabric, revealing something about the people.[11]

Woo was not sure what to make of his experience. It revealed "something," he realized, but what? In a neighborhood approach to journalism, the Kiwanis Club would not necessarily get coverage every time it met. But its institutional significance as community connector would be acknowledged, and the Kiwanis Club and other community-building and -defining organizations would never be marginalized or discounted. Woo, ironically, had discovered the value of the ordinary.

When the neighborhood becomes a focal point of news coverage, journalists cannot escape encounters with the "ordinary," in part because that is the world most people inhabit. Ordinary does not mean, however, uneventful or insignificant. Ordinary people leading ordinary lives need to be heard, seen and attended to. In a sense, the ordinary Jane or Jamal—their travails, triumphs and tragedies—are a microcosm of human existence.

Rather than shun the ordinary, *through the ordinary* journalists can learn what is really important in a community or neighborhood. People care about climbers lost in a snowstorm in the Rockies, and they rejoice if the story ends happily and empathize if it does not. But people lost in a mountain of bills or a blizzard of bureaucratic red tape need attention, too, and their stories will resonate with nearly everyone in the realm of the ordinary.

As for the ordinary Jane or Jamal, what can journalists expect to learn? David Johnson, a writer for the *Lewiston* (Idaho) *Morning Tribune*, believes "everyone has a story," which is the name of his weekly column. In a profile, the *New York Times* said he has written about "an elderly couple whose aches and pains made them too tired to spit, let alone want to live; a woman whose husband ran a hose from the exhaust pipe of his pickup truck into the cab and died to the sound of country music three weeks earlier; and a couple whose daughter-in-law drowned their granddaughter, thinking the baby was possessed by demons. The child is buried in their backyard."[12] Johnson found those stories by choosing names at random from telephone directories in the newspaper's circulation area.

Covering neighborhoods, however, should not be the reporter's version of "Pin the Tail on the Donkey." With news space and broadcast time generally scarce, news organizations cannot risk wasting precious resources on games of chance. A strategy is needed to help journalists decide where to go, who to see, what to ask and, finally, what to report.

Goals for Neighborhood News

A word of warning before we explore the following goals of neighborhood news: *Do not consider these goals as journalistic gospel.* In fact, discuss and debate what follows, because journalism, if nothing else, resists conformity. The goals suggested here, while not handed down from on high, possess intellectual and professional legitimacy, grounded as they are in the theory, philosophy and practice of journalism.[13]

Goal 1: Facilitate community building.

Goal 2: Promote understanding.

Goal 3: Question stereotypes.

Goal 4: Celebrate diversity.

Facilitate community building

Mention "community building" to some journalists and they will blanch in alarm: *News organizations should not engage in community building, which gets too close to making the news instead of reporting it.* Nonetheless, news organizations cannot deny their role in a community's decision making and agenda setting, says journalist James Fallows. "One of public journalism's basic claims is that journalists should stop kidding themselves about their ability to remain detached from and objective about public life," he says. ". . . They inescapably change the reality of whatever they are writing by whether and how they choose to write about it."[14]

"Facilitate," a word some consider jargon, does, however, adequately explain and qualify the role of news organizations in community building. Facilitate implies helping others help themselves. A newspaper or broadcast station can assist the community without sacrificing fairness and balance.

The first and most fundamental way news organizations can facilitate community building is to amplify the voice of the people and signal to public officials and institutions what its citizens want and need. Community building starts when people know they are being heard and listened to by the powers that be. Conversely, a community risks disintegration when lines of communication fail or do not exist.

So what, then, constitutes community building? Certainly, it includes a literal definition. News organizations can, indeed, assist in economic and physical development, such as exploring how a community can create new jobs or expand health services. Proactively, news organizations sometimes help identify and prioritize a community's agenda. In a few cases, news organizations have sponsored community forums or formed focus groups to determine what matters most to citizens.

Beyond concrete efforts, a news organization can help its community build in less tangible ways. If a community is suffering in grief or festering in anger, a news organization can—and should—lend a helping hand.

After September 11, 2001, the *New York Times* profiled the office workers, firefighters, passengers and police officers who died that day in a long-running series called "Portraits of Grief." A *Times* editor later said the series was a means of giving solace to the families, to which a media commentator added: "The real significance of this series is to clearly give solace to a community—not simply the community of New York or those who knew the victims personally but the entire national community for which the remembrances have become a powerful sacrament."[15] Journalists should not stand by, like strangers, when they know something is tearing a community apart. While they cannot be expected to make things right, they at least need to acknowledge that a condition exists and enable people to figure out how to react or what to do.

Reporter Rodney Thrash acknowledged an open wound in his community and brought it into view in an article that explored why African-Americans shed tears over a videotape of a disruptive 5-year-old girl being handcuffed and held in the back of a police car outside her school. The article gave people—both black and white—with various opinions a chance to vent. The central theme of the article, however, was captured in the headline: "The prism of the past: For some African-Americans, the case of an out-of-control kindergartener becomes far more complicated when seen as history repeating itself."[16] Residents continued a dialogue about the episode at school board meetings and community forums in an attempt to change police policies and address underlying problems, including conditions at local schools.

Another form of community building involves cultivating a sense of pride. Journalism often covers the ugly side of life. Should it accentuate the good going on in neighborhoods? Obviously, community-building efforts depend on a motivated, energized cadre of residents. News organizations cannot ignore negative news, but they can concentrate on highlighting the assets and accomplishments of a community, which generally outweigh the detrimental side.

A proud neighborhood usually is a prosperous neighborhood, even if its residents are poor by economic standards. Telling the story of neighbors working side by side to clear a trash-strewn lot or paint the homes of elderly shut-ins can generate an infectious spirit of good will that spreads into other neighborhoods as well.

Stories about the good will and good deeds of people working to reduce illiteracy, feed the poor, protect foster children or care for abandoned pets also build community through boosting hope. When news accounts convey an impression that our world is filled with sadness, cruelty and pain, people are left with the feeling there is no end or solution in sight. Journalists can help the community from giving up on itself.

Promote understanding

What is going on, really, in neighborhoods? In a commuter society, people whiz by parts of the community, getting a blurred picture at best. Neighborhood coverage occurs best along sidewalks, at a walking pace. A useful analogy comes from famed CBS reporter Charles Kuralt (1934–1997) as he described his reporting style for the series "On the Road": "I have tried to go slow, stick to the back roads, take time to meet people, listen to yarns, notice the countryside go by, and feel the seasons change."[17] His meet-listen-notice-feel model fits well for reporters covering neighborhoods.

QUOTABLES

"Good journalism—in a newspaper or magazine, on television, radio or the Internet—enriches Americans by giving them both useful information for their daily lives and a sense of participation in the wider world. Good journalism makes possible the cooperation among citizens that is critical to a civilized society. Citizens cannot function together as a community unless they share a common body of information about their surroundings, their neighbors, their governing bodies, their sports teams, even their weather. Those are all the stuff of the news. The best journalism digs into it, makes sense of it and makes it accessible to everyone." (p. 10)

—Leonard Downie Jr. and Robert Kaiser, *The News about the News,*
New York: Alfred A. Knopf, 2002

A close-up, personal approach to neighborhoods offers reporters a chance to gain understanding of their own. Understanding can be disturbing if grounded in grim reality. Jonathan Kozol spent two years in New York's poor, drug-invested Mott Haven neighborhood for his book, *Amazing Grace*, which focuses on the sad lives of the neighborhood's schoolchildren, who, despite incredible hardships, still strive to succeed.

Significantly, Kozol faults the way the press handles the neighborhoods he knows best, like Mott Haven, saying reporters and editors tend "to sweeten and romanticize our cruelty to children." He decries what he calls "happy ghetto stories" about people beating the odds or the renovation of a block of buildings. News organizations cannot sanitize reality, he says.[18] A realistic, first-hand experience promotes understanding for both journalists and the people who seek out the news.

First, journalists themselves must achieve authentic understanding. It does not always come easily, as Reena Shah Stamets learned in reporting about motherhood in Kenya, where many women have eight, nine or 10 children. Her experience applies to neighborhood settings as well. "Some journalists parachute in and ask, 'Why do you have so many children?'"[19] Stamets knows deep feelings do not surface immediately. Groundwork comes first, which explains why for one of her Kenyan stories she planted corn with the women of a rural village. By sincerely taking part in the lives of ordinary people, reporters can establish a rapport needed to gain a wider, deeper understanding. Then they can spread understanding to others, as Stamets did.

Journalists promote understanding simply by giving us intimate insights into the lives of others and how their lives often touch ours. What is it like to be jobless, earn a college degree at the age of 80 or watch your third-generation business go up in flames? Through stories like those, we not only acquire understanding about the individuals involved; we gain understanding of universal feelings of both failure and accomplishment. We find out that the experiences of people in the news, while very personal, touch other lives. Journalists who promote understanding try to provide a larger context for individual stories. What is it like to be jobless, for example? On a blog site, Genevieve Roja exposed her anger about unemployment:

> While the President is horseback riding around his Crawford, Texas, ranch during his month-long hiatus, my fellow unemployeds and I try to land the job of today, rather than the job of our dreams. That's what happens when you're out of work—you take the measly scraps and wait for the steak dinner. . . . I can tell you a lot about the daily struggle of an unemployed. It is a constant period of personal re-evaluation and daily affirmation. It's learning to forgive myself, telling myself it wasn't my fault I was let go, that I'm good enough and smart enough, and by golly, someone *will* hire me someday. It's difficult hanging onto hope when you've been out of work for almost a year.[20]

Her experience, shared by tens of thousands, should be in the news, Roja says, as much as coverage of the fighting in Iraq, but journalists rarely find joblessness "sexy or scary." Her comments reflect her sense of frustration. The story is hers, but it is ours, too. We need to understand before we can comprehend, judge or respond. Context, too, promotes understanding. The jobless individual usually does not face the experience alone. Parents, spouses, children, friends and the larger community are drawn into the story as well.

Question stereotypes

The neighborhood approach educates people, especially those outside the neighborhood as they peer in through the window of the news. Reporters help outsiders by exposing stereotypes and myths that distort reality and undermine community cohesiveness. For example, in certain African-American neighborhoods, people carry on a tradition of the tree gathering. Under the shade of a large tree, men, women and children engage in the friendly sharing of food, fellowship and emotional support; it is a tradition rooted in African culture.

To the culturally uninformed, an outdoor congregation of blacks might be misunderstood. Reporter Peggy Peterman's story about a local tree gathering she attended explained the meaning of the occasion and, most importantly, taught a lesson about clichés of vision—how we sometimes see and define on the basis of biases and stereotypes.[21]

Stereotypes based on race or ethnicities certainly require attention. But journalists cannot afford to overlook less pernicious yet equally misguided depictions of other groups or categories of people. The elderly apply here. In her book *City of Green Benches*, anthropologist-journalist Maria Vesperi explained why people fail to listen to the elderly, assuming they belong only to the past, not the future. Her observations apply to journalists, because they, too, might be inclined to avoid or disregard older people. Vesperi, in explaining the struggles of an 82-year-old widower, Mr. Dawson, to get his views heard much less taken seriously by a social worker assigned to help him, wrote:

> The Messrs. Dawson of this world seem doomed to be abandoned in mid-sentence. Others invariably find them tedious, difficult to follow, boring. At worst they are labeled "wanderers," that is, incapable of remembering the original context of a conversation. I would suggest, however, that the tendency to tune out this type of monologue is a central factor in our cultural construction of Mr. Dawson and the well-meaning outreach worker failed to communicate.[22]

Vesperi said people like Mr. Dawson become supplicants and must recreate their "selves" in dealings with others. Seniors in other cultures stand a much better chance of being seen, heard, understood and respected.

Journalists, like the rest of society, can also succumb to stereotypes by engaging in tokenism, labeling or generalizations: an artistic, sensitive gay man; the youthful-looking, spry 95-year-old man who bicycles around town; the courageous youngster fighting leukemia.

As stereotypes succumb to the truth, previously strained or tenuous relationships within a community have a chance of improving. Questioning stereotypes also heightens a community's appreciation of its diversity.

Highlight diversity

Diversity comes in different forms, such as *multiculturalism*, a loosely constructed social attempt to increase our awareness and appreciation of the culture, heritage, perspectives and attitudes of others unlike ourselves. Diversity can conjure up negative images of politically correct speech and mandatory lectures on sexual harassment. Diversity, of course, comes with positive associations, too.

In neighborhood journalism, diversity deserves attention because it defines and, usually, unites people. In some neighborhoods, diversity is *the* defining feature, such as the Cambodian enclaves in Lowell, Mass., where people share an ethnic, cultural and religious background. In other neighborhoods, the diversity amounts to a tossed salad of different colors, languages and traditions, such as New York's Astoria, where a Greek-owned restaurant is next door to a Chinese merchant's novelty store and a Czech beer garden is across the street from a mosque.

Diversity does not always result in harmony. Ignorance or misunderstanding over diversity can result in divisiveness. When people genuinely appreciate diversity, however, it contributes to their pride about the community and builds bridges within and between neighborhoods. To help a community appreciate diversity, journalists should view the term through a wide-angle lens.

Diversity should not be narrowly construed as merely supplementing the news with diverse voices and faces—women, blacks, Hispanics. Robert Maynard, the late editor of the *Oakland Tribune*, encouraged diversity coverage along society's major fault lines: race, class, gender, geography and generation.[23] Diversity should be an inclusive term for journalists, encompassing a diversity of views, attitudes and lifestyles. Diversity in the news also includes people who do not own cars, read newspapers or sleep in a bed.

Leigh Stephens Aldrich, author of a diversity handbook for media, says diversity in journalism "places an emphasis on accepting and respecting differences by recognizing that no one group is intrinsically superior to the other." She warns that when the news omits groups and people in favor of stories about white males, the result is denigration and marginalization. Omission, she says, is a big problem of news organizations.[24]

Diversity stories can backfire if not done well and sensitively. Reporter Stephen Magagnini entered Sacramento's Hmong neighborhood gradually and carefully.

Magagnini wanted to explore and explain life inside a rather closed society and the internal problems, such as a high rate of gang crime, plaguing the community. He called it a "long incubation process." He attended events, sought the help of a mentor and sat at kitchen tables just to chat before he did any focused reporting.

In one of a series of stories that won Magagnini an ASNE writing award, he wrote:

> In the back room of a south Sacramento welfare office a quiet revolution is under way.
>
> A dozen Hmong women sit around a table, eating strawberries and trying to solve the mounting problems facing Hmong families in America.
>
> Tonight they are learning how to say "I love you" to their children. While many American parents say "I love you" as often as "Good morning," few Hmong are comfortable with the expression—as if to say it would somehow devalue it.
>
> Slowly, the crushing burden of Hmong womanhood unfolds. Debbie is missing tonight; no longer able to cope with her 10 children or the shame of her rumored affair, she has tried to hang herself. Meanwhile, three of Nue's four teenage sons are AWOL, and after 19 years, her arranged marriage is crumbling.
>
> Though nearly every woman in the group is in the throes of a personal crisis, an aura of strength and optimism fills the room. . . .[25]

Journalists cannot clumsily enter a neighborhood and in a few hours come up with a diversity story worth telling. The result would be worse than doing no story at all.

Strategies for Neighborhood-Based Stories

Journalists should first do their homework by conducting an inventory of the neighborhood's civic resources—people, institutions, businesses, organizations and groups. The Harwood Group recommends that journalists follow a process called "mapping." Its publication, *Tapping Civic Life,* identifies five potential layers of influence in a community: *official*, *quasi-official*, *third places*, *incidental* and *private*.[26]

Official includes elected officials or government institutions. Quasi-official often includes neighborhood associations, advocacy groups and urban or municipal leagues. Third places, like churches, fraternal halls, beauty parlors and coffee shops, support the gathering of people to talk and listen. Incidental covers spontaneous but frequent encounters of two or more people on the street corner, at the grocery store or across the backyard fence. Finally, the private layer occurs inside the home, around the kitchen table or on the patio.

Each of these levels of human interaction plays a role in neighborhood life, although the influence or dominance of one category vis-à-vis another will vary as neighborhoods vary. But a mapping model helps journalists recognize that civic life occurs nearly everywhere, and it encourages them to go beyond the official and quasi-official categories as they pursue stories and insights.

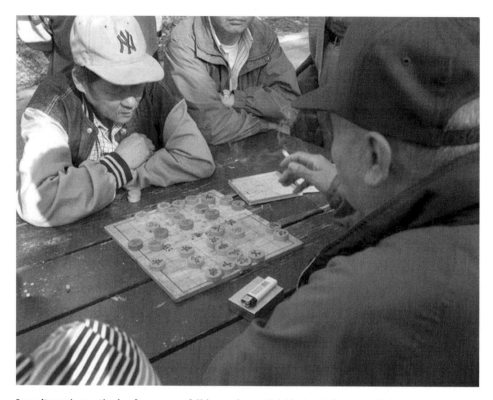

In a city park, a gathering for a game of Chinese chess   Neighborhoods feature gathering spots, where people meet, talk and build relationships. They include coffee houses, beauty parlors, street corners and park benches. Reporters attuned to neighborhood news visit gathering spots and find stories not usually found in city hall. (Photo by Robbie Arkovich.)

REPORTER'S TIP FILE

Getting to know you

Here are some steps to get acquainted with a neighborhood.

Reconnoiter. Drive around the perimeter of your neighborhood, and then make your way into its center. Take note of street names, churches, parks, lakes and other physical and geographic elements of the neighborhood. Take photos or make sketches.

Measure personality. Get a sense of the neighborhood's personality. Is it, for example, a place strewn with kids' toys and juggle gyms? Is it a place of front porches and potted plants? Is it quiet? Shady? Congested? Homey? Think of an acquaintance's personality: a sense of humor, quirkiness, and a friendly manner. Neighborhoods can be assessed in similar ways; just don't go overboard in personification.

Locate gathering spots. Identify the gathering places in the neighborhood—social, cultural, athletic, religious, organizational. Gathering places reveal the degree and flavor of community life. Do people gather in the evening at a park to escape the heat? Do older men meet at McDonald's to drink coffee, share stories and nourish their spirits? Do people linger at the beauty parlor for conversation and company? You can start by merely observing with your eyes and ears. Call it public eavesdropping. Gathering places are barometers of community life; they are also sources and indicators of news, for people discuss what's going on in their neighborhoods and beyond. Be sure to look at notices tacked to bulletin boards or taped to storefront windows.

Sample things. Sample the neighborhood by shopping at an ethnic market, getting a haircut at Bill's Barber Shop, eating homemade corn beef hash at the corner café early in the morning. Take in the sights, sounds and smells of the neighborhood. Look for the distinctive; a Walgreen's is a Walgreen's wherever you go. Get out of the car and enter the neighborhood on foot.

Take a pulse. Discern patterns of movement in and around the neighborhood. Is there a central business zone or hub of commercial activity? Does a main road run through the neighborhood? Do people walk to and from stores, churches and schools? Can you buy a gallon of milk without driving to Publix?

Pinpoint landmarks. Determine landmarks of the neighborhood. Perhaps it's a park memorial to World War II veterans. Historical sites and buildings come to mind, too. Some landmarks might amount to kitsch, such as the Tastee Freeze shaped like an ice cream cone.

Meet and greet. Talk to people in the neighborhood. Here's where you shed your inhibitions and discover that people like to talk about themselves and where they live. Try random encounters, such as the mail carrier or convenience-store clerk. Schedule visits with people of leadership or influence. Someone will represent the neighborhood on the city council or commission. The heads of civic and charitable groups often know the neighborhood intimately. Don't overlook the elders of the community. You're in search of people who can answer your questions about the neighborhood and help you determine what's gone on and what's going on—issues, problems, visions.

Find a guide. From your explorations, determine who might be someone in the community who can be your guide and advisor. In close-knit ethnic neighborhoods, for example, residents tend to view outsiders with caution. If someone they know and trust accompanies a reporter, doors are more likely to open and people are more inclined to speak candidly.

Do some reading. Ask the local librarian to recommend books or archives about the community. Check out online resources provided by the city, Chamber of Commerce or library Web sites.

Tapping Civic Life also provides a typology of leaders: *official, civic, connectors* and *catalysts*. The categories further help journalists understand the dispersal of influence in a community. Official leaders might include, for example, a community college president, school board members, city council members and department heads, state lawmakers and chief executives of major businesses. Civic leaders typically come from the ranks of the religious community, civic organizations and neighborhood associations.[27] The categories of "connectors" and "catalysts" help elevate the status of people who do not possess a title or garner headlines—at least as news is conventionally defined. The connectors and catalysts, however, deserve special attention under the neighborhood approach to journalism. Connectors circulate throughout the community, holding joint memberships in groups, attending meetings and participating in community events. Accordingly, they carry messages and spread ideas back and forth in their encounters with people and groups. The catalysts are those respected for their expertise, historical perspectives, wisdom and ability to explain, negotiate and persuade.

Resist trying to fit people into one category or another. Rather, identify people others seek out for advice or in times of trouble. They are news resources well worth the effort to know and interview.

How do you, then, get to know who's who and what's what in civic life? The "Reporter's Tip File" (p. 144) suggests a get-acquainted exercise. Beyond that initial step, the challenge is developing a deeper relationship. Reporters cannot, as they sometimes do when covering breaking news around the world, drop out of the sky and expect welcoming arms and intimate dialogue. Those who take the time and effort to learn about the hopes, dreams and worries of people realize the conventional steps of gathering "information" and quotes may not be enough to get stories with credibility and meaning. The Harwood Group offers good advice:

> The most fruitful insights from tapping into civic life emerge when journalists actively engage people in uncovering the essence of what they are thinking; the tone in which they speak; the language they use; the experiences and values that shape their thoughts. This takes building trust with people, perhaps even an ongoing relationship.[28]

Developing something other than a passing acquaintanceship is not simply a matter of spending time with people. When building a relationship, people talk, listen and explore, and gradually they build enough trust to let others into their lives. Journalists, though, are by trade accustomed to directed, controlled communication for their own purposes, mainly to get a story.

Reporters who listen more than talk, and talk to learn and understand, not merely gather information, can expect, eventually, fuller disclosure and cooperation from people they depend upon for stories and features.

REAL-LIFE LESSONS

The Department of Journalism and Media Studies at USF St. Petersburg assigns its students to cover the city's Midtown community through its Neighborhood News Bureau. Midtown comprises the once-booming African-American economic district of 22nd Avenue South. After a fatal police shooting ignited angry protests and acts of arson, the city looked at ways to heal the wounds through a concerted effort to rejuvenate the quality of life in Midtown. At about the same time, the journalism director at USF St. Petersburg sought ideas about how news organizations could better connect with their communities. One idea stuck: Let's set up a neighborhood news bureau of our own.

In 2001, the department established the NNB to train students, expose them to diverse perspectives and experiences, produce stories and features about Midtown for local news organizations and help the community by reporting news and views rarely covered in mainstream media.

When the NNB dedicated its Midtown newsroom in 2006, journalist Eric Deggans, who heads the Tampa Bay Association of Black Journalists, offered his approval: "Students will learn the craft while trying to tell the toughest stories out there—urban poverty, education struggles, drug problems—and when they hit a real journalism job, they'll have benefited from meeting the kinds of folks mainstream journalists don't often encounter, except while covering a murder or arrest."[29]

Over the years, USF St. Petersburg students have illuminated Midtown and other neighborhoods by producing stories such as these:

"Hugs the rule at school for homeless"

"'Missionary' labors to help his neighbors"

"22nd St. S.: Proud past, hope for future"

"Drug Busters: Armed with bullhorns and wearing hardhats, men, women and children march through city neighborhoods, shouting down drug dealers where they live"

"Lola Mae on patrol, looking out for others"

"A golf course Jim Crow built"

The lesson: *The students learned the value of challenging stereotypes and sampling diverse people and places. "I saw parts of the community I have not consciously ignored, but I saw them in a limited light because I hadn't experienced them before," said one student. Another added, "It opened my eyes. You drive by a playground and you see black kids playing ball and you wonder, what they are going to do next? Now I know something about their aspirations."[30]*

Other schools have tried similar projects, but with mixed results. At Syracuse University's Newhouse School, professors Steve Davis and John Hatcher decided to send 30 newspaper and magazine majors to a neighborhood near campus quite unlike where most of them grew up. "It costs $35,000 to $40,000 a year to go to school here—about $10,000 more than the annual household income on the largely minority South Side," they noted. They learned that students experienced discomfort, even fear, interviewing people unlike themselves. The students turned to conventional sources with titles and official status, avoiding "everyday people with stories to tell." Davis and Hatcher also concluded that neither journalism schools nor newsrooms assigned enough challenging, get-out-of-your-comfort-zone stories.[31]

Stories from the Neighborhood

An old (1958–1963) TV crime drama that focused on the lives of the detectives of New York's 65th Precinct ended each episode with the tag line: "There are 8 million stories in the naked city. This has been one of them. . . ." What about neighborhood stories? Are they infinite in number? Probably. But journalists can narrow the task by thinking in terms of specific categories, such as stories with a historical angle.

Using history as the focal point, here are subjects worth pursuing:

What's in a name?

Every neighborhood has its named streets, public buildings, community centers and parks—Austin Strauble Airport in Green Bay, Wis.; the Howard Franklin Bridge in Tampa; and Laclede's Landing in St. Louis. "The story behind the name" helps new-comers get a sense of who contributed to the community and why. Moreover, the stories sometimes uncover little-known details about the person whose name graces the city park or library. If you do not know the whole story about a noted former citizen, you can be sure many residents are likewise uninformed.

Anniversaries

Look for anniversary dates of events or births. The standard milestones of anniversary reflections covered by the press are 25-, 50- and 100-year marks. For example, when were the public schools of a community first integrated? Perhaps an anniversary date is coming up. The birthday of a founding member of the community allows journalists to present a history lesson.

Neighborhood elders

Oral history encourages people to reveal the memorable experiences of their lives. Studs Terkel won the Pulitzer Prize for *The Good War*, an oral history of women and men swept into the turmoil of World War II. He interviewed, for the most part, ordinary people—a Red Cross volunteer, a gay Marine, and a Japanese schoolboy, among others—who told emotionally powerful stories about their wartime experiences.

Oral history serves a community by preserving the wisdom and memories of its citizens. Oral history also helps connect the present to the past. A neighborhood elder, for example, might be asked how walking the neighborhood in her youth differs from today.

Then and now

Trend stories based on a historical context are also worth doing. The city of St. Petersburg became a destination for retirees on modest fixed incomes in the 1920s through the 1980s. Today, though, it is a Mecca for retirees with massive portfolios who live in high-rise condos along the waterfront. The then-to-now approach also helps people see how a community evolved. How, for example, did an abandoned military barracks grow into a bustling urban university campus?

A sampling of neighborhood stories, all of them produced by journalism students at USF St. Petersburg, offers other themes and approaches to neighborhood coverage.

Here are leads or brief segments of a range of topics that apply four goals of neighborhood-oriented journalism—building community, promoting understanding, celebrating diversity and questioning stereotypes.

Therese Mattioli spent time at St. Joseph's Catholic Church for her piece, "Heavenly Harmony: Gospel Choir Brings Notes of Celebration to Catholic Service." Here is an excerpt:

> . . . About halfway through the rehearsal, Pastor Callist Nyambo arrives. While choir members work to perfect a particular section of a song, Nyambo and Cynthia Williams (choir director) confer about Sunday's gospel. Together they stand at the piano, heads together, flipping through "Lead Me, Guide Me," an African American hymnal. . . .
>
> He briefly joins in the rehearsal, singing a cappella in his native Swahili. As he finished, there is good-natured criticism from the choir. Williams asks him to try again. "This time when you sing it, try to stay with me, okay?" she chides. They both laugh.
>
> . . . About 120 parishioners arrive Sunday to celebrate the 9 a.m. Mass. Gladys Kendall McGuire joyfully awaits the service. She's been attending St. Joe's for about eight years. "It's the spirit. You leave feeling so uplifted. When you leave, you *know* you've been to church."
>
> Pews have been replaced by neat rows of cushioned chairs, each backed with a kneeler. Families, couples and individuals of all ages and races are seated together. There is no sense of segregation, no division or difference. There are just people coming together to celebrate Mass. . . .

Mattioli's story highlights St. Joseph's racial harmony as well as its popular gospel choir.

Neighborhoods almost always feature churches that provide spiritual and charitable care. A story by Jordan Dye, "Feeding the Body and the Soul," tells about one of them:

> On a typical Sunday morning at St. Petersburg's Bethel African Methodist Episcopal Church, young ushers in crisp white shirts and pressed black slacks circulate collection plates among the congregation. The Rev. Harry Dawkins ask that they donate $3 toward what he calls the "benevolent collection."

The benevolent collection, Dawkins said, serves two purposes. It supports a weekly Sunday breakfast for church members and the homeless, prepared and served by volunteers in the church's large meeting hall. The remainder of the collection is directed toward an emergency fund for parishioners unable to pay their water and power bills.

Signs of the church's interest in community are posted everywhere—employment notices, voter registration brochures and fliers of community organizations. The parishioners extend their ministry well beyond Sunday worship and the walls of the church.

. . . Malcolm Flakes, a church steward, said the breakfast is a type of ministry. "If we can feed their stomachs," he said, "perhaps we can feed their souls too."

The businesses of a neighborhood warrant attention, too. They often illustrate the special bond of both working and living in a community. Bruce Barton, owner of Bruce's Auto Body & Repair, grew up just a few blocks from his shop. Reporter Mindy Tanenbaum learned that Barton was proud of his roots and his role in the community, as reflected in this excerpt:

. . . He's brought his nieces and nephews in to the business. "Hopefully, they'll take it over someday," he said. "If not, maybe they'll start one of their own."

Barton said he tries to support the community that has supported his business for so long. The plaques in his wood-paneled office thank him for his generosity and support. They've faded from the sun, but Baron's sense of pride hasn't. "It is gratifying to work in the community where you grew up," he said. "We try to give back when we can."

Another broad category with a neighborhood theme would be people helping others. You can find such everyday heroes at food banks, free clinics, soup kitchens and disabled services.

In Childs Park, neighbors help neighbors, and so it was on a recent evening when a friend brought the Rev. Willie Whiting his dinner.

Whiting, 53, also known as "Tub," is in the caring business himself. . . . Tub works four jobs, he says, but he sees them as a means to help the youth and others. "It takes a village to raise a child, and I'm part of that village."

—Jacqueline F. Dupuis

Come December, Max Perez will be able to switch on his radio and finally hear something meaningful to women and men who toil in the produce fields of Immokalee, Fla.

The Coalition of Immokalee Workers, . . . probably best known for leading the Taco Bell boycott, has gotten Federal Communications Commission approval to start up a low-power FM station.

All this thrills Perez, spokesperson for the workers coalition. Perez, 23, is a third generation farm worker who knows the workers' plight and recognizes the need for a united voice.

"On the radio all we hear is just music, nothing that has to do with our situation and problems," he said. "This station will be workers talking to workers, so we can start to analyze and figure how to change things."

—Theresa Sterling

Angel Toro rolled down the window of his white Ford Ranger pickup and listened. He could smell it. He pulled over to the side of the road, and reached for his aluminum Maglight and searched. Finally he found his quarry.

"We've got some water over here," Toro said.

You should know the city of Tampa enforces its one-day-a-week watering restriction and that Toro, a water-enforcement officer, is serious about water conservation.

"It's a resource," he said. "We need to conserve it."

—Jordan Dye

Finally, neighborhoods take unconventional forms, as Moshood Fayemino discovered at a housing complex occupied largely by immigrants from around the world:

Joy Simic calls it her own odyssey. She can never forget the events that forced her, as a teenager, to leave her native Yugoslavia six years ago.

"I was only 14, didn't actually know when the religious war started but recalled Dad had to fight; he never returned," Simic said in a sad voice. But living here brings her comfort.

Yohe Mboye, his wife and their 2-year-old daughter fled tribal bloodshed in the Democratic Republic of Congo. He won admission to the United States in a visa lottery. He considers himself lucky.

Barbara Flemings migrated to the United States from Belize. "I came with my elder sister for the proverbial American Dream." She thinks she's found it.

Today, all three live in the Park 46th Avenue apartment complex in Tampa, which, with its ethnic and nationality diversity, resembles a United Nations Assembly.

Every neighborhood teems with people, conditions and activities that call out for news coverage. The neighborhood approach brings journalists into communities and in ways not usually found in conventional beat and general assignment coverage. At its best, news helps people understand what's going on in our interconnected lives so that we can confront and solves problems (or avoid them); reach decisions and form opinions; explore and debate values; and achieve personal and community fulfillment and happiness. In short, news should be relevant, even essential, in our lives and relationships.

Will a neighborhood approach define journalism in the near future? That's unlikely. But should journalists seriously consider it as the model for local news? Yes, emphatically.

Exercises

1. Visit a neighborhood in which you're a stranger, walk around and find a story subject that you think fits the neighborhood goals in this chapter. Then do the story and run it by the neighborhood people you interviewed for their take on how well you represented the neighborhood.

2　Heighten your cultural awareness by attending an event or going to a place outside your comfort zone. Attend a tent revival. Sample food at an ethnic restaurant off the beaten track. Eavesdrop on conversations of chess players at a city park.

3　Follow the advice of the Partnership for a Walkable America and find out how friendly a neighborhood or part of the community is to pedestrians. Pick a place to walk, such as the route from a family's home to a neighborhood school. Then follow a checklist you can download online at www.walkinginfo .org/walkingchecklist.htm.

Notes

1. Gary Ross Mormino, *Immigrants on the Hill: Italian-Americans in St. Louis, 1882–1982* (Columbia, Mo.: University of Missouri Press, 2002).
2. Justin George, "Pains of Progress," *St. Petersburg Times*, Dec. 6, 2006, p. 1E.
3. Jane Jacobs, *The Death and Life of Great American Cities* (New York: Random House, 1961).
4. Hmong Cultural Center, St. Paul, Minn.: http://www.hmongcenter.org/index.html.
5. David K. Perry, *The Roots of Civic Journalism* (Lanham, Md.: University Press of America, 2003), pp. 11, 12.
6. Michele McLellan, "Savannah's Neighborhood Newsroom," ASNE: http://www.asne.org/ credibilityhandbook/savannah.htm.
7. Nick Madigan, "Video Stories Put Newspapers on a Whole New Page," *Baltimore Sun*, Sept. 24, 2006.
8. Paul Swider, "Sembler, Neighbors Spar over Tyrone Proposal," Neighborhood Times, *St. Petersburg Times,* Feb. 26, 2006, p. 13.
9. Howard Troxler, "18 Mostly Vacant Acres Put City Council in Tight Spot," *St. Petersburg Times*, March 2, 2006, p. 1B.
10. William F. Woo, untitled address to the California Society of Newspaper Editors, Napa, Calif., April. 25, 1997.
11. William F. Woo, "Understanding Our Neighbors," *St. Louis Post-Dispatch*, April 19, 1992, p. B.
12. Tina Kelley, "'Everyone Has a Story,' as One Reporter Proves," *New York Times,* March 29, 1998, p. 16, Section I.
13. See Rob Anderson, Robert Dardenne and George M. Killenberg, *The Conversation of Journalism: Communications, Community, and News* (Westport, Conn.: Praeger, 1994).
14. James Fallows, *Breaking the News* (New York: Pantheon Books, 1996), p. 260.
15. James Fallows, "Howell Raines Owes Me an Apology," Slate.com, posted Dec. 3, 2001.
16. Rodney Thrash, "The Prism of the Past," *St. Petersburg Times,* May 10, 2005, p. 1E.
17. Charles Kuralt, *On the Road* (New York: G.P. Putman's Sons, 1985), p. 14.
18. Michael Quintanilla, "Look at Undercovered Communities, Kozol Asks," *American Editor,* June 1996.
19. Quoted in *The Conversation of Journalism*, p. 88.

20. Genevieve Roja, "Take This Jobless Recovery and Shove It", AlterNet.org, posted Aug. 11, 2003.
21. Peggy Peterman, "A Tree Stands Alone," *St. Petersburg Times,* May 26, 1992, pp. 1D, 2D.
22. Maria D. Vesperi, *City of Green Benches* (Ithaca, N.Y.: Cornell University Press, 1985, reprinted 1998), p. 55.
23. Sally Lehrman, "How to Cross Your 'Faultlines,'" SPJ.org, http://www.spj.org/dtb2.asp.
24. Leigh Stephens Aldrich, *Covering the Community* (Thousand Oaks, Calif.: Pine Forge Press, 1999), pp. 4, 7.
25. Keith Woods, ed., *The Best Newspaper Writing of 2001* (St. Petersburg, Fla.: The Poynter Institute for Media Studies, 2001), pp. 226, 256.
26. The Harwood Group, *Tapping Civic Life* (Washington, D.C.: The Pew Center for Civic Journalism, 2002), pp. 10, 11.
27. *Tapping Civic Life*, p. 17.
28. *Tapping Civic Life*, p. 8.
29. Eric Deggans, "The Birth of a Journalism Dream," The Feed, posted Oct. 1, 2006, http://blogs.tampabay.com/media.
30. G. Michael Killenberg and Robert Dardenne, "Instruction in News Reporting as Community-focused Journalism," *Journalism & Mass Communications Educator*, Spring 1997, pp. 52–58.
31. Steve Davis and John Hatcher, "Reporting out of the Comfort Zone," *AJR*, December 2005–January 2006, p. 64.

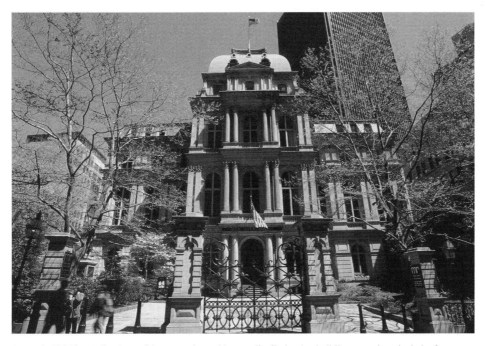

Boston's Old City Hall   Opened in 1865, the architecturally distinctive building served as the hub of municipal government until 1969, when the present city hall replaced it. Today, Old City Hall houses businesses and organizations. For journalists, city hall, whether modest or ornate, remains an important news beat and a place they know intimately. (Photo courtesy of Richard Burton White.)

The business of government is conducted at polished walnut desks beneath the fresco-adorned ceilings of massive statehouses. It also is conducted at folding tables set up on the patched linoleum floors of cinder-block community halls.

No matter what the setting, and no matter who governs, the average citizen wants to know an essential point about the business of government: "How am I going to be affected?" That question should guide all government reporters, whether they cover sessions of Congress or meetings of the village board. Here is how Mark Davis of the *Tampa Tribune* keeps his perspective on government reporting: "You sit in some old county commission meeting, and they're talking about developmental impact or some old crummy ordinance, and you forget that basically they're dealing with people.

Somebody's going to be affected, and you have to keep your eye on those details: who the people are, how it's going to affect them for better or worse, and how they view it."[1]

As Davis knows, the key to effective, appealing government reporting is the people factor. First, tell the news of government *through people*. Second, relate news of government *to people*. Writing coach Don Murray adds this advice: "Invite the reader in—it's the reader's government."[2]

Government reporters who care about "inviting the people in" avoid becoming pipelines for "officialdom." Officialdom is not so much a place as a state of mind. It is a stultified realm populated by politicians and bureaucrats who speak *governmentese*, a hybrid of jargon and gobbledygook. Reporters have to function in officialdom, but they must not succumb to its numbing influence. Otherwise they are apt to end up writing by formula, concentrating chiefly on meetings and events, relying on a handful of favored official sources and dealing in the inanimate objects of government—bills, reports, studies and pronouncements. The dull stuff.

Too many news accounts of government are poorly written and poorly read. Readers often skim government stories, assuming they offer little of interest or value. But government is not a vast, barren wasteland. For resourceful and enthusiastic reporters, there is action, intrigue, drama and significance on government beats, as Mark Davis demonstrated in his five-part series "Anatomy of a Road." By turning what could have been a tedious subject into a lively journey through a tangle of heavy machinery and traffic jams, Davis won an American Society of Newspaper Editors award for government reporting.

Mark Davis and other reporters who have shared his experiences know the task is not easy. Government at all levels is becoming increasingly complex, specialized and far-flung. To find important stories, reporters must sift through layers of bureaucracy—agencies, commissions, boards and departments. Moreover, much of the debate, bargaining, compromise and decision making of government occurs away from public view. Simply covering meetings and events is not enough. To do the job adequately means understanding the intricacies of policy making, legislation, public finance, law and politics.

Veteran journalist and teacher Rob Armstrong urges journalists to become experts in civics—all journalists. "It is difficult to overstate the importance of basic civics—knowing how government works—to journalists," he says. "It doesn't matter where you work or what your area of specialization. . . . Civics is part of your daily work. If you don't understand civics it will be impossible for you to explain it to your audience."[3] The most successful government reporters learn to attend to both the important actions of government and the significant issues and problems affecting—or soon to affect—citizens.

Journalists rightly keep close tabs on government, but increasingly, the private sector—all entities outside government, such as corporations, banks and non-profit organizations—occupies significant space and influence in the public sphere. When Wal-Mart comes to town with plans for a supercenter, for instance, city hall might unfurl a "welcome" banner of tax breaks and land subsidies. At times, the encroachment of the private sector comes by government initiative, through a concept called *privatization*. Under privatization, federal, state, county and local governments contract with businesses or organizations to operate landfills, house the homeless, guard buildings and store digital data, for example. The private sector, while not accountable to the public by the ballot box, clearly shapes legislation, budgeting and land use at all levels of government and warrants unrelenting attention by journalists, even those stationed far from the corporate towers of Big Business.

Chapter 6 begins with and focuses heavily on city hall, where many reporters, some while still in school, start their careers. City hall coverage is at the core of government reporting and prepares journalists for other beats.

Covering the City and the Hall

A city hall reporter ought to be a walking encyclopedia of community life. Intelligent, accurate, thorough coverage begins with a foundation of knowledge. Do not assume you know the city until you can answer the following questions—and many others:

What is the city's history? Who founded it and when? How did it get its name? Who were the leading settlers? What were crucial events in the city's history? What does the city's history say about its *present* and suggest about its *future?*

Who are its people? What are their geographic and ethnic roots? What is the city's demographic profile? Where do people live? Is there segregation by race, ethnicity or age? Discrimination? Are segments of the population frustrated? Involved? Angry?

What about development? Is the city growing? Stagnant? Withering? Is there a sufficient tax base to maintain city services? Which businesses and institutions are the largest employers? What's the jobless rate? Are people taking out building permits? Business licenses? Does the city have a master plan for development? If so, what does the plan propose?

What's the condition of the city's infrastructure? Are water and sewer lines adequate and in good repair? How about housing? Roads? Bridges? Public buildings? Who does the inspecting and how diligently?

What about amenities and services? Is it a good place to live in terms of health facilities, police protection, arts and culture, transportation, recreation, social services and education?

Who are the political, social and economic power brokers? Who are the opinion leaders? The religious leaders? Who are the experts and authorities?

Although you cannot learn about a city overnight, there are shortcuts. Often the city government or Chamber of Commerce prepares a community profile for use in planning and economic development. Get a copy and read it. A good deal of basic information about government is now available on Web sites. Of course, check out online resources. Then shut off the laptop and go exploring. Ask to accompany a social worker as she visits clients. Ride around town with a supervisor in the streets department. Drop by the municipal recreation center and explore the city parks. Invite a housing-rights activist to give an assessment on the city. Chat with the city's unofficial historian. Share a cup of coffee and a view of the city's future with the executive director of the Chamber of Commerce. Discuss the city's progress with a labor union official.

QUOTABLES

"It's a continuum here at City Hall. You need to present the readers with a sense of where things have come from. You can't just do a story that says, 'Here's what happened today.' You can't write your stories in isolation, or you do a disservice to the readers. The frustrating thing about young reporters is that they don't have a sense of history."
—Fran Cohen Spielman, *Chicago Sun-Times*, quoted in Terry Stephan, "City Beat,"
Northwestern, Summer 2000

If you make an effort to know the city, you will better understand personalities, events and activities; ask more penetrating questions; acquire the background to issues and problems; build a file of valuable news sources; and discover untold stories. For example, you might find out that dozens of older residences still lack indoor plumbing—or that no new homes have been built in the city in the past six months, all of which could surprise even the most well-informed citizens.

Functions and Role of City Government

Reporters who carefully monitor a city's functions understand the greatest concerns of citizens. In an ideal sense, cities function to ensure order, provide essential services, nurture civic life and protect public health, welfare and safety—with varying degrees of success and efficiency. When a city fails to perform its basic functions, that is usually news.

An urban scholar studying government-citizen contacts in Kansas City found that people were most often concerned about service problems, such as uncollected trash or barking dogs. Next in degree of concern were safety problems, like fear of walking city streets at night. Least frequently mentioned were social problems—for instance, unsupervised teenagers.[4] Should reporters, then, devote more attention to junked cars than aimless youths? Remember that each city has its peculiar problems. In some cases, cities conduct surveys or form committees to measure citizen attitudes to municipal services or prioritize plans for the future through what many communities call "vision" statements. Surveys and vision statements provide clues, but to really understand citizens and their concerns, leave city hall and visit neighborhoods: Talk to people and listen to what is on their minds. (Chapter 5 focuses on neighborhoods.)

Knowing a city also involves understanding its relationship to the state. Cities are not autonomous entities that can do as they please. In fact, political scientists sometimes describe cities as "creatures of the state" because, in many cases, charters granted by state legislators define a particular city's powers, functions and structure of government. For example, most states, by statute, determine how cities set tax rates, annex land and borrow money. Certain cities, though, operate under a principle known as *home rule*. States with home-rule charters allow cities a greater degree of self-determination, particularly in selecting a form of government and method of elections. Home-rule communities still must abide by the state's constitution and statutes. If nothing else, home-rule cities enjoy a psychological sense of freedom. If your city has a charter, be sure to study it.

REAL-LIFE LESSONS

Keeping an eye on the mundane is a requirement in city hall coverage. Sometimes it is just a matter of making sure public officials are doing their basic duties. The IRE (Investigative Reporters and Editors, Inc.) recognized the *Rocky Mountain News* for its story "Council missing in action." Reporter Daniel J. Chacón noticed a lot of absenteeism at committee meetings, so he started counting heads. He found the city's 13 council members had missed 18 to 81 meetings of regular, joint and special committees between mid-2003 and September 2006. The member with the worst attendance record missed 81 of 289 meetings during that span.

Here's how Chacón put the problem into context:

> On Tuesdays and Wednesdays year-round, decisions affecting thousands of Denver residents are hashed out in a small room in the City and County Building.
>
> Council members, usually in groups of six or less, pile around a table, often with mayoral appointees, department officials, business leaders and others by their side.
>
> But council members don't always show up, raising concerns that the vetting of major decisions is getting shoved to regular council meetings, one of the last steps in the process.
>
> . . . Council members can catch up on missed meetings by reading the minutes, watching broadcasts on Channel 8 or on the city's Web site, and talking to those who participated.
>
> But some acknowledge that poor attendance may be delaying work that's supposed to be done in committee, which ranges from simple single-family rezoning requests to more complicated publicly financed projects.[5]

The lesson: *By checking minutes of the committees, the reporter discovered a problem that, on the surface, seemed relatively insignificant. But important city business goes on outside the regular city council meetings. By his vigilance, Chacón did his job of informing citizens about the performance of their elected officials. He also helped educate the community about the inner workings of the council at the committee level.*

The Structure of City Government

In part, journalists are responsible for the structural characteristics now widely found in city governments. Lincoln Steffens and other muckrakers helped expose the shame of the cities—the graft and bossism of the late 19th and early 20th centuries. They wrote about election fraud, bribes, influence peddling, patronage, nepotism and other sins of the boss-led political machines that controlled many big cities. Their stories helped fuel a reform movement that tried to rid cities of corruption and chaos and restore honesty and efficiency in government. The reform package often included non-partisan, at-large elections, city manager-council structure and civil service merit employment, all intended to make city government more democratic, professional and honest.

Actually, reform presented its own problems, some of them unanticipated. For example, with management of government in the hands of unelected professionals, city officials began to be less directly accountable to the people; you cannot vote a city manager out of office. By ousting boss-controlled political cronies from their patronage jobs in city hall and replacing them with bureaucrats, government tended to become less responsive to complaints. In the old days, people knew whom to call to get a pothole repaired or a stop sign installed. And when at-large elections replaced election by wards or precincts, some neighborhoods and classes of citizens lost their direct representation on the city council.

Most cities now operate under one of three common forms: *mayor-council, city manager-council* and *commission*. City hall reporters need to know the characteristics, strengths and weaknesses of each form of government, since the structure of government tends to create different sets of tensions over who wields power, sets policy and makes decisions.

The *mayor-council* form includes two main variations—weak mayor and strong mayor. The distinction pertains to the powers held by a city's chief executive. As a rule, strong mayors are authorized to hire and fire administrators, initiate policy, prepare and administer the budget and veto legislation. Weak mayors frequently are ceremonial figures with little administrative power. An administratively strong mayor, however, could be ineffectual as a politician, just as a weak mayor may possess influence and power that go beyond heading the 4th the July parade. Personality, ability and political connections help determine whether, in practice, a mayor is strong or weak. Henry Maier, mayor of Milwaukee for 28 years, observed: "The mayor of New York has considerable strength by statute. And Mayor (Richard) Daley of Chicago had the weakest power by statute in the U.S. So which is the strong mayor?"[6] Mayor Daley dominated Chicago politics; his son, the present mayor of Chicago, also wields considerable power. As Maier suggests, do not put too much stock in "statutory power."

The *city manager-council* form is common in midsized cities of 25,000 to 250,000 population. It began as a product of reform, but today it makes sense for cities that are governed by part-time mayors and legislators who often lack the expertise or time to oversee day-to-day operations. A competent, professionally trained city manager can bring cost-effective, expert administration to a city.

City managers often run the show, particularly if the mayor and council members are busy at their full-time jobs. Reporters, naturally, will turn to city managers for opinions, reactions and information related to city government. But keep in mind that a powerful, policy-making city manager may be knowledgeable, witty, urbane *and* politically savvy, at least in dealing with the mayor and council. But is he or she as attuned to citizen concerns or as knowledgeable about the community?

Keep in mind as well that many city managers lead a nomadic life, relocating frequently because of career ambitions, a tiff with the city council or election of a new administration. This is the price of being a hired hand. City managers often will admit that it is a precarious, stressful position. "People expect you to do miracles," said Robert Obering about his tenure as city manager of St. Petersburg, Fla. "Then if you have a city council that doesn't like you very much, that's much more stress. If you have a split council, they will put the city manager in between."[7] He served for six years before resigning under fire. City managers walk a tightrope and are cautious about what they say and do. Reporters should not overly rely on the city manager as a source for news or insight. As always, seek a diversity of viewpoints.

The *commission* form is an awkward breed of government. By most accounts, the commission form developed in 1900 after Galveston, Texas, struggled to recover from a hurricane that killed 6,000 of the city's 37,000 residents and destroyed half of the city's property. The state legislature appointed a five-person commission of business leaders to run the city. Each commissioner directed a municipal department. But as the commission form evolved and spread to other cities, its disadvantages became apparent. Not all commissioners, even those who are successful in the business world, prove to be adept at managing municipal departments. In addition, the commission form fails to provide for a separation of powers between executive and legislative functions of the commissioners and leads commissioners to frequent turf battles. The mayor, often holding no more power than the other commissioners, may lack authority to intercede when commissioners fail to act in the best overall interests of the community. Today, fewer than 200 cities, mostly small communities, operate under the commission form.

The structure and size of city government also influence how much day-to-day contact reporters can expect with officials. In big cities, the mayor's office may be structured like the White House, which means a reporter must deal with a chief of staff, an appointments secretary, a press secretary and assorted aides before—or instead of—seeing the mayor. As a result, some big-city reporters must either be satisfied to ask questions at the mayor's occasional press conferences or wait for a personal interview, which might have to be scheduled well in advance. Big-city mayors are busy, but they are also in a good position to dictate and manage media coverage, particularly by staging events and "happenings" for television coverage. At the other extreme, small-town mayors answer their own phones and share coffee and chitchat with reporters. And if you miss the mayor at city hall, she can be reached at her full-time job as a State Farm insurance agent.

Council members, sometimes called aldermen, usually are available and eager to talk to the press. Even in the largest of cities, few are full-time lawmakers. But they are politicians, and, if they wish to remain in office, they need to be visible to their constituents.

The mayor meets the press A phalanx of reporters and camera crews questions Chicago Mayor Richard Daley and other state and local officials at a press conference announcing a new drug-abuse treatment program for inmates of state prisons and local jails. Mayor Daley draws a crowd, but even small-town mayors can expect a steady stream of queries and interview requests from reporters. (Photo courtesy of the National Institute of Drug Abuse.)

Who's Who in City Hall

Regardless of the size of the city, certain officials—both elected and appointed—play key roles as newsmakers and information providers. In midsized or small municipalities and villages, the office of the *city clerk*, often adjacent to the front lobby of city hall, is the hub of activity. (In the case of a village, substitute "village" for "city" in the titles.) Here is where you will find the bulk of the city's records, such as minutes of council meetings, applications for building permits, lists of property-tax assessments and sets of ordinances. In smaller communities, the city clerk may be the only full-time elected official. In almost all cases, the clerk knows who's who and what's what in city hall. The clerk is one of the first people you should get to know on the city hall beat, especially when you need background information, access to city documents, schedules of meetings and copies of agendas.

The *city attorney* (sometimes called the corporation counsel) is a source of information on nearly every facet of city government, including ordinances, municipal bonds, contracts and labor negotiations. You can anticipate that other city officials, including the mayor and city manager, will seek the city attorney's advice on a wide range of issues and problems. Usually, the city attorney is an appointed official on a retainer who serves at the pleasure of the administration. In large cities, it is a full-time position. City attorneys tend to be politically astute and well connected, but most prefer to remain in the background, staying clear, if possible, of tugs of war over city policy. When there is a division among city council members and the mayor, you might be able to tap the city attorney for a moderate, less partial viewpoint although it may be given off the record.

Municipal money flows to and from the *city treasurer*. That does not necessarily mean the city treasurer is a fiscal expert. In fact, many city treasurers are elected officials who know only the rudiments of accountancy and budget management. In large cities, the city treasurer frequently oversees a professional staff and a multimillion-dollar budget. Even when there is no reason to suspect problems, the city treasurer's office requires constant vigilance. Conscientious city hall reporters routinely inspect invoices, purchase requisitions, bills and monthly budget updates.

Municipalities that seek orderly, sound development often hire a professional *city planner*. Part of the city planner's job is to design and implement a blueprint for land use and growth called a *master plan*. City planners frequently find themselves in controversies over rezoning, annexation, condemnation of property and other touchy aspects of city growth.

Operation of city services is delegated to department heads who are likely to be well-trained professionals. Nearly all cities have a *public works director* or city engineer responsible for, among other things, water and sewage-treatment facilities, which are subject to increasingly strict, complicated and expensive requirements set by federal and state agencies. Other common municipal departments include housing, recreation, streets and public safety.

In new communities, such as Sandy Springs, Ga., and older, traditional cities, such as Indianapolis, fundamental functions of government now are controlled by private companies under a managerial philosophy known as *privatization*—turning over responsibility for services from the public to the private sector. Sandy Springs, an unincorporated but thriving suburb of Atlanta, had contracted with Fulton County for the bulk of its community services, but residents felt shortchanged by the county, so they incorporated as a city in 2005 and contracted with professional firms or nearby governments, including the county, to do the city's traditional jobs.

Cities have long contracted with outside firms for such services as vehicle repair, telecommunications or park maintenance. But under recent cost-cutting trends, cities have privatized more vital services, such as waste disposal, tax assessment, social services and, in a few cases, police and fire protection. The proponents of privatization cite improved efficiency and economy; opponents fear cities, to save a dollar, will surrender part of their autonomy and accountability in a government-style "outsourcing" scheme. Whether privatization works or not, it is part of contemporary municipal governance and warrants careful attention from journalists. Of course, private firms hired by cities and other government units often fall outside open-meetings and open-records laws, so reporters trying to monitor their performance can expect roadblocks.

How to Cover Council Meetings

Covering city government means going to meeting after meeting. Too often, the meetings are overly long, slowly paced and sparsely attended, unless a controversial issue is on the agenda. Dreary as this may sound, dedicated reporters approach government meetings with a serious sense of purpose. They know they have a responsibility to the public to report the activities of government. With many city council meetings now aired on the local public-access channel, citizens can watch the mayor and city council spar from the La-Z-Boy. Reporters, however, know that cablecasts do not substitute for a vigilant press. They also know that what happens at a city council meeting may reveal the tip of a larger story. What if an engineering report, given scant attention by the council members, reveals a serious, impending shortage in the city water supply? Unless reporters are present—and alert—the story may go undetected, which could be exactly what city officials hope will happen.

Experienced city hall reporters also know that much of the work, discussion and resolution of differences over ordinances and other municipal business occurs at meetings of the *standing committees* of the city council. Standing committees, most often comprised of council members who either are assigned or volunteer for service, do the preparatory work on matters such as drafting ordinances, planning and research for budgets, reviewing bids and purchase requests, and hiring, dismissing and evaluating employees. The standing committees ultimately report to the city council. Cities typically, as well, form *advisory committees* of lay people to help deal with important issues such as economic development, housing and public transportation. Learn about the committees and advisory groups under the auspices of city government, and cover their meetings, because the seeds for stories often germinate at the committee level.

Preparation

Preparation is a key to competent coverage of city government meetings. A starting point is careful review of the agenda and the packets of materials the council members receive in advance of meetings. The packets contain, among other things, copies of reports, correspondence and proposed ordinances. Most often, the city clerk's office prepares and distributes the packets. Increasingly, cities post agendas and other relevant meeting material online at the city Web site.

Even veteran reporters review material prior to meetings, and they frequently rely on informative sources in city hall to help provide background and explanations for items on the meeting agenda.

Preparation includes, at times, *advance stories* to alert citizens about what is going to happen at the city council meeting. Advance stories also help reporters stay on top of their beats. By talking to council members and city officials prior to a meeting, you can begin to anticipate, plan and organize meeting coverage.

What to Expect

Government meetings are not reported in chronological order; otherwise, most leads would begin: "The City Council opened its meeting Tuesday night with a solemn pledge of allegiance, followed by a snappy roll call and unanimous approval of the minutes."

The order of business will vary, but generally meetings include these categories: petitions and communications, reports of city officers, council committee reports, new business and old business. Time may be reserved at the beginning or end of meetings for citizens to speak from the floor.

In small and midsized communities, the mayor presides over meetings of the city council. In larger cities, an alderman, elected by his or her colleagues or by citywide vote, may preside as president of the board of aldermen or council. Whoever presides usually controls the pace, tone and flow of meetings.

City council meetings often are informal and disorganized. People, including council members and reporters, move around the council chambers, shuffle papers, clear throats and carry on conversations when others are trying to speak and conduct business. For the uninitiated, the apparent lack of decorum may be disconcerting, but it usually is not worth reporting—unless, of course, a meeting turns into a three-ring circus of epithets and incivility. It happens, as Heron Marquez Estrada of the *Star Tribune* in Minneapolis reported in her coverage of a suburban city's escapades:

> The first speaker before the Maplewood City Council threatened to sue. The second wanted to turn City Hall into a community center for Little Canada or St. Paul.
>
> To an outsider, things may have seemed unusual at last week's council meeting.
>
> But it was just another Manic Monday in Maplewood, a city of 37,000 where the City Council is at war with its constituents, its staff and itself.
>
> Since a new council majority took over in March, there have been numerous accusations: personal and political vendettas, bullying of staffers, arbitrary firings, conflicts of interest, office break-ins, secret meetings in violation of state law.
>
> "It's so incredible what's going on there, that people can't believe it's true," said Sherrie Le, who was fired in August as Maplewood's director of human resources.[8]

With meetings now carried live to homes in the community, public officials usually show restraint, but the business of running a city gets intense at times.

Legislative Process

The meat of most city council sessions is passage of *ordinances*—the laws of municipalities. Ordinances originate in several ways. A citizen, for example, may approach a city council member, asking for a parking ban on the north side of a dangerously narrow stretch of Elm Street. Or a problem may arise, such as keg parties at city parks, requiring specific rules governing consumption of alcohol on municipal property. Regulations coming from a federal or state office, like the U.S. Environmental Protection Agency, might require passage of a new ordinance detailing how, say, sewer lines are installed. In some cases, ordinances satisfy a public official's whim or address a pet peeve. In suburban Chicago, the mayor of Evergreen Park spent more than an hour stuck at a railroad crossing by a stopped freight train. Soon afterward the village board passed an ordinance calling for a $100,000 fine against trains that unnecessarily blocked crossings.

In its earliest stage, an ordinance may be scribbled in pencil on the back of an envelope. Eventually, it is refined and put into legal form and language by the city attorney or the city manager. Once introduced before the city council, the proposed ordinance receives what is called the *first reading*, and normally it is perfunctorily passed on first reading so that it may move to the next stage, which usually is review by a standing committee of the city council. If, for example, the ordinance involves parking, it is sent to the committee responsible for streets. In special cases, the standing committee holds one or more public hearings to allow citizens an opportunity to respond to the proposed legislation, particularly if a tax levy or expenditure of public money is involved.

As a proposed ordinance undergoes review, it can be modified or refined before returning to the full city council for the *second reading*. At this point the proposed ordinance normally is subject to discussion and debate by members of the entire city council, who may seek additional amendments or alterations from the floor or return it to committee. Some cities require a *third reading*, followed by a majority vote of the council, to pass an ordinance. The process is deliberately slow so that citizens and lawmakers alike can read, consider, amend or reject legislation. In an emergency, an ordinance can be passed on first reading, but usually a two-thirds vote is required to prevent laws from being "railroaded," or rushed, through the city council. The final steps of the process include approval by the mayor, who may have the power to veto the legislation, and publication of a legal notice of the ordinance in a local general-circulation newspaper.

Understanding the process is important, but, above all, reporters must know the origins and motives behind any important piece of legislation. Who, for example, are the opponents and sponsors, including those in the forefront and those behind the scenes? David Broder, a political correspondent for the *Washington Post*, once described coverage of Congress in terms that apply, as well, to coverage of city government: "When I started working on Capitol Hill, the wire service did a lot more of what I would characterize as railroad timetable reporting of Congress, which tells you what train (or bill) has just left what station and what its next stop will be. It tells you a little bit about what's on the train, but almost nothing about how the train was put together and why it is carrying that particular cargo."[9] Reporters who provide consistently accurate explanations attend committee meetings where they can better observe how the train is put together, learn what it is carrying and find out where it is headed and why it is headed there.

Do not confuse ordinances with two other official actions subject to a vote of the council—*resolutions* and *motions*. Resolutions are used to set city policy (telling the street department to cut high weeds on vacant lots and bill the owners) or express community sentiment (declaring the council's moral support for the United Way campaign). Motions made and approved by the council usually direct city administrators to take action on a variety of routine matters, such as instructing the city clerk to rehire two part-time employees or authorizing the treasurer to pay the city's monthly bills.

Writing Meeting Stories

For inexperienced reporters, the greatest challenge of meeting coverage is determining what to emphasize among a number of actions of apparently comparable importance—or unimportance. As the meeting progresses, dozens of agenda items may be swiftly dispatched to committees or disposed of with little comment and no vote. Do not assume such matters are inconsequential. Conversely, do not assume a lengthy, heated debate over a request by the fire chief to attend a convention in Las Vegas is important. Stay alert and ask questions if you are unsure of what is significant and what is not. Let the people factor guide you. As a rule, the news value of city business increases proportionately with the number of people affected.

QUOTABLES

"Remember that each story is a conversation with the reader. The reader isn't passive, but is asking questions. It is your job to anticipate those questions and answer them [p. 167]. . . . It is amazing how often as a journalist I found that a story had five key questions. These were not the questions I wanted to ask or even the questions my editor told me to ask. They were the questions that the reader would ask and if I did not answer them the readers would be unsatisfied. . . . I would take a minute before starting a quick daily story, a six-week magazine story, or a year-long book project to ask five questions my readers would ask. I still do this. I have to keep learning.

"On a story about an addition to a high school, the questions might be:

What's it cost?

Where's the money coming from?

Why is the addition needed?

How will it help students? Teachers?

Is there a temporary alternative?

"When I come to write the story, I order the questions in the sequence I think the reader will ask them. In some cases I type them into the copy, then cut them out in the final editing." (pp. 39, 40)

—Donald M. Murray (1924–2006), *Writing to Deadline,*
Portsmouth, N.H.: Heinemann, 2000

It is much easier to determine significance when you are familiar with the background of major business before the city council. That is especially true regarding matters the council has discussed repeatedly over the course of months or even years. Because there is no need for council members to review the history of a long-standing agenda item, they compress details, speak obliquely and still understand each other—losing reporters who fail to do their homework.

Government officials also speak in bureaucratic shorthand. In the course of a few rapidly delivered sentences, a city official might refer to "IEPA," "C-3 zoning," "special-use permit" and "non-performance bonds." To survive, you must be conversant in the language of government. If necessary, ask public officials to help you define specialized terms in lay language.

Another challenge of writing meeting stories is to translate the legalese of ordinances into plain English. Ordinances normally are collections of "whereas" paragraphs that explain the background and rationale of the legislation. They lead to the "therefore" clause: "Therefore, be it ordained by the City Council of Pottsville. . . ." After that, the details of the ordinance are enumerated by series of sections. When ordinances are especially long and technical, do not be too proud to seek the city attorney's help.

With any major legislation, you will want to explain the background, anticipate the impact, gather reactions and provide the analysis, none of which is to be found in the text of the ordinance. One reason that accomplished city hall reporters do their homework is to prepare themselves to flesh out the story. By itself, an ordinance provides little more than the story's skeleton. In fact, with a controversial ordinance, reaction-background coverage begins with its first reading. If, for example, the city council proposes to ban overnight parking of all trucks, including pickups, on residential streets, there will be no shortage of reaction. Just be sure to seek reaction both inside *and* outside city hall.

To some extent, what you write—and how you write it—depends on a number of external factors. Among them are the amount of news space in that day's paper, your editor's desires and needs and news developments elsewhere that are competing for space. It is vital for beat reporters to consult with editors frequently, especially to plan and coordinate meeting coverage. Consultations between reporters and editors should be a mutual enterprise, with ideas flowing in both directions.

Most city hall reporters for newspapers prefer to present council news in several small doses rather than cram everything they know into a comprehensive piece. When coverage is limited to a single, long story, readers may overlook other important city business reported deep in the story. If forced to go with a single piece, be sure to insert a paragraph near the lead of the story to summarize major developments. Here is an example:

> Despite objections from local merchants, the city council voted unanimously to increase parking meter rates downtown from 10 cents to 25 cents an hour.
>
> In a meeting marked by angry debate, the council also approved a zoning variance that will allow Pizza Palace, Inc., to build a restaurant adjacent to Washington grade school and granted a liquor license to Mayor John Williams' son-in-law.
>
> The strongest protests, however, came when the city council prepared to act on parking rates. . . .

Sometimes, particularly in small communities, there is not much on which to pin a lead. One possible solution is to find a connection among otherwise unrelated, minor actions, as the opening of the following story does:

> In a brief but busy session last night, the city council took several steps to replace wornout equipment.
>
> Among other things, the council:

- appropriated $1,000 to buy tires for a city fire truck
- authorized the city clerk to call for bids on a police car
- asked the city engineer to estimate the cost to replace a faulty sewer pump at the Beacon Hills lift station
- approved a low bid of $10,500 for a new tractor for the streets department

News emerging from city council meetings seldom is momentous. Even when more pressing issues beg for attention, much time and effort may be given by the council to seemingly mundane matters, such as sewer backups, junked cars and potholes. But life's mundane side occasionally produces everyday irritations that should not go unaddressed or unreported.

No matter the topic or issue, the top city hall reporters find ways to engage readers through vivid writing. Chip Scanlan of the Poynter Institute compares a straight summary lead—the kind that tops many city council stories—with one that uses narrative style to convey the same point. Would you prefer the following lead? he asks:

> A Putnam County resident warned county commissioners yesterday that a snake- and rat-infested abandoned house on her street poses a threat to children and threatened to prove it by presenting officials with a bounty of dead varmints she's shot at the place.

Or, he asks, would you prefer this one?

> Dodie Griffin sits on her concrete porch, aims her Mossberg shotgun across the way and blasts her target.
>
> Over the last few years, she's bagged a slew of snakes and rats that take refuge most of the time in an abandoned house next door.

She told Putnam County commissioners Monday how she had thought of gathering up her dubious bounty and plopping it onto the desk in their chamber.

But she thought better of it and addressed the commission without visuals aids. This time.

The second lead appeared on a story by Heather Svokos published in the *Charleston* (W.Vir.) *Gazette*. "At first glance her (Griffin's) story was one I had told several times before about an abandoned building: Children will fall through the floor to their death! Cut themselves on broken glass! And God knows what else! Sometimes that's powerful enough. But like I said, it's been done so many times, I wanted a new twist."[10]

REPORTER'S TIP FILE

Don't neglect the "small stuff"

Sometimes little steps in the preparation and coverage of a meeting make a big difference in getting the story done well.

Don't be late

Arrive at least 30 minutes early for a city council meeting. If nothing else, you may need the extra time to battle traffic or find a parking space. More productively, you can use the time to gather background information, conduct interviews or engage in useful small talk.

Get a good seat

Position yourself close to the action. A table for the press may be provided, but is it the best vantage point? Try to get an unobstructed view of the council so you can better see and hear what is being discussed. If you have never met the council members, do not assume that the person sitting at a desk marked "Alderman Mary Davis" is Mary Davis. Learn the identity of all the city officials prior to the start of the meeting.

Line up sources

After the meeting, line up people you need to interview. You might say, "Councilman Perkins, I have to ask the mayor a few questions, but if you could wait, I'd like to talk to you, too." If people are in a hurry to leave, find out where they will be later and how you can reach them by phone or e-mail.

Work the audience

Talk to citizens who attend. Find out who they are and why they are present, even if they were silent during the meeting. They still may have a story to tell. "Few people come to a meeting for entertainment," says Fred Palmer, managing editor of the *Johnson City* (Tenn.) *Press-Chronicle*.[8]

Who's absent—and why?

Identify in your meeting story any city council members who were absent, and find out why they were absent. Do not be satisfied with a vague explanation, such as, "She's away on city business" or "He's attending to a personal matter." The council member away on "city business" might be meeting with representatives of a corporation who are scouting the city for a factory site. The council member attending to a "personal matter" could be at a college graduation or in the hospital for cardiac tests.

Financing City Government

Running a city is big business. In 2004, the budget for the City of Chicago passed the $5 billion mark. Three hundred miles downstate, the general fund (operating) budget of Collinsville, Ill., population 25,000, topped $15 million in 2006. Municipal finances, however, actually are not complicated once you become familiar with their four basic components—*revenues* and *expenditure* and *budgeting* and *borrowing*.

Revenues and Expenditures

For most communities, property taxes constitute the main source of revenue, although increasingly, especially in suburban cities with profitable shopping malls, the *sales tax* is overtaking the property tax. The property tax remains a crucial and controversial source of revenue, partly because it is a tax that city officials can manipulate to help balance the municipal budget. Indeed, understanding the budget-making process begins with an understanding of property taxes.

Property tax
The property tax is based on a unit called a *mill*, which is one-tenth of a cent (penny), but most commonly, the tax rate is expressed as $1 of $1,000 of assessed valuation of the property being taxed. The *assessed value* generally is based on a percentage of the fair market value of the property. County or municipal assessors inspect and photograph real estate property, noting, among other things, lot size, square footage of living space, type of construction and condition of nearby property as factors in determining the market value. When a home is sold, the purchase price normally is used to set a new assessed value. Otherwise, property is supposed to be reassessed every few years to account for appreciation and improvements that might affect the market value. Assessments of commercial, industrial and farm land are more complicated, based on various formulas to determine income-earning use or potential.

Setting the tax rate
The tax rate is set by a city or county official, such as the county clerk, based on information provided by the taxing body. The mayor, budget director and other

municipal officials figure the city's revenues and expenditures and then calculate how much in locally generated property-tax revenue is needed to balance the budget. Once collected, tax revenue often goes into a general fund, although sometimes a city's tax rate is subdivided, and revenues are diverted to several separate funds dedicated for special use, such as employee pensions or library expenses.

Most city residents live within the boundaries of several taxing authorities, so a typical homeowner may pay taxes to the city, county, township, airport authority, sewer district, community college district and the local school district, which usually requires the largest share of the tax dollars. A sample tax bill, based on a $100,000 home assessed at 75 percent of its market value ($75,000), breaks down this way:

County	3.56 per $1,000 assessed valuation
Township	1.09
City	1.18
School	4.34
Community college	0.27
Airport district	0.18
Sewer district	0.23

Reading a tax bill

The total comes to a tax rate of $10.85 per $1,000 of assessed valuation. Multiplied by 75 (75,000 divided by 1,000), the taxpayer's bill comes to $813.75. Another method used to determine tax bills is to create a *millage rate* by dividing the total mills (10.8) by 1,000, which comes to 1.085—the millage rate. The next step is a simple calculation: the millage rate (1.085) $\times$ the assessed value ($75,000) = tax bill ($813.75).

Taxing bodies—cities, counties, special districts—vary considerably in how the tax bill is calculated, organized and presented, so do not expect the sample used here to neatly match a tax bill in your community. Get someone to carefully explain the process to you and, if necessary, to go over a tax bill, line by line.

Property-tax issues

Long before the taxpayer revolts of the late 1970s, property owners protested the inequities, financial burdens and corruption associated with the tax-assessment process. Among a litany of complaints are these:

- Property is not always assessed uniformly or accurately.
- There is little incentive for owners to improve property if it means an increase in taxes.
- The poor and people on fixed incomes are hit hardest by the property tax.
- Dishonest public officials continue to assess private, commercial and industrial property for political favor or personal gain.

For homeowners, however, one of the most controversial aspects of the property tax is *equalization*. When assessments in a county or city fail to correspond with selling prices of property, state or county officials are empowered to raise or lower taxes automatically and uniformly by a legal means sometimes known as a *multiplier*. In theory, multipliers and other instruments of equalization are supposed to maintain equity in assessments from county to county or city to city, but in practice, multipliers penalize property owners whose assessments already are in line with prevailing market values. The real estate boom of recent years, fueled by low interest rates and housing speculators, resulted in higher assessments for all property owners, but older residents on meager pensions have suffered the most.

Other revenue sources

Other major revenue sources are the city's share of various state-collected taxes on incomes, motor fuel (gasoline), tobacco and alcohol. Government officials lump these as "intergovernmental transfers." A few large cities, such as St. Louis, impose an earnings tax on all people who work in the city, regardless of where they reside.

Grants and aid from state or federal agencies, user charges, impact fees, licenses and franchise fees also constitute income for cities, but as revenue sources, they generally are not as dependable or substantial as taxes. City officials try to avoid funding programs with grant money: They usually come with strings attached, and they can be cut off at any time by Congress or the state legislature. In 1986, Congress eliminated the federal revenue-sharing program that many cities depended on as a major source of outside funding. Most user fees are generated by city-owned utilities, which frequently augment income by selling water or electricity to homes and businesses in unincorporated areas. In some areas, developers and builders must pay impact fees to help finance public roads and utilities needed to service new developments. Licenses range from auto stickers to liquor-sale permits. And franchise fees often are collected from cable operators, ambulance services and other companies that seek special or exclusive arrangements to do business in the city.

Reporters need to monitor all aspects of city finance. But tax levies and assessments deserve extra attention, largely because they nearly always generate debate and disputes. Do not underestimate the emotional and economic impact of taxes. When city officials propose a half-cent increase in the city's share of the state sales tax, it is of less consequence for a merchant selling greeting cards—or for customers buying the greeting cards. But applied to someone who sells $25,000 automobiles, increasing the sales tax from 6 to 6.5 percent adds $125 to a customer's bill, which is enough to drive some customers to a car dealer outside the city limits. Whenever taxes go up or down, do your best to determine what the change means in dollars to the average citizen.

Outlays, spending

Of course, nearly all of a city's income is quickly converted to expenditures. For most cities, the largest outlay—often one-third or more of the budget—goes to fire and

police protection. In addition, cities that borrow money through the sale of municipal bonds may earmark 5 percent or more of the budget to retirement of debt, which
could be substantial if the city decides to finance a major project, such as a sports
complex or convention center. Other big-ticket items are employee pensions and
insurance policies.

As cities age, more money has to be spent on replacing, repairing or upgrading the
infrastructure—expensive physical facilities, such as water lines, sewers, streets and
bridges. New needs also arise and call for new services, such as care for the homeless
in big cities. And some variables are beyond the control of city officials. One of them
is the weather, which affects spending on road repairs and snow removal.

City hall reporters cannot be expected to examine and assess every expenditure,
but they can and should be experts on municipal fiscal policies, procedures and
records. Clark Mollenhoff (1921–1991), a prize-winning investigative reporter before
he turned to teaching, encouraged reporters to concentrate on how equipment is purchased, contracts are awarded and bills are paid.[11]

Bidding and contracts

Knowing bidding procedures is particularly important. Most cities are required by law
to seek competitive bids for all purchases over a set amount, such as $1,000. The bid-
ding process is designed to ensure that both the city and its vendors operate fairly
and honestly—something that does not always happen. At times bid specifications
are written in a way to favor a particular vendor; occasionally, someone in city hall
conspires with a vendor to fix a contract by improperly disclosing the amount of the
competitors' sealed bids.

Cities also contract for services, ranging from vending machines in public buildings
to telecommunications. Contracts, despite the appearance of legal exactness, can work
to the city's disadvantage if not well drafted. Sometimes comparing contracts (which
should be public records) among cities helps spot flaws or irregularities.

Always be alert for conflicts of interest or questionable spending. Is the city, for
example, buying insurance from an agency co-owned by the mayor's son-in-law? Is
it paying $15 for brooms that should cost $5? Are officials spending lavish amounts
on travel expenses? Often a city council will pay hundreds of accounts by voice vote.
Reporters, however, should spot-check payments. Moreover, they should check the
monthly budget for spending patterns. (Is the city headed toward red ink on telecommunications?) And they should examine any audits closely. If an outside, independent
audit has not been conducted in years, they should find out why.

Corruption is not the only reason for your vigilance. By incompetence or neglect,
city officials may not be handling public money wisely or economically. Are the city's
surplus funds, for example, sitting idle in a non-interest-bearing account? Could the
police department save money by hiring its own mechanics rather than sending patrol
cars to an auto dealer for repairs? Is the city getting its fair share of revenue from the
franchise agreement with the cable company?

Borrowing

A city borrows money for many of the same reasons its citizens borrow—to make improvements, build facilities, pay off an unexpected expense, buy a needed piece of equipment or weather a temporary financial shortage. When cities or other government bodies, such as school districts, encounter a cash-flow problem, they generally borrow money from a local bank and repay it as soon as tax revenues come due. Most short-term borrowing is by way of *tax-* or *revenue-anticipation warrants*. It is not uncommon for a government body occasionally to need to borrow money while awaiting tax receipts, but frequent short-term borrowing suggests deeper fiscal problems that should be examined.

Bonds

For large, long-term projects or problems, cities usually issue *municipal bonds* to raise needed money. There are two principal types of bonds—*general obligation* and *revenue*. General-obligation bonds are guaranteed by the municipality and backed by its taxing powers. A general-obligation bond might be used to build a new city hall. Revenue bonds, however, are not guaranteed and are repaid by revenues the project generates. Revenue bonds might be used, for example, to finance building a municipal skating rink or expanding the airport, with user fees and other income brought in by the project, such as food-concession contracts, used to help retire the debt. A fairly recent development by cities to manage money from revenue-producing projects is the *enterprise fund*. Enterprise funds generally are segregated from other funds and accounts of the city so that revenues generated by the project go directly to funding the project's operation and paying off debt service or securities issued to finance the project.

Municipal bonds are usually sold in denominations of $5,000 or higher, and they may be repaid or retired over a period of 20 years or more. They offer a lower pretax return than some other types of investments, but the interest they pay is not usually taxable. Because investors today are able to choose from a number of tax-deferred or tax-exempt options, municipal bonds are less attractive than they once were.

Two other methods of borrowing are *special-assessment bonds* and *industrial-development bonds*. When a project, such as installing a sewer line to a newly annexed neighborhood, primarily benefits one segment of the population, the property owners may be asked to bear the cost of the project through a special assessment. By sponsoring tax-exempt industrial-development bonds, cities encouraged the construction of numerous private projects, ranging from luxury hotels to furniture factories. Businesses and developers once flocked to these bonds because they could build projects with money borrowed at below-market interest rates. Federal laws, however, now limit the amount of tax-exempt funds that may be used for private development.

Borrowing factors

Some communities believe in a pay-as-you-go policy. But when cities do borrow, they encounter factors that affect all borrowers: interest rates, borrowing power and credit ratings. High interest rates may force a city to postpone projects, and state laws set ceilings on the amount of money a city is allowed to borrow. Moreover, the city's financial condition affects the bond rating it receives from investment services, among them Moody's or Standard & Poor's. An "Aaa" rating from Moody's, for example, reflects a solid fiscal base and record and helps sell a city's bonds. A "Caa" reflects a weak fiscal base and record, thus making it harder to attract investors. Watch the city's borrowing practices. Like its citizens, a city might indulge in impulse spending on unwise or unneeded projects that threaten to put the community too far in debt.

The Budget-Making Process

Reporters who fail to follow the budget-making process from start to finish will not be able to adequately interpret the final product when it is presented to the people and the city council for reaction and adoption. The annual budget represents a city's estimate of expenditures and revenues for operation of the municipal government and its services. The budget covers either a calendar year or a fiscal year, which is usually July 1 to June 30 of the following year. The budget-making process begins in the executive branch and is overseen by the mayor and the mayor's staff. (The budget process of municipal government resembles the process for state, county and federal units of government as well.) In general, the municipal budgets evolve in these stages:

- submission of proposed spending plans for the year by department heads to the mayor, city manager or budget officials
- assessment of anticipated revenues for the year
- meetings and conferences between department heads and budget-making officials
- drafting of the budget
- submission of the budget and budget message by the mayor (or designee) to the city council
- study, debate and adjustments by the city council
- public hearings
- adoption of the final budget

Reporters ought to be stationed at every stop along the route.

Each city goes about preparing and adopting a budget in its own way, but nearly all city officials *strive* for a balanced budget that maintains existing services and provides for wage increases for municipal employees—without raising taxes. They do not always succeed.

If revenues cannot keep pace with the costs of government, which is often the case, city officials have little choice but to raise taxes, find new revenues or make cuts. Often equipment and supplies are the first to be trimmed. Plans to hire new employees or launch costly programs are likely to be postponed. Who wins or loses the budget-cutting game may indicate who wields the greatest or least power in city hall.

As the proposed budget is developed and debated, it helps for reporters to retain a degree of healthy skepticism. Are fiscal conditions as dire as city officials proclaim? Guard against either understating or overplaying budget-making rhetoric.

It is also important to see the budget as more than a spending blueprint or a set of numbers. According to Dave Herzog of the *Providence Journal*: "It's an operating plan. It sets out the [community's] vision. A budget is a very political document."[12] Reporters should examine and assess those values and priorities to determine whether they correspond with the needs and demands of the community. Are the city's priorities misplaced if $250,000 is allocated annually to manicure the city's golf greens while nothing is spent for after-school programs?

Once completed, a big-city budget can fill several dictionary-sized volumes. A village budget may be held together with a paper clip. Regardless of the budget's size and bulk, citizens—as always—will be concerned about how they are going to be affected. Reporters who regularly attend budget meetings and hearings will not be in a last-minute rush to decipher the pages and columns of figures and percentages. In addition, the budget message by the mayor or chief financial officer will help highlight major points. Nonetheless, a careful review of the final budget is essential.

All budgets include two parts—revenues and expenditures—but the organization, format and detail of budgets vary considerably. Usually, revenues and expenditures are listed for a number of funds or accounts. The largest of these is the *general fund*, which includes most of a city's operational costs, such as administration, public works and public safety. Some cities have dozens of lesser funds, covering everything from retirement and pension programs for public employees to support of the municipal band.

The budget submitted to the city council for consideration might be divided into several columns for ease of comparison and study. Here is a sample section for the municipal swimming pool of a small city:

Budget categories	Current budget	Department request	Mayor's recommendation
	FY 2007	FY 2008	FY 2008
Payroll	$75,000	$82,000	$75,000
Repairs	10,000	15,000	5,000
Utilities	3,500	4,000	4,000
Advertising	500	1,000	750
Supplies	7,000	7,000	7,000
	$96,000	$109,000	$91,750

Notice the column marked "Mayor's recommendation." Under a weak-mayor system, budget preparation and recommendations might come from a special committee of the city council instead of the executive branch. But many municipalities operate under the *executive-budget plan*, which means the budget is prepared by the mayor or a budget officer, who is an employee of the executive branch. The chief executive's control over the final budget varies.

Notice, as well, that the proposed expenditures for the swimming pool are individually specified. This is an example of a *line-item budget*. Line-item budgets emphasize costs and purchases, as opposed to services, and tend to lock cities into spending patterns. A more flexible alternative is the *performance budget*, under which a department receives a lump sum for the operation of its various activities. Suppose usage of the swimming pool is down from last year's attendance figures. Under a line-item budget, the pool supervisor might be limited to spending $500 on advertising. But under a performance budget, he would be able to make adjustments, such as ordering fewer supplies and increasing advertising.

A reporter's analysis of the budget begins with several central questions:

- How does the budget compare to the budget from last year or the year before?
- What, if any, services and programs are being cut or added?
- What taxes and fees are being added, changed or increased?

Of course, answering these questions thoroughly and clearly may require dozens of hard-earned stories spread over a period of weeks. Using the swimming pool example, if the mayor's recommendation holds, the recreation department will have to live with a smaller budget than the previous year, and some planned repairs will have to be put off.

Helpful, informative budget coverage humanizes, explains and anticipates the city's fiscal condition, which, in turn, takes time, effort and enterprise. Focus on the implications for those in the community who can least afford higher fees or reduced services—the aged, the poor, the young.

Here's how *Seattle Times* reporter Sharon Pian Chan reported the city council's approval of the budget:

> Despite a new state law that could cut $20 million from the city's 2008 income, the Seattle City Council decided to spend $5.9 million on public safety and cut electricity rates an average of 8.4 percent in its 2007–08 budget.
>
> Mayor Greg Nickels had proposed adding six new police officers, and the council added 31 more for a total of 37 new police positions. Community members who lobbied the council consider the hires a good start.
>
> On Monday, the council formally passed a $1.6 billion budget that would raise and spend $803 million next year and $813 million in 2008 for the city's general fund, the discretionary part of the budget that pays for most services.

The city could lose $20 million in revenue in 2008 because of a law passed by the state legislature that changes how business-and-occupation taxes are distributed. The mayor hopes the law will be repealed. But if it remains in place, he and the council will have to find spending cuts.

"When we're counting pennies to get a police officer or a human-services provider, that $20 million can be quite a mountain," said Richard McIver, budget chairman.

Some budget highlights:

- Public safety: $2.9 million to hire 31 new officers; $840,000 for youth programs in Rainier Beach and Madison Valley; $409,000 for late-night recreation programs; $300,000 for youth-employment programs; and $405,000 to help victims of domestic violence.
- Seattle Center: $4.5 million to rehabilitate the monorail; $1.2 million for new maintenance positions.
- Human services: $450,000 for youth tutoring; $270,000 for SOAR early-education program; $200,000 for senior-service centers; $300,000 for Chief Seattle Club, which serves Native Americans; and $250,000 for Nisei Veterans. Among other programs to receive funding are the low-income meal provider Meals Partnership; mortgage counseling with a focus on preventing predatory lending; and health-worker education on how to work with lesbians, gays, bisexuals and transsexuals.
- P-Patches: $160,000 to buy property for a P-Patch [community garden] at 25th Avenue East and East Spring Street; $35,000 to prep the P-Patch grounds at 51st Avenue South and South Leo Street and another in High Point.

Nickels is expected to approve the budget.

"We're very pleased they made very few changes to his proposal," said Marianne Bichsel, Nickels' spokeswoman. "We think we're going to make real progress with issues that are important to the mayor—homelessness, transportation and public safety."[13]

Chan's story—not the first or last word on the budget—puts the city's financial situation in understandable terms and provides the context for unsettled issues, including a potential loss of state funds. While budget coverage may culminate with the adoption of the city's *budget ordinance*, it should not end there. Citizens certainly want to know how public money is supposed to be spent, but they also want to be assured that budgeted money actually is being spent properly and wisely. As the fiscal year unfolds, be alert for rates of spending and whether they are under or over budgeted amounts of the previous year.

Cities and Land Use

Cities address planning and zoning in different ways. Some rely on a professional administrator to plot the city's course of development. Other communities prefer to place planning in the hands of a commission, usually comprised of citizens appointed by the mayor or council. Still other cities have both a professional planner and lay commission.

179

Occasionally, a single body oversees a city's planning and zoning, but most often there is a separation of responsibility. The separation is logical: Planning establishes priorities and policies for a city's land use and development; zoning, by means of various ordinances and codes, enforces city planning.

The practice of giving citizens key roles in planning and zoning began as an attempt to minimize the influence of politics and private interests. But no matter where a city places responsibility for planning and zoning, politics are involved and battles ensue. In fact, the composition of many planning commissions—realtors, bankers, engineers and land developers—ensures conflicts of interest and potential corruption.

Planning and zoning disputes often involve big stakes—property values, jobs, housing—and little consensus. One segment of a city may value rapid growth and industrial development; another may cherish a tranquil status quo. A condominium builder could profit from a rezoning decision that allows him to build beside a subdivision of expensive single-family residences; the homeowners' property could decrease in value if the rezoning is approved. Residents may band together to oppose plans to build low-income housing in their neighborhood; civil rights activists may band together to promote housing rights.

Disputes often end up before the *zoning board*, sometimes called a *zoning board of appeals*, which must decide how—or whether—to enforce land-use laws. Most commonly, the board is asked to consider a rezoning petition or a request for a *variance*, an exception to a zoning ordinance or building code. A typical rezoning petition might be brought by a homeowner seeking to change a single-family designation to a multiple-family, which might result in an influx of rooming houses into a single-family neighborhood. An applicant for a variance or a *special-use permit*, another type of exception to land-use laws, might seek permission to convert a garage of a single-family home into a beauty shop. Sometimes the rezoning process requires on-site public hearings, which can yield lively human-interest stories.

Many zoning and planning issues ultimately end up before the city council, which acts on recommendations from planning and zoning bodies. The city council usually is authorized to overrule the zoning and planning bodies, but a vote of two-thirds of the council might be required. If the stakes are high enough, a land-usage issue can be counted on to attract a crowd of vocal proponents and opponents. Even when a land-use decision attracts little attention, reporters should be wary. If big money is involved, there is always the possibility of graft and illicit dealing.[14]

City hall reporters deal with two other land-related issues—annexation and eminent domain. *Annexation* is the process by which cities acquire additional territory. Most often, people residing in an enclave adjacent to the city will either court annexation or agree to overtures from the city. At times, land-hungry cities on either side of a piece of property will compete for annexation, particularly if the land has great tax-generating potential. Rarely, though, can a city absorb another area against its will; normally, a referendum by both sides is required. Although annexation may look good in theory, officials sometimes discover too late that there is a high price for bringing city services to fringe areas.

Eminent domain gives municipalities and other government bodies the legal right to take private property for public use, such as widening a road or building a stadium. The power of eminent domain expanded dramatically in 2005 when the U.S. Supreme Court ruled the city of New London, Conn., could seize homes in a neighborhood for *private* redevelopment to boost the economy and tax base.[14] Critics said the ruling, *Kelso v. City of New London,* undermined the constitutional rights of property owners, causing homeowners across the country anxiety that local authorities would move against them, too. Several states passed statutes to ban eminent domain for redevelopment except to eliminate blight. City officials, however, seem reluctant to use their power under *Kelso*, knowing eminent domain, no matter who benefits, does little to enhance a city's image with residents. Displaced property owners are supposed to receive just compensation for their property, but when people are forced to give up a beloved home or a business, they tend to fight back—and citizens tend to side with them.

Local Government

Local government comes in a variety of sizes and forms. There are county government, township government, regional government and the largest category of all—special-district government. In a metropolitan area there may be dozens—perhaps hundreds—of government bodies supported in whole or in part by tax revenue. Some small, obscure units of local government operate in near seclusion; only rarely do outsiders attend meetings, even when important issues are on the agenda. It is important for journalists to give attention to *all* government bodies entrusted to serve the public.

County Government

The role and power of county government vary from urban to rural areas. County government may be important or powerful in a sparsely populated region and, in fact, may be central to the lives of people living there. In metropolitan areas, county government not only provides essential services, such as police protection and road maintenance, to unincorporated areas, but it also typically assumes responsibility for areawide problems or operations, such as jails, airports, parks and flood control.

County governments (called "parishes" in Alaska and Lousiana) differ in organization, but most share these features: a chief executive; a legislative body, named variously the county board, county commission or board of supervisors; a half-dozen or more elected officials, such as sheriff, coroner and recorder of deeds; and a number of appointed officials, who oversee departments and services, among them libraries and roads.

In rural areas, the offices and departments of county government are likely to be housed in the courthouse, which may be an old, ornate edifice of doric columns and limestone that occupies the center square of town. In fast-growing metropolitan counties, government business is more likely to be conducted in modern, corporate-style buildings that may be attractive and efficient but lack the lore and appeal of the old courthouse.

Regardless of where government business is conducted, you can expect the atmosphere in a county building or courthouse to be politically charged. Unlike the non-partisanship of many city governments, most elected county officials proudly campaign and vote along party lines. Workers in the offices of elected officials often earn and keep their jobs through political loyalty, which may include a monthly contribution to the boss's re-election fund.

Reporters covering the county beat frequently are responsible not only for government news but court news as well. (The judicial system is covered in Chapters 8 and 9.) Part of the job naturally entails meeting coverage. Although frequently larger in size, the county legislative branch operates like a city council, with much of its work being done by standing committees. In the organization and conduct of business, meetings of a typical county commission and a typical city council display few differences.

The county's chief executive may be elected at large or selected by the membership of the county board. Chief executives often lack direct power or control over the county's elected officials. But if a chief executive controls the legislative branch, which controls the budget, then the power of the purse strings applies. The political clout of many county executives goes far to compensate for any built-in administrative weaknesses.

County beat reporters should monitor all county offices and services, but several merit special mention. One is the office of *county clerk*, where most of the county's records are stored. Besides maintaining minutes and records of the county legislative body, the clerk's office usually holds license records, birth, death and marriage certificates, voter registrations and campaign-disclosure reports. When reporters are unsure where to find a piece of information or the answer to a question, they usually start with the county clerk's office.

Another key office is the *recorder* (register) *of deeds*. It may not be a daily stop on a county reporter's rounds, but the recorder's office can help you find out who owns and who is buying and selling property in the county. Deed records, for example, will reveal whether foreign investors are buying thousands of acres of local farmland. *Revenue* (or document) *stamps*, a fee paid to the county by sellers of property, indicate the sale price, which often is not listed in public records. A common charge for a revenue stamp is $1, with each stamp representing $1,000 of purchase price. A deed transfer that requires 100 revenue stamps means the property sold for $100,000. Buyers have been known to buy extra stamps on their property to make it appear more valuable than its actual price.

The *county treasurer's* office is also an important stop on a reporter's beat. The treasurer, of course, generally handles the county's fiscal transactions through payments by checks called *warrants* and keeps track of the budget funds. But the office also is valuable for its tax-related records. They usually include assessment books for all property in the county, filings of people protesting taxes and records on property owners who are delinquent in paying taxes. Records on unpaid taxes might, for example, indicate that a prominent business in town is failing.

Counties, like many other large units of government, often have a department, independent of the executive branch, to monitor the fiscal activities of other departments and public offices under its jurisdiction. Heading the department is an official usually called an *auditor* or *comptroller*. Financial records, including copies of vouchers (receipts or statements certifying an expenditure or receipt of money) and purchase orders, are kept by the auditor, who also periodically checks the efficiency of services and the need for purchasing supplies and equipment. The auditor's office is a principal source when reporters are investigating the management and use of the public's money.

Some counties have a *supervisor of assessments*, whose office oversees property assessment throughout the county. The supervisor of assessments' office often includes a board to review complaints from citizens who believe their property assessment is too high. Because of the potential for corruption and controversy in tax assessments, the office bears watching.

Several other offices that typically fall under the county beat, including the sheriff's department, coroner's office, prosecuting attorney and clerk of the court, are discussed in detail in other chapters.

Township Government

Township government is largely an old-time form of government that manages to stay alive in several states. (It is also a six-mile-square unit of measurement in U.S. land surveys.) Years ago, when people were scattered across the countryside, hours by horse or wagon from the county seat or nearest city, township government served them best. With urbanization, the role of township government has diminished, but in some unincorporated areas outside the boundaries or attention of other government bodies, the township remains an effective provider of services, particularly road maintenance, public aid and support for such improvements as sewer systems.

Township government often gives citizens a direct say in decision making through a vote at annual or semiannual town meetings. The township hall may be one of the few places where reporters can still see grassroots democracy in action.

Regional Government

Regional government units, normally comprised of elected officials from local governments in a region, serve to address areawide problems and issues. Some are merely quasi-governmental bodies that undertake studies, issue reports and suggest cooperative ventures. Others go beyond those roles and administer programs and disperse grant money.

Regional bodies came into existence beginning in the 1950s, partly as a means of unifying and coordinating the fragmented web of local government. The concept spread as federal officials tied more aid and grant programs to areawide cooperation among local government officials. If local officials wanted federal money for rapid-transit systems or air-pollution control, they were told they had to work together. In some instances, though, regional agencies only intensified infighting and conflict over who gets what. Many of them have been allowed to expire, especially since the demise of federal revenue sharing in the 1980s.

Special Districts

Special districts are units of government that possess taxing authority. Many exist to provide services to a large region. There may be hundreds of special-district bodies of varying size and authority within a metropolitan region, serving such purposes as mosquito abatement, sewage disposal and public housing. In some areas, special districts enable residents outside the reach of municipal services to organize and raise tax money to provide, for example, fire protection. (The most common form of special unit—the school district—is discussed in Chapter 10.)

By sheer numbers alone, special districts pose challenges for news coverage. On a given Tuesday, a popular night for meetings, several dozen special districts might be in session in your community. But special districts cannot be ignored or given cursory attention; to do so would invite expansion of a hidden layer of government with great power but little accountability to taxpayers.

Special districts sometimes vie for tax dollars and control to the detriment of other units of government. In 2007, New York Gov. Eliot Spitzer asked the legislature to help him consolidate some of the state's 4,200 independent taxing districts, which he called "too many, too expensive and too burdensome," *Newsday* reported. "You have vested special interests who have been operating these districts as their own personal fiefdoms for over 50 years, some of them 100 years," said Nassau County Comptroller Howard Weitzman. "There's an institutional bias against giving up this power."[15]

Before prejudging special districts as tax-revenue sponges, consider that in some cases they were formed by local residents when requests for state or county assistance for a sewer system, fire protection or other type of vital public service operation went unanswered.

Covering State and Federal Government

For most reporters, experience in public affairs reporting begins with city hall or the courthouse, and only after years of proven service is a reporter assigned full time to the statehouse. Few reporters have the opportunity to cover the federal government from Washington, D.C. A beginning reporter's coverage of state and federal government typically is done locally or as part of a temporary assignment.

State Government

A state capitol is an imposing sight of marble floors, mosaic walls and dark-stained woodwork. It is a dignified setting for a process that is not always pretty to behold. As an old statehouse saying colorfully puts it, "If you love sausage and law, don't watch either being made."

If laws are like sausages, then each is made from many ingredients. Lawmakers, the governor and the governor's staff are involved in lawmaking, as are the staffs of state agencies. Behind the scenes, but not too far behind, are the lobbyists. In fact, in some state capitals there are three or more registered lobbyists for every lawmaker. In general, lobbyists possess a tarnished reputation, but reporters quickly learn that some lobbyists are gold mines of information.

A movement spearheaded by California voters in the late 1970s restored a Progressive Era strategy to empower citizens to make law—the *citizen initiative*. The citizen initiative (also known as a ballot initiative) allows the people of a state—and in some cases even residents of a city—to force a vote and either make or amend a law. Nearly half of the states allow for citizen initiatives of one kind or another. The initiatives have covered a range of issues, some of which legislators either avoided or voted down, such as legalizing medical marijuana and same-sex marriage; capping property taxes and government spending; and adding amendments to the state constitution. The citizen initiative promotes direct democracy, but critics say it also subverts the authority of elected officials. Moreover, special-interest groups often fund and control what are ostensibly grassroots, citizen-inspired movements.

Much of state government coverage naturally focuses on the legislative process. The flowchart on page 186 shows how laws progress through the Illinois General Assembly, which is a bicameral (two-house) legislature, comprised of a 59-member Senate and a 118-member House of Representatives. The process is complicated. At any point along the path to passage, a proposed piece of legislation, called a *bill*, can be killed or left for dead. Bills that run the entire legislative gauntlet are often the products of compromise and bargaining by many players. The legislative process is similar to what happens when a city council passes an ordinance; bills receive readings and go through committees where they may be reshaped by amendments. But there are differences. Chief among these is the requirement that *both* houses of a bicameral legislature must approve the bill. If there are disagreements, the bill may be sent to a joint *conference committee* that attempts to work out a version acceptable to both houses.

Legislators' positions on a particular bill usually are based on political considerations. For one thing, legislators weigh how a bill is going to be received by constituents

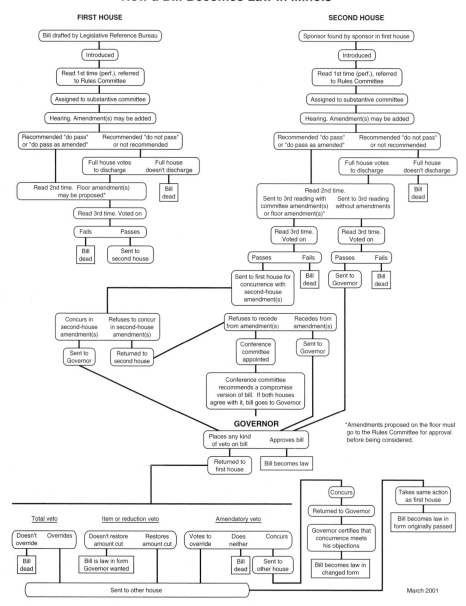

How a bill becomes a law in Illinois   Before it becomes law, legislation follows a complex set of stages, from its introduction to its approval by the governor. Reporters cannot be content to follow the hearings and votes as a bill winds its way to passage as a statute. They must also report who benefits from the legislation and how it affects citizens. (Image courtesy Illinois General Assembly.)

in the home district. Sometimes legislators support a colleague's bill with the understanding that the favor will be returned at a later date. Throughout the process, lobbyists are at work to either kill or advance legislation. A legislator is most vulnerable to pressure by lobbyists who represent a contributor to the legislator's election or re-election.

When the trucking industry, for example, backs Sen. Thompson, the senator's support on industry-related matters is expected in return. Lawmakers who accept campaign contributions from organizations seeking influence over legislation often find themselves in compromising positions. Sen. Thompson personally may believe the large cross-country trucks operating on state highways endanger motorists, but his campaign "debt" forces him to vote against a bill that would restrict the weight and length of tractor-trailer rigs. Reporters covering the legislature should know which senators and representatives are beholden to special interests.

A key player, of course, is the governor, who influences legislation by many means, among them arm-twisting of legislators to support or defeat a bill. The governor's ultimate power is the veto, which the legislature can override with usually a two-thirds or three-fifths vote of its members. Competent statehouse reporters thoroughly understand the legislative process and know all the players.

States enact thousands of new laws each year. Not all can be reported, but the news media provide a service by informing the public about the major laws, especially as they are about to take effect. On New Year's Day, when new laws become effective in many states, news organizations will provide capsule descriptions of important pieces of legislation, usually under categories, such as "motor vehicles." In California, for example, Jan. 1, 2007, marked the implementation of mandatory jail terms for convicted street racers who cause bodily injury; longer suspensions for drunk driving convictions; and a one-year probation period before newly licensed teenagers can drive after 11 p.m. or transport passengers under the age of 20 without an accompanying adult.

Statehouse reporters get a good deal of newsgathering assistance, which they need to keep track of the steady stream of legislation. State-run online information services help journalists and lawmakers alike by publishing daily schedules of meetings and providing updates and chronologies of bills. At a glance, reporters can tell where a subcommittee on agriculture, for example, is holding a hearing on inspection guidelines for imported fruits and vegetables. Less valuable but useful are the press releases and reports pouring daily out of state agencies, departments and the governor's office. In some states, reporters operate out of offices, provided at taxpayer expense, in the capitol building that are wired with closed-circuit audio or television systems to allow reporters to work in their offices while still monitoring sessions of the House and Senate.

Although it may take years to understand the intricacies of state government and develop the sources and background needed to cover the statehouse properly, reporters who become entrenched in the job tend to acquire habits of coverage and lose a fresh perspective. That is why reporters are now spending less time on the statehouse beat before moving on to other assignments, a cycle that is largely by design. Younger, mobile reporters sacrifice the close relationships journalists of previous generations shared with legislators. As one observer notes, "The distance between press and politicians has widened in the past generation, pushed by evolving ethical standards on both sides, [resulting in] a mutual wariness that has mounted over the years with each new scandal."[16] But the loss of "coziness" in statehouse journalism has advantages that probably outweigh the disadvantages.

Reporters are correct to concentrate on the governor and the legislature for news, but important work of government goes on in dozens of other buildings and offices in a state capital city. In most states, the Department of Transportation is the largest executive-branch department in terms of budget and number of employees. Other major, newsmaking departments deal with corrections, public welfare and child abuse and family services. The state organizational directory, often known as the "blue book," describes the full range of governmental operations, including administrative agencies and commissions. Even obscure units of state government hold news potential. The Internet has helped reporters keep an eye on state government through official state Web sites.

The executive branch includes the governor's cabinet of elected or appointed officials, such as the lieutenant governor, secretary of state, treasurer and attorney general. Because the office focuses on substantial legal matters, the *attorney general* tends to generate more news than other cabinet officials. In several states, an increasingly active role for the attorney general is consumer protection through high-profile prosecution, for example, of insurance frauds and nursing-home violations.

Because coverage of many administrative agencies and executive departments, even the larger ones, is infrequent or sporadic, stories abound outside the legislative chambers for reporters who make the effort to collect them. Remember that when the legislature passes a law, responsibility for its implementation most often falls to a state department or office. After the fanfare of the bill's passage subsides and the law takes effect, government reporters should continue coverage to determine how well the new legislation or program is working. Too frequently, such follow-up reporting is absent.

Administrative agencies and departments also offer bountiful opportunities for feature stories, especially ones that tell readers or viewers how various components of state government work. What, for example, does the public health department do? In many states, the department provides prenatal care for mothers with high-risk pregnancies. What does that responsibility entail? Another common function of the public health department is milk and food inspections. How is milk tested—and for what? A reporter's role includes educating citizens about the processes and functions of government.

Some government stories are so close at hand they tend to be overlooked. As metropolitan editor of the *Des Moines Register*, Richard Paxson regularly tapped a simple source of good stories:

> Almost every weekday in our newsroom, a big envelope arrives from the state unemployment agency, containing dozens of written decisions from hearing officers on whether out-of-work Iowans should get jobless benefits. Most of the cases are appeals from unemployed workers who originally were turned down. Others are from businesses protesting the awarding of benefits because it raises their taxes.
>
> These decisions provide terrific keyhole peeks into the workplace. . . . Some of the stories make you angry—like the nursing home worker who got unemployment benefits even though she was fired for hanging paper cups from the ears of a victim of Alzheimer's disease.
>
> Many make you laugh—like the baker who was fired because he bared his behind to co-workers so often that they adopted "Blue Moon" as their theme song. . . .
>
> Almost every reader can relate to such stories because almost everyone has a job and a boss.[17]

As Paxson points out, it pays to check out what at first glance might appear to be "junk mail" (or e-mail) from state offices.

Coverage of state government goes on well beyond the city limits of the state capitol. Scattered throughout the state are branch offices of departments and agencies. Legislators, too, operate offices in their home districts. Not all actions or policies of state government originate in the statehouse and flow downward to regions and communities. The conduit linking government and the people is two-way, and news can be covered from either end. An agriculture agent, whose office may be a few blocks from your newspaper or broadcast station, might be working with local apple growers to control the spread of a plant blight that threatens to damage next season's crop. Local reporters who build and nurture contacts within branch and regional offices of state departments will be rewarded with good stories and news tips.

Federal Government

Experienced Washington correspondents acknowledge that federal government is too big and complex to ever understand fully. Besides the 15 departments of the executive branch, the federal government operates more than 60 independent or quasi-independent agencies, ranging from the Central Intelligence Agency to the Tennessee Valley Authority.

The White House is the glamour beat of federal coverage, although coverage of the president and his staff is so tightly managed that enterprise reporting is difficult. What amounts to "news" too often is generated by staged events, like a presidential appearance to welcome a visiting dignitary or news briefings conducted by White

House staffers. According to political scientist Timothy Cook, White House reporters have more contact with *their own colleagues* than with other news sources. "They are quickly aware of the stories and angles pursued by their colleagues and cannot help following each other's leads. . . . Because of the beat, then, the White House press corps is a textbook example of pack journalism. . . ."[18] In many respects, the White House is less complicated to cover than other federal government assignments but, in the long run, is probably less satisfying as a beat.

Congress, on the other hand, offers almost too many sources and too many possibilities for news. So much is happening on Capitol Hill, primarily the "nuts and bolts" variety of government business, that reporters find it easier and more appealing to focus on "sexy" issues, according to Tom Freedman, a former legislative aide for a New York congressman. As he recalls:

> While Washington's establishment—its politicians, reporters and administrators—is whipped into motion by the mere whiff of an emotional issue or scandal, there is no reward in today's Capitol for fixing the broken mechanics of government or solving the huge problems that haunt us. . . . There was always extensive press coverage at [congressional] hearings if a star from the entertainment world, or better yet, a dramatic hooded witness was testifying. . . . In Washington, there is widespread acceptance of the idea that the public doesn't want complicated news.[19]

Do people prefer simpler news—sexy news? Reporters have been known to underestimate the public's interest in hard news. Solid government reporting, told in a style and language people can understand, will find an audience. Based on information from the National Highway Traffic Safety Administration, Chip Scanlan of the Knight Ridder Washington bureau highlighted the high fatality rate in minivan accidents. Scanlan, now a faculty member at the Poynter Institute, humanized the story with this opening:

> To Alan Janofsky, his new Chevrolet Astro minivan was a dream vehicle—with enough interior space to use in his cosmetics business and ample room for his two daughters to spread out on trips.
>
> But the van frightened his wife, Barbara. "I have a feeling if we ever get hit broadside, it's going to flip over," she recalled warning as they drove it home from the dealership. "It's your imagination," he said.
>
> Eight months later, Barbara Janofsky's fears came true.

The story went on to dramatize the growing number of accidents, pointing out that minivans, despite their popularity with families, continue to be exempt from safety standards required for automobiles.[20]

Despite the wealth of stories elsewhere in Washington, the White House and Congress attract the greatest attention, partly because they are convenient to cover. According to veteran White House reporter Lou Cannon, "Off Capitol Hill, with the exceptions of the White House, the State Department and the Defense Department, coverage of the vast, overlapping federal bureaucracy is sporadic at best and non-existent at worst."[21] As a result, important news or actions of the federal bureaucracy may go unreported until a scandal or disaster surfaces.

The tentacles of federal government crisscross the nation; offices are not relegated to metropolitan areas. A quick check of the local telephone directory will tell you which agencies and departments are in your area. Sometimes reporters overlook local federal operations, such as the U.S. Postal Service, the Veterans Affairs hospital or the Civil Aeronautics Board office at the airport. There are also the district offices of members of Congress, which are usually staffed year-round. Congressional aides in district offices can reach Washington quickly by telephone, computer or facsimile machine. Sometimes the district aides are former journalists who are sensitive to newsgathering needs and deadlines.

All reporters ought to be alert for ways to localize developments in Washington. If Congress is considering an important piece of legislation, the political editor should tell the public where their legislators stand. When the Department of Interior promulgates a new regulation on camping in federal forests and parks, the outdoors writer can explain its impact on the region.

Several sources of information can help local reporters stay abreast of developments in Washington. Among the more important are the *Congressional Record* and the *Federal Register*. Regular reading of the *New York Times*, the *Washington Post*, news magazines and specialized publications, such as the *National Journal* and *Congressional Quarterly*, also yield ideas for local reports on the activities of the federal government. Internet Age reporters do not have to be ensconced in a Washington, D.C., bureau to reach newsmakers, collect data or write stories about Congress, the executive branch or the federal bureaucracy. Especially helpful is Thomas, an online service launched in January of 1995 to make federal legislative information available to the public. Named in honor of President Thomas Jefferson, Thomas (http://thomas .loc.gov), maintained by the Library of Congress, provides complete texts of bills and the status of legislation. Easy to use, it also links users to a variety of federal government documents and information.

Government reporting does have its dull side at times. Sitting through a public meeting might require several cups of strong coffee and a firm resolve to find a way to enliven a story of what transpired. But by casting themselves as guardians of the public's right to know, journalists assume an obligation to spend hours, if necessary, listening to windy lawmakers or poring over tax rolls. When dull meetings or dusty records yield nothing more than a news-digest item, reporters can at least say they did their duty as society's watchdogs and surrogates for the people.

No matter where you are stationed and no matter what you cover as a beat, keep this thought in mind: If government is *of* the people, *by* the people, and *for* the people, reporters should bring government at all levels *to* the people through appealing, useful and informed coverage.

Exercises

1. Develop a state-of-the-community feature based on an interview with the mayor, city manager or another key municipal official. Concentrate on major conditions, such as city services, crime, economic conditions, city finances, public housing, homelessness and social services. Examine both positive and negative sides of the city's condition.

2. Profile a state agency or office in your area. Explain its functions. Introduce key personnel and show them at work. Perhaps the state Department of Agriculture has a livestock and poultry inspector stationed nearby. Besides describing the inspector's work, accompany her on rounds, such as a check of an egg-producing complex where you will see the process that leads to tomorrow's omelets.

3. Localize a story out of Washington, D.C. You will probably want to focus on a federal law or regulation that will affect your community.

Notes

1. Don Fry, ed., *Best Newspaper Writing 1989* (St. Petersburg, Fla.: Poynter Institute, 1989), p. 297.
2. Donald M. Murray, "Making Politics Dull," *Writing on Writing,* September 1988, pp. 1, 5.
3. Rob Armstrong, *Covering Government: A Civics Handbook for Journalists* (Ames, Iowa: Iowa State University Press, 2002), pp. xi, xii.
4. Elaine P. Sharp, "Citizen Demand-Making in the Urban Context." *American Journal of Political Science,* November 1984, pp. 654–670.
5. Daniel J. Chacon, "Council Missing in Action," *Rocky Mountain News,* Sept. 5, 2006.
6. Jane Mobley. "Politician or Professional? The Debate over Who Should Run Our Cities Continues," *Governing,* February 1988, p. 48.
7. Amelia Davis, "City Managers Learn to Live with the Job," *St. Petersburg Times*, May 22, 1989, p. 3.
8. Heron Marquez Estrada, "Suburb's City Hall Discord Brings Call for Probes," StarTribune.com, posted Dec. 17, 2006.
9. David S. Broder, *Behind the Front Page* (New York: Simon & Schuster, 1987), p. 224.
10. Chip Scanlan, "Lemonade from Lemons: Finding Stories in Meetings," Poynter Online, posted Feb. 26, 2003.
11. Clark R. Mollenhoff, *Investigative Reporting: From Courthouse to White House* (New York: Macmillan, 1982), pp. 361–368.
12. Quoted in "Writing Tips," *Providence Journal,* 1998.
13. Sharon Pian Chan, "City Council Approves $1.6 Billion Biennial Budget, *Seattle Times,* Nov. 21, 2006.
14. *Kelso v. City of New London*, 545 U.S. 469 (2005).

15. Reid J. Epstein, "Spitzer Targets Tax 'Fiefdoms,'" *Newsday,* Jan. 7, 2007, p. A20.

16. See Brant Houston, Len Bruzzese and Steve Weinberg, *The Investigative Reporter's Handbook,* 4th ed. (New York: Bedford/St. Martin's, 2002).

17. Richard Paxson, "The Best Local News Idea I've Had in Five Years," *ASNE Bulletin*, April 1986, p. 5.

18. Timothy E. Cook, *Making Laws and Making News* (Washington, D.C.: Brookings Institution, 1989), p. 34.

19. Tom Freedman, "While Journalists Chase 'Sexy' Issues," *New York Times*, Sept. 16, 1990, p. A14.

20. Christopher Scanlan, "Critics Question Safety of Popular Minivans," *Miami Herald*, Aug. 14, 1989, p. 1A.

21. Lou Cannon, *Reporting: An Inside View* (Sacramento, Calif.: California Journal Press, 1977), p. 196.

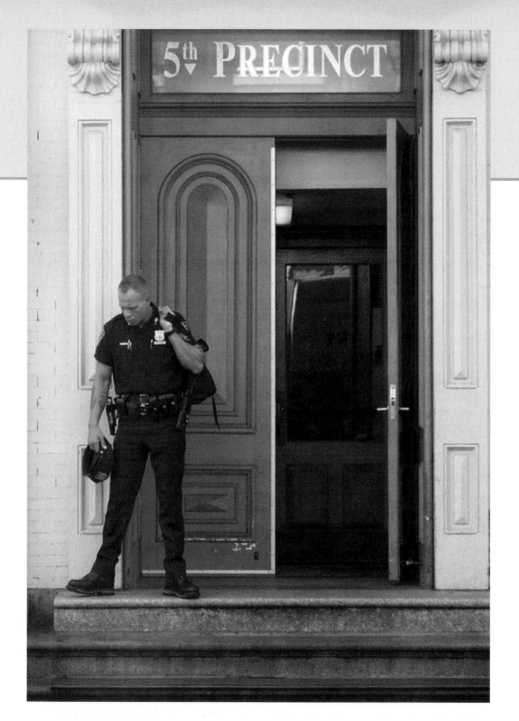

Shift ends at the 5th Precinct   I shot this photograph in July 2001, only two months before the tragic events of that fateful day every New York police officer experienced. It was just a grab of a photograph as I walked by the precinct house with my family, so I never spoke with the officer. I did not realize how powerful the image was until I got home and looked at it more closely on the computer screen. I returned to New York City many times over the next few years and always wanted to bring the officer a copy, but I hesitated. The 5th Precinct is in Chinatown, only blocks from the World Trade Center. A number of their officers perished September 11, and I was afraid to learn the officer's fate. Finally, in October 2004, I got the courage to walk into the precinct house. As I entered the front doors, I saw the wall of photographs of the officers who died that day. I scanned each photograph looking for the now very familiar face. He was not on the wall. I left the copy for him and later found out he enjoyed receiving it. (Text and photo by Robbie Arkovich.)

Public Safety: Crimes to Corrections 7

Edna Buchanan knows the police beat, having spent more than 20 years covering murders, muggings and mobsters in a city made infamous by the television program *Miami Vice* and now by *CSI: Miami*. Here is how she once described the job:

> Nobody loves a police reporter.
>
> You are often an unwelcome intruder. People blame you for the bad news. It is human nature. Somebody gets in trouble, you report it and he turns on you as though it were your fault, not his, that he is into this mess.
>
> The job can be lonesome and arduous. I have been threatened with arrest, threatened physically, had rocks thrown at me. I've gotten threatening letters, subpoenas and obscene phone calls, some of them from my editors.
>
> It is tiring, haunting and truly wonderful.[1]

Buchanan elevated the stature and visibility of the police beat by winning a Pulitzer Prize in 1986 for her crime coverage in the *Miami Herald* and by writing a lively book about her work, *The Corpse Had a Familiar Face*. As the magazine *presstime* noted: "For a while it was a stepchild beat. Then Edna Buchanan won a Pulitzer. Now covering the police beat is glamorous."[2]

For Buchanan, now a best-selling novelist, and a handful of other reporters, the police beat is the ultimate assignment. Yet many of journalism's finest, who started out on the police beat, saw it mainly as a prerequisite to more respectable, substantial assignments. Russell Baker, later to achieve fame as a *New York Times* writer and columnist, went to work on the police beat at the *Baltimore Sun*, not knowing that "a police reporter was the lowest form of life in the *Sun*'s universe."[3] In those days, as Baker quickly learned, police-beat reporters rarely wrote their own stories or worked out of the main office of the newspaper. Baker wanted to be a newspaper *writer*. Phoning in details about a holdup or murder to the city desk, where a rewriteman would rapidly mold them into a story, was not his idea of a career in journalism.

The police beat remains a training ground for many young reporters, who now usually do their own writing on laptops tied to the main office by modems. Still, there is a lingering stigma about police reporting. It is not a beat most reporters volunteer for or fight over. The work is tough and stressful. Much of the job involves writing about life's ugly side. Paradoxically, the job calls for sensitivity and compassion mixed, at times, with toughness and detachment.

Done well and done right, the police beat is more than a rite of passage or a rung on a career ladder. It is a valuable job, full of drama and societal significance. Enterprising police reporters quickly graduate from chasing sirens or listening to police-band scanners. They humanize the beat by including coverage of everyday crime as it touches everyday people. They describe and explain crime and law enforcement in useful, intelligent, responsible ways. They are curious and vigilant, going beyond the surface facts.

When a drunken-driving suspect dies after being subdued by police officers, police reporters ask "Why?" and "How?" The questions, in turn, lead to a story about a controversial police policy on use of chokeholds.

When three accidents occur at the same intersection in less than a week, they test the casual theories of patrol officers ("There's just too much traffic there") and question engineers and safety experts.

When a clerk at a convenience store is robbed at knifepoint, they do not rely on an antiseptic police report. They visit the scene and sensitively ask the attendant to relive the experience. As with most reporting, there is always a degree of uncertainty. Did I get the story right? Have I been fair to all parties? Should I do more? Edna Buchanan explains why that is particularly true on the police beat:

> You never know if you are really finished. There is always something to check, another detail you might glean that could change everything. A newspaper story can ruin a life or come back to haunt it twenty years later. . . .
>
> Police reporters deal with lives, reputations and careers. So you keep on—ask one more question, knock on one more door, make one last phone call, and then another.
>
> It could be the one that counts.[4]

This is excellent advice for *all* reporters on *all* beats.

Crime and the Mass Media

Is crime in America as bad as it seems? The statistics certainly are alarming, as illustrated by the Crime Clock, a visual device the FBI uses in its annual *Uniform Crime Reports*, a nationwide, cooperative statistical effort of more than 17,000 city, university and college, county, state, tribal and federal law enforcement agencies that voluntarily report data on crimes brought to their attention. Over the years, the UCR has become a leading social indicator, used by criminologists, sociologists, legislators, municipal planners and the media to study and assess crime in the United States. The Crime Clock converts crime occurrences to minutes and seconds; for example, a property crime may occur every three seconds or a rape every five minutes. Naturally, people begin to wonder, "Will I be the next statistic?"

Statistics, of course, can be misleading or overstated. Big-city murder rates, for example, leave the impression that the streets of Chicago, Los Angeles or Washington,

D.C., are littered with bodies. Actually, Americans are much more likely to die in an auto crash than at the hands of an unknown assailant. Without a doubt, crime is a real problem in America. No town or city is crime-free, although some are vastly more dangerous than others. By way of comparison, in 2005, Morgan Quitno Press, in its widely cited annual report, ranked Camden, N.J., population 80,125, the most dangerous city in the United States and Newton, Maine, population 83,570, ranked the safest.[5] The statistics stand out in stark contrast:

Murders
   Camden—33
   Newton—1

Rapes
   Camden—47
   Newton—6

Aggravated assaults
   Camden—898
   Newton—92

Robberies
   Camden—707
   Newton—15

Nationwide in the 1990s, rates for violent crimes declined or held steady until 2005, when the FBI reported a 2.5 percent increase, with robberies, aggravated assaults and murders leading the way.

Despite all the sobering statistics and studies, should people be putting bars on their windows and handguns under their pillows? No, say criminologists like Valerie J. Callanan, author of *Feeding the Fear of Crime*, who blame the mass media for creating excessive, unwarranted fear and anxiety about crime.[6] There is no denying that crime news dominates television newscasts and grabs headlines in newspapers and magazines, especially accounts of violent attacks against people. That is to be expected; these are the crimes the public finds most menacing and disturbing. Several years ago, a pregnant young doctor was raped, strangled and fatally beaten in her office at New York's Bellevue Medical Center. Commenting on the horror of her death, a magazine writer said, "A murder in a hospital? A murder in the cathedral? The mind keeps a list of safe houses in the world, and it is shaken when sanctuaries are violated."[7] As life's sanctuaries are being violated, the press cannot be expected to sanitize or ignore what is happening.

Obviously, the press plays an important role in informing people about the scope and seriousness of crime. It is sometimes hard, though, for reporters to know when they have gone too far—or when they have not gone far enough. A low-key approach to coverage might lull people into a false sense of security. If tourists are being mugged in a popular downtown entertainment district, the story should not be buried in the crime roundup column on page 5A. On the other hand, sensationalized treatment of crime news might unduly frighten people, perpetuate stereotypes or cause societal tensions where none need exist. Moreover, by reporting some criminal acts, do journalists exacerbate conditions or contribute to copycat crime? Did cocaine use, for example, spread partly because of media publicity? When news accounts described how someone slipped cyanide in Tylenol capsules, did the mass media encourage others to poison consumer products? Often, it seems, crime reporting is a case of damned if you do, damned if you don't.

Reporters who cover crime must understand crime—as well as it can be understood. This much is known: Crime is everywhere. It can be found in hamlets and luxury high-rises as well as city streets and housing projects. Criminals and their victims come from every segment of society. Crime is also relative. In a small town, an armed robbery will be given the highest priority by police. In a big city, police must practice a form of medicine's *triage*, deciding which cases are most urgent—and which to deal with as time and resources permit. Press coverage follows a similar pattern. An armed robbery is front-page news in a city of 4,000; in a city of 1 million, a similar armed robbery may go uncovered by the press.

There is much about crime that is unknown or unexplainable. What are the causes of crime? How can crime be curbed? There are no ready answers or quick fixes; if there were, society could begin to control crime as it controls measles or air pollution. Police-beat reporters must continue to seek answers and explanations, even though they can expect to be forever perplexed and troubled by much of what they see and report. Think about the journalists in Camden, N.J., and Newton, Maine, and the challenges they face in attempting to explain the disparity of crime in their communities. But they must try.

A model for reporters writing about crime is the work of Leon Dash, who won a Pulitzer Prize at the *Washington Post* for his exhaustive study of a family trapped in a generational cycle of crime and poverty. After publication of his series, people would ask Dash, "What is the solution?" His response: "There isn't one clear answer—the many problems in families like Rosa Lee's are too intertwined. The third-grade reading levels of Washington's criminals, however, do offer one clue: They tell us when the criminals stopped learning." Education, he concludes, while not the answer in all cases, can save many people from a life of crime.[8]

Behind the Badge

Police officers are nearly always on guard—watchful, suspicious, cynical. It is a survival instinct. Not surprisingly, neither police officers nor reporters demonstrate much trust or understanding in their mutual relationships. Author Joseph Wambaugh, once a Los Angeles police officer, put it this way: "Cops generally trust the press about as much as they trust politicians, judges, lawyers, psychiatrists and the Red Army [under the Soviet Union's communist regime]."[9] Two experienced reporters echo Wambaugh's observations:

> To most police officers a reporter is welcome only as long as he is not only anti-crime, but pro-police. Let that reporter turn a critical eye on the department or any of its knights in blue and immediately the reporter becomes an enemy to be shunned, misled and even arrested, if possible.
>
> No matter how noble a cop might be, he knows that out there among the public are lots of people who fail to appreciate him, who misunderstand him, who instinctively dislike him. At the top of the list of unfriendly people—just below professional criminals—are most journalists.[10]

Considering such bleak assessments, can reporters ever expect to relate to law enforcement officers and vice versa? The answer is yes—at least in terms of a professional relationship. Building the relationship is usually the reporter's responsibility, and a starting point is understanding the fears and pressures facing the police.

Listen, for example, to a patrolman with 18 years on the Detroit police force talk about daily effects of stress: "You run into people that think that you should be invincible, okay? You should be afraid of nothing. You've got a gun on your side. Well, you know, on TV it all looks so good. Pull the gun, the guy runs, shoot him, you know? You see, you have to live with that."[11]

Listen to another police officer, Robert Stewart of St. Petersburg, Fla., as he described living with the memory of killing a man. "It leaves home with me every day, and it comes back home with me. It's something that I had never wanted to have happen in my career."[12] His chilling story illustrates the reality facing everyone in law enforcement. It was about midnight and Stewart, home and off duty, had just paid a pizza delivery man. The delivery man returned to his car, but he didn't leave. He stood in the street, alongside the car, which Stewart thought was strange. Then Stewart heard another voice and sensed something was wrong. As Stewart, armed, approached the car, he saw a figure crouched nearby and realized the delivery man was being robbed. "I grabbed him [the robber] and told him to drop the gun," Stewart recalled. "As I was trying to put him in a neutral position, I saw a gun come up to my face. . . . I never even remember pulling the trigger." For a split second, Stewart was not sure whether he or the robber had been shot. Another police officer adds, "After you shoot someone, things will never be the same. It's almost a loss of innocence involved. You'll just never look at life the same way."[13]

Many police officers never draw their service revolvers in the line of duty, much less fire them. Indeed, police work can be generally dull and uneventful. But even in the smallest communities, even when answering a call about a family spat, police officers never know whether this will be the day their luck runs out.

QUOTABLES

"The police work of action, of confrontation, and force, the roundhouse punches and high-speed chases, is what makes both the movies and the news—and, now and then, means everything in real life, our real life, too. But what you say and how you say it comes into play far more often than anything you do with your stick or gun, and can prevent the need for them. . . . A talker can do things, or undo them: I know cops who have talked would-be suicides from rooftops, and who have convinced raving gunmen to release child hostages. More often, you talk people into talking, only talking, instead of screaming and waving a knife." (p. 19)

—Edward Conlon, *Blue Blood*, New York: Riverhead Books, 2004

The pressures build in other ways. After dealing with fatal accidents, child molestations, rapes, drug dealers and lie after lie, police find it difficult to see the decent side of life and the good in people. "I think you can't help but get a little callous to it after a while," says another Detroit officer. "You just see so much stuff, and I think the hardest thing is trying to remember that you are dealing with people out here all the time."

Mark Baker, author of *Cops: Their Lives in Their Own Words*, found that police officers often see the world as nothing but falsehood, evil and death, which helps explain why they sometimes appear hard-edged and unfriendly. As Baker got to know police officers, his opinion of them changed: "Having tasted the casual violence and bone-numbing boredom they experience, I am better able to understand their point of view. I don't fear police as a group as much as I used to, because I now know a good number of them as individuals. When I see a police officer today, I look at his face, not at his uniform."[14]

Journalists who make a sincere attempt to understand the person behind the badge can anticipate better relationships and ultimately better news coverage. A word of warning: Do not join the police team. Maintain a *professional* relationship and distance. And maintain a critical eye in monitoring the performance of the police.

Inside the Police Department

With any beat, you start by learning the lay of the land. For a police department, that includes its organization, facilities, communications system and operating policies.

Organization

The *police chief* is at the top of the organizational chart. Often attached to the chief's office is the *internal affairs* unit, which is entrusted to rigorously and independently investigate possible cases of police misconduct. Occasionally, a separate civilian board addresses complaints against officers, but all law enforcement agencies should have a formal process for investigating questionable behavior by police, and reporters should monitor internal discipline and professional standards carefully and continuously.

The police officer's wife   It takes a special kind of person to be a police officer's wife. It takes a special kind of person who can send her husband off to work each night with a smile on her face, carefully hiding her fears of *what if*. It takes a special kind of person who can keep the house and the family moving along while the police officer sleeps all day after working all night. It takes a special kind of person who can tuck the kids in bed every night alone while making them understand daddy loves them even though he is not there to tuck them in, too. All police officers should be so blessed to have such a person in their lives. (Text and photo by Robbie Arkovich.)

Another important person reporting to the police chief is the public information officer (PIO), generally responsible for day-to-day contact with the press. A good PIO will balance the needs of the department with those of the reporters seeking assistance. In major crimes, the PIO will be at the scene to provide breaking details.

Many departments are organized along similar lines, with three main bureaus or divisions under the chief of police: patrol, investigations and administrative services. The *patrol division* handles most day-to-day operations. There are usually three eight-hour periods or shifts of patrols a day, each overseen by a *shift commander*. The patrol bureau might also include a K-9 (police dog) unit, a traffic branch and a unit for reserve officers. The patrol division can include elite units, such as SWAT teams, that garner glory and news clips, and other highly trained teams, including, for example, DUI officers with expertise in high-tech blood-alcohol analysis and training in legal affairs, including court testimony when driving-under-the-influence cases go to court, as they often do.

The *investigative division* often includes separate units to deal with juvenile offenders, narcotics cases and crimes against persons or property. Some departments have an undercover intelligence-gathering branch under the investigative division. Larger departments can afford a crime-analysis laboratory unit.

Service divisions usually handle administration, records, communications, training and community programs, such as Drug Abuse Resistance Education (DARE), which in several states brings uniformed police officers into grades from kindergarten through high school for a curriculum designed to prevent use of drugs and alcohol. A related operation, called school resource officer program (SRO), places uniformed police full time in high schools and sometimes in middle and elementary schools to provide protection, resolve conflicts and teach students to respect the law.

Whether it falls under patrol or service divisions, a politically popular philosophy and approach to law enforcement—typically called *community policing*—assigns specially selected and trained officers to beats in designated neighborhoods. Community policing is rooted in the belief that the legendary officer of yesterday, who strolled the sidewalks, eating an apple and kissing babies, brings the police and the public closer together. Departments with community policing operations expect officers in the unit to work independently and creatively to solve problems and act as a liaison between the residents and city hall on a range of public service duties, not just crime fighting or prevention.

Community policing is not always popular with the rank and file, and for various reasons. In part, it is viewed as social work rather than policing. Moreover, in some departments patrol officers consider the community unit a posh assignment that drains resources and personnel from what they consider the primary work of policing. Given both its good and bad reviews, community policing should be considered a potential pressure point within a police department.

Do not be satisfied with simply knowing the organizational chart. Learn the duties and responsibilities for all units and offices within the department. If the department, for example, has a research unit, its work could include interesting, important studies into crime trends and psychological profiles of criminals. Ask questions and learn about how the department operates. Take advantage of programs that allow you to shadow police officers, such as a ride-along. Study the police budget and how it is subdivided; compare the budget to those of other comparable police departments.

Facilities and Equipment

Police department facilities vary, depending on the size of the community and the size of the city budget. Usually, though, a police station has *holdover cells* to confine prisoners temporarily until they can be taken to a county or regional jail. Another common facility is an *evidence room*, where drugs, weapons and property connected with crimes are stored prior to a case going to court. Examine all sections of the police station, if possible, and learn how facilities are used. But the evidence room and holdover cells are particularly important, because these are places where improprieties are likeliest to occur. Suspects are sometimes neglected in holdover cells; firearms and drugs are known to disappear from evidence rooms.

Reporters can also learn about a department—its strengths, weaknesses and approaches to law enforcement—from taking stock of its equipment. Does the department have the latest in radar guns to catch speeders? Does the city provide top-of-the-line bullet-resistant vests to all officers? Has the department invested heavily in riot gear and high-powered weapons? Is it stockpiling guns and vehicles that it is allowed to seize from drug suspects? What happens to money seized from drug dealers? Can it be used by the department to purchase supplies and equipment? The answers to questions like these may reflect a department's priorities and lead to important stories.

Over the years, the computer has become the most important piece of police equipment. Do not expect to find sophisticated systems in place at the local police department, but major cities and county, state and nationwide law enforcement agencies have invested substantially in crime-fighting technology. The widespread linkage of computers has been the impetus for police agencies, large and small, to build intelligence files and dossiers on suspicious persons. For example, the local police, called to question a shoplifting suspect, complete a field-interrogation report, noting, among other things, a distinguishing physical feature—a tattoo of an eagle on his right wrist. The information goes into a database. Months later, a woman in a neighboring suburb may fight off an attempted rape and remember her assailant's eagle tattoo. A computer check quickly pulls up the name of a possible suspect.

One of the showcase operations belongs to New York City Police Department—the Real Time Crime Center. Officers at the scene of a violent crime can feed the address, descriptions of suspects and other initial information, such as license plate numbers, into the $11 million system of integrated databases, capable of searching through 120 million criminal complaints, arrests and 911 call records compiled in the metropolitan area, and additionally ties into 5 million state crime files, 31 million crime files nationwide and an astounding 31 billion public records. Information culled from data-bases, along with intelligence derived from additional digital tools in the system, such as satellite imaging, registries of nicknames and tattoos and computerized maps of crime patterns, flow from the center by phone, fax or PDA to investigators in the field. Police Chief Joseph D'Amico said information that would take hours or days to access, assemble and assess is now available to detectives within minutes, ready to use.[15]

Communications

At the heart of most police operations is the communications center. In smaller departments, one person—usually known by the job title of *dispatcher*—may serve as receptionist, watchman and communications operator. Within the dispatcher's reach are television monitors, radio microphones, computer terminals and telephones. In the period of a few minutes, a dispatcher might greet a visitor, take a call about a stolen bike, run a computer check of a license plate number and dispatch a patrol car to investigate an activated burglary alarm. In large departments, the job is much the same; there are simply more dispatchers.

Federal grant money has enabled nearly all police agencies to tap into computer-ized crime data from state records centers and the National Crime Information Center (NCIC) in Washington, D.C. The computer is especially important in protecting police on patrol. An officer making a traffic stop, for example, can either use a dash-mounted computer terminal or radio a dispatcher in headquarters to run a com-puter check of a license plate or a driver's license. Within seconds, the request will be answered by state computers or the NCIC, providing the officer with a variety of information, including whether a license plate is connected with a crime or whether a driver is wanted on criminal warrants. Crime-information computers also hold data about stolen property and missing persons.

Reporters, however, cannot, in all cases, expect direct access to information in crime computers. About 30 states now allow public access to criminal data, usually for a fee. Moreover, most states provide the names of those being imprisoned, often through the corrections department Web site. However, restrictions still apply widely, especially regarding an individual's criminal history of arrests, charges and convic-tions, or what officers still refer to as a *rap sheet*. Release of such information to the press might later make it difficult to find jurors who have not been prejudiced by the disclosure. Police chiefs do not want judges or district attorneys accusing them of botching prosecution of a criminal case.

Telephone calls to the police often involve routine, non-emergency matters: "Someone's illegally parked outside my business" or "Those teenagers next door are hav-ing another wild party." Because no one knows when the next call will be serious and urgent, many departments tape record *every* call. With the increasing use of cell phones, along with 911 systems to quickly summon emergency help, drama is being preserved, including, at times, the dying words of murder victims. Although police tapes are not considered public records in all jurisdictions, reporters should always ask to review or transcribe newsworthy calls and persist with higher authorities when the request at first is declined. Besides their potential news drama, the tapes may determine whether the police or other emergency agencies responded quickly and appropriately to an emergency. (Video recorders mounted in patrol cars also provide an additional form of response record, provided they are made available to the press and public.)

Since the communication chaos surrounding the September 11 terror attacks, another toll-free system—311—has spread to cities around the country.[16] Some 311 systems handle calls for all municipal services. Employees also are trained to deal with 911 emergencies.

In addition to taped or digital recordings of 911 and 311 calls, the dispatching center usually keeps a digital record of four stages of a call: when it is received, when an officer is dispatched, when the officer arrives at the scene and when the officer is freed from the call—a chronology of police response. Another communications tool, the global positioning system (GPS), installed in patrol cars or handheld within a pocket computer, helps track the movement of officers in the field, pinpoint addresses and direct pursuits. It, too, can help provide details for a story about police response.

In metropolitan areas, police departments are often interconnected by a joint radio frequency to coordinate operations, such as setting up roadblocks or directing a high-speed pursuit. At times, though, a fugitive will escape because police departments are not properly equipped to quickly share information by radio. Tragically, New York authorities learned during the attack on the World Trade Center that communication breakdowns cost lives. After the South Tower collapsed, firefighters in the North Tower were told to evacuate, but many did not hear the order because they were on different radio channels or the radio channel they were using was overwhelmed by emergency people trying to talk to one another. They died as a result, according to a commission created to investigate the September 11 response.[17]

The public listens in on police radio communication by way of scanners. But lawbreakers use scanners, too, so when police require secrecy in the field, they turn to encrypted channels or use cell phones. Web sites, as well, are increasingly used by police agencies to communicate with the public to announce crime-fighting programs, seek tips on active cases, such as a missing person and post, in real time, dispatched response calls online. Not all law enforcement officials, however, embrace the idea of scanners or Webcasts of active calls, believing they compromise the safety of officers and hamper police work.

Reporters need to know how the communications system works and what type of information it yields.

Operating Policies

Knowing the department also means knowing its operating policies, particularly ones governing police conduct and procedures. For example, what kind of professional training and psychological screening does the department require of its new officers? What is departmental policy on the types of weapons and ammunition officers may carry—and their use of those weapons? Does the department have guidelines on methods to subdue violent suspects? Clear, strict policies covering police behavior indicate whether a department is serious about preventing brutality or unjustified in use of force. In the absence of rules and policies, abuses occur. After a suspect in New York died while hog-tied—his arms and legs bound together behind his back with plastic restraints—the city police commissioner admitted he never realized police routinely but unofficially used such a restraint. New York City subsequently banned the practice.[18]

Law enforcement agencies now are debating use of the Taser, a hand-held, gun-shaped weapon that delivers an electric shock of up to 50,000 low-amperage volts via two wire-connected, stainless steel barbs that pierce the skin. The Taser is meant to subdue potentially dangerous or violent subjects when other means of control fail. It is considered a non-lethal weapon, but Amnesty International reported 61 deaths in the United States attributed to the Taser in 2005.[19] Law enforcement organizations usually include the Taser as part of a "matrix" or "continuum" of levels of force to apply in risky situations. *Use-of-force guidelines* vary in scope and specificity, but generally all include at least five levels of escalated response: (1) the presence of uniformed officers on the scene; (2) the use of verbal commands, such as "sit down" or "step out of the car"; (3) physical contact, like "softhands" to move or direct an individual; (4) non-lethal weapons, including the Taser and pepper spray; (5) and, as a last resort, deadly force by firearms.

Police officers authorized to use the Taser usually must themselves experience the pain of the electrical jolt. Question the policy and practices in the use of non-lethal weapons, but, conversely, do not judge the police too quickly or harshly when they use force. In seconds, a reasonable-sounding and -acting person can go beserk, grabbing a police officer and putting the officer in grave danger.

In urban areas especially, the department's pursuit policy warrants attention. A surveillance group, PursuitWatch.org, estimates more than 450 people are killed annually in high-speed police pursuits; the National Highway Traffic Safety Administration statistics put the number at about 350 annually. News accounts focus on innocent bystanders killed or injured in police chases, and usually the pursuit is over a minor traffic infraction, not a serious crime such as armed robbery, carjacking or homicide.[20] As a result of accidents and the subsequent civil lawsuits they generate, some police departments have instituted strict guidelines to limit pursuits to felony cases. Car thieves, in particular, benefit from tightened rules; they simply speed away when spotted by a police officer, who, in frustration, must watch their taillights disappear.

In some areas, an unwritten, unofficial "policy" covers a controversial practice called "racial profiling." No universal definition exists, but generally the term means stopping, questioning and searching someone on a public highway, city street or airport concourse based on the individual's race or ethnicity. Young black males, in particular, get targeted. If the practice exists in a community, it should be exposed.

Working with Police

Twenty-five years ago reporters could walk into most police stations and freely inspect copies of incident reports. No more. Scanning digital video cameras guard exits and entrances to police stations. Visitors, including reporters, are stopped in the front lobby and asked to state their business by clerks or police dispatchers protected behind bulletproof glass. Then they must go through metal—and chemical—detection devices.

Access to records is also more restricted than in the past, when reporters could simply go to a counter and flip through a stack of police incident reports. Today, incident reports often are screened and in some cases withheld from journalists. Many departments filter news through the public information officer (PIO), blocking reporters from talking directly to patrol officers or detectives. At times, the police exhibit a siege mentality.

Once a reporter is a known quantity, however, access to people, places and records is easier and rules are more readily bent. But it takes time before a reporter is trusted. And some reporters, especially those who get facts wrong or violate confidences, never gain police cooperation.

The Blotter

Covering the beat begins with access to police-blotter information. The *blotter* is an old term to describe a book in which police recorded criminal incidents and arrests. Today, blotter information usually is recorded in a computerized *incident log*. The log generally contains a brief summary of an incident; for fuller details, police and reporters alike must refer to a written incident report completed by the officers handling the case, although they, too, are likely to be processed and retained by computer.

You will find that access to records varies from department to department, and even from reporter to reporter. Some differences are a result of statutory provisions— or interpretation of statutes. State open-records laws vary on the types of police information that are considered public domain. Moreover, some laws are ambiguous in their treatment of police records. Learn about the laws that govern access to records in your area. To help reporters, the Reporters Committee for Freedom of the Press (www.rcfp.org) keeps tabs of public-record access in a state-by-state report.

When police-press relations are badly strained, reporters may be permitted access to incident reports only at a designated time and place—say, once or twice a day at the public-information office. Increasingly, nearly all police officials are concerned about protecting the privacy and safety of victims, witnesses and juveniles, so reporters might have to settle for edited versions of incident reports with certain names and addresses deleted.

As a rule, reporters are entitled to details immediately surrounding an arrest, including:

- identification of the suspect by age, address and occupation
- the substance or text of charges against the suspect
- names of arresting officers and law agencies
- time, date and place of the arrest
- descriptions of weapons used or possessed by the suspect
- information regarding how the suspect was taken into custody, such as pursuit or resistance

Additional information will be harder to come by, particularly if it jeopardizes a suspect's rights to a fair trial by an impartial jury. As a result, police often will not disclose the following information:

- the contents of any statement, confession or admission made by a suspect
- opinions about the suspect's character, guilt or innocence
- the results of investigative procedures, such as polygraph examinations, ballistics tests, fingerprints or laboratory evidence
- statements concerning the credibility of prospective witnesses in the case
- the prior criminal charges and convictions of the suspect

In dealing with timid or lackadaisical reporters, police will be inclined to withhold more and more information. Reporters sometimes are obligated to fight for access to police records and information, including the names of victims and witnesses.

To gain the fullest amount of information, especially where open-records laws are vague or weak, reporters must also develop a number of reliable contacts within the department, particularly with detectives who investigate crimes. A good network of sources ensures against being shut out if policies change or unfavorable press coverage chills access to the police chief.

In small departments it is important to build rapport with police dispatchers, who frequently are keepers of the incident log. Because dispatchers are at the center of operations, little escapes their attention. When police withhold arrest information, sometimes the county jail's daily log of prisoners will be available in person or online. But realistically, there will be times when nothing you say or do will yield answers and information, even from your unofficial sources.

Stories from the Police Beat

News organizations have widely divergent approaches to covering the beat. Some papers, for example, report every traffic accident, from fender bender to fatality.

Others cover only unusual accidents or ones resulting in injury or death. By policy, a big-city daily may publish the name and address of everyone arrested for driving under the influence; a midsized paper may be sporadic in DUI reportage. Television journalists look for crime incidents that lend themselves to visual treatment; therefore, a spectacular pile-up on the interstate usually gets more attention than a new method to use hair samples to test for the presence of drugs.

Getting beyond the obvious

Access to incident reports is merely the starting point for a reporter. Police reports provide the skeleton of a story. That is to be expected. Most police officers dislike doing paper work, which probably explains why their reports sometimes can be incomplete and inaccurate, with misspelled names, wrong addresses and skimpy details. A report lacking in detail, however, does not necessarily signal a bad attitude; police intentionally withhold information from a report if they expect to testify or give a deposition. The rationale? They do not want to give defense attorneys the opportunity to nitpick every detail in the report. The reporter's job is to verify police information, visit the scene, talk to victims, witnesses and officers and then produce a readable, accurate account of what happened and why it happened.

REPORTER'S TIP FILE

Lessons from the beat

Stephen Buckley offers a list of tips based on his experience as a police-beat reporter at the *Washington Post*.[21] Here's a summary of his advice:

Cops are human. Get to know them. Like everyone, they respond to reporters they know. Tell them a little about yourself. Ask them about their families. And of course, ask them about the work. Steve Aspinall, a detective from the St. Petersburg Police Department, said a reporter once called him in the hospital where he was a patient. After that, no matter what he was doing, he always returned that reporter's calls.

Always go to the scene. This is where you get the details that the public information officer can't provide. The blood on the sidewalk. The howling, disconsolate mother. The stunned friends. Perhaps the eerie quiet that settles over the neighborhood. And most importantly, you sometimes find witnesses at the scene. They may be able to tell you only how many shots they heard or how loud the shots sounded, but you can't write great stories without those kinds of details.

Never assume people don't want to talk. Sometimes, particularly after an especially horrifying crime, victims and their relatives—and a suspect's relatives and friends—don't want to talk. But many, many times, they do talk to reporters. Sometimes, they even talk for hours. The point is: Don't try to guess. Ask. You never know.

Spend time in neighborhoods. Particularly spend time in those known for high crime. The temptation is to avoid these communities. The truth is that they often offer rich stories—stories of people trying to save their children; stories of people trying to drive out criminals; stories of people who've seen their beloved communities crumble. Get to know the activists, longtime residents, mothers (mothers talk because their top priority is to save their children, so they're often willing to risk the scorn of neighbors by talking to reporters). The best police stories are almost always in the neighborhood.

Look for patterns. Police departments often have daily logs that they allow reporters to go through. Go through that log. Check to see whether there's been an unusually high amount of crime in a normally quiet neighborhood. Or maybe you'll notice that a normally dangerous community turns quiet for a few weeks. Or maybe you'll see that all the homicides in a neighborhood seem to have the same m.o. (i.e., three cases over a few months in which young professional women are strangled). Don't wait for the cops to put those things together. Be your own detective.

Read police news in out-of-town papers. Often, crimes move in trends. If you live in Harrisburg, Pa., and you hear that heroin is making a big comeback in Pittsburgh, ask detectives if they're seeing more heroin on the streets of Harrisburg these days. Crime-fighting strategies also move in waves. If you read that the San Jose, Calif., police department has started to employ something called community-oriented policing, make a note of it. Chances are lots of other departments either have started to do the same or are considering taking that route.

Police-beat coverage involves far more than daily inspection of police reports and coverage of news items they yield. It includes stories about unpaid traffic tickets, police training, neighborhood crime-watch programs, dangerous intersections, missing children and the recovery of accident victims. Stories emerge, too, from knowing what police are talking about out of earshot of supervisors. Their conversations sometimes end up online, so reporters should regularly tap into a Web site, such as www.leoaf fairs.com, and visit message boards. Much of the chatter, usually done anonymously, is about routine gripes—endless paperwork and inept bosses. But occasionally, a message board raises serious concerns. In Washington, D.C., for example, police officers discussed the shortage of on-board computers in patrol cars, one saying the department needed "to drag itself into the 21st century."

The best stories, however, usually are found outside the confines of police headquarters and on the streets, where reporters can hear about crime and law enforcement from the experiences of experts on the subject—people who live in public-housing complexes, work at all-night gas stations or drive cabs.

Capturing the drama and pathos

The stories coming from the beat ought to overflow with drama and pathos. Too often, police-beat stories are cold and mechanically written. They have a sameness about them, as if composed by a computer; only the names, dates and places change. Police-beat reporters should always humanize coverage, no matter how "routine" a story might first appear. And they should always consider the victim's perspective.

The victim, for example, may be the owner of a ramshackle one-chair barbershop on the edge of town. Three times in the span of a month, neighborhood youths break into his shop, stealing from the petty-cash drawer, breaking into a gum-ball machine and taking bottles of after-shave lotion. Against a backdrop of armed robberies and sexual assaults, his loss, of course, is insignificant. But stories like his should be told periodically to remind us that *all* victims of crime pay a price and have feelings.

QUOTABLES

"The irony of crime beat journalism—maybe all of journalism—is that the best stories are really the worst stories. The stories of calamity and tragedy are the stories that journalists live for. It gets the adrenaline churning in their blood and can burn them out young, but nevertheless it is a hard fact of the business." (pp. 8, 9)
—Michael Connelly, *Crime Beat: A Decade of Covering Cops and Killers*, New York and Boston: Little Brown and Company, 2004

Journalists, at times, underplay crime stories, withhold grim details or report with unnatural detachment. In some cases, their behavior is overcompensation for critics' charges that the press and public gorge on crime fare. Then, too, a few reporters become so blasé or callous about crime news they stop being astonished or outraged by it; the burn-out rate on the police beat is high. Still others fear offending sensitive readers, which is a legitimate concern when not taken to an extreme. Whatever the reason, by de-emphasizing crime news, reporters inadvertently insult already injured victims and their families. And by withholding details, they deprive the citizens of information they ought to hear or read. Consider this account from a metropolitan newspaper:

Two North Side women—one of them nine months pregnant—were the victims of sexual attacks Wednesday, police said.

A 19-year-old North Side youth was charged Wednesday afternoon in the sexual assault and vicious beating of a woman, 32, and the beating of her two children—a girl, 10, and a boy, 5—who live in his neighborhood.

Buried eight paragraphs into the story were details of the "assault" and "vicious beatings." At 12:30 a.m., an intruder broke into the 32-year-old woman's home and sexually assaulted her with a board, which he then used to beat her and the two children. All three suffered skull fractures; the mother lost an eye, a lip and part of an ear in the beating. The 12-paragraph story contained not a single direct quote from anyone—police, victims, neighbors or family of the victims.

More commonly, police-beat reporters fail to capitalize on the human-interest value of everyday police stories, such as vehicle accidents. Treated in a routine, unimaginative manner, the report of a tanker-truck accident might go this way:

> A fuel tanker spun out of control and rolled over on Interstate 222 near the 54th Avenue exit Friday, gushing fuel onto the highway.
>
> A passerby helped the driver, Henry Smith, 48, of Middletown, crawl away from the wreckage. He was listed in good condition Saturday at St. Joseph's Hospital, where he was treated for four broken ribs.
>
> No other vehicles were involved in the accident, which tied up traffic for an hour. City firefighters washed the fuel from the highway.

But when a reporter does his or her homework, the human interest surfaces, as in this version of a tanker accident:

> The sound of a tire exploding boomed in Connie Murray's ear as she drove south on Interstate 222 Friday afternoon. Moments later, in her rear-view mirror, she saw a fuel tanker spin out of control and roll over.
>
> "The whole thing looked like a total mess and the cab was on its top," said Mrs. Murray. A private-duty registered nurse, she was on her way from her home in Jonestown to St. Joseph's Hospital.
>
> "All I could think of was, how was I going to get the driver out of the cab?"

The story told *how*.

Now and then, a police story is suitable for light treatment. After taking three police cars on a wild, reckless chase that ended, luckily, without loss of life or limb, a 20-year-old motorcyclist said to one of the police officers, "Man, you aren't going to give me a ticket, are you?" "No," said the officer, "we're giving you 21 tickets." For the most part, your treatment should be serious; crime seldom is a laughing matter.

Press-Police Relationships

It should come as no surprise that police officers have little regard for reporters who make mistakes, ask stupid questions, renege on agreements, get in the way at crime scenes or endanger victims and witnesses. The more you know about police work and criminal procedure, the less likely you will make mistakes and damage your reputation with police officers. Do not, in particular, use legal terminology carelessly. Assault and battery, for example, sound like they go together—as a single charge. But they are distinct criminal offenses that may or may not go together. *Assault* is an attempt or a threat to injure a person; *battery* is actually striking someone. Know the traffic laws to cover accidents properly. What, for example, is the difference between *reckless* driving and *careless* driving? News organizations that use scanners to track police activity recognize the codes used commonly as verbal shorthand, including the

"10" and "11" codes and other numerical terms, like "211" for "robbery" or "510" for "speeding or racing vehicles."

At accident or crime scenes, remember that police and emergency personnel are under as much pressure to do their jobs as you are to do yours. They are particularly concerned about maintaining the "integrity" of crime scenes. If you are among the first persons to reach a fire or crime scene, do not tramp about or touch anything. By barging in, at worse, you could damage evidence; at the minimum, you are going to irk police officials. Police also frown upon door-to-door canvassing of a neighborhood by reporters at a crime scene, such as a vehicular homicide, home invasion or murder. Police, from experience, believe the first statement from a witness is usually the most reliable. If a journalist gets to a witness before they do, police fear their follow-up might be tainted either by a reporter's leading questions or by the witness's tendency to alter the account each time it is retold. Nonetheless, big-city news organizations expect reporters to seek out neighbors for the details needed to produce fully developed stories.

REAL-LIFE LESSONS

Reporters on the police beat learn the hard way, at times, when they get too close to a tactical operation, such as a hostage standoff, and end up being accused of reckless, dangerous behavior. A convict disarms a courtroom bailiff, flees in carjacked auto with the driver as a hostage and gets stopped by police inside the driver's house. When the news reaches newsrooms, reporters mobilize. News helicopters hover overhead to beam live reports back to the station. Photographers on the ground, with either video or digital cameras, crawl as close to the action as they can without getting caught by police. Print reporters, knowing the hostage location, search for phone numbers and try to call for an interview with the suspect or victim. In the heat of a dramatic, breaking story, good jugment can be the first casualty—and, if luck holds out, it will be the only casualty attributed to the press.

Consider what happened when Nester DeJesus shot a pursuing Tampa police officer after DeJesus and his girlfriend, Paula Gutierrez, held up a bank. As they fled, the couple took a hostage and holed up inside an apartment. When police negotiators reached DeJesus by phone, DeJesus and Gutierrez kept asking about the female officer's condition. The negotiators intentionally would not tell them. Then a local news outlet reported the officer had died. "Why are you lying to me?" Gutierrez screamed. "We just heard on Bay News 9 she's dead!" Hours later, after DeJesus had committed suicide, Gutierrez had surrendered and the hostage was rescued unharmed, the police blamed the press for making a dangerous situation potentially worse. "Once they know someone is dead," a tactical team leader said, "it's easier to kill again."

The lesson: *Journalists should know how their actions can endanger lives and should wait, in most cases, until the crisis is resolved before releasing news or taking steps that could impede the police or incite the suspect. "My goal is to urge journalists to think about these situations before they're in the minefield," says media ethicist Bob Steele.*[22]

Keep your cool at all times. Do not automatically get testy and demanding when police officers refuse to answer every question you put to them. Generally, police welcome media coverage of unsolved crimes, for it often helps them generate tips and make arrests. Sometimes, though, they must suppress key evidence or information to rule out bogus confessions. If every detail of a crime is broadcast or published, police can anticipate getting calls from people who, for whatever reason, admit to crimes they did not commit. Reporters are trained to seek specific details, but when a suspect is still at large, they might have to be satisfied when police simply say the murder weapon was a "large-caliber revolver" or a "blunt instrument."

For many police officers, the worst offense is for a reporter to prove to be untrustworthy. Journalists who violate a confidence, break an agreement about release of information or act irresponsibly in coverage can expect retaliation from the police. In some cases, police departments blackball untrustworthy journalists; in other instances the retaliation happens, but it is less obvious, such as making the offender wait for hours outside a crime scene and then giving him just scraps of information.

Police officers are known to test newcomers to the beat by passing along a juicy but fabricated piece of information, with the stipulation to the reporter that the information is off the record. "If [the police] see it in print," says Joseph Halliman of the *Indianapolis Star*, "that reporter is burned for the rest of the time he's down here. They'll never talk to him or her again."[23]

It is all part of dealing with police officers. Edna Buchanan's observations are worth sharing:

> Persuade them that you will be fair, absolutely accurate and can be trusted to protect your sources.
>
> It is inevitable that we clash from time to time. When it happens I do not take complaints to their bosses or mine. . . . It is better, whenever possible, to handle [complaints] yourself, person to person. Police officers perform under pressure. So do we. We should be able to work things out without ratting on each other. Nobody likes a crybaby, especially cops.
>
> I like to let them know that our jobs are a lot alike. If we wanted to be loved, they would be firemen and I would teach kindergarten. We both have to do things we don't like. We are both just doing our jobs.[24]

There is a delicate balance to press-police relationships. That balance is severely tested when law enforcement officials ask you to withhold information or help them set a trap for suspects. Are there ever times when reporters should cooperate with police? If so, when does cooperation cross the line to co-option? Two examples, each based on actual incidents, underscore the problems inherent in answering those questions.

Three times in the space of a week, an abusive-talking man wearing a ski mask has broken into apartments in a six-block area, robbing two elderly women and being scared off in the third incident. Police ask you to hold off on a story about the robberies another day or two so undercover officers, staking out the neighborhood apartments, can catch the man. What do you do?

A detective asks you and the editor of your newspaper to plant a bogus story that says a local businessman is missing and presumed to be the victim of foul play. The plan is to entrap the businessman's partner, who has offered a hit man, actually an undercover police officer, $5,000 to carry out the killing. What do you do?

If you polled editors and reporters at random, they would struggle over these scenarios, arriving at a variety of decisions based on a variety of reasons. While there is no definitive rule to cover police requests for press cooperation, the primary duty of the press is to serve the public's right to know, not function as an arm of law enforcement. Reporters who decline to cooperate with police risk a loss of cooperation in return. But reporters should never abandon principles and credibility to avoid offending the police.

Danger Zones

The police beat requires great care in coverage. Here are a few areas where dangers lurk.

Arrests, Warrants and Rights

From the first day on the job until the last, a police reporter must know and remember that there is a big difference between being *arrested* and being *charged* with a crime. When police arrest someone, they detain the person as a suspected lawbreaker. A flexible legal yardstick called *probable cause* is supposed to help police officers determine whether there are sufficient grounds for an arrest. While there is no uniform definition for *probable cause*, it basically amounts to circumstances and facts that would lead a reasonable and prudent individual—in this case, a police officer—to believe someone has committed a crime. If a woman cries out, "Stop, thief!" and officers catch a teenager two blocks away clutching her handbag, the police might decide that possession of the handbag is probable cause to arrest the teenager, particularly if the victim says, "That's the one!" However, a police officer's determination of probable cause may differ from probable cause as seen by a judge, who may conclude the arrest was unwarranted and release the individual. In addition, the facts and circumstances that led to the arrest could quickly change; the victim, for example, might waver on her once-sure identification of the purse snatcher.

To be legally safe and ethically responsible, avoid printing, posting online or broadcasting the name and address in an arrest report until formal charges are filed in an official court document, which typically is a *warrant* issued by a judge that names the accused and specifies the charges against him. Once a news report prematurely identifies and links someone with a crime, the damage may be irreversible. The more serious the crime, the greater the damage. Even a report of a shoplifting arrest can cause pain and problems for the individual involved and his or her family. If circumstances dictate that you must report an arrest immediately, try, if possible, to withhold the suspect's identification or blur it by saying, for example, "Police arrested a 35-year-old accountant Monday on suspicion that he is the Oceanview cat burglar, responsible for 20 break-ins locally."

Occasionally, police publicly identify someone as a "person of interest" in a criminal invesigation. Do not leap to publish, air or post the name. The term, critics say, allows law enforcement officials to draw attention to individuals without formally charging them. Often, the police hope news coverage will stir up witnesses and evidence to give them the legal justification for an arrest. Journalists should question police motives and recognize the potential damage they might do if the "person of interest" turns out innocent of involvement.

Once charges are filed, however, reporters should pursue the case aggressively. Nevertheless, there must be limits to coverage, based on a concern for the rights of accused persons. The U.S. system of criminal law rests on the principle that all accused persons are presumed innocent until proven guilty. The principle of a *presumption of innocence* is reinforced by rules and procedures designed to ensure that criminal defendants can exercise their constitutional rights to be tried according to due process of law and before an impartial jury. Journalists should not intentionally jeopardize those rights by publishing inflammatory hearsay or other inadmissible information, even if it comes from the police. What to publish—and what to withhold—may present difficult choices for reporters. Do you, for example, publish the contents of a murder suspect's rambling confession statement, leaked to you by a source in the department? When in doubt, share your indecision with editors and colleagues and allow them to help you weigh options and make a decision.

Crime Data

Stay abreast of local crime numbers. Ask your agency for monthly or quarterly updates if it customarily releases only annual statistics. Every crime reporter should be familiar with the two forms of national crime statistics: the FBI's Uniform Crime Reports and the U.S. Justice Department's crime victimization numbers, both of which can be found online.

Get to know your agency's statistical guru, but have other sources who can offer independent analysis of the numbers your agency provides. Reporting on crime statistics is tricky. For one thing, crime data are based on *reported* incidents. Since a number of crimes, for various reasons, go unreported, the statistics do not necessarily provide an accurate picture of a city's or region's crime rate. Careless use of percentages adds to the problem of interpreting crime statistics. If a community, for example, experiences nine slayings in a year, up from six the previous year, stories and headlines might emphasize "a 50 percent increase" in the murder rate. With such small numbers, stressing the increase in terms of a percentage tends to be misleading.

Still another problem is lack of adequate analysis of statistics. Raw numbers and percentages alone cannot reveal much about patterns of crime in a city. A more useful account identifies and assesses important factors in determining patterns, such as location, time of day and types of victims. Explanatory stories—accompanied by graphs, maps and other visual devices to explain the crime rate and compare it to previous figures—put the statistics into context.

Reporters are justified in being skeptical about crime figures and police rhetoric. Law enforcement has its political side. Police officials want to look good, so there is a temptation to pad arrest figures or downplay serious crimes. To provide balance, check with insurance companies to see whether they have more reliable data on thefts and burglaries in the city.

Bias and Labels

Stereotypes influence public perceptions of crime. Some people associate crime with skin color and neighborhoods. When a woman is abducted from a suburban shopping mall parking lot and raped, they will assume the victim is white and a black man assaulted her. If a drug dealer is shot to death outside a public-housing building, they will conclude that the killer and the victim are black. In other cases, stereotypes cause us to write off certain crime as insignificant or inevitable; after all, do not some "elements" of society invite or cause trouble? This kind of racist or ethnocentric thinking can be found everywhere, including newsrooms.

Especially troublesome is how stereotypes affect our impressions of black-against-white crime. Columnist Ellen Goodman addressed the problem by describing an encounter on a dark city street:

> One night last winter, a young and white friend left a movie theater and headed down the street to her car. Out of the corner of her eye, she anxiously tracked two black men walking until they were right in front of her.
>
> Finally, eyes cast down, she heard their laughter and when she finally looked up at one of the men, her fear met his smile. He was a colleague from work. In the moment of that exchange, he read her expression. Everything passed between them. Hurt. Anger. Understanding. Sadness.
>
> That's what crime does. That's what racism does. That's how hard it is to tell them apart.[25]

Actually, crime statistics suggest that most crime is *intraracial* (white against white; black against black), not *interracial* (white against black; black against white).[26] Occasionally, though, racism is at the root of criminal violence. Two separate episodes suggest that the press is not always consistent in dealing with racism and crime. When a gang of young whites in the New York City community of Bensonhurst killed a 17-year-old black in August of 1989, race became the focal point of intense media coverage. *Bensonhurst* practically became synonymous with racism. But earlier, in Cleveland, when a black mob killed a young white man, his death, as one critic put it, "occasioned a great silence." Editors of the *Cleveland Plain Dealer* de-emphasized the racial angle, even though the black reporter covering the story said, "There's no question that it was racial. Anybody that can't see that is blind."[27]

A writer who studied the Cleveland killing and compared it to another racial attack of whites against blacks in New York City's Howard Beach area commented:

> Twenty-five or 30 years ago, the mainstream American press did a lousy job of being fair to minorities. . . .
>
> News people eventually confessed past sins and repented. And they—the good ones, at least—have tried to make amends. . . . And yet, perhaps news organizations have gone so far in making amends that they now routinely miss certain kinds of stories—stories that revolve around this unpleasant fact: While whites can be racists, so can blacks.[28]

Reporters are wrong to devalue a criminal act—either by underplaying it or by not reporting it all—based on where it happened or to whom it happened. Is the mugging of a black grandmother any less disturbing than the mugging of a white grandmother? When a prostitute is murdered, is it any less tragic than the murder of a nun? Is publicity more warranted for a missing teenager from an affluent suburb than one missing from a trailer park?

Nevertheless, being strictly non-judgmental in crime coverage presents its problems. Did the black mugging victim live in a neighborhood where attacks occur daily? Prostitutes work in areas and engage in activities that put them at risk; they get beaten, robbed and murdered. Nuns usually are not at such risk, and if one is killed, it is unusual and therefore considered bigger news. Crimes against prostitutes—and against street people, the poor, blacks and Hispanics—undoubtedly are underreported by the press because, ironically and sadly, crimes against certain categories of people are so commonplace that they *lessen* in news value.

The question of racial identification is even more complicated. In a world still full of hatred and prejudice, how do you determine when—or whether—race is a factor in a criminal act? Moreover, if the press identifies most victims, witnesses and suspects by name, address, age, sex and occupation, should not the public be provided with racial identification as well? In a controversial book, *Coloring the News*, William McGowan contends the press too often unwisely withholds racial indentification to avoid accusations of racism.[29] But cannot racial identification *dispel* stereotypes as opposed to perpetuating them?

Clearly, these are difficult questions that defy ready answers. Perhaps they are best addressed through advice from civil rights leader Benjamin Hooks. In the late 1970s, Hooks, director of the NAACP, stressed the importance of the media's role in race relations. "The press," he said, "becomes a major link between black and white communities. It can either reinforce prejudices, racial stereotyping and the status quo, or it can take on the role of broadening the horizons of its readers."[30] Thirty years later, his words should inspire reporters to seek fairness and balance covering *all* crime news. That includes paying attention to *all* victims of crime.

Handle with Care

Crime news should always be handled with care, but there are times when reporters must be especially sensitive.

Victims' rights

To begin with, reporters should recognize that crime victims have certain rights. The principal right is to say no to interviews. Other rights include being able to grieve in private, to refuse to answer certain questions, to know the proposed angle or approach to the story, to select the time and place for an interview and to request a specific reporter as the interviewer.

Try hard to imagine the victim's experiences and feelings; take care in asking questions. When in doubt, ask for the advice and cooperation of a trained counselor who helps victims of crime. Many communities now have victim-assistance units, either independently operated or attached to the local police department. These counselors will tell you that crime victims and their families may be physically and emotionally stunned by what happened; they are vulnerable. Reporters, therefore, must guard against causing additional hurt—a second victimization—by their behavior.

Every victim of a serious crime suffers in some way. Do not assume that an unbloodied victim is unhurt. Psychic and emotional injuries are as painful and real as physical ones. A victim of a holdup, for instance, might be ridden with guilt for not resisting. Reporters should not compound the guilt by insensitive remarks ("At least you weren't hurt") or insensitive questions ("Didn't you fight back when the holdup man hit your son?").

Sex crimes

Rape, incest and child molestation are among the most serious and traumatic of crimes. The victims of sex crimes must be, whenever possible, spared further pain or the possibility of harassment, intimidation or threat of another attack. In most cases, the names of sex-crime victims are voluntarily withheld by the press. There are exceptions, such as a rape-murder or an assault on someone so prominent the identity cannot be protected. Infrequently, a rape victim voluntarily goes public with her ordeal to help other victims.

Once again, arriving at ironclad rules is impossible and probably unwise, even when it comes to something so traditionally accepted as protecting the identity of rape victims. Geneva Overholser, a former editor, believes the news media need to reconsider not naming those who bring charges of rape. While acknowledging the painful issues of naming names, such as twice-victimization and reluctance to report rapes in the first place, Overholser makes this point: "Journalists cannot choose the one adult in a criminal trial who deserves protection."[31] Other proponents of openness believe withholding the identity of rape victims perpetuates the notion that there is some blame, disgrace or stigma attached. Finally there is the question of whether keeping victims anonymous dulls and dehumanizes our views toward rape. Some critics contend that the public needs to know that real people—your child's teacher, a friend's mother, an executive at your bank—are attacked. Despite these different viewpoints on identification of rape victims, most news organizations will not reveal names.

Identification of witnesses and victims

Editors and reporters usually protect the identity of victims and witnesses if there is any possibility that they might be emotionally or physically harmed by the publicity. If a nurse escapes an attack by a rapist, reporters should not give the assailant another chance to attack by publishing her address; if a frail, elderly couple is robbed, do not mark them as a tempting target for other thieves; if a witness can identify gang members who beat a street person, do not help the gang harass or threaten the witness into silence. When police ask you to withhold information, listen to them, but before agreeing or disagreeing, consult with your editors.

It is rare when the identity of a crime suspect is withheld, but it happens, and perhaps it should happen more often than it does. Newspapers, for example, routinely withhold the names of juvenile offenders. At times, the names of parents accused of child abuse are withheld until more evidence is acquired. Or when incest is the charge, usually you cannot identify the assailant without indirectly identifying the victim. These exceptions aside, often the newsroom policy is "show no favorites" and "treat everyone equally." A shoplifter is a shoplifter; a child molester is a child molester.

Punishment by publicity

An equal-treatment policy, however, fails to account for a problem known as *punishment by publicity*. The term is based, in part, on the possibility that mere publication of a suspect's name, address and alleged offense constitutes a harsher penalty than that meted by the sternest jury or judge. In cases of acquittal or dismissal of charges, the "sentence" imposed by the press cannot be easily repealed, even by a follow-up story or a retraction.

A related problem involves the often unclear distinction between what constitutes a criminal condition and what constitutes a medical or psychiatric condition. Is an accused arsonist, sex offender or thief evil—or mentally or physically ill? Police are not trained to determine the difference; neither are reporters. Should people with mental or medical problems—and their families—pay an additional penalty of press publicity? Is there harm in withholding identity until more facts and answers can be obtained? These are questions police-beat reporters should seriously consider before going public with sensitive information.

Dealing with death

One of the hardest assignments for any journalist is to interview and collect information from people still reeling after the tragic, sudden death of a child, spouse, parent or friend. Such assignments often go to police-beat reporters. Yet some of the most touching, effective stories about tragedies are based on interviews with survivors. In Oldsmar, Fla., a 5-year-old kindergartener died after she darted into the path of a van. By interviewing her father, reporters learned he was not allowed to accompany his daughter on the medical helicopter. Instead, he and his wife raced by car to the hospital, where they learned she was dead. "It would have been nice to be with her instead of being stuck in traffic," he said. "It's a hollow, sad feeling."[32] Evocative words like his help us feel the loss.

You might wonder, "Why do reporters bother people at such times?" Reporter Charlotte Sutton offers this explanation that reporters should find reassuring: "No reporter wants to be outdone on a story. But competition isn't the only reason for what can look like cold voyeurism. It seems wrong to let pass the violent death of a good person without saying more about the victim than his name and age. To do that would almost be like equating a tragedy with any routine entry in the police blotter."[33]

REPORTER'S TIP FILE

Talking to people in pain

There is no right way to approach people in grief. Try to be professional, yet compassionate. Briefly offer condolences, then gently and slowly proceed with your questions. A starting point is background information about the deceased. Facts of the accident or tragedy should be elicited carefully, so as not to cause pain. Ask for pertinent details without dwelling on gory particulars. Remember, there are other sources—police, medical examiners, emergency crews, friends and other family members—for many of your questions.

Listen and react non-judgmentally, particularly in regard to suicides. Often, suicide survivors experience fear, guilt, rage and depression. Rather than bluntly ask, "Do you know why your son killed himself?" probe gingerly and indirectly. Henry Seiden, co-author of *Silent Grief: Living in the Wake of Suicide*, offers advice for friends of suicide survivors that applies, as well, to reporters. Say something like, "It's the why of this thing that's really hard to understand, isn't it?" he suggests. "This," says Seiden, "lets the woman know you're there and helps her clarify what she feels."[34]

Let your humanity guide you. How would you want to be treated?

Public-Safety Agencies

While city police may remain the focal point of your coverage, you must develop contacts with other public-safety agencies that deal with crime, accidents and disasters.

State Police

The state police do more than nab speeders and handle traffic accidents. The state police often are among the best-trained and most comprehensive of law enforcement agencies. Unfortunately, too many journalists know the state troopers only as "Smokies" who patrol the highways and interstates.

The highway patrol may be one of several diversified divisions under the department of state police. In Illinois, for example, other elements include a Division of Internal Investigation, which handles police or official misconduct in cities or counties statewide, and the Division of Forensic Services, which operates crime laboratories around the state.

The work of the state police includes gathering criminal intelligence for dissemination to local police units; investigating auto theft and "chop shop" operations, where stolen cars are cannibalized for parts; regulating gambling and race tracks; inspecting trucks that transport hazardous wastes; reconstructing vehicle accidents; training new troopers and local police officers at the state police academy.

All reporters who cover law enforcement should make it a point to know the people and functions of the state police and visit the regional headquarters regularly, whether or not it is under their beat.

Sheriff's Department

Reporters assigned to cover the county courthouse sometimes get a bonus—coverage of the county sheriff's department. The size and role of the local sheriff's department will vary. In rural areas, it may be the main branch of law enforcement in a sparsely populated but geographically large county. In urban counties, sheriff's deputies may be limited to law enforcement in unincorporated areas that lack a municipal police department. In addition, the sheriff's department normally operates the county jail, since few cities can afford or justify their own facilities to hold suspects awaiting judicial action.

Nearly all police agencies are touched by politics, but that is particularly true of sheriff's departments because most sheriffs are elected, not appointed. Many sheriffs must stand on their record before voters every four years. Political pressure cannot help but influence a sheriff's behavior, decisions and relations with mass media. Raiding the sheriff's own Elks' Club, for example, and seizing its backroom slot machines may be proper law enforcement but dumb politics, so with some so-called victimless crimes, the sheriff might adopt a see-no-evil stance. But he may, again for political reasons, arrest clerks at several video shops for renting obscene tapes.

Politics mix with police work in other ways. If the sheriff is Republican and the County Board is predominately Democratic or vice versa, the department's budget may become a political pawn. When an incumbent sheriff is defeated or resigns, you can expect major administrative changes in the department. The new sheriff probably will replace key aides and officers with his or her own politically loyal people, which, among other things, means reporters must rebuild a network of news sources.

Federal Law Agencies

Homeland Security

The Department of Homeland Security supplanted the FBI as the nation's top law enforcement agency in 2003, the year of its creation, when it assumed control over a number of federal operations, including the U.S. Secret Service, Coast Guard, FEMA (Federal Emergency Management Agency) and the Immigration and Customs Enforcement Service (ICE), a revamped, hybrid of the former U.S. Customs Service and Immigration and Naturalization Service. President George W. Bush said he established the department because the threat of terrorism required a unified effort to protect the nation and its people. The secretary of Homeland Security oversees 180,000 employees and holds cabinet rank in the president's administration. The secretary's authority includes unprecedented access to electronic databases, wiretap information and raw investigative files of the FBI, the CIA and other federal intelligence organizations. Among the department's responsibilities are the protection of the nation's borders, transportation facilities and infrastructure; coordination of intelligence data; education of first responders; distribution of federal emergency resources in disasters and attacks; and institution of guideliness to combat bioterrorism.

Federal Bureau of Investigation

When we think of federal law enforcement, most of us picture the Federal Bureau of Investigation (FBI) and rightly so. It remains the most celebrated federal police force. Its 12,600 special agents, all trained at the FBI Academy in Quantico, Va., operate out of 56 field offices around the United States and 50 international offices at U.S. embassies. Thousands of other FBI employees support the agents in the field, checking fingerprints, conducting scientific tests of evidence and maintaining computer records of arrest warrants and stolen property through the National Crime Information Center.

The typical FBI agent is well educated, well trained and very disciplined. Agents reputedly are closemouthed, but they can be good news sources under the right conditions. Like all police officers, they will be cautious until they feel a reporter can be trusted. Remember that their work is largely investigative, and therefore they cannot reveal many details without jeopardizing an investigation.

At times, FBI agents will leak—most often under a condition of anonymity— incriminating information about individuals under investigation. Whenever that happens, reporters ought to warily question the FBI's motives. In the past, particularly under the administration of J. Edgar Hoover, the FBI's founder and long-time director, the FBI used reporters to uncover information or put pressure on a public official suspected of being corrupt or tainted. Reporters should not allow themselves to be manipulated by the FBI or *any other law enforcement agency*.

Specialized agenices

The FBI is part of the U.S. Department of Justice, as are two other agencies with an increasingly important role in law enforcement—the Drug Enforcement Administration (DEA) and the newly reformulated Bureau of Alcohol, Tobacco, Firearms and Explosives, which had been under the U.S. Department of the Treasury. The Treasury Department law enforcement includes the Internal Revenue Service, responsible for investigating tax fraud.

Many other federal departments have law enforcement components, such as the U.S. Postal Service, which investigates illegal use of the mail. In addition, the president appoints approximately 100 U.S. marshals, backed by more than 3,000 deputy marshals, to transport federal prisoners and to enforce federal law. In the past, U.S. marshals have been used to control riots, implement court-ordered integration of schools and protect commercial airliners from skyjackers.

In the 1980s, the federal government mobilized to combat violent crime in the United States by establishing the National Center for Analysis of Violent Crime (NCAVC) and the Violent Criminal Apprehension Program (VICAP). Both units collect and assess data and help local police agencies solve, apprehend, prosecute and, ultimately, prevent violent crime. The NCAVC includes the FBI's highly publicized criminal profiling operation and the VICAP uses vast database resources to track down serial criminals.

Crime Laboratories

Today's sophisticated crime-fighting equipment and scientific methods would astound Sherlock Holmes, but Holmes never sat in front of a TV for programs like *CSI: New York*. Nearly everyone now knows how computer-powered sensing devices analyze and identify drugs; physical anthropologists reconstruct unidentified skeletal remains; and scientists link suspects to crimes through use of genetic DNA "fingerprints" taken from blood, semen or saliva samples.

Part of any police reporter's beat is the local crime lab. Only the largest of municipal departments have their own labs; most others rely on state, regional or federal labs.

Laboratory work begins at the crime scene, where evidence is carefully gathered and catalogued. The process can be flawed. In some instances, the police initially may decide a sudden death resulted from an accident or natural causes. Evidence is not immediately collected or secured. By the time police conclude a crime was committed, the evidence may have been mishandled or removed. In other instances, sloppy police work results in mislaid, damaged or incomplete evidence.

Once collected, scientific analysis of evidence is entrusted to crime laboratory technicians, whose effectiveness and thoroughness, obviously, are dependent on how effectively and thoroughly evidence was collected. Well-equipped laboratories can conduct ballistics tests; analyze blood, hair and saliva samples; administer polygraph examinations; classify drugs; examine documents; identify fabrics and other materials; and process, evaluate and compare fingerprints. Reality contrasts with the apparent speed and efficiency of TV's prime-time crime labs; in real life, tests and analyses often take weeks to complete, partly due to backlogs caused by stretched-thin staff.

Experienced police reporters know how tests are run and what they yield. Fingerprints, for example, can be collected and processed in a half-dozen ways, including the use of Super Glue, which helps detect fingerprints on metal and many other surfaces. (The Super Glue is heated on a piece of aluminum foil, and the fumes then adhere to the fingerprint residue, causing the prints to become visible.) In comparing prints taken at a crime scene to those taken from a suspect, police and prosecutors usually want a full enough print to make at least eight distinct points of comparison; the higher the number of comparison points, the better. Fingerprints remain an important tool to link a crime with a suspect, but other identification methods, including teeth imprints, lip, palm, heel and toe prints and, most recently, DNA tests of the body's unique genetic code, are used as well.

Reporters ought to observe how tests are conducted or, if possible, participate in tests, such as taking a polygraph examination. (How often do journalists refer to polygraph examinations without knowing the procedures, uses and limitations of the examination?)

With criminal cases pivoting frequently today with evidence collected, assessed and verified at trial by crime technicians, journalists inspect lab facilities and monitor procedures to ensure criminal prosecutions are not tainted by a law-and-order mentality, incompetence or outright corruption.

Medical Examiners

The "death detail" belongs to medical examiners and coroners. Medical examiners are usually appointed, professionally trained public servants; in many states they are required by statute to be a licensed physician, preferably a forensic pathologist, whose medical specialty is to determine causes of death. Coroners, however, are usually elected and often lack formal medical training. Few states require elected coroners to be physicians. Many coroners, in fact, are full-time funeral directors or mortuary employees, which poses a built-in conflict of interest if they solicit business while on official duty. Keep in mind that coroners, however, can be dedicated, honest and competent, and medical examiners, despite their academic and professional credentials, can be lackadaisical, corrupt or inept.

Both medical examiners and coroners are responsible for issuing death certificates and determining the "cause" and "manner" of deaths that do not appear to have been from natural causes. The *cause* refers to the medical reason for death, such as a gunshot wound or heart attack. The *manner* refers to circumstances that led to the death— accident, natural cause, suicide or homicide. Determining cause and manner of death is not always an easy task, and coroners, while they may have considerable practical experience, are limited in their resources. An autopsy, augmented by tests conducted by criminal lab technicians, may be required. Even after an *autopsy*—a pathologist's careful, video- and audio-recorded medical examination of the external and internal condition of the body—the question of cause and, more often, the manner of death may remain undetermined. On occasion, controversial findings may prompt legal challenges by dissatisfied family survivors or dubious law enforcement officials.

To aid in closing a case, some jurisdictions provide for a *coroner's inquest* before a jury. Evidence, witnesses and test results are presented to the jury, which tries to decide on the questions of cause and manner of death. Normally, such inquests are open to the press and public; moreover, they may yield more details about a case than the police are willing to release. The contents of an autopsy report, for example, might be presented at the inquest. In some states, autopsy reports, particularly audio- and videotapes, along with still photographs, are not covered by the open-records law.

Coroners and medical examiners work closely with the police and sometimes provide the key to solving a crime. A medical examiner in New York, for example, found a contact lens in one eye of a woman who had been raped and strangled. He told police to search the suspect's car for the other lens. They found it, and the lens helped bring a conviction in the case.[35]

Fire Departments and Emergency Services

September 11 elevated the public perception of firefighters to heroic stature. The police usually get most of the attention and the headlines. Now and then, a firefighter will be pictured rescuing a baby from a burning building or snatching a pet kitten from a tree limb. But most of the time, firefighters and emergency-medical technicians (EMT) aid people at great risk—anonymously. Reporters do not get to know them as they do the police. They should, of course. After the mind-searing events of September 11, we cannot help but remember the hundreds who rushed to the World Trade Center and died trying to save lives.

Beyond tales of their bravery in the face of disaster, firefighters and emergency crews—more recently described as "first responders"—are valuable sources in the relatively mundane world of traffic accidents and crime. Frequently, they arrive at the scene ahead of the police and are the first to assess the situation and talk to victims and witnesses. Cool and well trained, they are highly reliable sources, as well. They also may be freer than the police to talk to reporters.

Reporters need to build contacts and observe the work of emergency personnel, like paramedics and emergency medical technicians (EMTs). Tour their stations, learn about their equipment, accompany them in training and in action. Well-informed reporters ask better, more focused questions; they know, for example, without asking, why firefighters quickly use axes or power saws to cut a hole in the roof of a blazing building. They know, too, that firefighters rely, as the police do, on accurate, detailed information, available through computer databases, about specifications and risks of dealing with emergenices in high-rise buildings, chemical plants and industrial complexes.

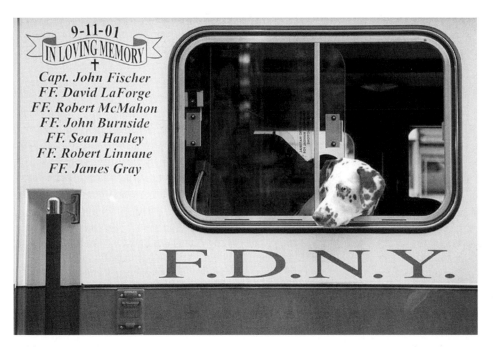

Dalmatian on duty   The black-and-white spotted Dalmatian has been associated with firefighters since the days of horse-drawn firefighting wagons. The oft-repeated story has the fearless Dalmatians racing ahead of the wagons, barking loudly. At the fire, the Dalmatian would soothe the jittery horses and keep them company. Today, the Dalmatian largely serves a ceremonial role and rides in the fire engine cab, such as this one in New York City. (Photo by Robbie Arkovich.)

At fire scenes and accidents, give emergency crews time and room to do their jobs. At first you might concentrate on talking to bystanders, witnesses, survivors—whoever can help you learn who, what, where, why and how. During a lull in the action or once the crisis stage has passed, then talk to fire officials and others involved in handling the fire or emergency. If you have cultivated relationships, the emergency crews will not be strangers.

REPORTER'S TIP FILE

When a disaster strikes

Earthquakes, plane crashes, chemical-plant explosions, bridge collapses and tornados occur quickly, with little or no warning. Since September 11, we guard against—but plan for—foreign terrorist attacks on American soil.

All news organizations should have disaster plans, as far as they can be developed. No amount of preparation can anticipate every development or every problem. But there should be at least a basic plan to provide for the notification, deployment and coordination of the news staff. A list of names, addresses and telephone numbers of key information sources—police, emergency services, hospital officials, state and federal disaster agencies—should be at hand. An emergency power system may be needed to stay on the air or to publish.

When emergency teams rehearse for a disaster, news media people ought to rehearse along with them, not only to assess the strengths and weaknesses of the agencies involved but also to test their own responsiveness.

When the real thing occurs, journalists must engage in calm, accurate reporting; otherwise they risk adding to the initial confusion, misinformation and anxiety. News organizations need to verify and reverify information before making it public. Do not overly rely on official sources, who often lack an accurate, overall picture. Hurricane Katrina exposed more than the weaknesses of the levees encircling New Orleans. The monster storm also established that local, state and federal officials were ill-prepared to react to Katrina's approach and respond after it hit, even days afterwards, as flooding and power outages left thousands in dire straits, without medicine, food and shelter. News organizations covering Katrina and other major disasters seem better equipped to measure the impact and identify problems.

Joseph Scanlon, an authority on disaster response, further cautions journalists to be patient. "Rather than harass already overburdened officials with demands for precise information—how many injured, how many dead, what's the extent of the damage—the media should understand even the best planned response effort will take time to learn precisely what has happened and what needs to be done."[36] Do not rush onto the air, newspaper or Web site with casualty and damage figures; in the confusion, you can expect that they will be inflated.

Be understanding about the emotional trauma likely to affect victims, rescue workers and journalists themselves who live through or witness massive tragedies. When a crippled United Airlines jet crashed in a cornfield at Sioux City, Iowa, in 1989, killing 111, secretaries typing body-identification tags at a makeshift morgue were so overwhelmed by the grim task that psychologists were called in to console them. And survivors who fled the burning wreckage felt ashamed that they left fellow passengers behind. Similar stories emerged in mental aftershocks of the 1995 Oklahoma City bombing, September 11, 2001, and the Indian Ocean earthquake in 2004.

Journalists covering disasters should focus on five stages of reporting:

- Determining the dimensions of the disaster
- Providing the public with safety information and advice from officials
- Alerting the public to present and potential dangers
- Calming the public by emphasizing positive aspects of the disaster, particularly who and what was spared
- Assessing the situation as to causes or, if complications that contribute negatively to the crisis arise, determining who is responsible for the complications

When the breaking news cycle runs its course, there is still work to be done, says Joe Hight, managing editor of *The Oklahoman*. "Use newspaper (or station) and online product to provide forums on what people are thinking, words of encouragement, and offer lists for ways people can help and how they have helped (acts of kindness). Find ways people are helping and report on them throughout the recovery process. This provides hope for the community."[37]

Jails and Prisons

While police-beat reporters or court reporters frequently *write* about penal institutions, too often no one regularly and systematically covers the penal system as a *beat*. The result may be missed opportunities for important stories and a serious breakdown in the press's watchdog role. While many penal facilities are well run and free of abusive treatment, abuses are more apt to occur when the public and press are not watching. In June 2006, a special commission on prisons, offered this observation:

> Most Americans feel that life in prison and jail does not affect them. It takes an awful event to remind people that the dangers inside can endanger them: a large-scale riot that threatens to spill over into the community; a corrections officer who is killed on the job leaving a family behind; the spread of infectious disease from cell block to neighborhood block. When the emotional reaction to the awful headline fades, however, we are left only with the sinking feeling that prison is a problem with no solution. The temptation is always to look away, hoping the troubles inside the walls will not affect us.[38]

An ACLU official who testified before the commission called for "light, light and more light" on prisons, coming, in part, from "courageous news reporting."[39]

Even more problems exist in detention or treatment programs for juveniles. Overcrowded county jails and the popularity of programs like "Scared Straight" and "Tough Love" prompted development of "boot camps" and "academies" to hold and treat troubled teenagers through military-style discipline and punishment, both physical and psychological. Journalist Maia Szalavitz estimates between 10,000 and 100,000 teenagers were being held in such facilities in 2006. "Exact numbers are impossible to determine, because no one keeps track of the kids in these programs, most of which are privately run," she says.[40]

In some cases, the facilities are government-run by state employees. A growing number of penal institutions, however, come under the supervision of the private sector by contract with government agencies. Other private operations oversee detainment of troubled teenagers arranged by parents and, in a few cases, ordered by judges who offer a boot camp as an alternative to a conventional juvenile facility (usually a wing or component of the county jail complex). Szalavitz said if the camp or academy offers "treatment," health insurance usually covers some of the costs. She calls it "a billion-dollar business."

Deaths of teenagers at camps in Arizona, Florida and elsewhere shed light on a relatively hidden corner of juvenile crime and punishment. Florida moved to shut down its state-operated boot camps when a 14-year-old boy died after guards, wearing drill-instructor uniforms, beat, kicked and slammed him to the ground. Oversight by public officials and the press becomes doubtful when juveniles of the community are transferred to out-of-state camps or academies.

Not all of the nation's 5,000 jails, prisons, detention facilities and penitentiaries are open to reporters (see Chapter 4); do not expect to be made welcome. Each year, more prisons come under the management of private companies, which compounds problems for reporters trying to visit or interview inmates. If reporters are allowed access, it may be limited to portions of the facility. Bans or unacceptable limits on access to facilities or prisoners should always be challenged. County jails tend to be more open than state or federal prisons, partly because many of the people detained in county jails are not serving time; they are awaiting trial or judicial action, and, until judged, they are presumed innocent. In most cases, if they had money or property to put up, they would be free on bail. As a result, detainees at a county jail may have comparatively liberal visitor and phone privileges.

Police-beat reporters are wise to make the county jail a part of their rounds. For one thing, crime occurs at jail—stabbings, rapes, murders. Usually, the crime is the work of the detainees, but guards commit crimes, too. Unwatched, jail crime may go unreported. In addition, good feature material is to be found in the jail, yielding stories on such subjects as "Scared Straight" tours for juvenile offenders, the traffic in contraband, prison ministers and their work, educational-vocational programs, letter-writing scams by inmates and overmedication and prolonged incarceration of mentally disabled prisoners.

A regular check of the county jail roster to see who has been admitted recently also serves as a back-up system, especially for reporters who suspect the police are withholding records of some arrests.

Do not be reluctant to seek interviews with suspects and inmates. In fact, you might want to encourage particular individuals to call or write you. Communication with an inmate might amount only to jailhouse jive. Then again, a memorable story could emerge.

That is what happened to Peter Franceschina of the *News-Press* in Fort Myers, Fla., when he interviewed, by telephone, Samuel A. Pettit, known as "Wild One," who spoke from the county jail. Pettit, accused of the murder of an assistant state attorney and the attempted murder of a female companion, another assistant state attorney, seemed to gloat over the killing, saying, "I think I should have done better 'cause she [the survivor] lived. . . . I would've killed her, too." In a chilling page 1 account, Pettit described his attack on the pair. Told of the interview, the prosecutor handling the case said, "That's amazing. I still can't believe prisoners in jail have phones. That blows my mind. He has not given us any statement, any statement about the shooting or a confession."[41] Although publication of a "confession" like Pettit's poses questions of free press versus fair trial and could result in the reporter being subpoenaed to testify in court, the episode is a dramatic example of enterprising prison reporting.

In some ways, covering the police beat is like running in a relay race. Police reporters cover crimes and arrests, then the baton is passed on to the courthouse reporters, who run the next leg of the process—coverage of the disposition of criminal cases. Often, however, it is an uncoordinated exercise in news coverage. The next chapter on the courts beat, therefore, begins with criminal law, then moves on to various aspects of civil law.

Exercises

1. See whether your city's police or sheriff's department has a "ride-along" program that allows civilians to go on patrol. Although a ride-along tends to be a managed experience, it is still a good way to meet police officers and observe how they go about their work.

2. Crime technicians often labor in relative obscurity despite the TV programs fictionalizing their work. Make arrangements to meet with a crime technician and tour crime-laboratory facilities. Among the interesting work to be observed is ballistics testing and drug analysis. You should find numerous possibilities for a feature story about the technician's role in criminal investigations.

3. Most communities now have counselors or specialists assigned to the police department who assist victims of crime. Interview a counselor and learn what the job entails. If it can be arranged, also talk to a crime victim who needed counseling.

Notes

1. Edna Buchnan, "Advice from One of the Best Police Reporters Around," *ASNE Bulletin*, April 1986, p. 10.
2. Rolf Rykken, "The Police Beat—Not Exactly a Dead Beat," *presstime*, September 1988, p. 6.
3. Russell Baker, *The Good Times* (New York: William Morrow, 1989), p. 53.
4. Edna Buchanan, *The Corpse Had a Familiar Face* (New York: Random House, 1987), p. 81.
5. "13th Annual City Crime Rankings," http://www.morganquitno.com/awards.htm#CIT.
6. Valerie J. Callanan, *Feeding the Fear of Crime* (New York: LFB Scholarly Publishing, 2005), p. 7.
7. Roger Rosenblatt, "Murder in the Safest Places," *U.S. News & World Report*, Jan. 23, 1989, p. 7.
8. Leon Dash, "Rosa Lee & Me," *Washington Post*, Oct. 2, 1994. Also see Leon Dash, *Rosa Lee: A Mother and Her Family in Urban America* (New York: Basic Books, 1996).
9. Joseph Wambaugh, *Lines and Shadows* (New York: Morrow, 1984), p. 24.

10. Harry Jones and Bill Farr, "Law Enforcement," in John Ullmann and Steve Honeyman, eds., *The Reporter's Handbook* (New York: St. Martin's Press, 1983), p. 329.

11. "Behind the Badge," *48 Hours*, CBS News, Jan. 5, 1989.

12. Tammerlin Drummond, "Killing Still Haunts Officer of the Year," *St. Petersburg Times*, March 7, 1989, City Times, pp. 1, 3.

13. David Klinger, *Into the Kill Zone* (San Francisco, Calif.: Jossey-Bass, 2004), p. 271.

14. Mark Baker, *Cops: Their Lives in Their Own Words* (New York: Pocket Books, 1986), p. 7.

15. Joseph D'Amico, "Stopping Crime in Real Time," *The Police Chief*, September 2006, pp. 20–24.

16. Patrick McMahon, "311 Lightens Load for Swamped 911 Centers," http://www.usatoday.com/news/nation/2002/03/05/usat-311.htm.

17. National Commission on Terrorist Attacks upon the United States, http://www.9-11commission.gov.

18. Bob Port, "Merits of Hogtying Suspects Debated by Police Experts," *St. Petersburg Times*, Feb. 16, 1989, p. 8B.

19. "USA: Renewed Call for Suspension as Taser-Related Deaths Pass 150 Mark," http://news.amnesty.org/index/ENGAMR510392006.

20. Neill Borowski, "Investigative Journalists Look at Police Pursuits," *The American Editor*, November–December 2005, p. 19.

21. Chip Scanlan, "Tips for Covering Cops," *Poynter Online*, Dec. 3, 2002.

22. Amy Herdy and Eric Deggans, "Police, TV Media See Shooting Differently," *St. Petersburg Times*, July 15, 2001.

23. Richard Kobel, "Some Agencies Seek Harmony in Police-Press Ties," *Law Enforcement Newsletter*, Aug. 25, 1988, p. 13.

24. Buchanan, "Advice from One of the Best Police Reporters Around," p. 12.

25. Ellen Goodman, "The Confusion of Racism and Crime," *St. Petersburg Times*, May 3, 1989, p. 18A.

26. U.S. Department of Justice, http://www.ojp.usdoj.gov/bjs/homicide/race.htm. Also see William Wilbanks, "Is Violent Crime Intraracial?" in Delos H. Kelly, ed., *Criminal Behavior*, 2nd ed. (New York: St. Martin's Press, 1990), pp. 94–103.

27. Ted Joy, "Why Was the Story Kissed Off?" *The Quill*, May 1989, pp. 20–23, 26–27.

28. Joy, p. 27.

29. William McGowan, *Coloring the News* (San Francisco: Encounter Books, 2004).

30. Quoted in John DeMott, "White Racism in the Newspaper," *The Masthead*, Winter 1981, p. 10.

31. Geneva Overholser, "Moving beyond Naming Names," *Washington Post*, Sept. 4, 2004, p. A31.

32. Angela Duerson Tuck and Stevan Allen, "Van Strikes, Kills Girl in Oldsmar," *St. Petersburg Times*, Oct. 28, 1988, p. 3B.

33. Charlotte Sutton, "Trying to Add a Human Touch to News," *St. Petersburg Times*, Nov. 13, 1989, City Times, p. 3.

34. "Christopher Lukas and Henry M. Seiden, *Silent Grief: Living in the Wake of Suicide* (Northvale, N.J.: Jason Aronson, 1997).

35. Ullmann and Honeyman, *The Reporter's Handbook*, p. 341.

36. Joseph Scanlon, "Media Cover Disasters by Rote," *content*, November–December 1988, p. 37.

37. Joe Hight, "Five Steps to Covering a Disaster Effectively," Dart Center for Journalism and Trauma, http://dartcenter.org/articles/special_features/covering_disasters.html.

38. *Confronting Confinement* (Washington, D.C.: Commission on Safety and Abuse in America's Prisons, 2006), p. iii.

39. *Confronting Confinement*, p. 78.

40. Maia Szalavitz, "The Trouble with Troubled Teen Programs," *Reasononline*, January 2007.

41. Peter Franceschina, "Pettit Admits to Killing Young Lawyer," *News-Press*, Fort Myers, Fla., Aug. 13, 1989, p. 1.

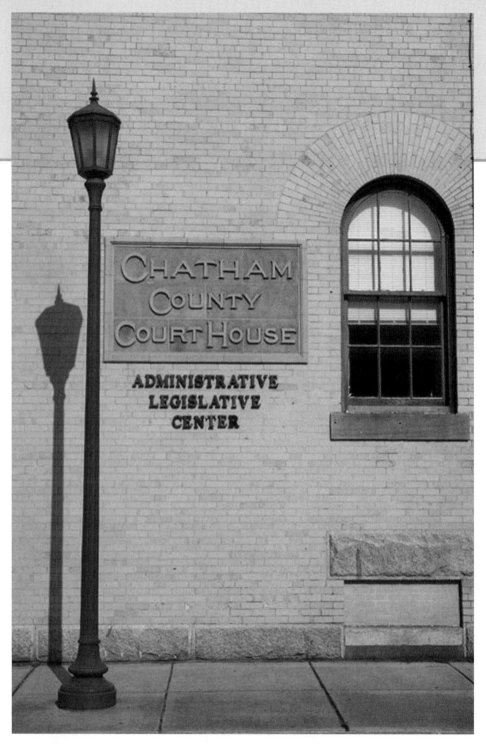

Shadows fall on Savannah's old courthouse American courts operate from venerable buildings that capture the history and pride of the community. Today's modern courthouses seldom match the character and architecture of the buildings they have replaced. Savannah's old courthouse remains in use as a government center. (Photo by Robbie Arkovich.)

Into the Legal Maze 8

Columnist Ellen Goodman often tells engaging stories about the law and its sometimes extraordinary implications. In one, she described the experience of John Moore, a 43-year-old Seattle sales manager whose treatment for leukemia included removal of his spleen. Moore's doctors, though, did not tell him that tissue from his spleen would be used for important research. The research led to development of a cell-line for treating cancer, which the doctors patented and negotiated into multimillion-dollar contracts with a bioengineering firm and a pharmaceutical company.

Moore eventually filed a lawsuit, arguing that he deserved to share in the profits. A California appeals court agreed, finding that blood and bodily substances are an individual's "tangible personal property." Goodman raises several issues in analyzing Moore's case, including whether it could lead people to "market their tissue as if it were pork bellies or wheat futures. If we discover the cure for AIDS in one person's blood, he or she can offer blood up for auction." To which she added, "None of this paints a very attractive picture."[1]

Goodman and scores of other columnists and reporters frequently focus on legal issues because they involve gripping tales of human tragedy—and folly. While trials seem to attract the most attention from the news media, court coverage involves much more than highly publicized spectacles before judges and juries. In fact, few legal matters—civil or criminal—ever go to trial. The vast majority of cases are settled or negotiated, sometimes just minutes before the jury is seated. Yet as scores of reporters recorded every salacious detail of the Michael Jackson child-molestation trial in 2005 or recounted each gruesome piece of evidence raised against Scott Peterson in the murder of his pregnant wife, Laci, in 2004, substantial portions of the legal beat remain in the shadows.

The preoccupation of press and public with the sensational side of the law sometimes deflects attention from thousands of day-to-day stories, played out not before television cameras and standing-room-only crowds of reporters and spectators, but in near-empty courtrooms, private conference rooms and judges' chambers. Many of these stories are as important and as intriguing as those emerging from more celebrated cases.

Ours is a litigious society, which is not necessarily a problem. As a nation of law, most often we seek justice and resolve disputes through a relatively civilized process of jurisprudence. But unwarranted and insignificant litigation can clog the courts, complicating the work of reporters and judicial officials alike. What happens when enraged Washington Redskins football fans go to court in an effort to overturn a referee's controversial touchdown call or a 24-year-old man sues his parents for $350,000 on grounds of parental malpractice? The courts must deal with an unusual assortment of legal issues, and because some of these issues are outrageously odd, the press reports them.

QUOTABLES

"Almost invariably, *every* story about public life in the United States, or private life interesting enough to get into the newspaper, will mention a law, a legal proposal, a bill in Congress or in the state legislature, or something a judge, a policeman, a court, a lawyer has done or said; or some statement from the president or other high officials, in any case always about some affair or situation or event done by, with, through, or against the law. In the world we live in—the country we live in—almost nothing has more impact on our lives, nothing is more entangled with our everyday existence, than that something we call the *law.*" (p. 3)

—Lawrence M. Friedman, *Law in America*, New York: Modern Libary, 2004

Actually, there is far too much happening in the courts for the news media to cover all that merits coverage. But included among the legal developments that *must* be covered are some of society's most controversial, far-reaching issues, which come before the courts for resolution. The challenges and complexities of our legal system demand that reporters be on duty as explainers, interpreters and watchdogs. In those roles, it is vitally important that reporters know the law in theory, principle and practice.

Lyle Denniston, long-time court reporter and author of *The Reporter and the Law*, reminds journalists to report legal news simply and clearly so laypeople will find it understandable and useful. Doing so requires special ability: "To be able to write simply, any journalist—on the court beat or elsewhere—must understand penetratingly. The language of the law and its processes can be excruciatingly precise and arcane. It is an accomplishment of major dimensions to translate it into the popular vernacular, and to lose nothing of consequence in the translation."[2]

Denniston values a balanced preparation of legal training and general knowledge so reporters can see the law in terms of its broad social utility. The common denominator for journalists is knowledge and respect for the law. The best court reporters know that hasty, ill-informed and sensationalized treatment does not serve the law or the public.

The law in all of its forms and processes cannot be explained adequately in a few pages of a journalism textbook. Indeed, what follows is a departure point for journalists who wish to cover the legal system intelligently and responsibly. By necessity, the chapter, in sections, reads like a civics book. Consider it a primer for reporters unschooled in our system of law.

The Judicial System: Structure and Process

The United States has 51 court systems—one for each state, plus the federal system. Although all share certain characteristics, each system exhibits differences in procedures, rules and terminology. In one state, for example, those who prosecute criminal cases are called *district attorneys*; in a neighboring state, prosecutors are called *state attorneys*; in the federal system, they are known as *U.S. attorneys*. An *initial appearance* and an *arraignment* usually are two distinct criminal proceedings, but in a few jurisdictions the terms are synonymous. Grand jury witnesses are banned from discussing their testimony outside court chambers in some courts—but not in others. Reporters must know the differences between systems and never assume that what is done in one jurisdiction is surely permissible in another.

Federal courts have jurisdiction over cases that arise under the U.S. Constitution and the civil statutes and criminal laws of the United States. Federal crimes include acts of treason, counterfeiting and interstate transportation of stolen property; crimes committed on federal property also fall under federal jurisdiction.

In civil law, federal courts exclusively handle bankruptcy, patent, copyright and trademark cases. Occasionally, federal courts resolve civil disputes between two or more states or take jurisdiction over civil litigation between citizens of two different states when damages sought exceed, at present, $75,000.

The jurisdiction of the state courts extends to basically any type of case that does not fall within the exclusive jurisdiction of the federal courts. Examples of cases within the jurisdiction of the state courts include crimes defined by state law, such as murder or armed robbery; tort and personal injury litigation; contract law; probate (validation of wills); family law, including divorce, adoption and child custody; municipal ordinances; and motor vehicle regulations.

To help the news media understand and report on the law, the federal Administration Office of the United States Courts publishes and regularly updates *A Journalist's Guide to the Federal Courts* (www.uscourts.gov). State bar associations often publish comparable guides, such as Florida's *Reporter's Handbook* (www.floridabar.org).

The federal system and a number of state systems use a three-tier structure: *trial courts*, *appellate courts* and a *supreme court*. Not all systems are organized this way; many have additional courts with limited or special duties, such as *family court*, which handles matters like non-payment of child support and adoptions, or *probate court*, which is responsible for supervising the disposition of estates and determining the authenticity of wills (see Chapter 9 as well).

In both civil and criminal law, nearly all cases—federal and state—begin at the trial level. Verdicts, findings, judgments and rulings made by trial courts may go on to an intermediate level of appellate courts, where they are reviewed for errors or misapplication of the law. Appeals courts, usually comprising three or more judges, do not retry the case, calling witnesses and examining evidence. Instead, sitting either on *panels* of less than full membership of the court or *en banc*, with all members present, they review the facts and the records of a case, deciding whether to uphold or overrule the trial court's action. Although civil and criminal defendants are free to appeal, normally there are no guarantees that a case will receive full review. Appellate and supreme courts exercise broad discretionary power in accepting cases.

The Long and Winding Road

Going to court seldom is a simple matter. Complications, for instance, can arise in determining which court holds *jurisdiction* over a legal matter. Ordinarily, state courts address civil and criminal issues dealing with state law or occurring within the boundaries of the state and involving citizens of that state. Federal courts address violations or questions of federal law or legal issues involving different states or citizens of different states. At times, the distinctions between federal and state jurisdiction become blurred.

In criminal cases particularly, multiple violations of federal and state law are possible, which means multiple prosecutions are possible as well. A husband and wife, for example, are abducted from a shopping center parking lot in New York. The husband is killed while the abductors are still in New York. The wife is taken to a remote area in New Jersey, where she is raped and murdered. State authorities in both New York and New Jersey could pursue charges against the abductors; U.S. authorities could do likewise because federal laws covering interstate crime apply. In criminal cases, jurisdictional problems usually are worked out among the prosecutors involved because of a common goal—the prosecution of criminal acts.

Civil law poses even more problems. When jurisdiction is not clear, lawyers and litigants in civil cases often will seek the court that appears to offer them a strategic advantage. Under the right circumstances, for example, rail or barge workers injured on the job may file suit in a court hundreds of miles from the site of their injuries or homes, provided the railroad or barge company operates within that court's jurisdictional boundaries. As a result, thousands of such lawsuits have ended up in the circuit courts of Illinois' Madison and St. Clair counties, which are known as "plaintiff's counties" for the high monetary damages juries there typically award in personal-injury suits.[3] Struggles over jurisdictional questions might lead to additional legal action, such as a motion for a *change of venue*—a request to have a case heard in another location.

Beyond problems over jurisdiction, the judicial path a case follows can be tortuous and unpredictable. Consider this example: An accountant files a libel suit in the local state court after the hometown newspaper publishes a story in which a half-dozen unidentified clients accuse him of fraud. One of the first steps by the accountant's lawyers is to ask the reporter to identify her unnamed sources. The reporter refuses, even after the trial judge orders disclosure. The judge finds her in contempt of court and orders the reporter to jail.

The newspaper's lawyers then challenge the judge's action through what is called an *interlocutory appeal*, which allows a higher court to settle a disputed point of law that could bear on how the case is tried. As a result, the battle over confidential sources might have to be resolved by an appellate court's ruling before the libel case can progress. Along the way, there may be numerous legal twists and turns before final resolution; it certainly is not a linear process. In fact, the case could meander through the courts for years before running its full course of motions, trial and appeals.

Finally, litigation often is costly, both emotionally and financially. Two dramatic examples in 1989 occupied the news on the same day—October 9. In Atlanta, testimony opened in the first of seven scheduled civil trials in a sex-abuse case involving ex-employees of a treatment center for troubled youths. Lawyers took three years preparing for the trial, which is not surprising for a case with 124 plaintiffs, 31 defendants and 10,000 pages of documents. In Los Angeles, final arguments started in a 30-month-long trial against preschool employees accused of molesting 11 children. According to news reports, it was the nation's longest and costliest ($15 million) criminal case and apparently remains so, although the O.J. Simpson murder trial in 1996 trial may have exceeded it in total costs. *USA Today* said Los Angeles Country spent $9 million to prosecute Simpson; Simpson's legal "Dream Team," led by famed defense attorney Johnny Cochran, probably upped the ante considerably.[4]

On appeal, cases like these may drag on for several more years, adding to an already heavy toll. Litigation in the Terri Schiavo case lasted nearly eight years. In 1990, at the age of 26, she collapsed in her Florida home and lapsed into a coma. In 1998, her husband and guardian, Michael Schiavo, petitioned the courts to remove her gastric feeding tube, which her parents fiercely opposed. By March 2005, the legal history around the Schiavo case included 14 appeals and dozens of motions, petitions, and hearings in the Florida courts; five lawsuits in federal district court; and four appeals for *certiorari* to the U.S. Supreme Court, all of which were denied. In related litigation, the Florida supreme court struck down legislation hastily enacted to keep her alive, and a congressional committee attempted to qualify Terri Schiavo for witness protection. With the appeal process exhausted, a Florida judge ordered the tube removed, and Terri Schiavo died 13 days later on March 31, 2005. The ethical and medical fallout continued long after the ligitation ended.[5]

Roots and Branches of Law

To this point, the word *law* has been used to refer to the U.S. system of courts and judicial processes governing them. *Law,* in another sense of the word, refers to the legally enforceable rules by which society lives.

U.S. law, in its broader meaning, is like a sturdy, pliable tree, with deep roots and a thicket of branches. At the tree's core is the United States Constitution—the law of the land. Forming the branches are state constitutions, federal and state statutes, local ordinances, court opinions, administrative rulings, executive orders and other legal pronouncements, which combine and, at times, interrelate to form our body of law.

Common law

Our legal system is rooted in *common law,* which originated in medieval England as a practical means for the king's courts to settle disputes that were not covered by written laws. Today, common law amounts to centuries of accumulated legal precedent, much of it based on sensible resolutions of conflicts. Under the common law of many states, for example, unwed couples who cohabit for a period of years are considered legally married—a "common law marriage." Judges continue to create and interpret common law because it remains a flexible, useful means of addressing life's unanticipated or uncharted legal problems.

Statutory law

Legislation passed by elected officials on the local, state or federal level of government is called *statutory law*. Statutory law is *codified*—that is, it is organized and maintained in books and volumes referred to as *codes*; statutory law includes criminal codes as well. Every year, thousands of new laws are created by local, state and federal legislators. The Pottsville city council, for example, enacts an ordinance requiring a building-safety inspection before any home in the city can be sold and occupied. On the same day, Congress passes a statute amending the federal tax code's provisions on interest deductions. Although both pieces of legislation would be widely reported— one locally, the other nationally—the public may be unaware and uninformed about most areas of statutory law, which on all levels of government is simply too voluminous to report in any comprehensive way.

Administrative law

Administrative law primarily encompasses rules and regulations formulated by state or federal regulatory agencies, such as the Federal Communications Commission or the Internal Revenue Service. These rules and regulations have a legal effect comparable to a statute. *Executive orders* fall in the same category. These are pronouncements issued by the president or, on the state level, by governors, setting policies and rules for the executive branch of government. The president, for example, might order all federal agencies to establish procedures to punish employees who leak sensitive information to the press.

Constitutional law

The U.S. Constitution and the various state constitutions define the powers of government and the rights of citizens. *Constitutional law* generally refers to judicial interpretation of the meaning and scope of these documents. Changing times and newly emerging societal problems pressure the courts to examine and re-examine constitutional law.

The judicial system ultimately touches each element of law—constitutional law, statutory law, common law, administrative law and executive orders—because all law is subject to legal challenge and review by the courts. The city council's ordinance on home inspections, Congress' statute on tax deductions and the president's order to plug leaks are bound to generate controversy and debate, probably leading to legal action of some sort.

All law, however, including law established by state constitutions, is subservient to the United States Constitution. No legislative body or agency can sustain a law that is in conflict with the rights and liberties guaranteed in the federal Constitution. Of course, thousands of legal disputes have focused on what the Constitution's words do or do not protect. The final authority is the nine-member United States Supreme Court, empowered to interpret the Constitution and decide all legal challenges, even if the result finds the actions of Congress or the president unconstitutional or over-rules the decision of a lower court or even one of its own decisions.

Principles, Characteristics and Qualities

Although not unchangeable, the law is quite stable, based on time-honored principles. One principle in particular distinguishes the judicial system: the *doctrine of judicial review*. Of the three branches of government—judicial, legislative and executive—the judiciary enjoys a special status because it alone can decide the meaning of state and federal constitutions. Therefore, a court, exercising its power of judicial review, can nullify the unconstitutional action of any government within its jurisdiction. Of course, a single court's power is not absolute and rarely unchallengeable, which is why the judicial system includes many opportunities to appeal decisions and rulings.

Another fundamental principle is *stare decisis*—the policy of courts to stand by precedent and adhere to points of law settled by previous court decisions. When a legal problem arises, judges and attorneys consider how other courts dealt with simi-lar problems. But even the principle of *stare decisis* bends. Precedent does not always fit a particular case, requiring courts to seek new solutions. Moreover, courts must depart at times from outdated or faulty precedent to ensure justice or to serve the public interest. If that were not true, America's public schools would still be racially segregated under the "separate but equal" doctrine.

Energizing and fueling the judicial process is the *adversarial principle*. Our system of justice, in fact, depends on each side in a civil or criminal action to fight with all its legal resources. Ideally, truth and justice emerge from such a spirited contest.

The system, though, is far from perfect. Consider some of its flaws and limitations:

The adversarial principle works best when the contest is fought among equals
The fact is, money often can buy better legal representation. An overworked pub-lic defender may see his indigent client for the first time a few minutes before a court appearance. In a nearby courtroom, an immaculately groomed criminal suspect huddles with a high-priced, influential attorney in private practice, paid a hefty fee in advance and backed by the research of a team of other lawyers and specialists. Assuming the state's evidence against both is comparable, which defendant stands a better chance of staying out of jail?

Truth and justice are abstractions
Whose truth? Whose justice? Somebody wins, somebody loses, and truth and justice do not always prevail. At times, technicalities and loopholes determine the outcome

of cases. A burglary suspect is freed because an inexperienced police officer conducted an improper search of the suspect's apartment; a factory worker who lost an arm in a plant accident loses the opportunity to sue because his attorney waited too long to file the case (although he later might be able to sue his attorney for malpractice). Unfortunately, the judicial system, like other areas of human endeavor, displays ignorance, ineptitude and dishonesty.

Ambiguity permeates the law

Many laws are subject to widely differing interpretations. William P. Statsky, an expert on legal analysis, uses the following statute section as a simple but effective example of this ambiguity:

> Chronic alcoholic means a person who, in consequence of prolonged excessive drinking, has developed a diagnosable bodily disease or mental disorder.

Statsky provides an 18-point list of ambiguities in the statute. For example, what does "prolonged" mean? A period of years? If someone drinks night and day for two weeks, is that "prolonged"? By the time Statsky finishes picking apart the passage, it is easy to see how it could be read in a dozen or more ways.[6]

Often the system must make pragmatic compromises simply to keep the wheels of justice from grinding to a halt. In criminal law, plea bargaining generally results in reduced charges and lighter sentences. In civil law, settlements and deals may or may not serve the best interests of the parties involved. Moreover, not every case can—or should—go to trial.

Politics and the law are frequently inseparable

Many state judges either are elected or must stand before voters periodically for *retention votes*. Prosecutors, too, are often elected officials; some possess ambitions to hold higher office, including a judge's post. As a result, courthouses can be hotbeds of politics, and court officials may practice the most expedient or personally profitable form of law. Measures passed by local, state and federal legislators often reflect the agendas of political organizations or special interests, adding another thick layer of politics to the law.

The law is dynamic

The world changes, people change, customs change, technology changes. The law must adapt. Medical advances alone have forced the courts to address extraordinarily difficult questions involving life-support measures, surrogate motherhood, fetal tissue and genetic engineering. A courthouse saying applies: "Hard law makes for bad law," meaning that rigidity and inflexibility in either wording or application of law can pose problems.

Despite its flaws and limitations, however, the law touches lives, often in deep, lasting ways. From divorce decrees to murder verdicts, people are affected, which is something reporters must never forget. Constantly focus on the law for its human implications. The *Chicago Tribune's* Linnet Myers, winner of an ASNE best news-writing award, is a model for producing stories such as this one:

> Murderers walk these halls, and the mothers of murderers, and the mothers of the murdered too.
>
> This is 26th and California.
>
> Step through the metal detectors and enter the multicolored stream of humanity that flows through the Criminal Court building each day. It is the largest felony-trial system under one roof in the United States. In 34 courtrooms, nothing but felonies are heard: murders, manslaughters, sexual assaults, armed robberies, burglaries, drug cases. Last year, 19,632 cases were heard here.
>
> Officially, it is the Cook County Circuit Court, Criminal Division. But those who work here refer to it by its near Southwest Side location, 26th Street and California Boulevard—known simply as "26 & Cal."
>
> Outside, on the building's noble limestone walls, are carved the Latin words *veritas* and *Justitia*—truth and justice.
>
> Inside is a world the average Chicagoan never sees.[7]

As Myers knew by experience, the realities of the law can make covering the courts exasperating and confusing; they also can make coverage challenging, exciting and rewarding.

Civil Cases

Because of extensive press coverage and treatment of criminal cases in movies and television programs, most people have a passing familiarity with the fundamentals of criminal law—from arrest to trial. Civil law not only is less visible; it also tends to be more complex. In civil litigation, one party—whether an individual, corporation, group or government—battles a second party to correct alleged wrongs or seek redress for damages. The variety of proceedings and legal subjects under civil law is practically limitless, with new areas of civil law emerging to meet new problems.

Among the most common civil suits are those arising from traffic accidents. In a typical scenario, a delivery truck and a compact car collide on an icy bridge, leaving the driver of the car paralyzed by a neck injury. The driver sues the delivery person, his employer and the truck's manufacturer, claiming several counts of negligence. If the court finds sufficient evidence of negligence, the jury or judge's award for monetary damages might run into the millions of dollars.

Civil actions involving recovery for damages come under a category of cases known as *at law*. Other actions at law include disputes over breach of contract, invasion of privacy, product liability, professional malpractice or defamation of character.

A second category of civil action is known either as *equity* or *chancery*. Frequently, equity cases involve a request for court-ordered protection against an existing or impending wrong. A historic-preservation group, for example, attempts to stop a shopping mall developer from bulldozing a landmark—a 150-year-old home—to make way for a parking lot. The preservationists ask the court to issue a *temporary restraining order* to gain time to mount a legal argument and develop a plan of action, such as relocation of the building to a nearby park. Later, before both parties, the judge might issue a *permanent injunction*, ordering the developer to leave the home intact. Most often, all factual and legal issues in equity cases are decided solely by a judge and do not go to a jury for determination.

Cases in the category of *extraordinary* (or special) remedy usually do not fit the normal conditions of a lawsuit in which damages are sought; often, special-remedy cases involve unusual or urgent issues, such as an alleged deprival of legal rights and liberties. In one widely publicized episode, the American Nazi party, aided by the American Civil Liberties Union, successfully contested the efforts of city officials in Skokie, Ill., to ban Nazis from holding a rally, wearing military uniforms and displaying the Nazi symbol, the swastika. The City of Skokie and the Nazis battled on two main fronts. The first centered on the anti-rally injunction obtained by the city; the second focused on three ordinances the city quickly passed to block the Nazis' plans to gather in uniform. The cases warranted immediate, expedited appellate review because of the serious constitutional questions at stake.

Other special-remedy cases include changing a name, dissolving a corporation and challenging the action of a government official through a *quo warranto* proceeding to determine whether the official has the legal authority to take the action in question.

Combinations and complications are not only possible, they are probable. An entertainer suing to recover money from a business agent accused of misappropriating funds might first seek an injunction to bar the agent from further access to the entertainer's financial and business records. In addition, initial actions sometimes result in a spate of related litigation, as the Skokie–Nazi cases illustrate; in all, a half-dozen courts—state and federal—became involved over a period of 18 months.[8] Because civil actions frequently overlap, a number of court jurisdictions no longer distinguish cases as belonging to "law," "equity" or "special-remedy" categories, which has helped to streamline civil law.

If a civil case goes to trial, it should be decided in favor of the party with the most convincing, credible evidence, or what is known as either *preponderance of evidence* or *greater weight of evidence*. This is known as the "burden of proof" for a civil case decision. The burden of proof for a criminal case is higher; the defendant must be shown to be guilty *beyond a reasonable doubt*.

Commencing a Civil Action

Often, the first impulse of an aggrieved person is, "I'm going to sue!" At times, threatening to sue is merely a way to let off steam. Many conflicts are resolved informally, without resorting to litigation. An out-of-court process called alternative dispute resolution (ADR) has developed recently as an important step to avoid litigation. ADR typically includes arbitration, mediation and conciliation through such means as face-to-face negotiations and, occasionally, binding agreements. To offset the crush of lawsuits, more states have begun experimenting with ADR programs. Some of these programs are voluntary; others are mandatory. For journalists, ADR raises problems of access to proceedings and records, which usually are confidential. The Reporters Committee for Freedom of the Press fears the growing popularity of ADR potentially creates a system of "secret justice," denying the public the details of important consumer information about hazardous products, such as Firestone's infamous tires. Reporters should still attempt to cover ADR negotiations, especially when the public needs to know what is going on, but they can expect less access than afforded when disputes enter the court system.[9]

With a few exceptions—mainly petitioning to small-claims court—commencing a civil action requires the aid of an attorney. If the attorney believes there are grounds for a lawsuit, or a *cause for action,* the next step is preparation of a formal, written *complaint* or *petition* that states the facts, arguments and damages or relief sought. The person initiating a civil action is the *plaintiff,* and the action is directed against the *defendant.* The complaint is received, filed, recorded in a *docket book* and given a *case number* by the clerk of the court.

Civil complaints follow a format and procedure prescribed by each court system. Complaints may range in length from several paragraphs to dozens of pages; usually, they are written in stilted, formulaic language. The complaint might begin: "Now comes the plaintiff, Jane Doe, by her attorney, John Smith, and for her complaint against defendant Mary Brown, states as follows:. . . ." In some complaints, the basis for the suit—the *cause of action*—is detailed in a series of numbered *counts.* The damages or legal actions sought by the suit normally are stated at the conclusion of the complaint: "Wherefore, the plaintiff claims damages in the amount of. . . ."

A typical story based on the filing of a complaint would take this readable form:

> BEVERLY, Mass. — Parker Brothers filed suit Tuesday against the manufacturer of a board game that allegedly uses elements of Monopoly.
>
> The lawsuit, filed in federal court in New York, charges the Elusive Dream Marketing Service of El Cajon, Calif., with unfair competition and trademark violations for distributing a game called Cityopoly.
>
> Also named as defendants were the F.A.O. Schwarz and Saks Fifth Avenue retail stores.
>
> Parker Brothers seeks an injunction against the alleged use of Monopoly elements, plus unspecified damages.

The story would include comments by spokespersons for the plaintiff and defendant, if available and willing to talk.

The filing of a suit is followed by service of a *summons*—a legal notice—to the defendant. A summons usually is delivered by an officer of the court or a sheriff's deputy.

At times, summons servers must resort to disguises or ploys to reach an evasive defendant. Once properly served, the summons cannot be ignored, no matter how frivolous or unfair the defendant considers the complaint. Failure to respond to the summons could result in the court entering *judgment by default* in favor of the plaintiff.

A defendant is entitled to sufficient time to prepare and file an *answer*. In the answer, the defendant denies the claims in the complaint or enters a defense to the claims. Thereafter follows a period of pretrial motions and a process called *discovery*, during which both sides, under court order, must exchange information and evidence. One method of information exchange is accomplished by *interrogatories*, which are written questions from one party to the other. Interrogatories are supposed to be truthfully and fully answered. Oral interviews under oath are called *depositions*, which allow lawyers to question witnesses and parties in a case to gain information later needed to represent their clients in court. Depositions can last for days and involve hundreds of pointed questions and testy responses.

The steps described amount to the simplest of scripts for a civil action. Frequently, civil action is complicated by the legal strategies employed. A complaint, for example, might prompt a *motion to dismiss* or a *demurrer*, a request to discontinue a case because the complaint is legally insufficient. Other maneuvers by the defendant might include a legal counterattack in the form of a *cross-complaint*. After the defendant files an answer, more motions, such as one for a *summary judgment*, could follow. A judge's summary judgment decides the case for one party based on the facts presented in the *pleadings*—the complaint and answer, although some judges expect full discovery before considering a motion for a summary judgment. Summary judgments promptly end claims the judge believes to be legally unjustifiable.

Some action in a civil case occurs in private out-of-court meetings and communications between lawyers for the parties, outside the sight and earshot of reporters. During the discovery stage, records may be produced and depositions taken that might not be open to the press. Depositions can be quite newsworthy, but often they are considered the private work product of the lawyer unless officially filed with the court. There also may be several private pretrial conferences by lawyers in the presence of the judge. Pretrial conferences can lead to *stipulations*, which are agreements by both sides pertaining to the proceedings or use of evidence, such as the admissibility of photographs, videotapes or digital images or medical records.

Civil cases frequently end in *settlements* to avoid a costly, risky trial; at times, settlements are reached while a trial is in progress. Generally, one side or the other makes a settlement offer early in litigation. The settlement conditions and requirements sometimes are stipulated and agreed to jointly by the disputing parties and recorded under a court order. In other situations, particularly when a lawsuit can be satisfied by payment of a set sum of money, the plaintiff and defendant can simply file a notice to dismiss the case.

Going to trial is somewhat like throwing dice—for both sides. An automobile manufacturer, sued by a man badly burned when the gas tank of his pickup truck ruptured in a rear-end accident, may emerge from a trial with no damages assessed— or $5 million. The same range of possibilities exists for the plaintiff. So a settlement of $750,000 is reached. Once again, the press may not be privy to the conditions of settlements, which are often reached in private conferences between the opposing attorneys and their clients. In fact, a firm stipulation in some settlements is that neither party reveal any details, particularly the amount of money paid out.

Covering the Civil Courts

Covering the courts means regular visits in person to the *clerk of the court's* office, although information, increasingly, is available online. Reporters on the court beat, in fact, may check with court employees and examine records several times a day, keeping abreast of pending cases and looking for new filings to report. Some reporters check records right before the clerk's office closes to make sure an attorney does not try to slip a filing past the press. For the most part, reporters enjoy ready access to court documents, although they may not be allowed to retrieve certain records online.

As civil actions are received by the clerk's office, they are, as mentioned earlier, given case numbers and recorded in either a handwritten or computerized log. Without a case number, it is more difficult to track down records. Knowing the names of the parties involved—*Jones v. National Tool & Die Co.*—may not be enough. Workers in the clerk's office are still likely to ask, "Well, what's the case number?" Court employees are busy, too, and do not appreciate being inconvenienced.

Journalists and attorneys alike keep track of court cases through what is commonly called the *docket* or *docket book.* Although the term "docket" has a number of definitions depending on the court or jurisdication, it most often means a calendar of the cases awaiting action in a court. Other meanings include (1) a brief entry of the court proceedings and actions in a legal case, (2) the book containing such entries and (3) a summary or other brief statement of the contents of a document.

REPORTER'S TIP FILE

Advice from the Bar

Journalists, jurists and attorneys in Maryland joined forces to produce a guide to court coverage. The following tips come from the online edition of the guidelines, available at www.legalguide.umd.edu.

Watch what you say around jurors and witnesses

It is natural to talk about what just went on in court, but during courtroom breaks, reporters, jurors and witnesses sometimes share the same hallway, elevators, restrooms and cafeterias. If jurors or witnesses overhear your conversations, a mistrial could result.

While court is in session, you must abide by the judge's rules

Some judges will prohibit anyone from leaving the courtroom until and unless there is a recess. Others will allow reporters and the public in and out of the courtroom as needed. Whatever the guidelines—and this includes where reporters or media artists sit—you must abide by them. Any significant problems can be directed to the court's administrative judge. (A special problem can arise if a court imposes a verbal or written restrictive order in a case. Reporters should legally challenge a judge's actions to restrict news coverage of a pending case. Chapter 4 gives advice on what to do when facing a restrictive order.)

Don't let your beeper or cell phone ring in court

Set your equipment to vibrate. Similarly, if you have a laptop computer, ask a deputy or the courtroom clerk if the judge will allow you to type in court—you may be relegated to the back row where you do not annoy others.

Do not conduct interviews in any part of the courtroom while court is in session

In the view of most judges, that would be like carrying on a discernible conversation during the middle of a religious service. When outside the courtroom, interviews can and should be conducted. The courthouse is a public building and the hallways are public areas. You have the right to request interviews; of course, participants in a trial have a right to refuse them.

Check documents, when available

You are permitted to read public documents relating to the case you are covering and may request them from the court clerk during a break in the trial. (Access to documents during the case might not be so free in certain courts or jurisdictions.)

Work with court personnel

Introduce yourself to the attorneys and check with them periodically on the status of any motions and the trial itself (e.g., the number of witnesses they plan to present, length of their presentations, the trial and hearing schedules).

Since reporters cannot attend all hearings or keep up with all legal moves and motions, they rely on court personnel and records to stay informed. In most civil actions, documents—such as complaints, pleadings and motions—are kept in a legal-size folder that is accessible to reporters, unless the folder temporarily is in the judge's hands. Customarily attached to the file is the *minute record*, a chronological summary of each stage of the case, citing, for example, when a summons was served or what a judge ruled on a motion to dismiss. As courts install computer systems, records are being stored in databases, making it more practicable for court officials and journalists to retrieve and analyze cases and keep tabs on cases going on in the courthouse.

Certain documents are particularly valuable. Access, however, can be a problem. Sensitive records may be sealed by the judge or put off limits by a court ruling. In a 1984 case, the Supreme Court said pretrial depositions and interrogatories "are not public components of a civil trial."[9] Nonetheless, as watchdogs of the judicial system, reporters should continue to argue for access to all court records. Remember that court records that are open one day may be closed the next if the judge decides to seal them. To guard against such a possibility, alert reporters immediately copy every relevant document filed in an important case.

Of course, patterns and frequency of courtroom coverage will vary, but reporters normally cannot spend hours listening to testimony that may not yield a story worth publishing. Indeed, they must be extremely selective.[10] The typical legal reporter usually pops in and out of courtrooms, covering important pretrial hearings or a key witness's testimony in a newsworthy trial. Of course, celebrated, significant local cases do draw full-time coverage; the day-to-day courthouse "routine" business of filings, motions and even jury trials does not. There is simply too much going on, but that can never be a reporter's excuse for inattentiveness. Citizens rely on courthouse reporters to stay alert and use their time wisely.

Monitoring all that goes on in the courts is not easy; in some jurisdictions, hundreds of cases may be filed in a single day. With so much going on, reporters need to cultivate people in the courts building who have a good sense of what is newsworthy and are willing to assist with tips and information.

Nearly all courts are inundated by litigation. The challenge for reporters is to decide which cases and legal developments warrant coverage. The news criteria for the courts beat include the old standards: timeliness, prominence, consequence, oddity, conflict, change and proximity. A single story might meet several criteria at once. A 52-year-old woman, for example, sued the heavy-metal band Motley Crue after suffering hearing damage at a concert. Although the suit eventually ended in an out-of-court settlement, the woman's attorney said the case, reportedly the first of its kind, quickly produced results around the country. It led several rock promoters to include noise warnings on the back of concert tickets and issue earplugs on request at theater entrances.[11]

Reading complaints and other court records often presents translation problems for reporters. In "legalese," for example, an auto accident description might read: "On the aforesaid date, the defendant did operate a motor vehicle in a southerly direction along and upon Main Street, in the 3200 block thereof, in a careless, negligent and intoxicated manner, so as to. . . ." Reporters must convert the language of lawyers into everyday English, avoiding legal jargon and technical descriptions of injuries or damages.

Writing for and about people helps court reporters cut to the significance of even the most complex of court cases. *New York Times* writer Andrew H. Malcolm humanized a lawsuit between AT&T and a handful of Ohio farmers in a clear story with an appealing opening:

> ATHENS, Ohio — In an old courtroom with peeling green paint, a college professor and some farmer friends are fighting with a giant telephone company over a hole in the ground.
>
> There is no grand constitutional issue at stake. Both sides fully expect the American Telephone & Telegraph Co.'s new fiber optic cable, 1 inch of rubber wrapped around 42 strands of glass, to go 4 feet under all those farm fields between Washington and St. Louis.
>
> There, beneath Don Flournoy's hay and Scott Ervin's cows, tiny bursts of light will carry 500,000 conversations simultaneously.
>
> What is at stake in this struggle seems more a point of personal pride or principle, with the farmers sending a message to someone, almost anyone, that they feel pushed around by strangers on their own land and they don't like it.[12]

You will not find any *wherefores* or *thereases* in Malcolm's reporting. The issues and history of the lawsuit are explained in lay language, resulting in a relevant story for city and country residents.

There is another aspect of humanizing court coverage: Reporters should never forget that emotions and reputations can be deeply affected by litigation. Care is needed at all times in court coverage but especially at the complaint-filing stage. Nearly anyone can find an attorney willing to file suit, no matter how silly or unfair the charges might be. It is also relatively easy for a reporter to scan a complaint, make a few calls and write a story focusing on the allegations and the damages sought. But a civil complaint merely *begins* the process of determining who is right and wrong or who is at fault and who is not.

Suits asking for multimillion-dollar judgments sound impressive and serious. They may not be. Avoid overreacting to the sheer amount of damages being asked. With the exception of *actual damages*, which are supposed to be based on measurable out-of-pocket costs or losses, the damages cited in a civil complaint may have no relationship to what is reasonable redress—or what the plaintiff ends up being awarded. Remember that by overplaying damages, you might cause readers and viewers—some of them potential jurors—to wrongly assume that a plaintiff's request for massive damages suggests grave wrongdoing on the defendant's part.

Calling the defendant for "reaction" to the complaint may seem to satisfy the reporter's duty to be fair, but often such an obligatory phone call merely is part of a tired formula for lawsuit stories. In fact, the defendant's first knowledge of the complaint may come from a reporter, leaving no opportunity for much more than a brief remark: "I can't comment until I read the complaint." For reporters, the temptation is to publish or broadcast charges in a complaint as soon as it is filed by the plaintiff;

to be fair to all parties, a more cautious, restrained approach may be required. Many lawyers and judges would prefer that journalists withhold a lawsuit story until the defendant legally "answers" the charges in the complaint.

When possible, talk to all sides involved in a legal dispute, although you should be prepared for rejection. Lawyers or participants may decline to comment for any number of reasons, among them the fears of being unprofessional, upsetting the judge, violating ethical codes or otherwise hurting their own case. On the other hand, some lawyers and participants will orchestrate press coverage to their advantage. Despite the legal profession's overall objection to "trial by media," some lawyers welcome a hearing in the court of public opinion.

Journalists should attempt to follow up on all lawsuit stories by reporting the final judgment or settlement. A lawyer emphasized that point for *Los Angeles Times* reporter David Shaw: "If a guy sues for $10 million and the court gives $1.98, you ought to print it. Otherwise, the public gets a mistaken, inflated impression of the value of even the most frivolous lawsuits and they file bigger and bigger lawsuits and the spiral of cost goes up and up for everyone."[13] Reporters also should track a reported case to its conclusion, particularly for the sake of the reputations of the litigants. If a lawsuit is worth reporting in the first place, let people know what happened to it.

Criminal Cases

In film and television, from *Perry Mason* and *12 Angry Men* to *Law and Order* and *Presumed Innocent*, criminal law is the star. So it is in real life.

In criminal cases, the government seeks to enforce laws and punish those who violate them. Attorneys employed by local, state or federal governments *prosecute* violators on the behalf of the citizens, which is why criminal cases typically are cited as "*The state* (or the people) *against John Doe, defendant.*" A criminal violation is classified as either a *felony*, which is a serious offense that can result in imprisonment of a year or longer, or a *misdemeanor*, a "petty" violation for which punishment is typically a fine or less than a year's imprisonment.

Police sometimes clash with prosecutors and judges over whether a case is strong enough to prosecute. In some jurisdictions, police must present all felony arrests to the prosecutor's gatekeeper, usually an assistant prosecuting attorney, who reviews the facts and preliminary evidence, determining whether the case merits prosecution. If so, the prosecutor's office will have to commit what may be already stretched, limited resources. At times, the decision boils down to the odds of winning or losing the case.

A linchpin of the criminal system is the principle of a *presumption of innocence*. In theory, at least, criminal defendants are not required to prove their innocence. The prosecutor must convince the court and jury that the defendant is guilty *beyond a*

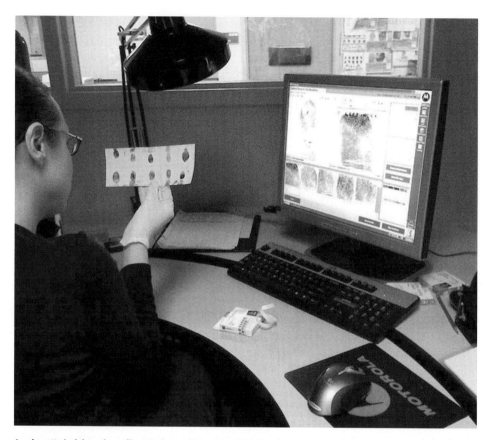

A crime technician views fingerprints   Fingerprint identification remains a central piece of evidence linking a suspect to a crime. Computers help sort through databases of fingerprints, but a technician's trained eye provides the human side of confirmation. Later, the technician might be called to court to testify about her role in handling the finderprint identification. (Photo by Robbie Arkovich.)

reasonable doubt. Jurors who have a reasonable doubt about guilt are instructed—and obligated—to find the defendant not guilty through an *acquittal*.

All criminal defendants possess constitutional rights, particularly those established by the Bill of Rights—the Fourth Amendment (which includes protection against unreasonable searches and seizures); the Fifth (protection against self-incrimation and double jeopardy, among other rights); the Sixth (the right to a fair, speedy trial and associated rights); the Eighth (no excessive bail or cruel and unusual punishments); and the Fourteenth (due process and equal protection of the law). These rights have been expanded by a number of court rulings, such as the U.S. Supreme Court's 1962 *Gideon v. Wainright* decision, which required states to provide legal counsel for indigent felony defendants.

The Genesis of a Criminal Case

A criminal case can begin in a variety of ways. Often, routine police work leads to arrests and charges against individuals caught committing a crime. In other cases, investigative work by the prosecutor's office—such as a "sting" operation to catch a public official taking a bribe—brings about criminal charges.

Arrests, searches and seizures

A key step in the criminal process is the issuance of a warrant of arrest or a warrant to search a person or property for possible evidence. An *arrest warrant* is issued by the appropriate court based on a demonstration of *probable cause* that the person named in the warrant committed a crime or violated conditions of parole or probation. Although its meaning and application vary, probable cause is generally determined by facts and circumstances that would lead a reasonable person to conclude that a crime had been committed.

Under federal and state constitutions, citizens are protected against unreasonable searches and seizures. When law enforcement officials ask a judge to approve a *search warrant*, they must clearly specify the person or property to be searched and identify what is being sought. They also must show probable cause for the search, as well as meet additional conditions set by particular courts or required in various jurisdictions. Comparable conditions, especially probable cause, apply to police requests for telephone taps or electronic surveillance.

Normally, a request for a search warrant is made and reviewed in an informal, confidential *ex parte* hearing, which means a one-sided presentation by the police or prosecutor. The individual named in the warrant is not present nor given the legal opportunity to contest the warrant. Reporters routinely should examine the *affidavits* on which requests for warrants are based. These sworn statements by law enforcement officials may contain important, newsworthy details not included in police reports, such as names and addresses of other persons connected to the suspect and the crime. Unfortunately for reporters, search warrants and the accompanying affidavits fall within a gray area of access, with courts divided on whether the press is entitled to such material.

If an arrest, search or seizure is done in an unconstitutional manner, evidence or statements so obtained may be inadmissible under what is known as the *exclusionary rule*. Defense attorneys frequently attack the legitimacy of searches and seizures, particularly those conducted without a warrant. Warrantless searches and seizures are permitted, but only under special circumstances. If evidence, for example, is found during a routine body frisk for weapons or if it is in plain view at the time of an arrest, it can be legally seized; of course, there is often controversy surrounding how *plain view* is defined.

A controversial method of warrantless search involves a police tactic called "knock and talk." Police officers, for example, acting on an informant's tip, knock at a suspected drug dealer's door and ask to come in for a talk, hoping that they will either see evidence or induce the suspect to voluntarily turn over contraband or make an incriminating statement.

The power of police to question suspects broadened in 2004, when the U.S. Supreme Court ruled against a cowboy named Larry Dudley Hiibel, who refused to identify himself to police officers in Nevada. The Court said police acted properly in demanding Hiibel's name after they stopped him on "reasonable suspicion" of criminal activity.[14] The *Hiibel* opinion expanded the *"Terry* stop" rule established by the Court in *Terry v. Ohio* (1964), which gave police the ability to stop and frisk someone for weapons when the officer had a *reasonable suspicion* that the suspect committed or was about to commit a crime. Most legal observers say reasonable suspicion permits greater leeway than does probable cause to justify a police stop.

Some criminal cases fall apart because of improper interrogation methods, including the knock-and-talk approach. For instance, if police question a criminal suspect in custody without a *Miranda warning* to explain the suspect's right to remain silent and right to be represented by a lawyer, any evidence and information collected as a result may be tainted under a legal concept known as *fruit of the poisonous tree*. If the "tree"—the illegally obtained statement—is poisoned, then the fruit it yields in the form of additional evidence is likely to be poisoned, too, and probably cannot be used against the suspect.

Lineup identification is another critical stage that can undermine the legitimacy of a case. Police cannot coach witnesses or allow them to talk among themselves as they try to pick out a suspect. Nor can they stack a deck so that a witness, who told police a holdup man "looked like a football player," cannot help but focus on a muscular suspect intentionally placed in the middle of a lineup of men with slight builds.

Interesting stories can emerge from clashes between the prosecution and the defense over the propriety of investigative methods and the validity of witness identifications. Competent defense attorneys will attack flawed police procedures or evidence through pretrial motions or, later, through post-trial appeals.

Formal charges

Whether criminal suspects are in custody or still at large, they must be charged formally before the judicial process goes any farther. Two charging procedures are commonly used: *informations* and *indictments*. An information is the prosecutor's means of alleging the commission of a crime and bringing a suspect to trial. Indictments come from a *grand jury*, a panel varying in size from 12 to 23 laypersons and appointed for specific terms of varying duration. The grand jury hears evidence presented by the prosecution and then decides, usually by a majority vote, whether there is sufficient probable cause to recommend that the suspect be charged. Some states require a grand jury hearing for all felony cases; in others, informations are being used more frequently than grand jury indictments to file charges against defendants.

An indictment, also referred to as a *true bill*, is only an official accusation; it is not a finding of guilt. All stories about indictments should stress that point. If necessary, reporters should include a definition of an indictment in grand jury stories. Otherwise, the presumption of innocence is undermined, and the common charge of "trial by media" becomes regrettably more valid.

Grand juries also investigate broader criminal problems, such as organized crime, gambling operations and governmental corruption. Another common function is overseeing public facilities and institutions, including jails and government-operated mental health centers. Thus, a grand jury inquiry might result in dozens of indictments in a drug-ring case or a recommendation for officials to improve medical treatment at the county jail.

The power of a federal or state grand jury goes beyond its ability to issue indictments; it includes the power to force the appearance of witnesses and suspects, even those not yet formally charged in warrants. A *subpoena* is a judge-issued order to appear before a grand jury or other judicial body. A *subpoena duces tecum* is an order to produce documents. Those who refuse to honor a subpoena are subject to a citation for *civil contempt* and jailing until they comply. (*Criminal contempt* applies to direct affronts to the court, such as an outburst during a trial, and is punishable by a set jail term or fine.)

A reporter who covers crime and corruption may someday face a grand jury subpoena. During the late 1960s and early 1970s, in particular, grand juries investigating militant groups, such as the Black Panthers, regularly called journalists to testify. The pattern continues, although the circumstances of cases have changed. Reporters subpoenaed lately, for example, were called by grand juries seeking to uncover the source of leaks involving national security; the anthrax attacks; and city hall corruption. According to a survey of news organizations conducted by the Reporters Committee for Freedom of the Press, 45 percent of newsrooms responding reported receiving at least one subpoena in 2001; the 319 news organizations responding reported receiving a total of 823 subpoenas that year. The RCFP concluded, "The significant burden that subpoenas place on the media has not been noticeably reduced or modified over the last 14 years."[15]

Reporters who receive subpoenas see them as intrusions on their newsgathering role. And at times, prosecutors or grand juries use subpoenas in an indiscriminate search for evidence, which critics label "fishing expeditions." But no one, including reporters, can ignore a grand jury subpoena. Even a patently frivolous subpoena is serious business that probably will require a lawyer's advice and assistance. Battles between the press and the judiciary are inevitable whenever reporters are subpoenaed and ordered to reveal names of anonymous sources or turn over confidential information. Most reporters will go to jail rather than break a pledge of confidentiality. (Chapter 11 addresses the legal and ethical issues of confidential sources.)

Because grand jury sessions are closed to the public and the press, coverage can be difficult. In some jurisdictions, everyone connected with the grand jury is sworn to secrecy. In others, reporters may be able to question witnesses after they testify. Often, reporters must wait patiently until the grand jury releases its report. When a grand jury inquiry is especially important, journalists may be tempted to approach grand jurors privately for inside information. But, if they are suspected of being involved in a leak of information from the grand jury, reporters can anticipate being subpoenaed and asked to identify their sources of information. Unless there is evidence of corruption or misconduct in a grand jury's handling of a case, reporters are advised to neither encourage leaks nor publicize them. Being first to break a story of a grand jury's indictment normally is insufficient reason for breaking the law.

In a few cases, the grand jury returns a *suppressed indictment* for criminal suspects still at large. Reporters who prematurely identify people named in suppressed indictments could give them an opportunity to flee.

Initial appearances

Regardless of the method used to bring charges, all accused persons are entitled to appear before a judge quickly to ensure that constitutional and due process rights are observed. In many jurisdictions, this proceeding is called an *initial appearance*. As a rule, judges use the initial appearance to determine the identity and age of the accused, read charges, inform the accused of his or her rights, determine whether the accused can afford to retain a lawyer and set bail, if it is permitted.

Most defendants are allowed to be free on bail while the case is pending. *Bail* is a written promise to appear in court as ordered. To ensure compliance, defendants must do one of the following: put up cash in the full amount of the bail; provide a percentage—usually 10 percent—of the cash bail; put up real estate of value equivalent to or greater than the amount of bail; or obtain a surety bond from a bail bondsman, who is responsible if the defendant fails to appear in court. Friends, relatives and neighbors of accused persons sometimes use their own property or cash to meet bond. If the accused flees, all cash and property may be forfeited to the courts. Determine who is liable if a defendant "jumps bail"; you may find a human-interest story.

Many states have made it easier and less costly for defendants to "make bail." Reform in bail rules has minimized the involvement of bail bondsmen, some of whom charge excessive fees for services, knowing that certain suspects have no other options.

In less serious cases involving first-time offenders, a court might accept a *signature* or *recognizance bond* that does not require money or property as a guarantee. Use of recognizance is based on the high probability that the defendant will honor the conditions of bail.

Many people, however, cannot make bail. Studies indicate that jailed defendants are more likely to be convicted and receive longer sentences than those released on bail. Evidently, defendants free on bail can better help in preparing a defense. Even when convicted, bailed defendants often can point to steady employment and good behavior while awaiting trial as reasons for probation or a minimum sentence.

Pretrial proceedings

Two other common pretrial proceedings are the *preliminary hearing* and *arraignment*. "Prelims," as they are called in courthouse jargon, serve the same basic purpose as the grand jury session—to determine whether evidence presented by a prosecutor as part of an information is sufficient to warrant a trial. A preliminary hearing differs from a grand jury session in that a judge makes the determination of probable cause. On advice of their lawyers, some defendants waive the right to a preliminary hearing, knowing that the prosecutor's office can easily establish probable cause for prosecution.

Rather than go through the formalities of a hearing, the defense attorney and the prosecutor's office simply get down to the business of a negotiated plea and sentence. In other instances, the defense may see the preliminary hearing as an opportunity to assess the strength of the prosecutor's case. If weaknesses are apparent, the defense could use them to its advantage during plea negotiations or, if need be, at the trial.

When the news media's interest in a case is particularly high, the pressure may convince the judge to ban the press and public from preliminary hearings. A judge who closes a preliminary hearing generally does so out of fear that prospective jurors might be prejudiced by the incriminating evidence presented by the prosecutor, including hearsay testimony, which is not admissible in a trial. The preliminary hearing often is a critical stage in the criminal justice process. Important pretrial motions to suppress evidence, for example, might be heard; conditions and agreements might be reached among the judge, defense and prosecution. With so many criminal cases ending in negotiated pleas, the preliminary hearing may be the last opportunity for journalists to hear evidence and rulings in a case.

The *arraignment* usually comes after an indictment is rendered or following a preliminary hearing. At a typical arraignment, the judge formally reads the charges, explains the consequences of a guilty plea or conviction, asks the accused to enter a plea and, if the plea is not guilty, sets a trial date. At this point, discovery generally becomes effective, although rules and procedures vary. *Discovery* in civil law and discovery in criminal law share a common purpose of a two-way exchange of relevant information, evidence and documents.

Several types of pleas are possible under criminal law. Some defendants stand silent or *mute* before the judge, who then enters a not guilty plea on the defendant's behalf. A *nolo contendere* plea is permitted in federal courts and certain state courts. Sometimes called a "no contest plea," a nolo contendere technically is not an admission of guilt and therefore cannot be used against a defendant in any civil actions related to the criminal case. Some states permit a plea of *not guilty by reason of insanity*, which often is used in murder cases. The plea has been used successfully by a battered wife accused of killing an abusive husband and by a young mother who killed two newborn daughters. It is a controversial plea, largely because the public perceives it as a convenient escape route for someone who has committed a terrible crime.

Although the likelihood of a trial increases for arraigned defendants who plead not guilty, negotiations between the prosecution and defense may continue, leading to a last-minute guilty plea.

Covering the Criminal Courts

Colleagues laud Linda Deutsch, the famed AP criminal courts reporter, for her talent at covering a complicated, emotionally charged case and capturing for readers both its drama and legal intricacies. "You have to be extremely focused," she says. "You can't miss a word or you might miss something crucial. . . . It also requires knowledge of the law, so it's very technical. If you don't understand what the legal terminology is—you're in big trouble."[16]

Big trouble occurs, as well, when reporters, due to bad judgment or careless reporting, publish, air or post information that damages the outcome of a criminal case.

REAL-LIFE LESSONS

Absolute accuracy remains the ultimate goal of all stories, but in criminal law, with lives at stake, there is little room for error. Journalists must be especially conscientious to avoid words or deeds that might subvert the quest for fair and just administration of the law. A respected reporter for the Raleigh *News & Observer* learned a hard lesson when he made a major mistake in coverage of rape charges against three lacrosse players at Duke University.

The reporter, Joseph Neff, had covered the case as it unfolded. An exotic dancer, hired to provide entertainment at a team party, said she had been physically assaulted and raped by three or more men. The prosecutor, District Attorney Mike Nifong, aggressively pursued the case despite questions about the accuracy and credibility of the dancer's accusations. In time, three Duke athletes were indicted on rape charges, and Neff reported the breaking news. The error occurred in the opening paragraphs of the story, when Neff said Nifong proceeded with rape indictments the same day he asked a police investigator to check if the accuser's injuries might have been caused other than by rape. In fact, Nifong asked investigator Michele Soucie for more background on the accuser nearly two weeks *prior to* the indictments.

By erroneously reporting that Nifong brought the rape indictments on the day he essentially asked Soucie to check on the accuser's veracity dramatically supported the theme of the remainder of the story—that the investigation and prosecution seemed flawed and ill-timed. Ted Vaden, the newspaper's public editor, discussed the error in a column:

> In the story, Neff set forth numerous other examples of a shaky prosecution case, but the erroneous information, coming at the top of the story, was Exhibit A. The story was accompanied on the front page by a reproduction of Soucie's notes, labeled "Excerpts from Soucie's notes on April 17."

... I think the error was substantial. It could at worst undermine some readers' confidence in the paper's reporting of this case and at the least contribute to a perception of journalistic sloppiness. We don't need either.

The paper should use the incident as an opportunity to redouble its efforts to ensure reporting accuracy—re-examining its fact-checking systems and holding sessions with all staffers to emphasize accuracy fundamentals. That is done here regularly, but not recently.

I also wondered: Can Neff continue to report on the lacrosse case with credibility among readers and the various actors in the lacrosse story?

... I think Neff should remain on the case. His mistake was one of carelessness, not of malice. Removing him would be a form of scapegoating, in the sense of blaming one person for an error that was allowed by a team of professionals. And it would be depriving the paper, and readers, of *The N&O's* best journalism.[17]

The lesson: *Mistakes happen when journalists forget that every fact must be double- or triple-checked. Intuition alone should have warned Neff of the improbability of Nifong's taking two contradictory steps on the same day. The damage done not only hurt the credibility of the reporter and the newspaper, it also undermined an already controversial prosecutor's case against the athletes.* As it turned out, in December 2006 Nifong dropped the rape charges although other criminal charges remained pending as of Jan. 1, 2007. Later in 2007 he withdrew from the case to face ethics charges brought against him by the state bar association.

Even mistake-free, enterprising reporting can flirt with irresponsibility. Just days after the murder of four family members, the *St. Petersburg Times* published a top-play, page-one story headlined "Sneak attacks took four in family, one by one." Graphic, detailed information about the slayings came from a note left by 20-year-old Richard Henderson Jr. and a taped confession he gave to sheriff's investigators. Reporter Brady Dennis wrote:

MYAKKA — When he had finished with the killings, 20-year-old Richard Henderson Jr. took a shower, crawled into his parents' bed and spent Thanksgiving night staring at the ceiling, he told investigators.

The bodies of his mother, father, brother and grandmother, each bludgeoned to death by a metal pipe, lay scattered through the small house on a quiet dirt road.

That evening, Henderson scribbled a note and signed his initials:

I knew I did it but I don't know why. . . . I didn't kill them out of hate but out of selfishness because I didn't want to die alone.[18]

The uncommonly specific account, provided by investigators, told how Henderson stealthily killed each member of his family. The story also carried details about

Henderson's past legal bouts for beating his teenage bride and bringing a gun onto school property. Moreover, the *Times* quoted an uncle who called Henderson the "bad apple of the family" who deserved the death penalty.

Reporters who cover the first days of a notorious criminal case should not allow their zeal for a good story to overcome their duty to honor the integrity of the judicial system. Many editors would consider the Henderson story exemplary reporting; judges would likely squirm over its potentially prejudicial impact on prospective jurors.

In an effort to come to a compromise on the free press v. fair trial front, police, courts, lawyers and journalists in several states operate under voluntary press-bench-bar guidelines for releasing details of a confession and statements about the suspect's character. For example, the state of Washington guidelines urge restraint:

> The release of certain types of information by law enforcement personnel, the bench, and the bar and the publication thereof by news media generally tends to create dangers of prejudice without serving a significant law enforcement or public interest function. Therefore, all concerned should be aware of the dangers of prejudice in making pretrial public disclosures of the following:
>
> - Opinions about a defendant's character, his guilt or innocence.
> - Admissions, confessions or the contents of a statement or alibis attributable to a defendant.[19]

Not all states, including Florida, follow a comparable set of guidelines, which attempt to balance the equally important interests of the First and Sixth amendments. Journalists concerned about doing the right thing can consider these guidelines from CBS News' "standards of self-restraint":

> There are clearly some circumstances where what we report in the way of crime news can result in a most serious miscarriage of justice. For example, if, prior to a trial, we detail the confession of the defendant or his/her prior police record, or present detailed "evidence" (interviews with people who allege that they have seen things or know things which establish the defendant's guilt), the result can well be that the courts will say that the defendant cannot get a fair trial. This is because the jurors, under our Anglo-Saxon system of jurisprudence, must render their verdict only on the basis of the evidence they hear in court. They cannot be infected by evidence that they have read or seen or heard outside the court, else the defendant is deprived of a fair trial.
>
> Again, for example, a defendant's prior police record is normally not permitted to be introduced as evidence in a trial—certainly not where the defendant does not take the stand. Similarly, we know that under Supreme Court decisions over recent years, many confessions are barred from evidence because they are not voluntary, or because the defendant has been held by the police too long without arraignment or without a lawyer. Hence, if we report in detail on confessions or prior police records, we may be informing

potential jurors of evidence most damaging to a defendant although, ultimately, that evidence never is presented to the jury and cannot, for good civil liberties reasons, be presented to the jury.[20]

Besides exercising care when reporting on potentially prejudicial pretrial disclosures, journalists need to ensure that justice is done as a suspect goes through the legal maze. Despite what news accounts and TV programs suggest, few criminal cases go to trial. In some jurisdictions, up to 90 percent end in either dismissal of charges or a negotiated plea of guilty—a *plea bargain*. To court critics, plea bargaining is an unsavory term; it suggests that criminals are getting off easy, which, indeed, sometimes happens. Without plea bargaining, though, legal experts agree that U.S. courts would be hopelessly snarled by a backlog of cases.

Building additional courtrooms and expanding the judiciary might reduce the number of plea bargains. But if more defendants enter the corrections pipeline as a result, what happens at the destination, where there are too few prison cells? Building more prisons would, in turn, ease pressure on the courts. Nevertheless, increasing the capacity and efficiency of the criminal justice system would not eliminate the need for plea bargaining. At times, there is little choice but to plea bargain. If, for example, the prosecution concludes that jurors will not believe a rape victim's story, a negotiated guilty plea on a reduced charge and sentence might be the only means to impose sanctions on the assailant in some way.

Under such circumstances, a plea bargain can appear to be unfair to the victim; that is why reporters should insist that prosecutors explain their reasons for a negotiated plea. Occasionally, prosecutors intentionally overcharge a defendant, citing as many offenses as possible, to encourage a guilty plea on a proper charge. By overcharging, prosecutors will argue they actually are not "bargaining away" anything.

Monitor the courtrooms

Prosecutors condone plea bargaining, but injustices are bound to occur, considering the high number of cases being negotiated within an already pressured, overburdened system. Realistically, too much is going on in most courthouses for any one reporter to monitor. But studying patterns and tapping the courthouse grapevine ought to reveal serious improprieties. Reporters, again, should persist in seeking explanations and particulars whenever charges are dropped or reduced, holding judges and attorneys accountable for their actions. Be aware that negotiated pleas are not always a "bargain" for defendants, some of whom receive bad legal advice and are pressured into a guilty plea. Consider, too, what happens when a defendant rejects a negotiated plea. Defense attorneys believe certain judges and prosecutors go harder on defendants who insist on a jury trial.

Obviously, these are potentially volatile subjects to raise with judges or prosecutors; you can anticipate that some of them will express outrage if their motives and integrity are questioned. But to effectively monitor the courts, reporters must be

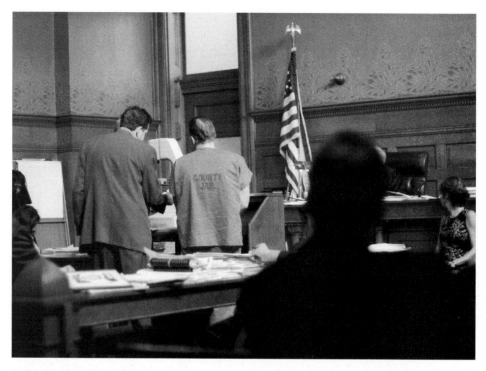

Facing the judge in handcuffs   Handcuffed and dressed in standard jail garb, an orange jumpsuit, an accused man makes an initial appearance in court. If it were a trial, the man would be dressed in a business suit; the jumpsuit would possibly suggest guilt to jurors. (Photo courtesy iStockphoto, ftwitty, Image # 2715910.)

aggressive, as officials of the Virginia State Bar urged at a seminar for news media: "Responsible journalists wouldn't dream of being satisfied with a partial and inadequate knowledge of either the legislature or the executive. Certainly, no seasoned journalist would ever admit to being awed, intimidated or mystified by the legislative or executive branches. The court system should be no different."[21] By asking tough questions, reporters usually serve the best interests of all concerned—the public, victims, defendants and officers of the courts. Whose interests are served by simply reporting that the "defendant pled guilty to reduced charges"?

QUOTABLES

"The courts in this country struggle daily to achieve the ideal of justice, often under less than ideal conditions. By and large, I believe that they do a good job of ensuring that rules and reason, not passion or privilege, determine the tens of millions of disputes brought to them each year. While far from perfect the American courts still play a major role in making our society one of the freest and fairest in world history.

"How the media portray us affects our ability to carry out our role, and it is not over-statement that the courts have not fared well in the media. Sensationalized reports on a handful of cases distort the public's understanding of their justice system. The paucity of coverage of courts' positive accomplishments further limits our ability to maintain public trust." (pp. 83, 84)
— Judge Judith S. Kaye, "The Third Branch and the Fourth Estate," in Robert Giles and Robert W. Snyder, eds., *Covering the Courts,* New Brunswick, N.J.: Transaction Publishers, 1999

Keep close contact with judges, lawyers and court personnel

A crucial part of a court reporter's job is to maintain close contact with judges, who, of all officers of the court, can appear—and sometimes are—the most intimidating. Although a few judges refuse to talk to reporters under any circumstances, many, if approached properly, will answer questions of clarification or provide off-the-record guidance and background for reporters. It would be appropriate, for example, for a reporter to ask: "Judge Baker, would you explain what an adjournment in contem-plation of dismissal entails? Is that like a no contest plea?" Be forewarned, however, that it is ethically improper for a judge to offer comments or opinion that might influence the outcome of *any* pending case; in fact, most judges would find it highly improper for journalists to solicit such comments. However, no amount of indigna-tion on a judge's part should deter reporters from asking questions meant to hold the judge accountable for his or her actions on the bench.

Court reporters must also work closely with attorneys in the criminal courts. In state court systems, persons who hold the title *prosecuting attorney* or *state's attor-ney* generally are elected to office and, therefore, pay attention to public opinion and press relations. The chief prosecutor can be an important source of information and commentary, but he or she is not likely to be in the thick of courtroom action. On a daily basis, you can expect to turn more often to assistant prosecutors, who do most of the courtroom work. Defense attorneys either are in private practice or serve as *public defenders*, who are employed by the state to represent indigent defendants. In most jurisdictions, the chief public defender is an elected official, accustomed to dealing with reporters.

For the most part, success at communicating with courthouse personnel depends on a reporter's personal reputation for accuracy and fair play. The extent and condi-tions of your communication with attorneys will vary from individual to individual and case to case. Some attorneys enjoy holding corridor press conferences; others pre-fer to talk quietly for background only; still others beg off entirely. Often, ethical considerations or office politics limit what attorneys say to the press; less frequently, attorneys are prohibited from talking about a case by a judge's restrictive order to curb potentially prejudicial publicity.

Intelligent questions rarely upset lawyers; dumb ones usually do. Defense attorney M. Hatcher Norris cautions reporters to avoid asking, "Is your client guilty?" "It's the worst question," he says. "What am I going to say? 'He's guilty as hell?' You don't really expect that answer, do you?" Norris further advises: "Don't ask us to characterize the evidence or witnesses. You're not going to get an answer. All you're doing is turning off the lawyer."[22]

A broad network of sources includes those in less lofty positions, such as court clerks, bailiffs and court reporters. Employees in the chief clerk's office not only help court reporters obtain case files. They also compile data and maintain calendars of court dates (dockets). In addition, the clerk of the court may issue detailed monthly reports on the disposition of cases.

Bailiffs aid judges and supervise courtrooms. When court is in session, the bailiff often seats the jury, announces the judge's entrance, maintains order, guards the courtroom doors, arranges seating for spectators and escorts witnesses to and from the courtroom. Befriend bailiffs. If so inclined, a bailiff can keep reporters informed, such as explaining why a trial is late in starting, when a particular witness is expected to be called or what issue the judge and attorneys probably are discussing in the judge's chambers. Bailiffs will not be inclined to confide in reporters they barely know or ones they feel are asking them to be disloyal to *their* judge.

Stenographers called *court reporters* are responsible for keeping a verbatim transcript of courtroom proceedings. Journalists who miss a portion of important testimony might convince the court reporter to repeat what was said. Since rules in some jurisdictions prohibit reporters from bringing a tape recorder into the courtroom, the court reporter's record becomes all the more important. If you are a stranger, it is much easier for the court reporter to say, "I'm sorry. I don't have the time." Complete transcripts of proceedings often can be purchased, but generally the cost and time of preparation negate their value as a news tool.

Periodically, visit offices and talk to courthouse personnel informally, not strictly in connection with a particular case or problem. You do not want to acquire a reputation as a reporter who comes around only "to get something."

Use online records and information—but not as a crutch

As courts increasingly go to computerized records, it is becoming easier for reporters to keep track of particular cases and to study trends and larger issues based on statistics kept by the clerk's office. Each state provides a certain amount of court information online, through either fee-based commerical services or their own Web sites. The federal district courts and bankruptcy courts can be accessed through a system called PACER (Public Access to Court Electronic Records—http://pacer.psc.uscourts.gov/). Reporters can retrieve useful information to guide and plan their coverage of federal cases, including such information as a listing of all parties and participants; case-related material (nature of suit and dollar demand); a chronology of events (motions, judgments) in a case; and a daily listing of new cases.

A virtual visit to the courthouse, while convenient and time-saving, cannot replace the real thing. Online, reporters do not meet people face to face, overhear courthouse gossip and witness the legal system ebb and flow.

Understand courthouse culture

Be prepared to wait for justice to be served; it is often behind schedule. Reporters find themselves spending precious minutes and hours in frustration, waiting for the judge and attorneys to get on with business. Court watchers attribute some delays to a condition called "courthouse time." If a hearing is scheduled to begin at 9 a.m., it may be 30 to 40 minutes before everyone is prepared to proceed. Delays apply to trials as well, but there is a tendency for judges and attorneys to be less punctual at pretrial hearings.

Pretrial proceedings tend to be relatively informal. The judge may wander in and out of the courtroom, engaging in small talk. The attorneys may kid each other and exchange documents, seemingly oblivious to the defendant, slouching in a nearby chair. At some pretrial or post-trial hearings, defendants may be manacled and dressed in sneakers and jail jumpsuit. You can expect a more serious tone and approach by all participants at a trial.

Although the number of civil and criminal cases going to trial represents a mere fraction of total business before the courts, trials often receive disproportionately high attention from the public and press. The trial—most notably the jury trial—still epitomizes the American system of justice in terms of both public perception and legal principle. Chapter 9, therefore, concentrates on trials.

Exercises

1 Try to follow a civil case from its beginnings. It may test your persuasive powers, but see if you can convince a local attorney to let you observe what goes into the filing of a lawsuit. For as long as your schedule permits, follow the case as it moves through the judicial system.

2 Ask the clerk of the court to arrange for you to review the records of a recently completed civil or criminal case that went to trial. Be prepared to wade through hundreds of pages of documents. Remember that the record probably will not include a transcript of the trial proceedings, which generally is prepared only when a case is being forwarded to an appellate court. Even without the trial transcript, the record should be substantial and interesting.

3 Interview a federal or state judge. Some may deny your request, but with persistence, you will obtain an interview. You might ask a local reporter to suggest an approachable judge. Be sure to avoid talking about any pending cases in the judge's jurisdiction. But talking about points of law and the judge's past experiences would be proper. After the interview, observe the judge in court. Drawing on information from the interview and your courtroom observation, produce a profile of the judge.

Notes

1. Ellen Goodman, *Making Sense* (New York: Atlantic Monthly Press, 1989), pp. 71, 72.
2. Lyle W. Denniston, *The Reporter and the Law: Techniques of Covering the Courts* (New York: Columbia University Press, 1992), p. 52.
3. See Thomas B. Littlewood, *Coals of Fire: The* Alton Telegraph *Libel Case* (Carbondale, Ill.: Southern Illinois University Press, 1988), pp. 6, 7.
4. *USA Today*, Oct. 9, 1989, p. 3; http://www.usatoday.com/news/index/nns062.htm.
5. John Leo, "End of the Affair," *U.S. News & World Report,* April 11, 2005.
6. William P. Statsky, *Legal Research, Writing and Analysis* (St. Paul, Minn.: West, 1974), pp. 392–394.
7. Don Fry and Karen Brown, eds., *Best Newspaper Writing 1990* (St. Petersburg, Fla.: Poynter Institute for Media Studies, 1990), p. 170.
8. Fred W. Friendly and Martha J. H. Elliott, *The Constitution: That Delicate Balance* (New York: Random House, 1984), p. 85.
9. "Secret Justice: Alternative Dispute Resolution," Report of the Reporters Committee for Freedom of the Press, 2001; www.rcfp.org/secretjustice/adr/index.html.
10. See Robert E. Drechsel, *News Making in the Trial Courts* (New York: Longman, 1983), p. 87.
11. Paul L. McGorrian, "How Loud? $30,000 Worth," *St. Petersburg Times*, April 25, 1989, sec. B, p. 1.
12. Andrew H. Malcolm, "Farmers Send a Message to A.T. & T.," *New York Times,* July 6, 1988.
13. David Shaw, "Media Coverage of the Courts: Improving but Still Not Adequate," *Judicature*, June–July 1981, p. 19.
14. *Hiibel v. Sixth Judicial District Court of Nevada,* 542 U.S. 177 (2004).
15. "Agents of Discovery," A Report on the Incidence of Supoenas Served on the News Media in 2001, available online at www.rcfp.org.
16. "Spirited Woman Q&A with Linda Deutsch," www.thespiritedwoman.com/newsletter/2005/10/december_2003.html.
17. Ted Vaden, "Lacrosse Error Clouds Story's Credibility," newsobserver.com, posted Aug. 13, 2006.
18. Brady Dennis, "Sneak Attacks Took Four in Family, One by One," *St. Petersburg Times,* Nov. 29, 2005, p. 1A.

19. "Considerations in Reporting of Criminal Proceedings," Washington Bench-Bar-Press Committee, www.wsba.org/media/benchbar/default.htm#crime.
20. Covering Trials, CBS News, July 30, 2006, www.concernedjournalists.org/node/184.
21. "Legal Aspects of Reporting and Editing News," Virginia State Bar, 1984, p. 5.
22. Quoted in "A Journalist's Guide to Federal Criminal Procedure," American Bar Association, videotape.

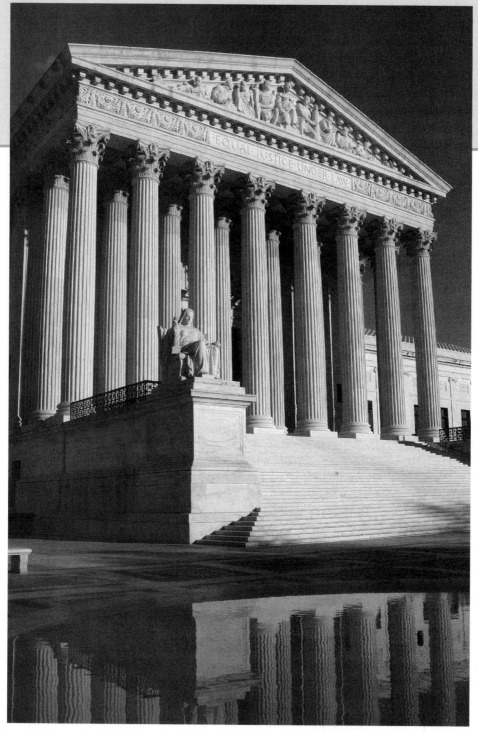

An imposing view of the Supreme Court The nation relies on the Supreme Court of the United States to guide us through legal and social issues of monumental importance. The Court's decisions reverberate as precedent through American courts. (Photo courtesy iStockphoto, DHuss, Image # 1493056.)

The Trial and Thereafter 9

Every year seems to bring its share of sensational trials. But 2005 set a standard for scandal and melodrama.

Early in the year, two Tyco International executives, Dennis Kozlowski and Mark Swartz, returned to court for a second trial on defrauding the company and its stock-holders of hundreds of millions of dollars, including $1 million doled out for a 40th birthday party on the island of Sardinia for Kozlowski's wife. A new jury found the two guilty of grand larceny and conspiracy.

In Birmingham, Ala., former HealthSouth CEO Richard Scrushy faced crimi-nal charges in a $2.7 billion accounting fraud. Prior to his trial, Scrushy joined the Guiding Light Church, a predominantly African-American congregation, and he toured other black churches, leaving large charitable contributions from his foundation throughout the city. During the trial, prominent black ministers sat in the courtroom in support of Scrushy; the press referred to them as his "Amen Corner."[1] Scrushy was acquitted on all 36 counts—prayers apparently heard and answered.

In the center ring, the circus trial of Michael Jackson on child molestation charges began early in February, drawing more than 1,000 journalists from around the world, who camped out in a media village surrounding the Santa Maria, Calif., courthouse. As the trial opened, Jackson's defense attorney named Elizabeth Taylor, Diana Ross and Stevie Wonder as potential character witnesses. After four months of steamy evidence and testimony, including appearances by Jay Leno, Chris Tucker and Macaulay Culkin, the jury acquitted Jackson on all 10 counts against him. Residents of the media vil-lage packed their gear and headed home.

As 2005 demonstrated, the criminal trial is the Big Show—the judicial system's scene stealer.

When most people picture a trial, they imagine suspense, tears, angry shouts of "Objection, your honor, objection!" and, perhaps, a surprise, last-minute confession. Real-life trials often fail to resemble the Hollywood or TV's *Law and Order* versions; they may move slowly and dryly, generating few sparks of excitement or nuggets of news. But since only a select handful of cases go to trial, there is usually legal signifi-cance and human interest—or both—in all trials.

Covering a trial is not easy, especially for newcomers to the court beat. While the judicial process itself is relatively uncomplicated, the legal strategy at work and the testimony of witnesses can be difficult to understand and report. Trial coverage also, at times, puts reporters in the position of trying to serve the public's right to know under the First Amendment without doing harm to a defendant's Sixth Amendment rights to a fair trial.

The verdict does not end the reporter's role or responsibility. Although news coverage tends to wane after a trial concludes, in many instances the human drama and legal maneuvers go on for years in a legal purgatory of motions and appeals.

The Big Show

If the trial resembles theater, then most reporters cover productions of the Community Players rather than Broadway extravaganzas. Although the settings and the characters change, civil and criminal trials follow a similar format. Certain cases, *bench trials*, are tried by a judge alone. Without a jury to impress, attorneys in a bench trial tend to be more restrained and less demonstrative. As a result, bench trials usually lack the tension and clashes of jury trials.

Defendants in criminal trials are constitutionally guaranteed a "speedy" trial, and in applying that guarantee most courts stipulate that cases are supposed to be tried within 60 to 180 days, unless the defendant seeks a *continuance* (delay) or agrees to a delay requested by the prosecution. Civil trials usually are not required to begin within a set number of days.

Once a judge is assigned to a case (which in some jurisdictions means being chosen by lot) and the trial date is set, the next step is jury selection. The trial itself commences with opening statements by the attorneys, followed by presentation of evidence, examination of witnesses, closing arguments, jury deliberation and the verdict or judgment. The sequence of these steps, however, may differ from court to court.

Stage Directions

When a high-profile case goes to trial, increasingly attorneys for both sides seek the assistance of trial consultants who help pick juries, prepare witnesses to testify, develop opening and closing arguments and arrange "shadow jurors" to watch the trial unfold and provide feedback along the way. Usually, trial consultants charge high fees, although occasionally they work *pro bono* as a free public service.

Debate over the use of paid consultants includes the issue of an inherent *unfair* administration of justice when one side or the other benefits from highly specialized, expensive trial preparation. As part of trial coverage, reporters should inquire about special resources the trial teams plan to draw upon. You might not find out, but it is worth asking. You might learn, for example, that lawyers for a teenage defendant on trial for vehicular homicide hired a communications professor to prepare the young man to perform well on the witness stand.

The Jury

In theory, the jury is the cornerstone of the judicial process; in practice, the jury system has weaknesses. One is public apathy; too many people try too hard to stay off juries, citing a litany of excuses when called to serve. Moreover, attorneys may try to remove potential jurors whom they consider too educated, independent or assertive for fear they might unduly influence fellow jurors. As one textbook for law students advises, "You want jurors whose minds can be molded."[2]

Concern over pretrial publicity also works against the selection of well-informed jurors. Consider the jury selected to hear the Oliver North case in 1989. According to published reports, the 12 jurors and six alternates selected showed little interest in or understanding of national news and knew only the sketchiest details about the highly publicized Iran-Contra scandal of the Reagan administration. In one observer's opinion, a typical jury consists of "twelve prejudiced, gullible dolts incapable of understanding evidence or law involved in a case."[3]

That assessment is too harsh and apparently unfounded. In *The American Jury*, a classic study of more than 3,500 trials, Harry Kalven Jr. and Hans Zeisel found that in about 80 percent of the criminal and civil cases examined, judges agreed with jury verdicts. More recent studies corroborate the Kalven-Zeisel findings. So despite criticism about who serves on juries and how they are chosen, more often than not, those 12 ordinary citizens listen, weigh evidence, deliberate and reach reasonable, fair decisions.[4]

The normal size for a trial jury, called a *petit jury*, is either six or 12 persons, depending on the type of case and rules governing particular jurisdictions. Several alternates are also selected in case illness or an emergency forces one or more of the original jurors to withdraw from the case. Jurors usually are selected from a pool of residents whose names are drawn from the roll of registered voters. Either in advance, by mail or at the courthouse waiting room, residents called for jury service might be asked to fill out a questionnaire to collect basic information, such as date and place of birth, employment history, education background. Journalists can expect access to a blank copy of the questionnaire; completed forms, however, are usually considered confidential. Occasionally, pre-selection questionnaires go into great detail. In the O.J. Simpson case, the juror questionnaire was 75 pages long.

Once at the courthouse, potential jurors, called *veniremen*, are welcomed by the judge, who may tell them about the case and question them before allowing attorneys to do their own questioning. The process of selecting a jury is called *voir dire*, a term that means "to speak the truth." Voir dire is an examination by the court to test the competence, ability and impartiality of persons called to serve as jurors.

During voir dire, attorneys for either side may exercise a number of *peremptory challenges* to "excuse" (remove) a venireman "without cause." Attorneys can cite an unlimited number of challenges "for cause," provided the judge agrees there is a good reason to doubt a venireman's ability to be fair and impartial. At voir dire, certain types of questions are standard. In criminal cases, for example, defense attorneys are likely to ask questions like these: "Do you know any party involved in this case?" "Have you ever been a crime victim?" "Have you read or heard news media accounts of the case?"

As attorneys question and challenge potential jurors, they may apply a mixture of science and intuition. In major cases, law firms sometimes hire psychologists or use consulting firms that specialize in jury selection and typically provide attitude surveys, computerized juror profiles and demographic charts. But hunches and stereotypes still prevail, even among attorneys who use scientific methods. Some prosecutors, for example, prefer black jurors, assuming that as residents of high-crime areas, they are steadfastly in favor of law and order. Conversely, other attorneys assume that blacks mistrust or dislike police officers and therefore will give more credence to the defendant's story. Something as inconclusive and subjective as body language or the tone of a venireman's voice might prompt an attorney to use a peremptory challenge. Several U.S. Supreme Court opinions, however, prohibit attorneys from using peremptory challenges to exclude potential jurors because of their race.

For high-profile trials, reporters cover the jury selection carefully, reporting the occupations and backgrounds of those selected. The composition of the jury may be an important issue as the trial unfolds or later on appeal, particularly if the defense claims the defendant's constitutional right to a trial by an impartial jury was violated.

In a celebrated case, a judge may try to protect jurors from outside pressure by keeping personal details, especially phone numbers and addresses, confidential. In rare instances, jury selection is conducted behind closed doors. Whenever a judge denies access to proceedings or trial-related information, news organizations should protest and seek legal assistance. But it is wrong to automatically condemn the judge's action; extenuating circumstances may put the jurors or the trial itself in jeopardy, possibly outweighing the public's right to know.

A jury selection and other pretrial steps offer reporters an opportunity to introduce the trial's main cast, especially the judge and the attorneys, and set the stage for what is to follow. Just after jury selection in the trial of Wayne Williams, suspected as the killer of 28 children and young adults in Atlanta, the *Chicago Tribune* painted this profile of Williams' chief defense attorney:

> ATLANTA — Alvin Binder is a lawyer who looks as though he stepped from the pages of a novel. He is a big showboat of a man who smokes expensive cigars from Chicago and calls young women "little lady."
>
> There is substance behind all this style, says a private investigator who works with him.
>
> In fact, some say, Alvin Binder is as smart as a professor and can be as tough as a junkyard dog that wags its tail before it attacks.

The story also included observations about the other attorneys in the case, the judge and background details, including reference to the judge's order that reporters not publish the names and addresses of the jurors selected. The *Tribune*'s reporter, Charles Madigan, remained on the scene to cover the trial as it unfolded.

Opening Statements

As law's Big Show, the trial becomes a dramatic production with the participants as actors, whether they care to play the role or not. The outcome of a trial is supposed to be determined by the jury's detached, logical assessment of the facts, evidence and testimony. As humans, though, jurors react to emotional arguments as well as reasoned rhetoric.

A prosecutor's or defense attorney's dramatic performance can be pivotal in an otherwise weak case. Although considered unprofessional for attorneys to perform for juries, it happens. The equivalent of acting classes for lawyers offers instruction on the importance of gestures, inflection, timing, props and attire. Occasionally, a shadow jury that matches the demographic-psychological profile of the actual jury is hired so the attorneys can rehearse opening statements and examination of witnesses, measure the shadow jurors' reactions and then, if necessary, adjust their strategy or delivery. An attorney's polished, eloquent performance might bomb with some juries; an "Aw-shucks,-I'm-just-a-good-ole-boy-myself" style might work best, unless jurors perceive it as an act.

Regardless of the style and approach used, opening statements must be confined to the facts and evidence that will be presented. In a criminal case, the prosecutor uses the opening statement to tell the jury how he or she intends to prove the defendant guilty "beyond a reasonable doubt." Court rules may permit the defendant's attorney to delay an opening statement until the prosecution presents its witnesses and evidence. Either side may waive the right to an opening statement.

The opening statement gives reporters a clearer idea of how the trial will unfold. In that sense, it is somewhat like a play program, listing the cast and scenes to follow. A word of caution: Guard against inflating the importance of opening statements or any other in-court remarks by the attorneys. Their rhetoric may be spellbinding, but it is not evidence, which is something jurors and reporters alike sometimes forget.

QUOTABLES

"The camera is the most honest tool of the criminal justice system, if it is allowed to show the public a trial, unadorned from gavel to gavel, in the courtroom—without the TV celebrities, without brain-dead interviews, without the second-guessing pundits. As citizens, we have the right to see our system, warts and all, to judge for ourselves. Nobody should have the power to deny us, the taxpayers, the right to watch what is happening in the courts we pay for, or should be allowed to tell us that by watching a trial on camera, in our homes, we are jeopardizing any other citizen's rights." (p. 11)
—Theo Wilson, *Headline Justice*, New York: Thunder's Mouth Press, 1996

Evidence and Witnesses

The main act of a trial is presentation of evidence and examination of witnesses. In criminal cases, the prosecution begins this stage of the trial; in civil cases, the plaintiff's counsel goes first, calling its witnesses for *direct examination*. In direct examination, each side, in turn, carefully asks questions of its own witnesses and experts to elicit testimony, building a chain of arguments in an attempt to lead jurors to a logical conclusion. The prosecution, for example, typically calls the arresting officer as a witness, asking such questions as, "Please describe what you saw when you arrived at the bank and saw a holdup in progress." There is an unwritten rule for attorneys in direct examination: Never ask a question unless you know what your witness is going to answer. Such answers become known before the trial from the lawyer's interviews with witnesses or depositions taken under oath.

After direct examination, the opposing side is entitled to conduct *cross-examination* of the same witnesses. A goal of cross-examination is to *impeach* (discredit) the credibility of witnesses and devalue the evidence. During cross-examination, questioning can get rough, as it did when a prosecutor cross-examined a 42-year-old woman accused of abandoning her newborn child in a trash dumpster. The prosecutor picked up a photograph of the woman's kitchen and began to question her:

> *Prosecutor:* "This is your kitchen?"
>
> *Woman:* "Yeah, it looks like it."
>
> *Prosecutor:* "When those kittens were born in that kitchen, you didn't put them in a box and throw them in a dumpster, did you?"
>
> *Defense attorney:* "Objection, your honor! He is goading the witness, and it's totally irrelevant."
>
> *Judge:* "Objection overruled."
>
> *Prosecutor:* "You didn't get rid of those kittens when they were born, did you?"
>
> *Woman:* "Oh, no, sir."
>
> *Prosecutor:* "That baby wanted you, didn't it? You held it?"
>
> *Woman:* "Only enough to clean it up."
>
> *Prosecutor:* "And then you just got rid of it and threw it like trash by the dumpster, right?"[5]

Exchanges between attorneys and witnesses usually are not so dramatic, but when they do reach this level of intensity, reporters can quote directly and let the participants' words best capture the moment.

Throughout the trial, the judge functions, in part, as a referee; that role is most apparent in witness examination, as the judge is often asked to either *sustain* or *overrule* objections from the attorneys. Many objections center on a witness's *hearsay* testimony or an attorney's *leading* questions.

Cross-examination may be followed by *redirect examination* and *recross examination*. The same process is followed when the defendant's witnesses and evidence are presented. Among those called to testify may be victims, plaintiffs (civil cases), experts and defendants, although in criminal trials, defendants can refuse to testify under the constitutional protection against self-incrimination.

Not all that occurs during presentation of evidence is obvious or spoken; some attorneys try to impress the jury with subtle, nonverbal messages. For example, a

The electronic courtroom   Today's courtrooms often combine traditional architecture and modern multimedia technology. At the U.S. District Court in Rhode Island, for example, the judge's bench is equipped with two flat-screen panels; one displays evidence, and the other displays testimony translated in real time from the court reporter's shorthand record. Both counsel tables are equipped with a flat-screen monitor, and the jury box is equipped—one for every two jurors—with monitors as well. With closed-circuit video, judges can also hold pre-trial hearings with jailed prisoners without the risk of bringing them to the courthouse. (Photos courtesy of Finegold Alexander & Associates, Inc.; copyright Peter Lewitt.)

factory worker suing over a job-related spinal injury gets these directions from his attorney: "Take your time getting to the witness stand. Let the jurors see how you walk. And bring along that cushion you use at home to sit on." Attorneys sometimes test the limits of propriety in trying to influence the jury. A prosecutor may play to the jury by dramatically handling and snapping shut a sawed-off shotgun used in a murder; another attorney may roll his eyes in mock disbelief as the opposition tries to make a point. Alert judges usually admonish attorneys who distract or disrupt courtrooms through overly dramatic behavior.

Closing Arguments

Closing arguments are characterized by impassioned appeals to the jury, or so people come to expect from fictional trials. In reality, not all closing arguments are moments of high drama, but they do give each side the opportunity to make a final impression before jury deliberations begin.

In their closing arguments, attorneys cannot stray beyond the issues or evidence presented in the trial. Each attorney usually tries to accentuate arguments that best support his or her position. If the judge gives *instructions* to the jury prior to closing arguments, the attorneys might also comment on the instructions and indicate how they apply to the evidence. Defense attorneys in criminal cases normally remind jurors that they must find the accused "guilty beyond a reasonable doubt"; otherwise, the verdict must be "not guilty." The plaintiff's attorney (or, in criminal cases, the prosecutor) goes first with a closing argument, followed by the defendant's attorney. The plaintiff's attorney or prosecutor may also be entitled to the last word—a *rebuttal argument*.

The goal of the defense is to plant the seeds of doubt; the prosecutor tries to remove doubt and appeal for justice, as Jackson, Miss., prosecutor Bobby DeLaughter did in the 1994 trial of professed racist Byron De La Beckwith, charged with gunning down civil rights leader Medgar Evers from ambush and leaving him to die in front of his three young children. Tried twice in the 1960s, all-white, all-male juries deadlocked on a verdict and De La Beckwith escaped conviction by mistrials. Thirty years after the assassination, De La Beckwith finally faced the prospect of punishment, and DeLaughter delivered a summation that enthralled jurors and journalists alike. He said, in part:

> This isn't about black versus white or white versus black. This is about something that is reprehensible to decent minds. This is about society, civilized society, versus the vile, society versus the reprehensible, society versus the shocking. This, ladies and gentlemen, is about the state of Mississippi versus this defendant, Byron De La Beckwith.
>
> . . . Medgar Evers didn't do anything of a violent nature to the defendant. What he did was have the gall, the "uppityness" to want for his people things like what? To be called by name, instead of "boy." To go in a restaurant, to go in a department store, to vote, and for your children to get a decent education in a decent school. For wanting some degree of equality for himself, his family, and his fellowman, and for them to be accepted as human beings with some dignity.
>
> . . . We have to learn from the past, folks, that where justice is never fulfilled— justice has sometimes been referred to as that soothing balm to be applied on the wounds inflicted on society—where justice is never fulfilled and that wound can never be cleansed, all it does is just fester and fester and fester over the years.[5]

The jury found De La Beckwith guilty, and he received a life sentence, dying in prison in 2001 of heart disease.

The Decision

Juries deliberate in secret. On occasion jurors are *sequestered* for the entire trial, which normally means they are confined to hotel rooms while not in court, isolated from family or other outside influences, such as news media coverage. The jurors are under the strict supervision of a bailiff or officer of the court. A jury also may be sequestered when its deliberations go longer than a day. Any attempt by outsiders to communicate with jurors is a serious matter and could lead to a *mistrial*.

During the trial of John Poindexter, President Reagan's national security adviser who allegedly lied to Congress in the Iran-Contra affair, a *Washington Post* reporter contacted several jurors to set up post-verdict interviews. The judge reacted angrily: "The reporter, we are told, just came back from Lebanon and didn't know the ground rules. If anyone . . . in government gave such a lame excuse, the press would be justifiably scornful and sarcastic."[6] Reporters, like everyone else connected with a case, must wait until the jury reaches a decision, no matter how long that takes.

The judge usually gives the jury its instructions after closing arguments. Although some jury instructions are "patterned" (standardized) to apply to an entire category of cases, judges usually are free to explain the jury's responsibilities in more detail. For example, the jury hearing the libel trial of Israeli general Ariel Sharon (later the country's prime minister) against *Time* magazine received a 64-page set of instructions from Abraham Sofaer, the presiding judge. Sofaer's instructions, in fact, helped clarify the question of "fault" in libel law and thereby became an important sidebar story in coverage of the verdict and a footnote in many media law textbooks.[7]

Reaching a decision is rarely easy for jurors, and it can be particularly agonizing in criminal cases. In a three- or four-day trial, the evidence and testimony might be sufficiently clear and convincing for a verdict to be reached in a matter of hours. Longer, more involved and less clear cases can take days to decide. After a period of time, the judge might recall the *foreman*, chosen by vote of the jurors at the outset of deliberations, to determine the jury's progress. At this point, the judge might decide to issue "blockbuster" or "dynamite" instructions, which urge the jury to do its duty and reach a verdict. For criminal cases, a verdict must be unanimous in most states. In civil law, a verdict or judgment may require agreement of only two-thirds or three-quarters of the jury. In the event of a *hung jury* (or deadlocked jury) that simply cannot reach agreement, a judge could be forced to declare a mistrial, which allows for the case to be retried.

Bench trials conclude with a judge's *finding*, which, at times, can be more suspenseful than a jury verdict because the judge is not compelled to decide immediately. Suspense might build for days or weeks before the finding is announced.

Reporting Trials

A trial unfolds in snatches of testimony and pieces of evidence. Each day brings its own news, but the news may be hard to detect. It is not like covering a baseball game. At a trial, who is scoring or striking out is not always obvious. Remember, too, that it is a grim, serious process.

With experience—and with insight provided by knowledgeable judicial sources—court reporters learn to recognize key testimony, evidence and strategy. Do not be embarrassed to seek help from court personnel and attorneys before, during and after a trial. Veteran court reporters sometimes get unsolicited tips. At the outset of a criminal trial, for example, the prosecutor approaches a reporter and says, "This is going to be an interesting case. We're bringing in the leading forensics expert on teeth-mark identification. You ought to catch her testimony." A judge presiding in a medical malpractice case volunteers: "The defendant is scheduled to take the stand after our noon recess. That ought to be lively."

REPORTER'S TIP FILE

A reporter's life in the courtroom

Theo Wilson's peers considered her a model reporter, and they especially praised her coverage of major trials, including those of O.J. Simpson and Charles Manson, the leader of a murderous cult. She died in 1997, just a year after publishing a memoir, *Headline Justice*. These tips come from her book and Linda Deutsch's foreword.

- Do not forget that real people, victims and defendants both, are dissected at trials. We see not only what they want us to see, but what is normally hidden from us.
- Nothing is ever predictable at a trial, and no two trials are alike.
- Never leave the courtroom except to file your story; you might miss a crucial moment.
- Don't give undue attention to out-of-court gossip; the only important facts are those which come from the witness stand to the jury's ears.
- Never forget that lawyers on both sides of a case are sales people, and those "secrets" they may want to tell you are designed to help their clients.
- And most importantly, never come to a trial with your mind made up: listen to the evidence as if you were a juror and report it with a fair, unbiased approach.[8]

Judges occasionally meet with reporters during a trial. Judge Hiller Zobel, in the trial of Louise Woodward, the British *au pair* convicted in the death of baby Matthew Eappen, met with journalists to help them get their accounts straight. In explaining procedure generally, he avoided getting into any specifics about the trial itself.[9]

Reporters with especially good contacts sometimes are able to discuss strategies or game plans with the attorneys involved. A few attorneys will open the door for fuller discussions of the case by asking reporters for informal opinions: "How am I doing? How do you think the jury reacted to my cross-examination of the victim's wife?" As a trial progresses, there may be many casual, off-the-record conversations between reporters and the judge or attorneys. The off-the-record stipulation may not be stated outright; it is one of those presumably "understood" conditions by which reporters and sources operate. To be safe and fair, reporters ought to know where everyone stands with regard to any conversations related to a trial. Whenever in doubt, always check with sources before quoting them by name in a news report.

A typical trial story opens with the most important development of the day; usually, the focus is on testimony. Here is how Linda Deutsch, legal reporter for the Associated Press, began one day's coverage of the tanker *Exxon Valdez* oil spill case, one of history's greatest environmental disasters:

> ANCHORAGE, Alaska — The skipper of the *Exxon Valdez* thought the seaman who was at the tanker's helm when it ran aground had problems steering and warned others to watch over him, the ship's second mate testified Wednesday.
>
> Both Capt. Joseph Hazelwood and third mate Gregory Cousins talked about problems with Robert Kagan's steering of the ship, second mate Lloyd LeCain Jr. testified at Hazelwood's trial.
>
> "How would you rate Mr. Kagan's abilities?" the prosecutor asked LeCain.
>
> "I'd say slightly below normal," LeCain said.

Included in nearly all trial stories is (1) a review of the charges or legal issues involved, (2) a summary of past developments and (3) a preview of what is expected to occur as the trial continues.

In another report on the Hazelwood trial, Deutsch helped readers easily see a pattern in past testimony and evidence:

> ANCHORAGE, Alaska — The *Exxon Valdez* could well have been an accident waiting to happen, according to testimony at the ship captain's trial.
>
> When the ship ran aground March 23, 1989, spilling 10.92 million gallons of oil into Prince William Sound, it carried:
>
> - A helmsman, Robert Kagan, who had well-known problems with steering.
> - A second mate, Lloyd LeCain, who allegedly had a history of mental problems. Capt. Joseph Hazelwood's defense attorneys have said LeCain boasted of being a submarine commander in the Falklands War, a Green Beret in Vietnam and a figure in the Iran-Contra affair.
> - Hazelwood, who has a history of drunken driving convictions and is accused of being intoxicated the night of the spill.
>
> As the prosecution ended its second week of evidence and prepared to wrap up its case, a picture emerged of a cohesive navigational team strengthened by highly educated and experienced officers but weakened by a troubled few.

Readable, informative trial stories also provide context and color. The context is provided through background information and history not found in the day-to-day testimony: Are the litigants in a civil suit former business partners? Is this case likely to set a legal precedent? Is there a connection between the present case and ones of the past? Color coverage focuses on the personalities, setting and mood of the trial—an Ivy League defense attorney versus the homespun prosecutor; the history of the old courtroom; the tension evident as the victim's and defendant's relatives glare at each other from opposite sides of the aisle.

A recent development injects an outside influence on trials in session. Legal commentators on cable news outlets, in particular, critique a trial and its participants as if doing a move-by-move color commentary of a gymnastics competition. Attorney Barry Scheck, part of O.J. Simpson's criminal defense team, believes lawyer-commentators bear responsibility for the nature of news coverage of celebrated trials. "We, as a profession, have to resist those people in the media that want us to come on when we don't know what we're talking about, or ask us for glib opinions that we shouldn't be giving. To be gratuitously critical or gratuitously knowledgeable, or pretend to be knowledgeable, is really dangerous."[10] Reporters should resist seeking instant analysis of ongoing cases from casual observers, no matter how impressive their legal pedigree.

At the conclusion of the trial, coverage continues as reporters attempt to elicit reaction from everyone connected with the case, including the jurors. In celebrated cases, some judges feel obliged to shield dismissed jurors from the press, telling them it would be "best not to answer" reporters' questions about the case. Convincing jurors that they have a *right to speak* to reporters may prove difficult, but always try; the results are often well worth the effort.

When the nation's longest criminal trial—a complex child-molestation case involving a Los Angeles preschool—ended early in 1990, seven members of the jury met with reporters. The director of the school and her son had just been acquitted on 52 counts of child molestation, and the jurors attempted to explain why. One juror said, "I believe the children believed what they were saying was true in the courtroom." But she added that she was not sure that "the children were telling what actually happened to them or if they were repeating what they were told by their parents and other people."[11]

By talking to jurors, reporters come closer to knowing what unfolded in the jury room. Your questions, for example, might reveal that several jurors felt pressured to go along with the verdict or, as in the preschool trial, that some objected to the way investigators handled the case.

Only rarely do courthouse reporters spend extended, uninterrupted periods at a trial or proceeding. An exception is the AP's Deutsch, who has covered the top legal stories of our times, including the trials of Charles Manson, William Kennedy Smith, Ted Kaczyzinsky, O.J. Simpson and Michael Jackson. She described her job and role this way:

> I'm the eyes and ears of the public. I'm there to say what happened, not to give any opinions on why it happened or who's responsible. I am an unbiased observer. TV cameras are not always there and even when they are people do not sit and watch every minute, they depend on the reporter to sum up what happened. You're taking a huge amount of

information. I fill two notebooks a day and bring it down to a manageable size where people can know what was said, what was important, what's happened, and if possible, how it felt to be in the courtroom when all of this happened. There are such dramatic moments that you have to talk about what it felt like to be there.[12]

News organizations around the world depend on Deutsch and her comprehensive coverage of major cases.

REAL-LIFE LESSONS

Responsible journalists are keenly aware that what they report and how they conduct themselves in dealing with court officials and participants can affect the outcome of a highly publicized trial. For example, publishing or broadcasting an incriminating story about the defendant's past troubles with the police either before or during the trial might expose jurors to prejudicial information.

In 2004, a New York state judge declared a mistrial in the corporate fraud case against two former executives of Tyco International, referred to in the chapter opening. The judge ruled as the jury, in deliberation after six months of testimony, seemed poised to reach a verdict. But several news organizations, including the *Wall Street Journal*, revealed a juror's name, alleging she made an "OK" gesture to defense attorneys, indicating she was holding out for acquittal. The situation worsened when the news accounts generated a flurry of Internet chat room talk, and the juror reported receiving a written threat.

CBSNews.com legal analyst Andrew Cohen called the press "outing" of the juror an act of journalistic irresponsibility. "I've covered high-profile trials for seven years and have never seen a juror identified publicly in mid-deliberations."[13] He feared the incident would give judges around the country an excuse to further limit public access to trials. In addition to the heavy responsibility of getting facts right, responsible journalists never forget that dissemination of prejudicial or damaging details can have dire results.

The lesson: *With the right to publish a potentially prejudicial story prior to a trial comes the responsibility to seriously consider a story's impact on the case. At the very least, a news organization should have sound, defensible reasons for going with a report that risks a mistrial.*

Verdicts, Judgments, Sentences and Appeals

The final scene of the trial is the reading of the verdict. Some verdicts are shocking surprises; some are anticlimactic. Trial's end is not, however, a time for a reporter's coverage to grow lax. Important details are yet to be learned and reported, with care, to the public.

Unless deadlocked, juries in criminal trials find the defendant either "guilty" (or guilty of a lesser included charge, such as a manslaughter charge in a murder case) or "not guilty" as charged. In bench trials, the term *finding* commonly is used instead of *verdict*. If the defendant is being tried on multiple charges, the jury might return a guilty verdict on certain counts and a not guilty verdict on others. After returning and reading its verdict, the jury's job usually is over, although certain states ask the jury to recommend punishment or, in a capital murder case, to decide whether the death penalty should be imposed.

For criminal cases, a "not guilty" verdict—an acquittal—ends the case; the prosecutor cannot seek a retrial on the same charges. But if other untried criminal charges are pending against the defendant, the prosecution is permitted to pursue them.

A conviction is likely to prompt one or more post-verdict motions by the defense. Most often, the defense makes a *motion for a new trial*, usually alleging procedural errors committed by the judge, such as allowing the prosecution to make an improper closing argument. Some states require filing of a motion for a new trial to preserve further rights of appeal. Another post-trial motion in both civil and criminal law is an *acquittal* (or judgment) *notwithstanding the verdict*. It asks the judge to disregard the jury's decision and declare a verdict or judgment in the defendant's favor. Since it is a motion judges rarely grant, it is news when accepted by the court.

If the post-trial motion is overruled, sentencing proceeds, with the judge normally asking for a presentencing investigation by state or federal probation officers. Unless the sentence has been negotiated in a plea-bargain agreement, there may be an *aggravation and mitigation hearing* to determine whether circumstances justify stiffer or lesser punishment. Because of mandatory sentencing rules, judges in both federal and state courts increasingly have less discretion in deciding on punishment. In some jurisdictions, being convicted of a serious crime—no matter who committed it and no matter what the circumstances—brings a set mandatory prison sentence with no possible probation, parole or early release. When judges do retain discretion, the presentencing report provides information about such factors as the defendant's criminal history, family situation, employment and prospects for rehabilitation. Sentencing on multiple charges may require the judge to decide whether prison terms should be *consecutive* (served in succession) or *concurrent* (served simultaneously).

Most negotiated pleas cover the charge and the sentence. Ordinarily, judges do not participate in plea discussions between the attorneys until a negotiated agreement is reached. Then, both attorneys usually ask the judge to follow the agreed-on charge and sentence. Some judges, however, insist, as they should, on checking the facts of the case and the background of the defendant. When defendants object to the prosecutor's proposed sentence, they sometimes opt for an *open plea*, which leaves sentencing up to the judge. If the judge does not accept the negotiated plea agreement, the defendant has the right to withdraw his or her guilty plea and go to trial.

Sentencing

No matter what form it takes, sentencing is not a simple process of meting out punishment. Sentencing guidelines and options are complicated, and reporters should never take this aspect of the criminal process lightly. Watch, especially, for sentencing disparities. Determine whether offenders who commit similar crimes under comparable circumstances receive similar punishment from court to court or judge to judge. Courthouse reporters quickly learn which judges are reputed to be "soft" or "hard" sentencers. But disparities are not always widely known or easy to detect. Sentencing ideally should be consistent, rational and fair; often, it is not, being the result of human judgments. One judge, for example, might consider a car thief's drug addiction a mitigating factor and lessen the punishment. But in a courtroom a few doors down the hall, another judge sees the offender's drug addiction as a reason to impose a tougher sentence. Sentencing by its nature attempts to individualize the punishment. Reporters ought to find out about the person sentenced and the judge's reasons for the sentences selected.

Sentencing stories should routinely explain terms and conditions of punishment. To merely report that "Joe Doe received a 10-year sentence" tends to be misleading. Frequently, well-behaved inmates receive credit for days of "good time," which could, in some states, reduce a sentence by 50 percent or more. If you are unsure how much of a 10-year term a convicted bank robber is likely to serve, ask the judge or corrections officials for assistance.

Finally, sentencing stories should, if at all possible, include the reaction of victims, families and offenders. The superficial emotions shown—or suppressed—at a sentencing hearing do not necessarily fully or accurately reflect feelings. Thorough reporters will ask questions sensitively and explore emotions after a sentence is imposed. For negotiated sentences, one question, in particular, should be asked: Did prosecutors and the judge seek reaction or input from the victim or his or her family in arriving at a plea bargain? The answer will likely be no. As courts rush to dispose of criminal cases, those who suffered because of a criminal act are sometimes overlooked. In their coverage, reporters should strive to avoid similar oversights. Victims seldom have any official role apart from that of a witness, although some jurisdictions now have victim-assistance programs and provisions for the victim to be heard at sentencing. It seems fair that they get a chance to comment, at least in news accounts.

Probation

Probation usually is among a judge's sentencing options. With probation, convicted offenders are placed under the supervision of a probation agency instead of being sent to prison. Probation is used in various ways. A judge, for example, could elect to set a burglar's penalty at five years in prison but suspend execution of the sentence, placing him on probation; if probation is revoked, the five-year sentence usually will be immediately executed. Other judges prefer to reserve the option to impose a sentence if probation fails; that approach affords the flexibility to impose a stiffer sentence than ordinarily given for a burglary conviction. Another variation is called *shock probation*, which involves imprisoning an offender briefly to demonstrate the

The Rock, a symbol of the nation's penal system The U.S. penitentiary known as Alcatraz and "The Rock" held American's most dangerous criminals, including gangster Al Capone. It closed in the 1960s. Now tourists visit the island and explore the cellblocks. While access to America's jails, prisons and penitentiaries often involves restrictions, reporters need to keep an eye on what goes on behind the guard towers and barbed wire. (Photo courtesy iStockphoto, khr128, Image # 838904.)

result if he or she violates the terms of probation. Increasingly, electronic transmitting devices, such as unremovable ankle bands, are being used to monitor the whereabouts of probationers, as well as offenders who are on parole or confined at home on "house arrest." Martha Stewart wore an electronic monitor as part of her sentence for obstructing the investigation of an illegal stock transaction. Electronic surveillance is not foolproof, but it offers another alternative to imprisonment.

With most prisons so overcrowded, judges regularly confront sentencing dilemmas: Imprisoning a 19-year-old car thief—a first-time offender—may mean that a 35-year-old armed robber with a long record gets an early release. With certain offenders, probation is an appropriate penalty. For example, is justice served by breaking up a single-parent family to jail a working mother convicted of passing bad checks? Not surprisingly, the U.S. Department of Justice reported that in 2004, of the 7 million under criminal court supervision, 4.15 million were on probation, about 60 percent of the total.[14] But probation often backfires, according to national crime statistics. One study found that 65 percent of convicted felons were rearrested, usually for serious crimes, while on probation.[15] The figures suggest that reporters are quite right to question officials rigorously and dig deeper into a case when previously convicted felons receive probation.

Ironically, despite its widespread use—or perhaps because of it—misconceptions about probation persist. Probation is not, as some people think, a free ride. Typically, probationers must submit to no-notice searches and drug tests, report regularly to a *probation officer*, undergo counseling and follow a strict set of rules governing where they can go and with whom they can associate. Often, probation officers play the combined roles of detective, social worker and counselor, watching over and caring for perhaps dozens of probationers at any given time. It is a demanding and frequently dangerous job. Reporters ought to know probation officers and appreciate their work.

Parole and Pardons

Few laypeople know how inmates become eligible for *parole* or a *pardon*, both extremely sensitive but shadowy areas of the corrections system. News organizations generally do an adequate job of monitoring criminal cases through the sentencing stage. But a gap in coverage often occurs when it comes to parole or other forms of early release based on good behavior and prospects for rehabilitation. Parole is a continuation of the sentence—but outside prison confinement. A pardon is an absolution of guilt and punishment for a crime and usually entails no conditions.

In a handful of cases, the parole or pardon process receives thorough coverage, such as the case of Sirhan Sirhan, who has sought early release several times since being convicted of the 1968 assassination of Robert Kennedy. But most often, it seems, the press ignores paroles and early releases until something goes wrong. A classic case was the early release of a convicted murderer named Willie Horton, who slashed a Maryland man and raped the man's fiancée after escaping on a furlough (a leave) from a Massachusetts prison. In the 1988 presidential campaign, George Bush repeatedly criticized his rival, Massachusetts governor Michael Dukakis, for that state's system, which allowed Horton out of prison.

Parole and pardon boards operate outside the normal parameters of the court beat, because parole is a function of the executive branch, not the judiciary. Who, then, covers parole boards—a legal reporter or a government reporter? Sometimes no one, which is why reporters covering the court beat ought to check personally—or through a colleague—the activities of parole and pardon boards at least monthly.

The process of deciding parole requests can be quite subjective and the criteria used vague or non-existent. Given the horror stories about freed convicts who, on release, return to a life of crime, parole and pardon decisions should be watched closely. Reporters, however, can anticipate obstacles. A number of states permit closure of meetings and records of parole and pardon boards in the name of privacy rights.

The Sentencing Reform Act of 1984 abolished parole in federal criminal courts in favor of determinate sentencing set by uniform guidelines; the term of imprisonment, therefore, is the actual time the person spends in prison. Several states have also abolished parole, especially for violent crimes.

Civil Verdicts and Judgments

As in criminal law, several motions usually follow the conclusion of a civil trial. These legal requests sometimes are required to reserve the right to appeal at a later date. But unlike criminal law with its outcomes of either guilty or not guilty, civil verdicts tend to be more involved. Reporting a civil verdict might include sorting out several types of damages, which are awarded as monetary compensation for losses or injuries to a plaintiff's person, property or rights through the defendant's unlawful act or negligence.

Three common categories of damages are compensatory, actual and punitive, but those terms differ in meaning from jurisdiction to jurisdiction, sometimes causing definitional confusion. In general, *compensatory damages* are awarded to cover losses or injury, including pain, suffering and disability, that are a direct result of the wrongful act. *Actual damages* cover tangible out-of-pocket losses that followed as a natural consequence of the wrongful act. *Punitive damages* are awarded over and above compensatory or actual damages to punish an offender for aggravated, willful misconduct. Another intent of punitive damages is to make an example of civil offenders to deter others from committing similar wrongs. While damages for tangible loss may amount to thousands of dollars, punitive damages often soar into the millions.

Jury awards that seem unrealistically excessive should not be overplayed by the press. The recipients of a $5 million award in a product-liability suit rejoice and celebrate, and news coverage makes them look like winners of a lottery jackpot. Years later, however, the case may still be on appeal and the plaintiffs have yet to receive a penny. Appellate courts frequently find jury awards excessive and reduce them substantially. A California jury, for example, awarded entertainer Carol Burnett $300,000 in actual damages and $1.3 million in punitive damages in her libel suit against the *National Enquirer*, which published a story describing Burnett as drunk and disorderly in a Washington, D.C., restaurant. An appeals court, though, trimmed the actual damages to $50,000 and the punitive damages to $150,000. Burnett and the *National Enquirer* eventually settled out of court, cutting short the cycle of appeals.[16]

Exaggerated media reports, critics say, also reinforce stereotypes about excessive judgments for what, on the surface, seem like trivial matters, such as the infamous McDonald's "hot coffee" case. In truth, when a New Mexico jury awarded 79-year-old Stella Liebeck, a retired sales clerk, $160,000 in compensatory damages and $2.7 million in punitive damages, it based its decision on solid evidence, including McDonald's in-court admission that it had known about the risk of serious burns from its scalding coffee for more than a decade. Liebeck suffered third-degree burns on her groin, inner thighs and buttocks when hot coffee spilled on her lap. On appeal, the parties reached an out-of-court settlement for an undisclosed amount.[17] Nonetheless, the myth of the multimillion-dollar cup of coffee persists.

In civil law, certain types of litigation do not involve a jury trial. Included under the non-jury category are equity actions, such as requests for an injunction. Regardless of who decides a case, there is usually a way for most court rulings and judicial decisions to be appealed to a higher authority. Whether an appellate court agrees to hear the case is another matter.

Appeals

After cases leave the lower courts on appeal, it is possible for them to disappear into journalism's twilight zone. Reporters who covered a case through the verdict and post-trial motions usually do not follow the case any further, partly because of geography and partly because of limited resources. The trial court may be hundreds of miles away from the nearest appellate court, and while nearly all news organizations cover the local circuit (or district) trial court, few station reporters permanently at appellate or supreme courts. Consequently, only the most publicized of cases are thoroughly monitored as they move through the appeals process. Even then, an appeals case may be passed along from reporter to reporter with little continuity in coverage.

The odds of losing track of a case increase if it happens to move from the state courts into the federal courts. (Appeals from a state court to a federal appellate court are possible when there are grounds to argue that the defendant's rights under the federal Constitution have been violated or denied.) Reporters assigned to cover the courts for a news organization need to meet regularly to share ideas and information and, with the aid of editors, coordinate long-term coverage of important cases.

To appeal a case, there must be a will and a way. Not all losers in a court case are eager to expend the time, money and energy on an appeal in the hope that somewhere, somehow and sometime they will be vindicated. Some litigants decide enough is enough. Even those with the will and resources to forge ahead may not succeed in obtaining a review of their case. There are few guarantees of an appeal in federal or state courts, although *one* appeal is a matter of statutory right in many jurisdictions. Most often there must be grounds for an appeal, and then the parties appealing must convince a court to review the case.

The appeals process usually begins with the appealing party—the *appellant*—filing a *notice of appeal,* a brief statement that may or may not specify the issues or points in question. The notice is followed by preparation of the *record* of the case, which usually includes the trial court's transcripts. The record accompanies the appeal. Normally, the next step is submission of the appellant's *brief,* which is a written argument of the issues to be decided on appeal. The other side—the *appellee*—is given time to file a brief to answer the appellant. After submission of the briefs, the appeals court may hold a hearing for *oral arguments,* at which both sides repeat or clarify points made in their briefs. The oral arguments also give the appellate judges an opportunity to question the attorneys.

Access to the records and proceedings of appeals courts is often broader than access to trial courts. A major reason is the absence of jurors, which, in turn, eliminates concern about the impact of prejudicial publicity. In any event, reporters covering the appeal of a major case should, at minimum, examine the briefs and attend the oral arguments. Particularly important cases might include *amici curiae* (friends of the court) briefs, which the appeals court can allow outside, interested parties to submit. The briefs, with their footnotes and numerous citations to other cases, often are as detailed, legalistic and ponderous as law journal articles.

The oral arguments, however, can be spirited jousts between and among the judges and the attorneys in the case. As veteran court reporter Lyle Denniston notes: "The hearing gives the reporter his first opportunity to gauge the potential reaction of the appeals court to the case." But Denniston quickly cautions that reporters should not assume that how judges react at oral arguments necessarily indicates how they will decide the case.[18] Reporters who study the briefs and attend hearings not only gain newsworthy information; they also prepare themselves for explanatory reporting once the appeals court reaches a decision.

A case, however, may linger in an appeals court for months before the outcome is announced. The outcome seldom is a landmark ruling; in fact, it could amount to an anticlimactic non-ruling, such as a simple confirmation of the lower court's decision without comment. Unless an appellate decision is announced with what amounts to a flourish of trumpets, reporters who are not especially alert and organized in their coverage can easily miss rulings.

State and federal appeals courts deal with newsworthy issues of considerable importance. But some journalists are concerned that appeals courts are not properly covered. John Seigenthaler, at the time editorial director of *USA Today*, commented: "Some news decision-makers have convinced themselves that if the story isn't about fads or fashions or jogging or junk food or polls or personalities, it doesn't touch the lives of readers." Seigenthaler particularly expressed concern about coverage of the federal appellate system—the "anonymous court," as one judge described it. Through interviews with judges and other court officials, Seigenthaler found that most media coverage ranged from "spotty" to "non-existent" to "very superficial" to "shallow at best."[19]

The federal system includes 13 circuits, called U.S. Circuit Courts of Appeal; some of these circuits encompass three or more states. All federal appeals within a circuit go to the circuit court's headquarters, which may be hundreds of miles from the court that originally heard the case and the news organization that originally covered it. In all, the federal appellate courts review approximately 65,000 or more cases a year. News organizations may want to cover the nearest federal appeals court, but the distance separating reporters from the source of the news, together with the size of the task, discourages thorough coverage.

Fortunately, digital technology encourages fuller coverage of all courts. Computer links with case-reporting data services such as findlaw.com, Westlaw and LexisNexis Academic make it possible for subscribers anywhere to obtain many court opinions soon after they are released and offer a bounty of additional information to help journalists cover and analyze judicial rulings.

The final step in the appeals process is the Supreme Court of the United States. Although asked to review as many as 7,000 cases a year by a petition known as a *writ of certiorari*, the Court usually issues full opinions for approximately 80 to 100 of these cases. The cases it does decide often are highly significant in both legal and societal terms. The Supreme Court obviously attracts news media attention, and most of its decisions are well publicized. A cadre of a dozen or so experienced reporters covers the U.S. Supreme Court full time. Their stories are widely disseminated through various news services, and, by most accounts, the coverage is quite good. Does that mean, however, that court reporters in Davenport, Iowa, or Bangor, Maine, should leave Supreme Court coverage to others? Reporters who want to keep abreast of legal precedent and measure legal impact will take the time to review the Court's decisions and, if appropriate, relate the Court's decisions to their own readers, listeners or viewers. That job is becoming easier for local reporters thanks to the Court's own Web site, www.supremecourtus.gov, and a privately funded site, www.oyez.org.

Finding, Reading and Explaining Court Decisions

Many, but not all, decisions of appellate courts are published and collected in volumes called *reporters*. The rulings of trial courts occasionally are "reported"—that is, published—but the vast majority of reported cases come from courts hearing appeals.

Bound sets of case reporters can be found in courthouses, law offices, universities and libraries. Usually, only law school libraries hold a complete collection of federal and state reporters, for there are hundreds of reporters with dozens of volumes. Journalists with access to Lexis or other database services can obtain full-text printouts of many federal and state court opinions without a trip to a law library or courthouse. Commercial newsletters, many published by the Bureau of National Affairs, provide weekly digests or full texts of important court decisions in particular branches of law, such as tax law or media law.

Nearly all cases are located and referred to by *citation*, which is a set of names, numbers and abbreviations. An early journalists' privilege case provides a typical citation: *State v. Buchanan*, 250 Ore. 244, 436 P.2d 729 (1968). The citation normally begins by naming the parties involved, with the appellant cited first. The number that follows—250—refers to the volume of *Oregon Reports* (Ore.) that contains the decision. The second number is the page on which the decision begins. For certain cases, there are multiple citations, indicating the case is published in other reporters. *State v. Buchanan*, for example, can be found in one of West Publishing Co.'s regional reports—the *Pacific Reporter*, second series (P.2d). Some reporters and law books are annotated, containing important explanatory notes about a particular case.

Ideally, reporters on the court beat should be well versed in legal research. More practically, what you cannot learn on your own, learn from a legal authority, such as a law school librarian. He or she can introduce you to many methods of examining and assessing the law.

Reading a court decision is not like reading a paperback novel. Decisions of appellate and supreme courts may be 50 pages or more of legalistic language and complicated arguments. Reporters who skim or flip to the last few pages to find out the outcome invite mistakes of interpretation and meaning. With experience, reading court opinions becomes easier, but it should never be a casual undertaking. A reporter who approaches a court opinion without a clue about its history or significance is asking for trouble.

Most opinions begin with background—the facts, chronology and issues of the case. The background, however, might be sketchy and require augmentation from other sources, such as previously published news stories. The background usually is followed by the court's rationale for its decision. Often, other cases germane to the present case are cited in support of the court's rationale. In stating its rationale, the court typically addresses the various legal arguments raised by the parties in the case, accepting or rejecting those arguments as it deems fit. Opinions generally end with the court's decision, or *holding*. Sometimes the holding is clearly marked in a synopsis of the court's position. In the classic 1964 libel case, *New York Times v. Sullivan*, for example, the Supreme Court said, "We hold today that the Constitution delimits a state's power to award damages for libel in actions brought by public officials against critics of their official conduct."[20] Of course, that summarized statement sheds little light on the importance of the case or the court's rationale. Usually, news stories must go well beyond simply reporting the holding.

The court's decision often includes further action to be taken in regard to the case. The most common actions are to *affirm*, or uphold, the lower court's ruling; to *reverse* the lower court and *remand*, or return, the case for appropriate action, such as a new trial; or reverse the lower court outright, which means there is nothing more to be tried or decided. There are combinations when the court is dealing with cases involving a number of rulings or issues.

The heart of most appeals decisions is the main or *majority opinion*. Appellate court decisions, though, usually involve a panel of three or more judges or justices, so there are bound to be differences of opinion, some of which could be significant and newsworthy. That is especially true of *dissenting opinions*, which reporters should heed and, if appropriate, include in their coverage of a ruling. A full decision might also include one or more *concurring opinions*, which are written by judges who agree with the holding and the action taken by the majority but see the issues or rationale in a different light. In a close vote of an appeals court, a concurring decision could be pivotal and crucial to the outcome of the case.

Poring over the record of a case is important. But useful, explanatory court reporting goes beyond the documents. Robert Coram, formerly a reporter for the *Atlanta Constitution*, reminds us: "Stories that are remembered are not those in which court records are parroted, but rather those in which a knowledgeable reporter went beyond the record and displayed initiative."[21]

Various law associations sponsor Web sites that provide background and analysis of the latest legal disputes, among them the American Association for Justice (formerly the Association of Trial Lawyers of America), www.atla.org. Reporters should also monitor law journal articles, which they can track using the *Index to Legal Periodicals*, and read periodicals, such as newsletters published by state bar associations.

Special Courts, Special Problems

As spectators and reporters flock to a murder trial two floors up, in the basement corner of the courthouse a judge assigned to probate court quietly does her work. Probate is one of several "other" courts that seldom attract much attention. Although often out of the way, special courts deserve coverage. Good stories and features are to be found in special courts, particularly in probate and two other areas—juvenile and bankruptcy courts.

Probate Courts

Each state regulates the disposition of a deceased person's property. The main role of probate court is to judge the validity of wills and supervise the administration of estates. Certainly, reporters will want to check probate court when a renowned citizen dies. News coverage should involve more than merely satisfying the public's curiosity about the lifestyle, money and heirs of the rich and famous, such as the turmoil in 2006 over former *Playboy* Playmate Anna Nicole Smith, the wife of an elderly Texas oil magnate who died in 2001 with an estate estimated at $1.6 billion. Smith died in early 2007, leaving her probate dispute in a legal limbo.

At times, provisions in the will and information about the estate reveal surprising, hidden aspects of the individual's life and relationships. In a sense, the will, if there is one, amounts to a person's last public statement and completes his or her record. Probate court also yields its share of human-interest stories: the apparent pauper who died, it turns out, with a million-dollar stock portfolio or the widow who left her sizable estate to a menagerie of cats, dogs and canaries. There are investigative possibilities, too. Occasionally, *administrators* or *executors*—those entrusted to carry out the will and administer the estate—divert money improperly into their own pockets.

Many people of wealth and power carefully prepare for the passage of property to heirs. When a person's preparation includes a will, it is said that he or she died *testate*; dying without a will is called *intestate*. In the absence of a will, state law provides for how an estate is to be distributed. When a will exists, determining the validity of its content and provisions often presents no problems. But occasionally wills are contested, such as when family members argue that a *codicil*—a modification to an existing will—unfairly changes who gets a share of the estate. Probate judges handle details and disputes over estates without the involvement of a jury.

Another function of probate court is to protect persons who are determined to be incapable of managing their own affairs. Children of elderly parents sometimes face the unhappy but unavoidable step of going to court to establish a mother's or father's incompetence. In such cases, a child, relative or trusted person is appointed *guardian* with the legal power to pay bills, manage property and administer fiscal accounts. It is a position of great trust that most people would never violate, but abuses occur, which is why diligent court reporters should monitor incompetency proceedings.

Juvenile Courts

All states have separate courts for *juveniles*, a designation that typically includes all children under the age of 18. The goal of juvenile courts is to *aid* as opposed to *adjudicate*. People tend to think of juvenile courts as forums for delinquency, and often they are. But juvenile courts deal with other types of cases, such as child abuse, lack of proper medical treatment, truancy and termination of parental rights.

Because juveniles are particularly vulnerable to the negative effects of publicity, the courts traditionally have been quite protective. Some critics will argue that juvenile officials are overly protective. Indeed, with strict confidentiality stressed in most juvenile courts, it is difficult at times for the press to perform its watchdog role.

Some states allow the press access to juvenile proceedings, although prohibitions on disclosure of the juvenile's identity or other confidential information generally apply. Access to records might be limited primarily to law enforcement officials or agencies that deal with juvenile matters. Moreover, paper trails can be wiped clean in jurisdictions that permit *expungement* (removal) of criminal records for juveniles who stay out of further trouble with the law.

Sensitive reporters, of course, consider the welfare of juveniles in their coverage and, most often, honor conditions of confidentiality, even with regard to juveniles accused of committing serious crimes. Names of juveniles do, though, appear in news accounts. Policies differ among news organizations; moreover, circumstances affect decisions to reveal identities. Under the law, however, it appears clear that it is not illegal for reporters to identify juveniles. In two cases in the 1970s, the Supreme Court established that journalists cannot be punished for or prohibited from disclosing lawfully obtained information about juvenile offenders. Civil liability, though, remains a possibility, especially over invasion of a juvenile's privacy.[22]

The toughest disclosure decisions usually involve particularly shocking crimes. The decision-making burden is eased if an accused juvenile is prosecuted as an adult. That happens if the prosecutor, through a motion, can convince a juvenile-court judge that the case warrants special consideration. Factors that determine whether a juvenile is certified as an adult include premeditation, extreme aggressiveness, age, prior criminal record and public safety. More often, though, juveniles are treated differently because they are children, and children make mistakes from which they can be expected to recover. Among the correctional options available to juvenile-court judges are placement in a foster home, assignment of community service or commitment to a detention facility, such as a military-style boot camp.

Despite the difficulties and sensitive matters associated with covering juvenile law, journalists must observe carefully, if not always report all that they observe. The juvenile justice system is one of society's pressure points. Crime, divorce, sexual abuse, drug abuse, runaways and teenage pregnancies frequently are either the causes or effects of juvenile problems. Important decisions affecting young lives are being made daily, often behind closed doors. The shield of privacy around the juvenile courts obscures as well as protects, increasing the likelihood of hidden problems. The argument that responsible news coverage serves the interests of juveniles therefore appears as strong as the argument for strict confidentiality.

Bankruptcy

Charles Dickens experienced the humiliation of a debtor's prison because of his father's financial problems. In Dickens' day, entire families lived in jails while the debtor was punished. It was a degrading and nonsensical way to deal with debtors, who obviously could not repay creditors from a jail. The specter of debtor's prisons encouraged the framers of the U.S. Constitution to provide for uniform laws governing bankruptcy under section 8 of Article I.

In today's climate of consumer credit, economic downshifts and job layoffs, debt is a problem of major proportions. But U.S. bankruptcy laws now allow individuals, partnerships and corporations relief from all or part of their debt in order to make fresh starts.

Although there are several types of bankruptcy cases under federal law, the three most common are "Chapter 7," "Chapter 13" or "Chapter 11" bankruptcies. Chapter 7 provides for *liquidation* of a debtor's assets, with the exception of certain exempt property, such as a home, and distribution of those assets among the creditors. A Chapter 13 bankruptcy, also called a wage earner's plan, enables people with regular income to develop a plan to repay all or part of their debts to creditors over three to five years in an installment plan. During this time the law forbids creditors from starting or continuing collection efforts. Chapter 11 provides for *reorganization* so that businesses, in particular, can continue to operate under a plan that determines the manner and amount of payments to creditors.

A Chapter 11 bankruptcy usually is handled by a court-appointed *trustee* whose duties include administering property, investigating financial conditions and overseeing implementation of the reorganization plan. Trustees in the reorganization of large corporations are often experienced managers or business executives. In Chapter 7 and 13 bankruptcies, trustees normally play a lesser role. All three types can be voluntary, when the debtor files for bankruptcy, or involuntary, when the creditors initiate the bankruptcy petition. In 2005, the federal Bankruptcy Abuse Prevention and Consumer Protection Act took effect, setting stricter requirements for Chapter 7 filings and more paperwork hurdles to discourage serial filers and other abuses of the law.

Where do journalists look for bankruptcy stories? When an unemployed sheet-metal worker with $10,000 in credit card bills declares bankruptcy, few news organizations could justify telling his story; there are too many more pressing, more significant stories to tell. In fact, the worker probably would not want his story told. But when the man's employer, which employs 800 other workers, files for bankruptcy, that is news—perhaps quite surprising news. Businesses and corporations sometimes quietly, without attracting much attention, fall into debt. A venerable downtown department store, for example, may seem to outsiders financially stable if not solid, until its owner petitions for reorganization.

Once an individual or company takes its financial problems into U.S. Bankruptcy Court, there is no hiding records and debt. The information debtors normally must provide includes the identity of company officials, the names of creditors and the amounts owed. Documents like these often lead to additional, newsworthy details about the company's financial woes and its impact on the community.

Much of the work of bankruptcy courts is done informally and not before a judge. Debtors and creditors, usually aided by the trustee, collaborate on terms. If all goes well, the judge's role is to approve arrangements and discharge the case. Along the way, there may be hearings, but there are no trials or juries in bankruptcy court. Moreover, bankruptcy is the exclusive domain of the federal court system. State courts retain some jurisdiction when creditors seek, for example, to garnish a debtor's wages or foreclose on his or her property. A petition for bankruptcy, however, *stays* (suspends) attempts by creditors to collect on a debt through state courts. In addition, state legislatures can establish statutory exemptions that protect debtors from loss of certain property, such as a home or tools of a trade. Often, debtors can choose between the uniform federal exemptions or the exemptions provided by state law, which can vary greatly.

This chapter and Chapter 8 primarily address the work of reporters assigned to the court beat. But *all* reporters should be able to find, read, interpret and analyze court decisions. In this society there is not a geographic or subject beat that is litigation-free. The baseball writer or book editor, for example, should be prepared to report on the law as it affects their beats. They cannot say, "Oh, that's something for the courthouse reporter." For one thing, the reporter assigned specifically to the courts might be tied up with several other pressing stories. For another, the court reporter may lack the background and news contacts to deal with, say, an antitrust suit by players against owners or a copyright case involving a biographer's use of a famous person's unpublished correspondence.

As Chapter 10 demonstrates, the challenges of special beats—from religion to business—include issues of social and *legal* significance.

Exercises

1 Ask a librarian at the nearest law school to show you reference books, law journals and case reporters available to help journalists cover legal news. Have the librarian help you conduct an uncomplicated search.

2 As an introduction to the criminal courts, spend several hours observing preliminary hearings, which are commonly held at a regularly scheduled time and courtroom. "Prelims" usually offer an intriguing cross-section of offenses, which, on a given day, could range from child abandonment to vehicular homicide. Select a case that particularly interests you and follow its outcome.

3 Scan the news for an important ruling by the U.S. Supreme Court or the state supreme court. (As an option, select a decision from a nearby state or federal appellate court.) Consider the ruling's local impact. Talk to people who might be affected and to those who have informed opinions about the ruling's meaning. Authorities are probably available on campus. Write a localized story about the case.

Notes

1. Brian Grow, "Richard Scrushy's 'Amen Corner'," *BusinessWeek* online, posted Jan. 20, 2006.
2. F. Lee Bailey and Henry B. Rothblatt, *Fundamentals of Criminal Advocacy* (Rochester, N.Y.: Lawyers Co-Operative, 1974), p. 285.
3. Seymour Wishman, *Anatomy of a Jury* (New York: Times Books, 1986), p. vii.
4. Harry Kalven Jr. and Hans Zeisel, *The American Jury* (New York: Little, Brown, 1966); Lawrence S. Wrightsman, Saul M. Kassin and Cynthia E. Willis, eds., *In the Jury Box* (Newbury Park, Calif.: Sage, 1987); Randolph N. Jonakait, *The American Jury System* (New Haven, Conn.: Yale University Press, 2003).
5. Michael S. Lief, H. Mitchell Caldwell and Ben Bycel, *Ladies and Gentlemen of the Jury* (New York: Touchstone, 2000), pp. 298, 301–302.
6. "Poindexter Judge Scolds Press for Calling Jurors," *St. Petersburg Times*, April 4, 1990, p. 4A.
7. C. David Rambo, "Judge's Instructions in Sharon Case Weighed by Libel Experts," *presstime*, April 1985, pp. 24, 25.
8. Theo Wilson, *Headline Justice* (New York: Thunder's Mouth Press, 1996).
9. Gary A. Hengstler, "Dealing with the Media," *Courts Today,* March–April 2006.
10. "Feeding the Ravenous Appetite of the Press," *Media Studies Journal*, Winter 1998, p. 106.
11. "Former Preschool Workers Acquitted of Molestation," *St. Petersburg Times*, Jan. 19, 1990, p. 2A.
12. "Spirited Woman Q&A with Linda Deutsch," www.thespiritedwoman.com/newsletter/2005/10/december_2003.html.
13. "Tyco Mistrial: Blame the Media," cbsnews.com, posted April 2, 2004.
14. "Almost 7 Million Adults under Correctional Supervison behind Bars or on Probation or Parole in the Comunity," press release, Bureau of Justice Statistics, Nov. 2, 2005, www.ojp.usdoj.gov/bjs.
15. Joan Petersilia, *Probation and Felony Offenders* (Washington, D.C.: U.S. Department of Justice, National Institute of Justice, 1985), p. 3.

16. "Burnett Settles Libel Suit," *Editor & Publisher*, Jan. 26, 1985, p. 33.

17. "Legal Myths: The McDonald's 'Hot Coffee' Case," *Public Citizen*, posted Nov. 30, 1999.

18. Lyle W. Denniston, *The Reporter and the Law* (New York: Columbia University Press, 1992), p. 198.

19. John Seigenthaler, "News Media Neglect Has Made the Federal Court of Appeals 'the Anonymous Court'," *ASNE Bulletin*, March 1989, pp. 4, 6.

20. *New York Times v. Sullivan*, 376 U.S. 254 (1964).

21. Robert Coram, "Assume That Assumptions Are Wrong," *The Quill*, February 1987, p. 17.

22. See *Smith v. Daily Mail Publishing Co.*, 443 U.S. 97 (1979), and *Oklahoma Publishing Co. v. District Court in and for Oklahoma County*, 430 U.S. 308 (1977).

Special Beats, New Challenges 10

On a playground, children mimic street life At play, children invent games for their amusement. Here they use chalk outlines of their own bodies and then label them with their names. Did they find inspiration in scenes from police investigations? (Photo by Robbie Arkovich.)

General-assignment reporters cover the day's news as it unfolds—from a hail storm in the morning to an American Legion convention that afternoon. They are valued for many reasons, such as the ability to transform a dull press release into a page-one story. Few assignments intimidate or deter competent general-assignment reporters, who can cover a first-grade play and the opening day of the state legislature with comparable verve and results.

General-assignment reporters do important work, but, increasingly, they lack the expertise to cover complex subjects and events. "Good general-assignment reporters—in print and television—are an invaluable asset," said *Time* and *Newsday* veteran reporter Richard Clurman (1924–1996). "But specialists are an imperative." As Clurman correctly noted, "Generalized knowledge or the ability to 'take the information down right' is essential but today it is insufficient. Very few big stories are any longer simple.

They are intertwined with economics, law, government, new technology, history, sciences. The essential homework on many an assignment can no longer be done by simply reading the clips."[1]

Journalists in the 21st century can anticipate more significant, rewarding roles in reporting the news. But to remain relevant and meaningful in a rapidly changing, diverse society, reporters should be masters of information and experts on particular subjects and issues. New York University professor Jay Rosen says journalism is becoming even more of a thinking profession. According to Rosen, "Reporters will have to be skilled in recognizing patterns, spotting connections, isolating and integrating key facts. The mind of a thinking journalist is an excellent device for reducing information, and this will be a vital service in the years ahead—reducing, rather than providing information."[2]

The journalist's ability to reduce and distill information will be needed for other reasons. Media observer Neil Postman (1931–2003) said we kept our eyes warily on 1984, but the Orwellian nightmare of an oppressive, Big Brother-controlled society never materialized. Instead, he said, we should have been heeding the words of Aldous Huxley's *Brave New World*. As Postman saw it, "[George] Orwell feared those who would deprive us of infomation. Huxley feared those who would give us so much that we would be reduced to passivity and egoism. Orwell feared that the truth would be concealed from us. Huxley feared the truth would be drowned in a sea of irrelevance."[3]

If we are closer to Huxley's world than Orwell's, today's journalists not only must skillfully navigate through a sea of irrelevance, they also have to be on guard for what Stewart Brand calls "toxic information," a byproduct of communications technology. Although toxins—disinformation, propaganda, political spin and other forms of media manipulation—are nothing new, Brand fears a future of bigger and more dangerous lies and deception. In his view,

> Two centuries of lively experience with the practice of free speech and press in America suggests that most information that might be considered toxic can be handled by the public kidneys. Yelling, "Fire!" in a crowded theater (unless there's a fire) has proven toxicity, however. There's insufficient time to sort out the truth of the matter before serious harm is done; could that happen in the crowded theater of world communication? Inevitably.[4]

The explosive growth of the Web has contributed greatly to the problem of toxic information. Besides providing news of importance and usefulness, journalists must do their best to keep information free of contamination.

The news beats and subjects addressed by journalists also reflect the changing world around us—unanticipated diseases spread by humankind's indifference to the environment; social tensions of immigration, race and ethnicity; the assortment of problems associated with poverty, homelesses and drug abuse. All these conditions—and more—require journalism's closest and best attention.

This chapter explores special areas of societal concern and the formidable challenges to news coverage they pose.

Medicine and Science

Elizabeth Whitney, who retired from the *St. Petersburg Times* after a distinguished career of reporting and editing, told her readers about a 15-year-old story she simply could not forget. Her experience began routinely enough, when she read a medical journal report about a remedy for traveler's diarrhea and children's diarrhea that could be made with ingredients found in anyone's kitchen.

Whitney called the chief of intestinal diseases at the Centers for Disease Control in Atlanta—a key source of information for medical reporters—to learn details. The doctor said the remedy was "a medical breakthrough" not then available in the United States. He gave Whitney the formula, which she published. Whitney recalled what happened:

> The day it was published, I was visited by a delegation of grim-faced pediatricians. They said my story omitted a crucial fact—that the formula had to be diluted with water. A child taking large quantities of the formula as given could develop salt poisoning which would cause brain hemorrhage, convulsions and brain damage.
>
> When I called the CDC chief, he said the local doctors were right and he had forgotten to mention the water. The next morning the Times published a prominent correction headed "Diarrhea remedy held dangerous."[5]

To her great relief, Whitney never heard about any child becoming ill from taking the formula, but she blamed herself for not knowing to ask whether the formula should be diluted. "Though I covered medicine for two years, I never overcame my discomfort with science. I asked to be taken off the beat."

In covering medicine, science and health, careful, precise reporting is an absolute necessity, not simply an ideal. As Whitney knew, making a mistake covering medicine and science can lead to far more serious consequences than an editor's scolding or a libel suit. People tend to put great faith in news reports about medical cures, wonder drugs, weight-loss programs, surgical procedures, tips for improved health and fitness and warnings about dangerous chemicals or treatments. Reporters who misinform or mislead in their coverage, however unintentionally, can do harm by raising false hopes or passing on bad advice. Worse, lives may be endangered. In an Internet age, reporters also need to combat misinformation about cures and treatments, some of them dangerous, spread by Web-based charlatans.

Medicine

AIDS remains a major topic of medical news, but in the beginning, with a few exceptions, the press slowly reacted to its presence, at first writing it off as an isolated disease of gay men. After 1985, however, coverage quickly expanded and gradually improved. Reporters who now cover AIDS on a regular basis are familiar with medical terms and sources of reliable information. They know, for example, that the correct name for the AIDS virus is HIV—human immunodeficiency virus—and that testing positive for HIV is not equivalent to having AIDS.

The AIDS crisis demonstrates the need for medical reportage that is clear and straightforward. In the early stages of coverage, newspapers and broadcasters avoided sexual terminology and descriptions pertaining to the transmission of HIV for fear of offending people. Reference was made to "bodily fluids" and "unsafe sex." Finally, news organizations began using graphic explanations, as the *Boston Globe* did in reporting that "no semen, pre-ejaculatory fluid or vaginal secretions should enter anyone's vagina, rectum or mouth."[6] In matters of life and death, delicacy and decorum must yield to the need for reliable facts. Stories continue to report treatment advances, especially new combinations of drugs to help those infected with HIV.

HIV/AIDS also illustrates several danger zones in medical reporting—the urgency of research in certain areas of medicine; the pressure on scientists to secure grants and win acclaim; and the tendency of journalists to look for "breakthroughs" and "cures." Obviously, reporters must first get the facts right. It is also vitally important for them to resist the urge—and the efforts of others—to exaggerate the importance of medical developments. In all areas of scientific reporting, reporters must proceed with caution and restraint.

Usually, findings published in a professional publication, such as the *New England Journal of Medicine*, are prescreened by experts who review a submitted article for the soundness of its methodology and conclusions. Not every study of importance, however, is carried by the leading journals. Can reporters judge research or medical reports for themselves? To a degree, yes, but safeguards should be taken. In *News & Numbers*, a guide to coverage of science and medicine, Victor Cohn (1955–2005) suggested questions that reporters can ask to gain understanding and to judge the validity of research.[7] If there is a study, Cohn said, obtain a copy. Ask researchers to explain and justify methods and procedures. If the research involves human test subjects, it is important to know the number of subjects and how they were selected and monitored.

As a final prepublication step, reporters should check with the researchers to ensure against errors in describing or assessing the study. If appropriate, reporters should also consult with other experts in the field for reaction and insight. Outside experts may save reporters from a serious blunder or mistake of judgment.

Medical coverage includes examination of the economics and ethics of care and treatment. The rising costs of hospitalization and medical procedures already is a societal problem of multiple dimensions. The U.S. Census Bureau puts the number of Americans without medical insurance at 15 percent of the population—about 45 million.

Millions more are underinsured, which means they cannot always afford to treat illness or seek medical assistance. Even those with health insurance through managed-care programs face restrictions on access to medical specialists and time limits on hospital stays under terms of their contracts. Occasionally, people do not get the care they need if the health-care provider refuses to pay the costs. Reporters ought to anticipate even more collisions of medicine, money and morals.

Medical reporters are responsible for monitoring a broad range of critical issues and concerns. No single reporter can begin to address them all, which is why most journalists should concentrate on news closest to home. One starting point is to obtain and examine mortality rates of local hospitals. As always, statistics should be approached skeptically. Although a high mortality rate might suggest a hospital is a death trap, other factors, such as the age and socioeconomic status of patients, might explain the figures. The mortality rate might also reveal a problem concentrated in one unit, not the entire hospital.

Another area to explore is the availability and quality of medical services. Some communities, for example, are without obstetric (childbirth) care because high rates for malpractice insurance have forced doctors to limit their practices to general medicine. Not all doctors do right by their patients. Medicine has its share of incompetents, drug users, molesters, quacks and mercenaries. State agencies and professional boards attempt to police medicine, but some bad doctors go undetected. Reporters on the medical beat must listen to patients, monitor lawsuits against physicians and check records of medical improprieties. The Alliance for Health Reform provides a handbook, *Covering Health Issues*, through its Web site, www.allhealth.org.

When new drugs, treatments and surgical procedures are announced, medical reporters should get details to the public quickly. With the national emphasis on good health, more people are alert for medical developments that affect them, family members or friends. Often they pass along information gleaned from news reports to doctors—not all of whom read newspapers, much less studies from medical journals. A story about a new method of cancer detection, for example, could save lives. Medical reporters should not assume that "everyone" knows about the latest cancer

Robots in the operating room The da Vinci robotic surgery system, used commonly to remove cancerous prostate glands, allows surgeons, positioned at a control station, to operate with great precision through the robot's arms and tools. With da Vinci, a surgeon could operate on a patient on the other side of the world. Doctors also use robotic surgery in heart, gynecological and gastric bypass operations, with added uses on the way. (Photo by Robbie Arkovich.)

news simply because the major media, particularly network television, gave it heavy coverage. Important medical stories deserve local coverage with local angles as well.

Finally, journalists need to look beyond traditional medical facilities to investigate the quality of care for the poor, homeless and the physcially and mentally disabled who are most likely to suffer neglect.

Science

Science coverage can range from mindboggling theories of cosmic evolution to studies about drought-resistant lawns. Obviously, scientific developments touch our lives in innumerable ways, but for most people, science news becomes a priority when it directly touches their lives. For example, people want to know if Splenda is a safe substitute for sugar or whether depletion of the ozone layer and global warming theories are as alarming as they sound. Consequently, a great deal of science reporting focuses on threats to humans and the planet. In covering such stories, reporters must be aware of potential for setting off false alarms or causing panic.

A pesticide, Alar, offers the anatomy of a so-called scare story. Alar, Uniroyal Chemical Co.'s trade name for daminozide, was used on apples primarily to improve color and prolong shelf life. Studies dating to the early 1970s suggested that large doses of daminozide caused cancer in laboratory animals. Little media attention was given to risks of eating Alar-treated apples until an environmental group called the Natural Resources Defense Council released a report early in 1989. The report predicted that 6,000 preschool children in America today would get cancer solely due to exposure to eight pesticides used on food, and it named Alar as the chief threat.

The NRDC report received widespread coverage fueled by a *60 Minutes* report, leading *New York Times* columnist William Safire to question whether journalists overreacted. "We are prone to be terrified of risk, any risk," Safire says, "and malleable media amplify the alarmists' cries." Environmental lobbyists like NRDC, Safire contended, undermine public trust in government scientists. "Government scientists have no monopoly on the truth," he says, "and it's healthy for them to be challenged—provided the alarm's coverage is accompanied by reassuring rebuttals."[8]

Today, Alar, according to Wikipedia, is shorthand among news media and food industry professionals for an irrational, emotional public response based on hyperbole rather than facts. Elliott Negin, reporting for *Columbia Journalism Review*, disputes the depiction of Alar as Chicken Little environmentalism and government regulation run amok. "There was indeed an overreaction to the *60 Minutes* report, as viewers confused a long-term cumulative threat with imminent danger. But Alar is a potent carcinogen, and its risks far outweigh its benefits." After extensive review, the Environmental Protection Agency banned Alar, saying "long-term exposure poses unacceptable risks to public health."[9]

Science reporters are under a doubly difficult obligation, says ABC correspondent Jeff Greenfield. "They have to interpret and understand very complicated disputatious material. Not only that, they have to render it in English without leaving the audience in the dark."[10] As Greenfield notes, sources of science information are often trade or industry groups that can be helpful but potentially biased. Turning to opponents, such as environmental groups, for reaction would add balance to coverage but not necessarily shed light. As a consequence, determining who is right and who is wrong—when to worry and when not to—can be difficult if not impossible. A free hotline (800-223-1730) operated by Media Resource Service (www.mediaresource.org), formerly a program of the Scientists' Institute for Public Information, can usually provide journalists with the names of experts on different sides of an issue.

Health

Many people are exceedingly concerned about staying healthy. They read labels and shun products that are fatty or laced with chemical additives. Those who zealously seek to be trim and fit are susceptible to dangerous weight-loss treatments or vitamin regimens. Reporters on the health beat must watch for the latest fitness trend and subject it to a thorough critique, not laugh it off as "wacky."

Health, like science and medicine, is another area where there are few unequivocal answers about what is good for us—and what is not. Should people be brooding about their cholesterol count? Does a high-fiber diet reduce the risk of cancer? If we turn to chicken instead of red meat, are we exposing ourselves to serious danger of salmonella poisoning? Studies and claims by experts vary and often contradict one another, leading columnist Russell Baker to say in exasperation: "Almost everything they say is good for you will turn out to be bad for you if you hang around long enough, and almost everything they say is bad for you will turn out not to matter."[11]

In 2007, the issue of trans fats in foods made headlines, especially after New York City banned trans fats, also known as partially hydrogenated oils, in restaurants and school cafeterias. Legislators in more than a dozen states called for similar prohibitions. *New York Times* writer Gina Kolata asked scientists what they thought, and one called trans fat the health panic du jour, and others downplayed the heart disease risk.[11]

REPORTER'S TIP FILE

Keeping a health-claims chronology

If both journalists and the public become exasperated over what is safe and what is bad for us, it stems from trying to keep up with the crush of competing health claims. Take coffee, for example; dozens of studies have examined the effects of coffee and caffeine. No reader or viewer can be expected to mentally log and compare each study. That job should be the reporter's. On any beat where a new study or report joins a growing stack of prior studies

---

and reports, reporters should periodically provide an accompanying chronology, identifying past findings and providing follow-ups on continuing research. Information on coffee, for instance, could be recorded and stored in a computer file or spreadsheet maintained by the reporter. Once a chronology is started, it becomes fairly easy to update.

A related problem worth the attention of journalists is the apparent peddling of prescription medicine and vitamin therapy—concerns that pharmaceutical companies, through TV advertising, are contributing to hypochondria of the latest popular ailments—restless leg syndrome, insomnia, acid reflux and allergies of all sorts. Besides drug ads to get patients to ask for name brands, salespeople flood doctors' offices and clinics with traveling shows of potions and pills. In a few cases, doctors and hospital officials succumb to gifts and others forms of inducement to use or prescribe particular products, including costly (but revenue-generating) diagnostic equipment. The drug and medical marketplace bears watching by the press.

Environment

Medical, science and health reporting overlap at times or intersect with another fast-growing area of coverage—environmental reporting. Much of what is considered environmental reporting focuses on humankind's abuse of nature, which includes pollution of water, land and air. The *Chicago Tribune*'s Casey Burko, one of journalism's first environmental-beat reporters, worries that too few reporters at smaller news organizations receive the chance to specialize in the environment.

He stresses the need for journalists to understand issues, not merely report the arguments or claims. Burko cites early coverage of nuclear power as an example: "We missed the boat on nuclear power because [we] became cheerleaders for technology. We just swallowed that stuff and didn't look at the downside at all."[12] Environmental reporters not only need to report today's problems and anticipate tomorrow's, they also should be determining whether programs and technologies offered as solutions to environmental problems are working, such as water-treatment plants.

The environmental beat may also include coverage of the use and transportation of chemicals. When mishandled, chemicals can poison water supplies, contaminate soil and cause health problems for humans and animals. Potential stories range from the dangers of lawn-spraying services to regulation of industrial byproducts. A related problem involves disposal and transportation of radioactive materials, such as waste from hospital radiology departments. Every day, radioactive materials are shipped through towns by truck or train, which means there is always the potential for a mishap. (Does your community have an emergency plan if toxins are accidentally released into the environment?) Reporters should also be prepared to react to environmental emergencies. A booklet produced by the National Safety Council—*Chemicals, the Press and the*

Public: A Journalist's Guide to Reporting on Chemicals in the Community—includes information on coverage of emergencies (www.nsc.org/ehc/guidebks/chemtoc.htm).

Environmental journalism includes sensitive, knowledgeable coverage of the larger world humans inhabit. Native American holistic philosophy offers an unconventional and potentially enlightening perspective for journalists. Geneticist David Suzuki said the chief of the Nuu Chah Nulth people in Canada once told him: "If the water can no longer support the salmon, if the land can't support deer and bear, then why do we think it will support us?" The Nuu Chah Nulth believe that all things are sacred gifts from the Creator and deserve to be treated with respect. The Nuu Chah Nulth phrase *hishuk ish ts'awalk* ("everything is one") refers to the belief of oneness between humans and their environment—land, water, animal and plant life. When reporting on the environment, stories often are framed through human eyes and experience. In the Native American tradition, a story about a woodland habitat endangered by a megamall might be told through the perspective of a northern spotted owl.[13]

Education

A typical education reporter can be found at 10 p.m. on a Tuesday night struggling to stay alert as she covers a marathon meeting of the school board. The next day she may be dodging a midmorning rush of university students as she heads to an interview with the school's president.

Education-beat coverage includes a mixed bag of meetings, bond issues, graduation ceremonies, homecomings, budgets, strikes and assorted controversies. It is an expansive beat that may range from preschool to the state capital. Education reporters can expect to encounter an interplay of many forces: unions, legislators, courts, school officials, parents, citizens and state boards of education. But in covering the groups and personalities, they must never lose sight of or contact with the main target—students.

Education on the Local Level

Newsday reporter Emily Sachar felt she needed remedial work in education writing, so she went back to school—as an eighth-grade mathematics teacher in Brooklyn. Prior to her journey into the classroom, Sachar had written frequently about the decrepit physical conditions of city schools and the tough job of being a teacher. Despite her past experiences, Sachar quickly discovered she really knew little about her beat. Her work as a teacher turned out to be exhausting, frustrating and disturbing. Particularly disturbing were the school district's lax requirements that allowed students to be promoted out of the eighth grade without having passed mathematics or language arts. "As a reporter, I had suspected that the promotional standards were weak. But, until I worked as a teacher, I had no idea what practical meaning the lack of standards has for kids."[14]

Sachar easily obtained a job because New York so desperately needed teachers. Not all reporters could—or would want to—go so far to learn their beat. But Sachar reinforces the value of direct observation and firsthand experience. Even a one-day visit is useful, says *Lansing State Journal* reporter Lisa Gutierrez: "Education reporters must get into the classrooms. Being there breathes detail and life into education stories. I would never have known a picture of Jesus Christ hangs next to the American flag in an award-winning Michigan teacher's classroom if I hadn't been there."

Gutierrez understands that meetings of the school board or interviews with the district superintendent rarely tell the whole story, much less reveal how administrative decisions affect students, teachers and parents. "Meetings reveal what administrators want the public to know," she says, "not necessarily what it should know. Meetings don't tell you that the budget cuts being discussed mean that students will keep using history books written in the 1960s."[15] Gutierrez regularly talks to teachers, students and parents, providing them with her business card and urging them to call with concerns or story ideas.

Education reporters, however, cannot ignore administrators as news sources or skip meetings. The presence of reporters at school meetings is particularly important for the sake of accountability. Unless a controversy over a tax hike or a book ban is brewing, school meetings are lightly attended. As with governmental meetings, reporters are there as the surrogate listeners and observers for the public. State open-meetings laws generally give the press access to school board deliberations but, at times, access is granted grudgingly and closed-door "executive sessions" are common. In some districts, reporters and school officials perpetually battle over access to meetings and records.

Invariably, a key source on the local education beat is the school superintendent, who is usually accustomed to meeting with reporters. Superintendents, however, face considerable pressure; the more pressure, the less likely they are to be candid and expansive in answering questions. While a powerful superintendent may rule a district with little opposition from the school board, circumstances and personalities might lead to frequent clashes and discord within the education hierarchy, further complicating news coverage. At the top of the hierarchy is the school board (or board of education), which is responsible for setting educational policy and making budgetary decisions. School board members are either elected or appointed laypersons who tend to reflect a cross-section of the community population—homemakers, insurance agents, dentists, factory workers. Are they, by education and experience, well suited to oversee the school system? That is something education-beat reporters should try to determine. As with coverage of any politicized beat, journalists need to know who wields power and how effectively that power is exercised.

The local education beat encompasses much more than the public schools, grades K through 12. Education begins in homes, where children ideally receive emotional and educational nourishment. Of course, home environments vary dramatically; an infant from a poor family might receive more verbal stimulation than one from a middle-class home, but the odds are against it. Comprehensive education reporting examines social conditions that eventually will be felt in the classroom, such as the alarming increase in teenage pregnancies and cocaine babies.

A community's education "system" also includes an array of private and special schools. Early childhood education is especially prevalent as parents seek places for their preschoolers. In some cases, the need is practical—someone must watch the children while the parents work. In other cases, parents enroll children in preschool programs because they believe it is a prerequisite for the academic and, ultimately, the professional success of their offspring. Private schools and parochial elementary and high schools provide options to public education. They should not be dismissed as havens for the elite or bastions of religious doctrine. In fact, many serve as innovative education models from which to draw lessons and make comparisons.

Non-traditional educational programs warrant regular coverage as well. These include schools for "special" children, whether gifted or mentally disabled. School districts nationwide use the *magnet school* concept to provide specialized education, for example, in the arts, information technology and health sciences. The programs also help naturally integrate the school system. Other popular alternatives to conventional schools include *fundamental* schools, based on strict rules and hands-on involvement of parents.

More controversial educational experiments involve charter schools and school vouchers. A charter school typically is designed and operated by educators, parents, community leaders and educational entrepreneurs. Ideally, a charter school uses innovative, non-traditional education methods to achieve results. While affiliated with local school districts, charter schools operate independently, although public school officials are expected to monitor their quality and effectiveness. Problems, however, include teachers without proper credentials, inadequate classroom facilities and budget mismanagement, including a few cases of outright fraud.

Under the voucher program, parents can apply state-funded monetary stipends toward the cost of tuition at private schools, including those operated by churches or religious groups. Touted as a way to help offer more educational opportunities to poor parents and their children, critics believe the system drains resources from public schools. In 2005, the Florida Supreme Court said the state voucher system, the nation's first statewide program, violated the Florida Constitution's requirement of a uniform system of free public education.

Vocational, trade and technical schools prepare an important segment of the population for the service-related jobs, although some trade school programs deserve special scrutiny for fraudulent claims about job-placement rates or dishonest practices, such as signing up "phantom" students for federal grants. Other areas of education include "elderhostel" programs for retirees who enjoy combining travel and study; the home-schooling movement; continuing-education programs for professionals; and adult-education classes.

Reporters who draw the boundaries of the education beat too narrowly will miss important stories.

State and Federal Involvement

Increasingly, educational policies are influenced by forces and factors outside the local community. While property taxes still constitute the major source of funding for local schools, the annual influx of state and federal money is critical for nearly all districts, particularly big-city systems. As government involvement spreads beyond local districts, politics and politicians play an even greater role in education, going well beyond debates on taxes and budgets.

Part of the attention being directed at education by the White House, Congress, governors, state legislators and assorted agencies can be traced to the publication in 1983 of *A Nation at Risk*, a report of the National Commission on Excellence in Education. Alarm over declining academic performance of students and teachers prompted politicians to form task forces and commissions, which in turn led to a spate of legislation and programs. In Florida and several other states, for example, legislators tried to curb high dropout rates by denying driver's licenses to anyone quitting school before the age of 18. Teachers and school administrators saw some of these efforts as needless meddling. Politicians justify an active role in school business, arguing that the condition of education is directly related to the social and economic well-being of the entire state.

The state's involvement in local education is substantial largely because of the governance structures and fiscal policies. Most school boards and districts are highly dependent on state funding. A handful of states have comprehensive boards of education that oversee and coordinate all public schools. In most states, however, there are separate boards and agencies for elementary-secondary education and higher education.

State boards, agencies and commissions engage in policymaking and planning, but nearly everything in education boils down to financing. On a national average, about 50 percent of school funding comes from state sources; 44 percent is locally generated principally by property taxes; and 6 percent comes from federal programs. State education boards normally recommend how state money should be spent, but ultimately the legislature and governor battle over the education budget. In covering school financing, reporters need both state and local sources. In all cases, reporters covering public education must know and report where the money comes from and how and where it is being spent. The public is always sensitive about how its taxes are handled, and rightly so.

The symbol of federal involvement is the Department of Education, created in 1980. Although it remains the smallest of the cabinet-level departments in terms of budget, it helps set priorities for education and provides funding for important programs, such as "Chapter 1" of the Education Consolidation and Improvement Act, which aids academically disadvantaged younger students with supplemental work in basic skills. Local schools depend on Chapter 1 funds to help children overcome those disadvantages.

Congress becomes involved by providing funding for the Department of Education. Less obvious is Congress' role in other education-related programs, such as the work of congressional committees and subcommittees. The Senate Agriculture Committee, for example, oversees school food programs that provide hot meals for students.

With education a pressing national issue, the White House, too, has gotten deeply involved, especially in promoting educational performance standards. In 2001, President George W. Bush introduced a massive federal reform plan called "No Child Left Behind" intended to reduce the achievement gap and raise achievement levels overall. The initiative gave state and local authorities more control over U.S. dollars and, in return, federal officials mandated more testing of student performance to provide accountability. Several states, including Utah and Virginia, represent a rising tide of opposition to the mandate on grounds that it is an unworkable intrusion on local school control.

Covering the local schools means covering federal and state influence along the way.

Higher Education

State involvement is especially apparent in regard to higher education. Public universities and colleges are highly dependent on state subsidies because, with the exception of two-year community colleges, they do not collect property-tax money. Appropriation bills for higher education sometimes become political hostages as legislators and the governor battle over budget priorities. Annual funding for higher education may be in doubt up to the final hours of legislative sessions. Critical books, such as 1990's *Killing the Spirit* by Page Smith and 1989's *Profscam* by Charles J. Sykes, have helped make the case that college students are not getting their money's worth. Unfair images persist of overpaid, underworked, tenured professors who enjoy sabbaticals and other leisure pursuits. Some politicians find academicians tempting and safe subjects, so they pander to public mistrust of what goes on at colleges and universities.

Regardless of the political unpleasantries involved, covering higher education can be an enjoyable, rewarding assignment. Today's colleges and universities reflect a new diversity in courses and students. With the pool of 18- to 22-year-old students dwindling, higher education is finding renewed life in older students who are returning to school. Some are women who have nurtured families and now seek careers outside the home; others are "lifelong learners"—men and women who enroll to stay intellectually active; and some are people who are making midcareer changes. Colleges and universities have reacted to a shifting clientele by offering a wider range of classes for part-time and evening students, some of whom take classes online from their homes or gather at distant-learning centers linked to the main campus by interactive cable hookups.

Thousands of potential human-interest stories are to be found in college classrooms. Other important, appealing stories can be found outside the classroom in faculty offices, research labs, clinics or auditoriums. Reporter John Carlson of the *Des Moines Register* tells about covering the University of Iowa:

> In the past year, I've stood alongside surgeons at University of Iowa Hospitals as they performed a rare 12-hour-long double-lung transplant and watched as physicists received and analyzed data sent back millions of miles from outer space.
>
> I have held the 300,000-year-old jawbone of an extinct ape and sat backstage as the Joffrey Ballet auditioned Iowa children for the company's performance of *The Nutcracker*.
>
> And I didn't come up with these ideas covering a dull faculty meeting or rewriting a press release.[16]

Worthwhile stories are not likely to emerge when a reporter simply drops by the campus for an occasional visit. Too much is happening—some of it out of sight—for part-time coverage to be effective. Moreover, part-timers cannot easily develop a mix of sources or build a reputation for reliability.

What's Wrong with Education—or What's Right?

"Crisis" seems to be the word most frequently used to characterize American education. In his book, *Among Schoolchildren,* based on a year of observing a fifth-grade class in Holyoke, Mass., journalist Tracy Kidder noted:

> The history of education in America is the history of attempts to reform it. The latest movement deplores high dropout rates and declines in the College Board scores of new teachers. Many tests and surveys show that large percentages of American youth come out of high school and even college incompetent in the three R's and ignorant of basic facts about history, geography, science and literature. The bad news has inspired many commissions and from them many reports that make use of the word "crisis." As in the late 1950s, these reports often invoke an external threat—not Soviet competition now, but Japanese economic power.[17]

Another journalist focused on education, Jonathan Kozol, first wrote about inner-city schools based on a year in Boston as a fourth-grade teacher. Later he wrote books filled with both hope and despair about schools in East St. Louis, Ill., and the South Bronx. In 2005, he published *The Shame of Our Nation*, subtitled *The Restoration of Apartheid in America*, arguing that despite the promise of *Brown v. Board of Education*, schools across America remain segregated and unequal.

Kosol vividly illustrates the impact caused by the vast differences in school funding between wealthy suburbs and those in a low-income section of the city. Kozol regrets the damaging effects of modern educational segregation on a child's intellectual development and the related damage to hearts and minds:

> What saddens me the most . . . is simply that these children have no knowledge of the other world in which I've lived most of my life and that the children in that other world

have not the slightest notion as to who these children are and will not likely ever know them later, not at least on anything like equal terms, unless a couple of these kids get into college. Even if they meet each other then, it may not be the same, because the sweetness of too many of these inner-city children will have been somewhat corroded by that time. Some of it may be replaced by hardness, some by caution, some by calculation rooted in unspoken fear. I have believed for 40 years, and still believe today, that we would be an infinitely better nation if they knew each other now.[18]

As urban cities continue to suffer economic setbacks and the flight of businesses and residents, schools and students suffer in turn. Early in 2007, Detroit school officials announced the planned closing of 47 schools over a two-year span. School closings and consolidations occur in nearly every area of the country, and they reflect more than budget deficiencies, the tip of the iceberg.[19] In several big cities, mayors or state boards have assumed control of troubled school systems, adding another layer of politics to education.

Reporters often feel overwhelmed in trying to assess what is right and, more important, what is wrong with education. Is it as bad as it appears? Should we despair? Looking for clearcut answers to such questions might be futile and fruitless. At best, reporters must keep a steady eye on what is happening immediately around them. That means critically examining teacher performance and training, curricula, student-achievement scores, counseling services, financial support and instructional materials and equipment. Something as seemingly inconsequential as classroom design might reflect a significant element of a school district's educational philosophy.

Reporters covering education must be as knowledgeable, well-read and alert to developments in their field as counterparts on the legal or medical beats. They must know, for example, how to read and interpret test scores, such as the Scholastic Aptitude Test (SAT), and how to understand budgetary processes and state-funding formulas. They must also be aware of what is happening behind the scenes, such as the debated but widespread use of drugs like Ritalin to control "hyperactive" children. Obviously, a reporter lacking a background in education cannot become an expert overnight. As a starting point, however, a concise overview of the beat and guide to coverage is available from the Education Writers Association (www.ewa.org) in Washington, D.C. The underprepared education reporter is at a distinct disadvantage, consigned largely to reporting the theories, observations, interpretations and explanations of others.

Education reporters who concentrate on the shortcomings and failures of our schools and de-emphasize the success stories can expect criticism. It is a valid criticism, considering the high number of news reports about drug deals, stabbings, rapes, truancy, drop-outs and illiteracy. Bad-news reporting is a common criticism of journalism, not one exclusive to the education beat. While the ugly side of education cannot, of course, be sanitized or ignored, reporters must remember that for every negative incident there may be 10 positive ones.

Religion, Values and Ethics

Religion news no longer languishes in journalism's backwaters. For years, many newspapers quarantined religion news on an inside page—the church page—of Saturday editions. Why? Partly because editors feared serious religious news would generate too much controversy and ill feelings among readers. Partly because they saw religion as "soft" news. And partly, perhaps, because journalists, as surveys indicate, are not active churchgoers compared to the general population.[20]

In the 1980s, the Jim Bakker episode demonstrated that religious news, although still controversial, was every bit as "hard" as news from the police beat, state capital or White House. Bakker and his wife, Tammy Faye, had built a fledgling Christian television show into a multimillion-dollar empire when accusations of Bakker's hushed affair with a 21-year-old church secretary and his extravagant misuse of church donations brought Bakker and his PTL ("Praise the Lord" or "People That Love") ministry into disrepute.

When Bakker resigned from PTL in 1987, he blamed the *Charlotte Observer*: "I am not able to muster the resources needed to combat a new wave of attack that I have learned is about to be launched against us by the *Charlotte Observer*, which has attacked us incessantly for the past 12 years."[21] The newspaper won a Pulitzer Prize for its efforts, and its coverage prompted news organizations to investigate the financial affairs of other ministries.

The Bakker investigation reinforced the point that religion stories can belong on front pages and at the top of newscasts. Often, however, it takes a fall from grace, such as the Bakkers', or the saintly deeds of a Mother Teresa to capture substantial coverage. Religious leaders and groups can be found at the forefront of social movements, financial empires, political intrigue and community activism throughout the nation and world. Consider the diverse beliefs and methods of such religious figures as preacher-politician-presidential candidates Jesse Jackson and Pat Robertson; evangelist Jerry Falwell (1933-2007), founder of now-defunct Moral Majority; Nation of Islam leader Louis Farrakhan; and the Dalai Lama, winner of the Nobel Peace Prize. Such an array of notable newsmakers alone suggests that media organizations need full-time religion reporters.

QUOTABLES

"I argue that journalists draw much of their professional inspiration from the Bible's prophetic complaints about moral corruption, as well as calls for reform that grew out of the Protestant Reformation, the Progressive and Populists movements, and the muckraker and Social Gospel campaigns in the United States during the late nineteenth century and early twentieth. By better understanding this history and the largely unexamined role that religion has played in the development of journalists' professional standards, journalists will, I believe, be better able to help renew their own faith, as well as the public's, in the journalistic enterprise." (p. 5)

—Doug Underwood, *From Yahweh to Yahoo!* Chicago: University of Illinois Press, 2002

There is no formula or traditional pattern for working the religion beat. For one thing, the beat lacks a central spot, like city hall, around which to organize coverage. But like most beats, it cannot be adequately covered by telephone from a newsroom. In fact, to achieve thorough, balanced coverage of religion, reporters need to expand their cultural and moral horizons, quell feelings of cynicism and take an ecumenical view of religion. Religion reporters should look for news in storefront churches as well as cathedrals and synagogues. They should attend tent revivals, bar mitzvahs and Jehovah's Witnesses' services, without passing unfair judgment about what they see or hear. They should recognize that God's work is being done in both cloistered convents and halfway homes for ex-convicts.

Newsday's Robert Keeler won the Pulitzer Prize for beat reporting in 1996 with his series on St. Brigid's Catholic parish—an in-depth examination of the spirituality of the parishioners. Keeler spent a year with the parish, attending services, meetings and small prayer groups. "It's hard to quantify an awakening of the spirit," Keeler admitted.[21] Founded in the 1850s for a largely Irish population, the congregation evolved into an ethically diverse church of 23,000 whose members include Salvadorans, Mexicans, Haitians and Filipinos.

Religion permeates other beats, such as politics, when reporters concentrate on the church-going habits or the moral positions of candidates for office. Judith M. Buddenbaum, author of *Reporting News About Religion*, sees fertile ground on the business, entertainment and education beats. "On the education beat, prayer and observance of religious holidays in public schools and state standards for parochial schools and home schooling are the most obvious examples," she says, "but religion can also be at the core of disputes over academic freedom, parental authority, discipline, curricular content, teaching methods and taxation."[23]

Occasionally, religion reporters must be prepared to disqualify themselves from stories that deeply touch their own beliefs. A reporter committed to the pro-life movement probably should not cover either an abortion-clinic protest or a pro-choice rally. The same view, of course, applies to a pro-choice activist.

Finally, all reporters, not just those on the religion beat, should neither judge too harshly the failings and flaws of "religious" people—nor accept their words and apparent good deeds uncritically. When it was disclosed during the 1988 presidential campaign that one of Pat Robertson's children was conceived out of wedlock, did some journalists privately gloat? When a cleric is arrested on charges of indecent exposure, is the press overly eager to publicize the offense?

On the other hand, the press cannot allow itself to look less critically because someone professes to do God's work. When Franciscan priest Bruce Ritter (1927–1999) was raising millions of dollars for Covenant House, a shelter for homeless youths, few news organizations questioned his growing power and influence. Until Ritter faced allegations of sexual and financial misconduct, says former *Washington Post* columnist Colman McCarthy, now a peace activist, the press took most of what Ritter said and did as "gospel." McCarthy advises reporters: "It shouldn't be a sacrilege to look at one of the haloed and wonder: If we give him a free ride, will we end up being taken for a ride?"[24]

Despite their small numbers, religion reporters are organized through the Religion Newswriters Association (www.rna.org), which, among its activities, holds an "Into the Darkness Award" to recognize the individual or group "that has done the most during the year to stifle the people's right to know." (The 2002 award went to the American Catholic hierarchy for its cover-up of the widespread clergy sexual abuse scandal.) The RNA can serve as a support group for reporters seeking guidance and ideas for covering religion-related news.

Campaigns and Elections

It seems as though the political beat is the pinnacle of reporting. It certainly has its notables—from Hunter S. Thompson (1937–2005), the iconoclast who reported for *Rolling Stone* and whose books include *Fear and Loathing: On the Campaign Trail '72*, to David Broder, the *Washington Post's* Pulitzer Prize-winning columnist whom a colleague described as "our most respected reporter and commentator on politics."

Yet with so many of journalism's stars on the political beat, why is campaign reporting, in particular, so frequently criticized as shallow or trivial, even by those assigned to cover the candidates and elections? There are dozens of explanations, apologies and excuses. Broder, for example, offers one view: "Because as campaign reporters we are very atypical—unlike most of our readers and even many of our newsroom colleagues—much of our output has an insider quality." The insider quality, Broder says, helps explain why reporters sometimes focus on minor incidents and disputes that are tangential to the central issues voters ought to know.[25]

Despite the stellar glow of the political beat, there is no mystery about covering campaigns and politics. Basically, campaign coverage is bread-and-butter reporting with few special requirements beyond a sense of history; a commitment to focus on the meat of issues, not the sizzle; skill at detecting "bull" when it appears, which will be often; and, most of all, a determination to report not tangential insider news, but news central to what voters ought to know.

Politicians and the Press

Politicians and journalists enjoy a symbiotic relationship at times. For reporters, the balance in the relationship should fall somewhere between chumminess and cynicism. Getting too close to politicians presents obvious problems of potential favoritism. An unrelenting adversarial relationship poses another set of problems. Reporters on the political beat must constantly suppress personal views—good or ill—of politicians. Covering politics requires that journalists remain true to their principal role of keeping the public informed.

The Character of Campaigns

The vernacular of campaigns includes lugs, roorbacks and spin control. They are unpleasant-sounding words that seem appropriate in the often unpleasant world of politics. Lugs, for example, are "voluntary" contributions government employees in an elected official's office sometimes must make to the boss's re-election fund. Roorbacks are smear charges leveled against a candidate in the final days of a campaign. Spin control, a strategy popularized by Ronald Reagan's White House staff, usually refers to efforts by political aides to contact reporters one-on-one and frame an event, report, speech or other news development within a favorable context.

Let's say a gubernatorial candidate issues a 20-page policy statement on tax reform. Spin control might involve the candidate's media adviser "helping" reporters determine which details to emphasize and why. As political reporters learn the latest language and games of politics, they often discover they amount to new terminology for old practices.

While some aspects of politics remain unchanged, technology continues to reshape campaigns and strategies. Television's influence is undeniable. Nearly all candidates for state or federal office make heavy use of 30-second political advertisements to win voters. Cable channels and Web sites have given politicians new venues for campaigning and, more significantly, a way to reach large audiences without going through the gauntlet of press questioning.

The use of media technology has increased the role of advisers who are skilled at marketing candidates through image making and opinion shaping. Media advisers suggest issues and themes for the campaign, direct political advertising, orchestrate staged news events (particularly photo or video "opportunities"), draft punchy one-liners and sound-bite comments sure to be quoted repeatedly in the news and rehearse candidates for media appearances.

At times it seems as though U.S. voters elect the best media adviser instead of the best candidate. Reporters cannot overlook the influence of campaign advisers; indeed, it is often part of coverage to profile the people behind the candidate. The focus, however, should always be on the person running for election, not those running the campaign.

The role of media advisers and other handlers—people who serve the candidate and protect him or her from harm—form a phalanx against the press tendency to engage in "gotcha journalism," that is, looking for character flaws and waiting for verbal slips of the tongue. Christina Martin, deputy press secretary for Bob Dole's unsuccessful presidential bid in 1996, said the press needs to allow a certain spontaneity in candidates' lives to permit them to go home early without reflecting on physical or mental health or state of mind. "Not everything—every movement, every breath—has a deeper meaning to it." Another Dole campaign official said if reporters continued their gotcha' tendencies, the candidate's "only response will be to slap on a bulletproof vest and try to communicate over the heads of reporters or through them."[26]

The never-ending cycle of news on the Internet and cable intensifies pressure on journalists on the campaign trial—whether local, state or national—to come up with something new. Critics call it "feeding the beast"—the media's insatiable appetite for tidbits of news.

Campaign Financing

The fallout of the Watergate scandal included widespread campaign reform on federal, state and local levels. Leading the list of reforms were limits and regulations governing campaign contributions by individuals, corporations and organizations, as well as laws requiring candidates to disclose the amounts and sources of campaign funds.

Spending limits vary according to state and federal laws. Typically, individual contributions to a candidate's election are restricted to $1,000 or less; for corporations or groups, the ceiling usually is $5,000 or less per candidate. But there are few restrictions on how much candidates may spend on campaigns. Political messages, even those that look and sound like product commercials, enjoy First Amendment protection. Moreover, election pragmatics enter into the picture; spending limits generally hurt challengers and help incumbents. A challenger to a well-established congressional incumbent, for example, might be forced to spend in excess of a million dollars simply to gain name recognition, much less get elected.

Money talks in politics as it does in other fields of endeavor. Money buys television advertising, the lifeblood of most campaigns. It also pays for billboards, fliers, office space, pollsters and travel. Without the ability to accumulate a campaign "war chest," few candidates for a contested office stand a chance of election. There are some refreshing exceptions, but they are usually candidates for the local school board, sewer district or city council.

To get a sense of the scope of campaign funds, consider that the 2004 presidential candidates exceeded $1 billion in spending, 56 percent higher than the 2000 election totals.

Campaign funds may come from a variety of sources. Some are self-generated by the candidate, who may tap personal wealth, take out loans or accept family gifts. Contributions from individual contributors can add up, particularly when solicited by a large direct-mail effort. Cocktail parties and fund-raising dinners also bring in contributions from individuals, whose chief reward might be a handshake and hastily taken picture with the candidate while passing through a reception line. Loyal, "electable" Democratic or Republican candidates can often expect additional contributions from the party treasury. Finally, large sums of money come from corporations and organizations, most notably funds dispensed by political action committees (PACs).

PACs represent a formidable force in campaigns, particularly on the congressional level. Under federal election laws, PACs can legally contribute no more than $5,000 to a candidate's committee per election (primary, general or special). They can also give up to $15,000 annually to any national party committee, and $5,000 annually to any other PAC. However, there is no limit to how much PACs can spend on advertising in support of candidates or in promotion of their agendas or beliefs. PACs must register with and file detailed financial reports of monies raised and spent to the Federal Election Commission, in Washington, D.C. The FEC reported that PACs raised $629.3 million, spent $514.9 million and contributed $205.1 million to federal candidates from January 1, 2003, through June 30, 2004. In all, during that span, PACs raised a total of $915 million.[27]

PACs represent a range of corporate, trade, labor or special interests. A PAC for automobile dealers, for example, might back candidates who support quotas on the import of foreign automobiles. Most often, PAC money goes to incumbents, especially those who hold leadership positions. Usually PACs support candidates, although occasionally PAC money is spent to defeat a candidate or wage a negative campaign. PACs or equivalent organizations also operate on state and local levels.

While money fuels campaigns, it also tends to leave candidates politically "in debt" and vulnerable to demands for paybacks. After all, those who contribute to candidates usually expect something in return. Part of the watchdog function of the press includes regular inspection of candidates' financial disclosure statements to learn who is contributing—and how much. A review of records might yield some surprises, such as a candidate who has received contributions from supporters on both sides of the abortion issue.

Disclosure statements are filed on a federal, state or local level, depending on the office being sought. For a city council candidate, disclosure records might be as close as a two-block walk to the county courthouse. A federal office seeker's file will be kept by the Federal Election Commission (www.fec.gov). Since most of the FEC's records are computerized, they are fairly accessible. Leads to sources of state and local campaign financing can be found at several sources, including a site sponsored by the Investigative Reporter and Editors organization, www.campaignfinance.org, and the Institute on Money in State Politics, www.followthemoney.org.

Once a reporter determines where records are kept, obtaining copies generally involves filling out a simple request form or logging in online. Keep in mind, however, that disclosure records may be neither complete nor truthful. Unscrupulous candidates look for loopholes or employ dishonest reporting practices to withhold information from the public and press.

Election Coverage

Reporters cover campaigns and elections primarily to help people learn enough about candidates and ballot propositions to make intelligent, informed decisions once they enter the voting booth. To do a thorough job, reporters need to dig beneath surface impressions to explore issues, qualifications and motives.

QUOTABLES

"Perhaps the most egregious weakness of those of us who cover politics is our lack of any sense of proportion. If a candidate misspeaks, God help him. Corrections and explanations are not allowed, lest we be accused of being 'soft' on one candidate or the other. There are,

of course, cases in which a minor episode may indeed reveal a basic inadequacy in a candidate. But there are too many in which candidates are doomed by a single sentence." (p. 263)
—Jack W. Germond, *Fat Man in a Middle Seat: Forty Years of Covering Politics,*
New York: Random House, 1999

Focus on facts, not on symbols, images and rhetoric, says political scientist James David Barber, who believes reporters too infrequently ask candidates the right questions—or test candidates' answers to questions. He offers two examples from the 1988 presidential campaign. To ask Jesse Jackson, "Reverend Jackson, what are the three things you're going to do when you get to be president?" invites a long, well-rehearsed discourse that sheds little light on the candidate's record or qualifications. But a specific question ("How did you operate Push/Excel?") based on solid research, might, Barber says, "change the nature of a campaign."

Barber's second example stresses the need to compare clever comments to past performance. When presidential-debate moderator David Brinkley (1920–2003) asked a panel of candidates, "Which of the pictures would you change in the cabinet room after you were president?" Paul Simon won applause and news coverage by saying, "I would take them all down. I would put up a picture of an Iowa housewife and of a coal miner from West Virginia. I would put up a picture of a kid from the Bronx, and so every time the president and his cabinet members came into that room they'd remember whom they were serving."

Barber reminds reporters that a candidate's quotable response may not reflect a true devotion to a cause or issue; although Simon in this case may have been quite sincere, check the facts and the record.[28]

With so much money and strategy devoted to TV and cable advertising, reporters find themselves, like movie critics, assessing the quality and content of candidates' messages. News outlets and public-service organizations help police campaign ads for truthfulness, such as www.factcheck.org, operated by Annenberg Public Policy Center of the University of Pennsylvania.

There are other distractions that reporters face when trying to stay focused on issues. One is the poll. Political polls are not without value in helping reporters gauge voter attitudes. The danger arises when the press relies too heavily on polls. Polls suggest certainty or exactness because they deal in numbers and statistics. But not all polls are created equal; they can be poorly constructed instruments of opinion measurement or skillfully constructed instruments of opinion manipulation.

Reporters who practice "precision journalism" and conduct their own polls are less susceptible to manipulation—but more susceptible to self-deception. Although few political reporters have time to do their own scientific polling, many news organizations now have an outside research firm or in-house research department on call. In any case, reporters must recognize the impact of polls and know how to read them.

Some polls are more credible than others, but in all cases polls tend to reduce campaigns to races, featuring "frontrunners," "long shots" and "dark horses." In covering polls ("Representative Denise Smith has a commanding lead over her opponent, according to a recent poll"), the press ironically may influence the outcome of future polls. As election day draws near, voters may react to poll results, elevating last month's "underdog" to today's "strong contender."

Naturally, journalists and voters are curious about who is going to win an election. But reporting a campaign as a horse race and attempting to predict outcomes put journalists at risk of being misled. Some campaign advisers, for example, believe in intentionally setting lower public expectations of a candidate's performance, saying in a grim voice, "It will be a close vote," when their private polls indicate a win is nearly certain.

There is also concern that polls and surveys discourage reporters from doing old-fashioned legwork. Polling expert Albert Cantril made this observation decades ago: "A generation ago when a political reporter got to a new state or location, he or she would usually call the local political organizations, labor unions, the chambers of commerce, the political party people, editors of local newspapers, to get some sense of what the texture was of what was going on in that area."[29] Now reporters covering major campaigns rely on poll printouts or turn to the candidates' polling experts for a picture of community attitudes instead of digging for stories and talking to people. Move away from the polls, the candidate and his or her inner circle and get among voters, advises David Broder.[30]

Nearly every presidential campaign illustrates how pursuit of scandal stories could lure political reporters away from coverage of more substantial questions. Evidence of a candidate's womanizing or heavy drinking, for example, is germane to what some call "the character issue." Still, reporters who operate as "morality police" ought to consider whether their time and efforts could be better spent on serious investigation of a candidate's ability and public performance instead of chasing rumors.

Campaign coverage should not end on election day. Although day-to-day responsibility for covering the newly elected official might shift to another reporter, someone—preferably the political writer—needs to provide continuity in coverage to see what happens to the former candidate's campaign pledges.

Probably no other beat enjoys as many reporting tools supported by news organizations, government agencies, non-profit watchdog groups and universities. For example, the Poynter Institute produces an *Election Handbook* that lists online and offline resources.

Business and Economic News

Once given stepchild treatment, the gray, dull business page—often little more than column after column of stock market reports—grew into well-written, well-edited daily sections, brimming with lively profiles, in-depth analysis pieces and attractive graphics.

People who turn to business reports usually are more than news "browsers." Many of them seek information to help make business decisions. And these information-seekers are not strictly corporate executives. The audience for business news is varied, and generally it is knowledgeable and discerning.

Those who rely on business news expect solid, accurate and responsible reporting; they are among the most careful and critical of news consumers. When a business reporter misreads a company's annual report, people will react, including the chief executive officer, who is not likely to be happy with news coverage in general. Mistakes just confirm his or her impressions that reporters cannot be trusted to report business accurately or fairly.

Business and economic news also touches many other beats—government, law, professional sports, medicine, to mention a few. When a credit union teeters on the brink of collapse after making bad loans, the impact is likely to reach far beyond its employees, stockholders and customers. Business reporters must see economic developments within the broadest contexts.

REPORTER'S TIP FILE

Getting in and getting news out of the corporate tower

On all beats, aggressive coverage is likely to generate occasional tensions between journalists and their news subjects. The business beat is particularly tension-ridden because, as one observer put it, "Businessmen rank journalists with bureaucrats and environmentalists as their most irksome tormentors."[31] The common complaint from the business world is that reporters are ignorant or biased—or both. From the journalist's perspective, top executives can be ruthless, greedy types, driven by a bottom-line mentality. Examples of both biased reporters and ruthless executives can be found, but neither image is fair.

Given the beat's climate of suspicion and hostility, a polite, patient reporter stands a better chance of success than a demanding, combative one. Business reporters, some of whom come from covering public officials, must remember that business executives are under no "right-of-access" obligation to grant interviews, answer questions or open files to the news media. A reporter will not get past the guard at the front gate if the chief executive officer declines to talk.

Complicating the situation is the aggressive stance certain business executives believe is necessary when dealing with the press. As a result, business reporters must be prepared for defensiveness and argumentation. Overcoming an executive's hostility might not be accomplished in the course of a single interview. But competent reporting over a period of time should improve relations. For reporters, there is a simple, initial step toward building rapport with business executives: Do your homework prior to an assignment. At a minimum, that means knowing the executive's background, the company's history and the products it makes or services it provides.

Reporters, of course, cannot begin to establish rapport when their requests for an interview are turned down or their phone messages go unanswered. At times, getting to a top executive is an involved, discouraging process of working through—or around—public relations people, whom some business reporters consider intentional obstacles to coverage. But an able, cooperative public relations person can make a business reporter's job easier by providing information and opening closed doors.

A realistic view of the PR role is needed; reporters must understand that public relations people owe loyalty to the employer, not the press. Does that make PR people "hired guns" or "hacks"? Let's try to be fair: Few in public relations take company loyalty to the point of lying or cheating, but shaping favorable coverage is part of the job. Realistic reporters—and realistic PR people—quickly reach an understanding about their respective roles.

At the other extreme are reporters who let PR staffers do too much. A study found two interesting tendencies of business reporters. First, they refer to documents less frequently than reporters do on other beats, despite the impression that business reporting involves a great deal of time sifting through reports, figures and numbers. Second, they rely heavily on press releases and press conferences.[32] The study offers no explanations for these patterns, but given the complexity of business and economic reporting, it seems reasonable to assume that reporters, especially inexperienced ones, will turn to the predigested information of press releases or the interpretations of public relations people or government officials when at a loss to understand fiscal reports or economic developments.

Obviously, reporters without proper preparation or knowledge of the business world lean toward dependency on the very people they are supposed to critically assess and question.

Into the Business World

Business reporters must deal with stock-market trends, government economic indicators, merger proposals, annual reports, takeover bids, trade deficits and corporate bankruptcies. Ideally, business reporters should be educated in law, accounting, business administration, finance and organizational psychology. A section of a textbook cannot adequately prepare a reporter for the business beat, but it can provide an overview and a starting point for coverage.

Most major businesses are organized as corporations, which means they have a board of directors and issue stock. There are two basic types of for-profit corporations—privately held (or closely held) and publicly held. A privately held corporation does not put its stock out for public sale; usually, there are a limited number of stockholders who are under legal restrictions about the sale or transfer of their stock shares. A publicly held company invites outside investment by a large number of shareholders. The crucial difference for reporters is that publicly held corporations must file extensive financial reports with government agencies, particularly the federal Securities and Exchange Commission (SEC); privately held companies face few reporting requirements.

Corporations raise capital by selling shares of stock. There is common stock, which amounts to units of ownership in the corporation. Those holding common stock also gain voting privileges to elect or remove board members and directors or to decide important fiscal matters. Common stockholders also receive a portion of the corporation's profits, called dividends. Preferred stock usually is distinguished from common stock by two features: Those holding preferred stock do not hold voting privileges, but they normally receive a higher, fixed and more secure return (dividends) on their shares.

The icon of American economy   The New York Stock Exchange shows its colors in a post–September 11 world. The terror attacks of 2001 buckled the nation's economy, but Wall Street went back to work within days. The iconic New York Stock Exchange often gets mentioned as a potential target of future terror attacks. (Photo by Robbie Arkovich.)

Investors make decisions to buy or sell stock in American companies based on a variety of financial information, including advice from stockbrokers, annual reports by corporations and, of course, stock-market performance as listed by the New York Stock Exchange (NYSE), the American Stock Exchange (AMEX) and the Nasdaq Stock Market (NASDAQ). Not all corporations, however, elect to have stock traded (or listed) on an exchange.

Business reporters are expected to check the financial health of companies and businesses in the community regularly. If publicly held, quarterly and yearly reports of earnings, losses, assets and liabilities are available from government sources. An important document is the 10K report, which businesses must file annually with the SEC; it is a public document. Other sources of information are records of lawsuits involving the company, reports in the trade press and data from investment services, such as Dun & Bradstreet and Moody's, and company-produced annual reports to stockholders.

Some newspapers take out a small amount of stock in major companies to ensure receipt of both annual reports and notices of stockholder meetings. In addition, former employees are valuable sources as are those who do business with the corporations, such as customers and suppliers. Few outsiders know as much about what is going on at General Motors as do the executives at Ford or Toyota.

Economic Indicators

Part of the business journalist's job is to report on the condition of the economy. Often, the job requires that reporters depend on figures collected and issued by government agencies. One set of figures is called the Index of Leading Economic Indicators, which, until 1995, was reported monthly by the U.S. Department of Commerce. It is now, however, compiled and publicized by a non-profit group, the Conference Board (www.conference-board.org). The index is supposed to forecast changes in the economy based on a number of national indicators of economic activity. Among them are new building permits, new orders for consumer goods and new claims for state unemployment insurance. Only a steady, three- or four-month rise or fall in the index percentage rate is considered a significant sign of growth or decline in the economy.

Other signals of economic conditions include the U.S. Consumer Price Index, which measures price changes for several hundred goods and services typically affecting consumers. The index gets particular attention because it serves as one measurement of inflation. The nation's unemployment rate, determined by the U.S. Department of Labor, also provides a gauge of the soundness of the economy. However, critics complain the jobless figures do not include the chronically unemployed who no longer seek a job. A third economic barometer is the gross domestic product (GDP), a figure reported by the Commerce Department quarterly that includes measurements of business investments in equipment and machinery; housing construction; consumer purchases; the balance of exports and imports; and purchases by government. The collection of data sets the total retail-price value of all goods and services produced by the nation's economy during a specific time period. While considered the best indicator of overall economic activity, the GDP provides a national picture. It does not, necessarily, reflect the economic standing of a particular community, which might be under- or outperforming the national economy.

Federal and state government reports can help business reporters compare and contrast economic conditions locally, such as the number of new housing starts and the rate of unemployment. Statistics and percentages, however, need to be humanized to show how economic developments affect people. Look for economic stories at distribution centers for free government food or at foreclosure sales on farm property.

Understanding the economy also involves knowing about money supply as determined by federal borrowing and the role of the Federal Reserve System, whose board of directors can influence the economy by regulating interest rates it charges when banks borrow money directly from the U.S. Central Bank. The Federal Reserve Board (also known by the abbreviation "Fed") often reacts to control both recession and inflation.

The board lowers interest rates to stimulate the economy; it raises interest rates to tighten credit when inflation becomes a problem. The money supply process is complex, but serious business journalists make the effort to learn about each twist and turn of the economy.

Labor and the Workplace

Unions that comprise Big Labor, among them the Teamsters and United Mine Workers, no longer possess the power and energy of the past. Mob corruption, foreign competition and recessionary spirals helped weaken previously powerful unions. But the demise of union strength and influence should not result in inadequate, stereotypical coverage of labor issues. Labor's image—especially in a high-tech, information- and service-driven economy today—cannot be reduced to a cliché of insatiable wage demands and violent strikes. The unions that represent workers in a range of occupations still have agendas that warrant fair, thorough coverage.

Younger Americans, including reporters, also need to remember what labor has done for them, such as the 40-hour week, sick leave, pensions and paid vacations. For example, the Newspaper Guild brought higher wages and stouter worker protection for journalists in general, not just those employed in so-called guild newspapers. On its Web site, the Newspaper Guild also takes credit for raising the standards and ethics of journalism and, more recently, fighting attempts to lay off newsroom personnel or outsource newsroom jobs.

Today and yesterday, a chief item on labor's agenda is safety in the workplace. Old dangers remain, such as those facing coal miners. New dangers involve hazardous wastes from chemical plants, repetitive-motion ailments for assembly line workers and birth and reproductive dangers from exposure to workplace contaminants. Journalists who work in pleasant, relatively risk-free environments must remember those who risk injury and long-term health problems each day. Business reporters who go no farther than the corporate offices will miss important stories that can be found only by going into factories and developing sources among workers.

Critic Michael Parenti says the news media in general give labor few opportunities to be heard. In his view, "The network evening news regularly reports the Dow Jones average and other stock market news but offers no weekly tabulations on industrial accidents, housing evictions or environmental violations. The major newspapers and weeklies have no 'labor' section to go along with their 'business' section. The Gross National Product is reported but there is no 'quality-of-life index' to tell us what the GNP takes away or fails to give us."[33] Parenti may overstate the case against the press, but he reminds business reporters that management's perspective sometimes dominates coverage.

Labor unions bring issues into the public arena, but the vast number of American workers, including immigrants without documentation, lack a unified, high-decibel voice to air their grievances and fight for their rights. Behind the walls of small factories and offices and out of sight, in our fishing waters and agricultural fields, men, women and children need the attention of journalists.

Diversity in Life and Perspective

By publishing a photograph of a newlywed couple, the *Everett* (Wash.) *Herald* took a small step in 1990 toward recognizing the diversity of its community. The decision to publish the picture required a period of soul searching, but the *Herald*'s managing editor, Stan Strick, felt it was the right thing to do. Why the soul searching? The photograph was of a lesbian couple, who had exchanged vows in a commitment ceremony before friends and family.

The decision provoked a strong reaction from readers, including several who threatened to cancel subscriptions because the newspaper no longer reflected "family values." As one subscriber put it, "It's not something I want my children to accept as normal life. I don't want my children to think that's the way God wants us to live." The pastor of a gay church, however, had this view: "I think it's healthy for society to see that there are gay people who are willing to commit to each other in a long-term relationship. For so many years all you saw was the seamier side. We indeed are a community of committed people."[34] Now the *New York Times* routinely publishes commitment or marriage announcements of gay and lesbian couples.

The *Times* and the *Herald* are among a large number of news organizations that try to achieve representative coverage that also recognizes differences among people. A responsibility for all journalists—specialists and general-assignment reporters alike—is to maintain a diverse perspective. Although news assignments offer a smorgasbord of people and places, journalists, despite the infusion of more women and minorities, tend to be a homogeneous group with little sustained involvement with the larger world outside its middle-class environment. Journalists will miss important stories unless they hear the voices and recognize the issues outside their immediate frames of reference. They must understand, relate to and accurately represent different generations, different races, different ethnic groups, different genders and different living conditions.

"Giving voice to the voiceless," a term used widely in books, articles and speeches, generally describes efforts by social reformers, charitable groups and civic-minded politicians to illuminate the lives and plight of people with meager resources and few advocates. Journalism owes loyalty to its audience of readers, listeners, viewers and subscribers, but it also serves those who never show up in readership or viewership audits. As a profession immersed in public service, journalism often brings the voices of the voiceless into the consciousness of those who do possess an ample voice—and the means to use it.

Journalism's emphasis on diversity not only helps draw attention on the truly voiceless segments of society; it also helps reveal what we share in common, once we understand one another better. Understanding, in turn, helps build community and improve communication; understanding also helps refute stereotypes and sweep away generalizations. Despite the melting-pot vision of social planners, America is undeniably multicultural. The authors of the book *Conversation of Journalism* explain how journalists can expose themselves to diversity and benefit from the experience:

> Journalists—all of us—can reduce our vulnerability to stereotypes by determinedly seeking multicultural experiences. These need not be in-depth projects, such as assigning a reporter to spend a month in public housing to produce a series of articles. Journalists might simply try more often to ride the bus to work instead of driving the freeway; sit in on morning gatherings of older citizens at McDonald's; attend Friday night football games at a city high school; talk to people living in a homeless shelter; or visit a hospice for AIDS patients. Although stories might emerge from such experiences, the main object is to infuse fresh attitudes that do not simply bolster previous expectations and conventional wisdom.[35]

Journalists, as they often do, disagree on what "diversity" in the news means—or should mean. Does it mean introducing diverse sources in stories? Yes, most journalists would agree. Bill Kovach and Tom Rosenstiel, authors of *The Elements of Journalism*, propose a transcendental type of diversity:

> The goal of diversity should be to assemble not only a newsroom that might resemble the community, but one that is also as open and honest so that this diversity can function. This is not racial or gender diversity. It is not ideological diversity. It is not numerical diversity. It is what we call *intellectual diversity,* and it encompasses and gives meaning to all the other kinds.[36]

Intellectual diversity encourages open exchanges and debate within the newsroom as editors, reporters and designers try their best to represent and serve the entire community.

Differences do exist, and journalists can help put cultural diversity into context. To some extent, any group of people—from the homeless of New York to Miami's Cuban community—develops distinctive values, styles of communication and patterns of behavior; in effect, despite obvious shared characteristics, various segments of our larger society therefore possess distinctive "cultures." What follows is a sampling of some distinctions and differences as they relate to journalists. It is not meant to be an inclusive list; it is meant to awaken and expand your awareness and sensitivity.

First, however, a word of caution: Guilt-ridden or quota-driven attempts at diversity are doomed to be seen for what they are. Journalism, with its reputation problems, cannot afford to produce stories about "articulate black athletes," "courageous single mothers," or "inspiring paraplegics."

The Homeless and Disadvantaged

The story of homelessness and poverty cannot be covered by 9-to-5 journalists accustomed to the comfort and security of their offices. Reporters must go to the source—into the streets—and not rely strictly on the pronouncements of politicians, government agencies or special-interest groups.

Advocacy groups, church leaders, politicians and police cannot agree on the number of homeless people—or why they are homeless. A 2006 study put the number of U.S. homeless at 744,000 on any given day, noting that most of them had mental, physical or medical problems, such as drug or alcohol abuse, that kept them out of the mainstream.[37] It is not easy to count the homeless and the "street people," but they exist in all cities, and their plight warrants coverage. Moreover, the statistics shift daily, as people fall into and out of homelessness.

In covering emotionally loaded issues such as homelessness, balanced treatment is essential. Reporters must be careful not to overreact to staged events, such as celebrities camping out overnight in cardboard boxes, or sensationalize accounts of families living in abandoned cars or elderly men and women subsisting on dog food. Although the public needs to hear stories of people on the streets and in trouble, coverage should be sustained and substantial, not primarily anecdotal and occasional. Journalist Michael Moss says the press is "far better at simply discovering the poor than we are at explaining the causes of poverty and exploring the solutions."[38]

Stories about the homeless and hungry sometimes overshadow a growing substratum of the population—the "underclass," a term used by sociologist William Julius Wilson in his influential book *The Truly Disadvantaged*. There is no universal definition for the underclass, but the designation suggests a category of people who are even more economically strained than the "lower class." Members of the underclass are often second- or third-generation welfare recipients trapped in a cycle of unemployment, poverty and despair, with little hope or motivation to improve their lives. The problem is compounded when news people begin to see the underclass as trapped in a hopeless state and fail to continue exploring conditions and solutions.

Class matters, as another social scientist, bell hooks, observes. She recognizes the plight of the poor and the homeless within the larger context of the millions of middle-class Americans who struggle in the face of plant closings, layoffs and soaring housing costs:

> Everywhere we turn in our daily lives in this nation we are confronted with the widening gap between rich and poor. . . . As a nation we have become passive, refusing to act responsibily toward the more than 38 million citizens who live in poverty here and the working masses who labor long and hard but still have difficulty making ends meet.[39]

While not living in tent cities or Salvation Army shelters, those hanging onto the lowest rung of the middle-class ladder are often one missing paycheck away from financial disaster.

African-Americans

The civil rights movement of the 1960s focused the nation's attention on racism and discrimination, leading to legal reform and economic improvement. But many of the most deeply rooted problems were only superficially treated by government programs and money, not cured or eradicated. Statistically, black Americans fall substantially behind whites in home ownership, wages and access to loans. In inner cities, where riots occurred 40 years ago, blacks and other minorities, especially Hispanics, account for nearly 80 percent of the population.

QUOTABLES

"When I was a boy, during the early years of the civil rights movement, I believed that by the time people of my generation came into positions of authority racial justice would have established itself in this country. Since I am a member of the Baby Boom generation, I believed, of course, that my age cohorts would make this happen through the pure rightness of our souls. Sadly this has not happened. We have not yet even agreed upon a definition of social justice, let alone made it manifest on earth. And helping move our society toward the elimination of racial bias now seems to me to be a lifework." (p. 107)
—Jack Fuller, *News Values,* Chicago: University of Chicago Press, 1996

The press long has been criticized for its treatment of black issues; at worst, the press has been blamed for perpetuating stereotypes, particularly in regard to crime news. It would help, of course, if more blacks opted for careers in journalism. Indeed, minority recruitment is a top priority for the profession, but blacks sometimes see media organizations as institutions of racism where chances for advancement are poor. According to one recent study, only 5.5 percent of the nation's 54,700 newsroom professionals are black.[40] Prospects for immediate improvement are not promising.

If reporting black issues remains the responsibility of a largely white, middle-class press corps (whose editors come from the same background), then heightened awareness and education are needed. From a black perspective, too much news focuses on negative images—criminals, welfare cheats, drug dealers. As a result, stereotypes persist and distrust between races remains high. As journalist Nathan McCall observes in his book *Makes Me Wanna Holler*, "The only stories the paper thoroughly covered about blacks related to protests, sports, discrimination, poverty, and crime. White writers and photographers seemed unable to conceive of black life being broader than that."[41]

A continuing obstacle to improved news coverage is the white journalist's lack of sustained contact with blacks, followed by lack of understanding of black experiences. White reporters rarely drive through black neighborhoods, much less hunt for stories that are behind the closed doors. Is it any wonder that white reporters face difficulties communicating with blacks or identifying with the issues and problems of the African-American community?

Occasionally a news report is revealing, such as a *Washington Post* piece about Michael McGee Sr., a black Milwaukee alderman, now a radio talk show host, who used rhetoric and outrageous behavior to draw attention to the problems of low-income urban neighborhoods. He has worn a bag over his head to protest racism and has threatened violence against whites unless $100 million would be invested in Milwaukee's black community within a five-year deadline. It might be easy for some people to dismiss McGee as a crackpot or a racist, but reporter David Maraniss' story showed another side to the man. In one scene McGee is making rounds in the community:

> McGee toured four blood plasma centers on North Avenue. At each he encountered dozens of black men waiting to be hooked to machines that extracted plasma in exchange for a $10 payment. The process takes about 40 minutes and leaves many men feeling dizzy. They are supposed to do it only twice a week, but many men roam from center to center, giving plasma several times a day to acquire money for malt liquor and cigarettes.
>
> "They milk these people," McGee said, his voice cracking. "They milk them like cows."[42]

The story captured both McGee's anger—and anguish.

Even the best intentions of white journalists sometimes go astray. Articles about black fashions or black filmmakers blazing "new trails" would be appropriate—once more central stories are told. A step toward better coverage of blacks is to open lines of communication by establishing bureaus or beats within black neighborhoods, not just at the local police precinct. Once into the community, reporters can cultivate a spectrum of reliable sources of information. (Chapter 4 discusses ways to cover the whole community.)

Another step toward improved coverage, suggests *Washington Post* reporter Courtland Milloy, is to report news of "the black middle class with the same sensitivity that most white people get." Milloy's comments are directed primarily at the Washington, D.C., media but relate to other cities as well. "Distorted and truly unfair images of the black community not only promote self-hatred," Milloy says, "they help to drive a wedge between the middle class and the poor, to say nothing of black and white. Because black people have been made to look so bad, so hopeless and helpless for so long, I believe that many of them have become just that."[43] Milloy's words offer a guide for coverage of blacks that is more balanced as well as more sensitive.

Gender

In the 1960s and 1970s, consciousness raising about the essential equality of the sexes enhanced the rights of women, but in its wake a new set of stereotypes and problems emerged. First came "Super Mom," who excelled at managing both job and family. Then came "Career Woman," who could match any man in terms of drive and savvy. Women rightly seek careers that match their talents, but many women also work because economically they must. These include both married women with children and single parents. News coverage, however, tends to highlight women who are well-educated, well-paid executives in pursuit of self-fulfillment, money and power.

Fewer stories examine the concerns of women who are worried, for example, about safe, inexpensive child care or who are returning to school at great sacrifice, perhaps surviving on food stamps.

Journalism remains a male-dominated profession, certainly at the news decision-making levels, and males do not always understand the issues that concern women. Will a male editor, for example, take a report about premenstrual syndrome seriously enough—provided he's aware of the report—to assign a reporter to do a story? Of course, women editors do not necessarily empathize with the woman at the checkout counter or the factory; they, too, may require fuller exposure to the problems of other women.

An enhanced sensitivity to the concerns of women includes awareness that, despite the feminist era, sexism—some of it unintentional—remains influential. Would either male or female journalists describe a man as perky or svelte? Would most stories about men include reference to a wife's job or position? All journalists must be careful to avoid images and language that diminish the credibility or seriousness of women.

There is another major shortcoming in the way the press treats—or fails to treat—women. Too many "authorities" quoted by the press are men. That fact alone does not mean journalists necessarily devalue women as news sources; sometimes a male is the best or only source for information or insight. But where there is a choice, how often do both male and female reporters turn first to a male spokesperson? The simple prescription to improve both the image and coverage of women is for reporters to decide to seek out women as news sources whenever possible.

People with Disabilities

America's disabled population is becoming an increasingly vocal and visible minority. Although some want the media to notice their problems and agendas, they do not appreciate being portrayed as extraordinary for doing what they consider the ordinary—succeeding in a job, raising a family or excelling in athletics. When reporting about disabled individuals, it is important to think of the person first, not the disability. Indeed, reference to a person's disability might be no more relevant to the story than the person's hair color or shoe size. When the disability is germane, reporters should view the disability as merely one aspect of the story, not *the* story. At all times, avoid terms or descriptions that might be considered negative or which suggest limitations, such as "wheelchair-bound" or "a victim of cerebral palsy." It is better to say someone "uses a wheelchair" or "has cerebral palsy."

Some people feel uncomfortable in the presence of those who are severely impaired, such as quadriplegics, and, as a result, treat physically disabled individuals as if they also are mentally disabled. An ill-at-ease reporter who acts unnaturally or clumsily when communicating with a disabled person puts an interview at risk. Usually, there is no need to treat a disabled person any differently than other news sources. If you cannot understand someone's speech, say so. If you must talk to a hearing-impaired person through an interpreter, remember to speak directly to the person you are interviewing, not the interpreter. Focus on the person, not the wheel-chair or the disability.

Disabled Americans are now protected under the Americans with Disabilities Act of 1990, which prohibits housing, employment and other forms of discrimination against people with physical or mental impairments. The law, for example, requires that all public buses, trains and subways and all new restaurants, hotels and stores (or those being renovated) be accessible to disabled persons, including those with emotional illnesses, epilepsy, drug addiction and alcoholism. Journalists can expect to encounter conflicts over implementation of the law's provisions. The Disabilities Act, like earlier civil rights legislation, will not automatically accomplish equality or end discrimination.

Older Citizens

Covering news of older people forces younger reporters to face mortality and confront such uncomfortable subjects as Alzheimer's disease. With the accelerated "graying" of our population, the issues and problems of age must be squarely addressed, not ignored because they are too disturbing or depressing to investigate.

Besides overcoming a generational reluctance to cover issues of age, journalists must recognize and attempt to dispel the myths of growing old. Some younger Americans, including reporters, resent what they perceive to be their tax "burden" for support of social-service programs. Despite images in recent advertising, many older Americans are not robust, well-to-do and living the good life. When older people bitterly complain about Medicare problems or their own tax burdens, reporters must be the first to take those complaints seriously. In some cases, the problems of the aged are hidden away in apartment buildings or nursing homes, where no one is going to be staging a protest or holding a press conference. Journalists should, as always, listen for the voices of those who sometimes cannot easily demand audiences for themselves.

When older people do make it into the news, stories that relate the "achievements" of older people often sound sappy or patronizing. They harp on "youthful" activities or images, such as a group of grandmothers "kicking up their heels" at an aerobics class or a "hot-sounding" band of "spry" octogenarians that plays at the nursing home. In one particularly insensitive episode, the *Sacramento Bee* ran the headline "Party Animals" over a picture of a couple at their 74th wedding anniversary; the caption led off, "Are we having fun yet?" The editors involved later apologized.[44]

More serious pursuits—and more serious, significant stories—frequently go untold. As the nation ages, journalists must devote increased coverage to areas such as "eldercare," retirement communities, health care and government services and de-emphasize stereotypical images of "sexy seniors" enjoying the "Golden Years." The authors of *Journalism Across Cultures* recommend another perspective: "Older people would be best defined by their lifestyle and income, ability and mind-set instead of their age."[45]

Reporters who turn to older people for stories learn to listen with special sensitivity. A model at communicating with his elders is physician Robert Coles, author of

Old and on Their Own. His stories are rich in human texture and full of valuable insights, such as his experience in asking folks, "How are you doing today?" ". . . So often I would realize that there are many answers to that question that might be coming," he says. One time, an octogenarian answered him: "It's ten o'clock (in the morning) and 'all's well,' but at ten-thirty, I could have another answer for you, because being old is like being on a swing: you go up, you go down." Coles realized her experience typified the life of older people, whose existences change from day to day. "She was referring to a complex mix of physiological, the neurological, the introspectively existential."[46]

Journalists should learn from Cole's powers of observation and insight, but he, in turn, learned by immersing himself in their lives. Reporters cannot waltz in and out and expect candor and richness of talk.

Children

Children depend on adults for help. But too many children are being battered and abused, and too many are troubled by drugs, peer pressures and split families. Journalists aggressively pursue such stories—after they surface. But instead of waiting to report the latest child-beating death or teenage suicide, they should be "patrolling" the world of children, alert for signs that society is not doing its job to protect them from danger. The sensational episode, such as a child abduction from a shopping center, can overshadow greater dangers existing in the home or other "safe" places. "Despite all the pictures of missing children on shopping bags and milk cartons, children are more likely to be kidnapped by their own parents than by strangers," say Richard Gelles and Murray Straus, authors of *Intimate Violence*.[47]

The old saying "Children should be seen but not heard" cannot be a guideline for journalists. Reporters, even ones who are not parents themselves, should remain alert to the changing, special problems and concerns of children, which means talking to children and, more important, really listening to them. In fact, many children are, indeed, unseen, isolated within boot camps, foster care and homeless encampments. Since 1993, the Casey Journalism Center has helped journalists keep abreast of children's issues and recognizes through an awards program exemplary reporting about children. Another source for data and story ideas is the annual report *America's Children in Brief: Key National Indicators of Well-Being* (www.childstats.gov) that compiles information from more than 20 federal agencies dealing with issues of children and families.

In 1990, the leaders of 71 nations adopted a declaration at the first World Summit for Children, pledging to fight hunger, disease and illiteracy affecting children. The summit focused on worldwide conditions, but it also helped illuminate problems in particular countries. According to a news report, one U.S. child in five is poor; one in five lacks health insurance. An estimated 100,000 are homeless. The United States ranked 19th in the world in combatting infant mortality and 39th for success in immunizing children.[48] Clearly, the plight of children is compelling not only in Soweto and Calcutta; it is also compelling in Detroit and El Paso.

Other groups that can be considered significant minority "cultures" in American life include gays and lesbians, Hispanics and Asian-Americans. They, too, contribute to our mosaic society. Reporters who accept diversity as a healthy societal condition will include the views and concerns of all cultural groups in their coverage. In coverage of all cultures, journalists need to take special care to avoid patronizing stories, culturally insensitive references or errors in fact, such as misidentifying a well-known minority figure. *Los Angeles Times* staff writer Agustin Gurza overheard a group of workers at a lunch counter laughing about the newspaper mistaking a photo of singer Paulino Rubio as Thalia, another Latin pop star.[49] Diversity in both perspectives and composition of newsrooms reduces the possibility of committing such cultural faux pas.

At times, journalists lean toward advocacy when reporting about the issues affecting children, disabled Americans or other minorities they see as underrepresented or victimized. That is understandable. Try, however, to stay focused and objective. Reporters should question the motives and arguments of any minority proponent as thoroughly and critically as they would those being espoused by a politician running for office or a bureaucrat explaining a controversial policy. In fact, most advocates for causes have learned to become politicians.

A multicultural perspective requires that journalists attempt to see the world as others see it. It also requires that journalists constantly recheck their perceptions, recognizing that the world changes. Language, for example, that was once acceptable may now offend because of stereotypes it evokes. It took time, but in the 1960s news organizations replaced Negro with black. In other instances, overused terms, such as Third World, can acquire pejorative meanings.

We exist in a fragile, complex cultural ecosystem that must be preserved, protected and promoted. A multicultural perspective should be global. The idea of the "shrinking world," although now a cliché, is real; the nations of the world are more interconnected and interdependent than ever before. Information technology is removing the few remaining barriers, making it possible to report about Cairo (pronounced Keye-row), Egypt, from Cairo (pronounced "Kay-row"), Ill., and vice versa. If properly tapped, knowledge and technology can expand the journalist's horizons, and the journalist, in turn, can expand the public's horizons. Opportunities abound for journalists to produce a more culturally diverse and representative news product: Take advantage of them.

Exercises

1   Attend a service at a church, temple, mosque or synagogue to sample the ceremonies and rituals of another religion. Prior to your visit, call the pastor, minister, sheikh or rabbi to arrange for an interview, possibly after the services. Discuss, among other topics, the role of the press in covering religion and how well that role is being carried out.

(2) Educators increasingly are taking steps to identify and help so-called at-risk students. At-risk programs usually focus on the elementary grades. Find out what the local school system is doing—or not doing—to reach drop-outs, pregnant teens, suicidal students, homeless children and other young people whose academic futures and personal lives are in jeopardy.

(3) Collect an oral history by interviewing several older members of your community. You might first call the local newspaper or talk to your professor to gather names of possible interviewees. One might be a former mayor; another, an early principal of the high school. Expect them to provide you with finely detailed, vivid accounts of the past.

Notes

1. Richard M. Clurman, *Beyond Malice* (New York: Meridian, 1990), p. 145.
2. "Six (or Seven) Things Editors Should Think About But Don't," *APME Redbook* 1989 (New York: Associated Press Managing Editors, 1989), p. 19.
3. Neil Postman, *Amusing Ourselves to Death* (New York: Penguin Books, 1985), p. vii.
4. Stewart Brand, *The Media Lab: Inventing the Future at M.I.T.* (New York: Penguin Books, 1988), pp. 258, 259.
5. Elizabeth Whitney, "A Look Back," *St. Petersburg Times*, Feb. 25, 1990, pp. 1I, 21.
6. See *Covering AIDS: A Handbook for Journalists* (Eugene, Ore: Pacific Media Center, 1987).
7. See Victor Cohn, *News & Numbers* (Ames, Iowa: Iowa State University Press, 1989).
8. William Safire, "Fruit, Panic and Public Policy," *St. Petersburg Times*, March 24, 1989, p. 21A.
9. Eliott Negin, "The Alar Scare Was for Real," *CJR*, September–October 1996, pp. 13–14.
10. Jeff Greenfield, "Good Science Reporting Requires More Than a 'Nose for News,' " *ASNE Bulletin*, October 1985, p. 32.
11. Gina Kolata, "The Panic Du Jour: Trans Fats in Foods," *New York Times*, Aug. 14, 2005, p. 4, week in review.
12. Marjorie Mandel Brooks, "Environmental Journalism," *Editor & Publisher*, April 21, 1990, p. 21.
13. David Suzuki and Peter Knutson, *Wisdom of the Elders* (New York: Bantam Books, 1992), p. xxxv.
14. Emily Sachar, "Teaching School for a Year Gave Reporter New Insights into Reporting on Education," *ASNE Bulletin*, January–February 1990, p. 23.
15. Lisa Gutierrez, "Editorially Speaking: Reporting from Classroom Breathes Life and Detail in Education Stories," *Gannetteer*, July–August 1989, p. 4.
16. John Carlson, "Editorially Speaking: From Giant Apes to Lung Transplants, the College Beat Can Be Exciting," *Gannetteer*, July–August 1989, p. 5.
17. Tracy Kidder, *Among Schoolchildren* (Boston: Houghton Mifflin, 1989), p. 301.
18. Jonathan Kozol, *The Shame of the Nation* (New York: Three Rivers Press, 2005).
19. Chastity Pratt, "Officials Announce School Closings in Detroit," *Detroit Free Press*, Jan. 5, 2007, p. 1.
20. David H. Weaver, Randal A. Beam, Bonnie J. Brownlee, Paul S. Voakes, and G. Cleveland Wilhoit, *The American Journalist in the 21st Century* (Mahwah, N.J.: Lawrence Erlbaum Associates, 2007), pp. 14–15.

21. Charles E. Shepard, "Jim Bakker Resigns from PTL; Jerry Falwell Assumes Leadership," *Charlotte Observer*, March 20, 1987, p. 1A.
22. Dana Deuell, "Pulitzer Prize Winning Reporter Robert Keeler Speaks to SPJ Members," *Newshawk*, University of Iowa, April 2001, p. 1.
23. Judith M. Buddenbaum, *Reporting News about Religion* (Ames, Iowa: Iowa State University Press, 1998).
24. Colman McCarthy, "The Fall of Father Ritter," *St. Petersburg Times*, March 23, 1990, p. 18A.
25. David Broder, *Behind the Front Page* (New York: Touchstone, 1988), p. 241.
26. Quoted in Ken Auletta, *Backstory* (New York: The Penguin Press, 2003), p. 230.
27. Federal Election Commission, www.fec.gov/press/press2005/20050412pac/PACFinal2004.html.
28. See *Covering Campaign '88: The Politics of Character and the Character of Politics* (New York: Gannett Center for Media Studies, 1988).
29. "Polling," *Problems of Journalism: Proceedings of the ASNE 1981 Convention* (Washington, D.C.: American Society of Newspaper Editors), p. 94.
30. Broder, *Behind the Front Page*, p. 243.
31. Kent MacDougall, *Ninety Seconds to Tell It All: Big Business and the News Media* (Homewood, Ill.: Dow Jones–Irwin, 1981), p. 7.
32. James T. Hamilton and Joseph P. Kalt, *Study of Economic and Business Journalism* (Los Angeles: Foundation for American Communications, 1987), p. 6.
33. Michael Parenti, *Inventing Reality* (New York: St. Martin's Press, 1986), p. 78.
34. Ferdinand M. de Leon, "Herald's Decision to 'Reflect Diversity' Stirs Controversy," *Seattle Times*, Dec. 7, 1990, Sec. C, p. 1.
35. Rob Anderson, Robert Dardenne and George M. Killenberg, *The Conversation of Journalism* (Westport, Conn.: Praeger, 1996), p. 91.
36. Bill Kovack and Tom Rosenstiel, *The Elements of Journalism* (New York: Three Rivers Press, 2001), p. 188.
37. "Study Finds 744,000 Homeless People in U.S.," *St. Petersburg Times*, Jan. 11, 2007, p. 8A.
38. Michael Moss, "The Poverty Story," *Columbia Journalism Review*, July–August 1987, p. 43.
39. bell hooks, *Where We Stand: Class Matters* (New York: Routledge, 2000), p. 1.
40. American Society of Newspaper Editors, http://www.asne.org/index.cfm?id=5663.
41. Nathan McCall, *Makes Me Wanna Holler* (New York: Vintage Books, 1995), p. 307.
42. David Maraniss, "McGee Steers with His Own Code of Ethics," *Milwaukee Journal*, July 22, 1990, Sec. J, p. 1.
43. Courtland Milloy, "For the Sake of Fairness, Let's Give the Full Story about Blacks," *Washington Post*, Jan. 18, 1990, p. 1J.
44. "They Were Just Funnin,'" *The Quill*, March 1990, p. 11.
45. Fritz Cropp, Cynthia M. Frisby and Dean Mills, *Journalism across Cultures* (Ames, Iowa: Iowa State University Press, 2003), p. 128.
46. Robert Coles, *Old and on Their Own* (New York: W.W. Norton & Co., 1998), p. 3.
47. Richard J. Gelles and Murray A. Straus, *Intimate Violence* (New York: Simon and Schuster, 1988), p. 18.
48. Reena Shah, "Leaders Embrace Agenda for Young," *St. Petersburg Times*, Oct. 1, 1990, p. 1A.
49. Daniel Hernandez, "Shades of Brown," laweekly.com, posted Dec. 20, 2006.

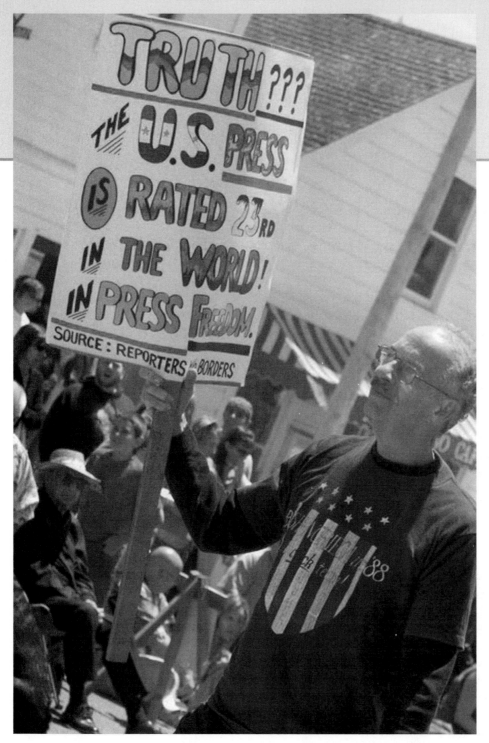

Fourth of July plea for truth in news   Marching in a July 4th parade in Mendocino, Calif., a man carries a poster suggesting the American press is not as free as some might believe. The poster refers to Reporters Without Borders, a group that monitors the state of press freedom around the world. (Photo courtesy of David Eppstein.)

Lessons in Law and Ethics

Stephen A. Cousley knows firsthand how litigation can smother aggressive journalism. As editor of the *Alton* (Ill.) *Telegraph,* he fought to prevent a $9.2 million libel award from killing his family-owned newspaper.[1] The *Telegraph* survived, but at a dear price.

The *Telegraph*'s troubles began with a confidential memo written by two of its reporters and sent to investigators for a Justice Department task force on organized crime. The memo outlined the reporters' suspicions about possible financial corruption involving a Chicago "family" of the Cosa Nostra, an Alton savings and loan and James Green, a Granite City, Ill., builder. The reporters were taking the tentative first steps—perhaps fruitless steps, they realized—required in investigative reporting. They still lacked enough verifiable evidence and documentation to print anything at all, but they hoped their contacts in the Justice Department would exchange information and provide leads. The reporters assumed the memo would be seen only by the investigators. They were wrong. In time, the memo reached the federal agency overseeing savings and loan associations, touching off a probe of the Alton firm and the termination of further loans to Green.

Somehow, Green obtained a copy of the memo, and he and several others implicated in the memo's accusations filed a libel suit in 1975. Few people, least of all Steve Cousley, expected the lawsuit to succeed, but when it went to trial five years later, the *Telegraph* lost decisively. Green's attorney convinced the jury that what the *Telegraph* did to his client was no different than allowing one of its delivery trucks to run recklessly over Green, leaving him crippled. While the case was being appealed, the *Telegraph* settled with the plaintiffs in 1982 for $1.4 million. In the meantime, the *Telegraph* already had undergone a personality change. Once aggressive in its news coverage, it had become cautious, even passive.

In a *Wall Street Journal* interview, Cousley said the *Telegraph* was like "a tight end who hears footsteps," meaning that his reporters and editors now anticipated being jarred by a tackler, leaving them reluctant to pursue tough stories.[2] Cousley later told another journalist: "All the ideals and principles in the world don't mean a damn when it comes down to hard economics. I like aggressive journalism. Newspapers have to keep doing their job; it's their constitutional responsibility. But when the trail of the story leads into the counting house and threatens the economic existence of the newspaper, watch out."[3] Eventually, the *Telegraph*'s mounting legal and financial troubles contributed to the sale of the newspaper to a privately owned newspaper chain managed by Ralph M. Ingersoll II. In 1986 Stephen A. Cousley resigned, marking the end of the 125-year association of the *Alton Telegraph* and the Cousley family.

What happened to the *Alton Telegraph* dramatizes the litigious climate of journalism. Its chilling effect is understood more viscerally by those who experience litigation than by those who understand it only in theory. While there may be some glory in carrying the First Amendment banner into battle, litigation (like warfare) usually is painful and costly. The price paid goes beyond lawyers' bills and damage awards. Media defendants also can expect their lives to be disrupted for months or years as they undergo intense scrutiny. In a lawsuit, nearly all aspects of a journalist's professional deportment and reputation are subject to question and attack. It is not an enjoyable experience.

In the 1964 landmark libel case of *New York Times v. Sullivan*, the Supreme Court affirmed a "profound national commitment to the principle that debate on public issues should be uninhibited, robust and wide-open."[4] Today that commitment is being tested as the public, press and courts disagree over just how uninhibited, robust and wide open that debate should be.

Media defendants cannot expect much sympathy or support from those outside the profession. Generally, the public shares the plaintiff's point of view: No matter how important a free press is to society, journalists should be held strictly accountable for what they publish or broadcast. Some people believe a stinging legal blow is needed on occasion to remind all journalists to act responsibly. Such a blow landed in 1990, when the *Philadelphia Inquirer* incurred one of the largest libel awards on record against an American newspaper—$34 million. Plaintiff Richard Sprague, a prominent lawyer and former prosecutor, sued over a series of stories that suggested he had interfered with a 1963 murder investigation. Speaking after the verdict, Sprague said news organizations must be punished for their falsehoods. "That is the message the jury wanted to send," he said. "They wanted to get the attention of the media around the country."[5] Sprague accepted an undisclosed out-of-court settlement in 1996, after a state court reduced the award to $24 million and the state supreme court denied review.

The Sprague payout, although substantial, fell well short of what the Media Law Resource Center, as of 2004, called the largest jury award in a libel suit, which topped $222 million against the *Wall Street Journal*. In 2000, the plaintiff, a Texas securities firm the *WSJ* accused of reckless, extravagant use of pension funds under its control, requested dismissal. What happened? In an unexpected twist, the trial court ruled that evidence deliberately withheld by the plaintiff prevented Dow Jones & Co., publisher of the *WSJ*, from fully defending itself in the case. No doubt a collective sigh of relief swept through the *WSJ* newsroom.

Two areas of press law—libel and privacy—receive special attention in this chapter. But an overarching issue connects libel and privacy: journalist-source relationships. Various dimensions of that issue will be explored as well.

Covering news of public affairs is not a job for timid souls who fail to ask tough questions and shy away from potentially explosive stories. Nor is it a job for gung-ho types who seek news with reckless abandon, hurting people and inviting lawsuits. Reporting public affairs requires aggressiveness and enterprise balanced by compassion, caution and common sense. Journalists of equilibrium possess an admirable sensitivity to the legal and ethical rights and wrongs of reporting of the news.

Unfortunately, there are few certainties or firm rules to follow. Media law is complex; media ethics is more complex. As journalists pursue stories, they often must enter a legal-ethical forest. Those who try hard to understand the law and navigate around hazards stand a better chance of reaching the destination all responsible journalists seek—a truthful story that can be told in good conscience.

Libel

For journalists, March 9, 1964, represents Liberation Day. On that date, the Supreme Court announced its *New York Times v. Sullivan* decision. *Times v. Sullivan* invited the press to practice an aggressive form of journalism, particularly in coverage of government and public officials. Errors are "inevitable in free debate," the Court's majority said, and to require that critics of government prove the truthfulness of every utterance leads to self-censorship. For freedom of expression to survive, let alone flourish, the justices concluded that "breathing space"—a tolerance for error—was needed. The Court provided that breathing space through the *actual malice rule* (or *New York Times* Rule), which requires public officials suing for libel to prove that a defamatory statement was published "with knowledge of its falsehood or with reckless disregard of whether it was false or not." The actual malice rule shifted the burden of proof in libel cases to public officials, making it more difficult for them to succeed in a libel suit against the news media, which, indeed, was the Court's intent.

As opinions of the Supreme Court and decisions of lower courts further defined and redefined libel law, the actual malice rule proved to be something less than invincible. Ironically, despite *Times v. Sullivan's* intent to encourage and protect robust coverage of public affairs, libel litigation increased.[6] Over the years, juries and judges have sided frequently with libel plaintiffs, ranging from entertainer Carol Burnett to factory worker David Rouch.

In Rouch's case, the *Battle Creek* (Mich.) *Enquirer* erroneously reported his arrest for the knifepoint rape of a 17-year-old babysitter; the mistake cost the Gannett-owned newspaper a $1 million libel judgment. In closing arguments to the jury, Rouch's attorney alluded to David v. Goliath. "Big Gannett, $364 million last year [and] David Rouch, $30,000 factory worker, 10 years trying to protect himself."[7] The David v. Goliath analogy touches a sensitive public nerve. "The average citizen and juror views the newspaper, its methods and motives skeptically," says editor Steve Wilson. "We are seen as the plaintiffs want us to be seen—a business with a greater desire to sell papers than to inform the public."[8] Even public figures are often viewed as victims of Big Media.

Statistics support Wilson's assessment. A two-year study of jury awards nation-wide, for example, found that in 54 libel or privacy trials, the plaintiff won in 42 of 48 jury trials and in 5 of 6 bench trials.[9] The study also found that most libel judgments were either reduced or overturned by appellate courts, but the promise of an appeals victory offers little consolation to journalists facing a lawsuit.

Elements of Libel

Knowledge of libel begins with an indefinite definition: In its broadest sense, *libel* is any published communication that is injurious to another person's reputation, occupation or social contacts. The meaning and language of libel law, though, vary from year to year and state to state, determined by both statute and court decisions.

Persons suing for libel generally must provide evidence that five elements exist: publication, identification, defamation, falsehood and fault. Each element can be tricky and imprecise for plaintiffs and defendants alike.

Publication

In most libel cases, a copy of the offending article or a videotape (or audiotape) of a broadcast establishes "publication." But as the *Alton Telegraph* case demonstrates, publication can include any communication for which there is a record, such as a memo, letter or notes, including electronic notes and records stored in a news organization's computer system. Publication occurs when someone other than the writer and the subject—a secretary, for example—sees or reads the communication.

Identification

People are usually identified by name, age, address, occupation and other forms of personal description. Identification, however, also can be established by circumstances or context. A police-beat story, for example, that reports the theft of equipment at a work site might quote the construction foreman as saying, "We think it's an inside job, probably involving a worker on the night shift." As everyone at the construction company knows, three guards regularly are on duty at night. The story casts doubt on the honesty of all three, and, although no names are used, dozens of people know the guards' identities.

Misidentifying someone is always embarrassing; it is legal dynamite when the story involves material harmful to a person's reputation. Crime reports, in particular, pose a constant hazard. A careless reporter covering the arrest of a man named Gregory M. Ingram on armed robbery charges checks the newspaper's library for previously published stories about Ingram, finds reference to a Gregory G. M. Ingram, the owner of a hardware store. Without confirming the identity of the man in custody, the reporter describes the suspect as a local businessman. It does not occur to the reporter that there could be two or more Gregory Ingrams; the similarity of the middle initials seems good enough. Not every case of misidentification leads to a libel suit, but few news organizations will tolerate careless, lackadaisical reporters who fail to check for accuracy.

Defamation

A story is not libelous unless defamation occurs. By most definitions, defamation amounts to a falsehood that causes perceptible injury to a person's reputation, such as being fired, losing clients or being ostracized. Not every falsehood, of course, injures. A story that inaccurately reports a jaywalking violation by Jon R. Chase is not likely to tarnish Chase's reputation. Falsely reporting Chase's arrest for driving under the influence of alcohol, though, is defamatory.

Circumstances may also affect defamation. For example, incorrectly reporting that Mary Davidson once had an abortion might not be defamatory, particularly if Davidson has made it known that she favors abortion as a matter of choice. But if Davidson is a legislator campaigning for re-election on a pro-life platform, the report will do damage and probably is defamatory.

Above all, defamation is a subjective determination. To say a politician has "failed to look out for the well-being of her constituents" might strike some people as harmless; to the thin-skinned, the words could be considered injurious.

Falsehood

The falsehood of defamatory statements used to be assumed. Under the common law of libel, it was up to the *defendant* to prove that the statements were *true*. In 1986 the Supreme Court required evidence of factual falsehood as part of a libel *plaintiff's* burden of proof. The Court went further to state that when evidence of truth or falsity is uncertain, the balance should tip in favor of true speech. Justice Sandra Day O'Connor wrote: "We recognize that requiring the plaintiff to show falsity will insulate from liability some speech that is false, but unprovably so. Nonetheless, . . . the First Amendment requires that we protect some falsehood in order to protect speech that matters."[10] Justice O'Connor's position is consistent with the *Times v. Sullivan* constitutional requirement that the plaintiff prove that the defendant made a defamatory statement with actual malice or negligence. The Court's ruling has given reporters added protection against libel suits.

Fault

The final element of a plaintiff's burden of proof is establishment of fault. The criteria for fault vary, depending to a large degree on the "status" (or category) of plaintiffs. In libel law, plaintiffs fall under two broad, often fuzzy categories: (1) *public official* or *public figure* and (2) *private individual*. The status of a libel plaintiff is critical because it determines which level of fault is to apply—the stricter standard of *actual malice* or the lesser standard of *negligence*.

Anthony Lewis, author and journalist

Anthony Lewis vividly recounts the story behind the landmark Supreme Court decision, *New York Times v. Sullivan*, in his book *Make No Law*. The book is must reading for journalists. (Photo by Stephanie Mitchell Courtesy Harvard News Office.)

Determining Fault: A Tough Call

In most instances, attorneys would prefer to represent a "private individual" plaintiff because of the less demanding burden of proving negligence instead of actual malice. As a result, one of the earliest battles in a libel suit is likely to be over the plaintiff's status. In defining *public official*, the Supreme Court has said that the designation "applies at the very least to those among the hierarchy of government employees who have, or appear to the public to have, substantial responsibility for or control over the conduct of governmental affairs."[11] The definition, however, is ambiguous. Many courts, for example, consider police officers to be public officials, but a handful of courts have held otherwise. Similar ambiguity applies to teachers or other public servants whose "responsibility for or control over" governmental affairs may or may not be "substantial." In short, the designation "public official" may be up for grabs.

The Supreme Court's 1974 decision in *Gertz v. Welch* helped distinguish the difference between a public figure and a private individual. A public figure generally falls under five categories: (1) someone of general fame or notoriety in the community;

(2) a person with pervasive involvement in societal affairs and issues; (3) an individual who invites public attention; (4) someone who thrusts himself or herself to the forefront to influence the outcome of issues; and (5) a person who is drawn into a particular public controversy involuntarily, although the Supreme Court has noted that "the instances of truly involuntary public figures must be exceedingly rare."[12]

Gertz by no means ended debate over public and private status. A succession of post-*Gertz* decisions both clarified and confused the issue. In one case, the Supreme Court said mere "media interest" in a person does not convert that person into a public figure, nor do those involved in litigation automatically become public figures.[13] In another case, the justices indicated that with a passage of years, someone who was once a public figure could revert to private-individual status.[14]

Plaintiffs deemed by a court to be either a "public official" or a "public figure" must prove *actual malice*, which has come to mean the defendant published a "calculated falsehood,"[15] proceeded with publication despite entertaining "serious doubts" as to its truthfulness[16] or engaged in conduct that constituted "an extreme departure from the standards . . . of reporting ordinarily adhered to by responsible publishers."[17]

The Supreme Court has not provided many examples of "extreme departures" from normal standards of journalism, leaving that responsibility to trial courts and juries. Obviously, one person's definition of "extreme departure" is going to be another's definition of "moderate departure." Even within the profession, journalists will disagree about what constitutes reckless disregard for the truth. Libel cases from federal and state courts offer little concrete guidance. For example, the Supreme Court, in one of its rare instances of specificity, said in a 1968 libel case that relying totally on an "unverified anonymous phone call" suggests actual malice. In the same decision, the Court said, less concretely, "Likewise, recklessness may be found where there are obvious reasons to doubt the veracity of the informant or the accuracy of his information."[18]

Most often, judicial guidance is in the form of what is *not* actual malice. Reckless disregard, for example, is not automatically established by a reporter's failure (1) to investigate charges, (2) obtain and present both sides of the controversy or (3) include material contradictory to the damaging statements. Reckless disregard obviously is difficult to establish but not impossible. Journalists who think the actual malice rule protects them from incomplete, sloppy reporting are only deluding themselves. Few juries are going to be understanding when journalists fail to do a conscientious job of being fair, truthful and thorough in news coverage.

That message came through when the Supreme Court affirmed a $200,000 damage award against the *Journal News* of Hamilton, Ohio. The newspaper reported that Daniel Connaughton, a candidate for municipal court judge, offered jobs to a grand jury witness and her sister in appreciation for the sisters' help with an investigation damaging to Connaughton's opponent. In his majority opinion, Justice John Paul Stevens said the key factor was the newspaper's failure to interview the grand juror's sister, whom Stevens called the "most important witness to the bribery charges." Failure to investigate is not in itself evidence of actual malice, Stevens said, but "the purposeful avoidance of the truth is a different category."[19] Since motive bears on a finding of actual malice, the Supreme Court has allowed attorneys for libel plaintiffs to vigorously inquire into the state of mind and decision making of journalists.[20] As a result, libel defendants can anticipate a barrage of dozens of questions from the plaintiff's attorney, such as: "Why did you interview Mr. Bowen, an enemy of the plaintiff, and not Mr. Clark, a friend?" or "Why did you include details about my client's tax problems but not details about his charitable work?"

QUOTABLES

"[I]f we take the libel suit too seriously, we are in danger of surrendering a wonderful part of our national identity—our strapping, scrambling, free-wheeling individualism, in danger of becoming less American, less robust, wild-eyed, pluralistic and free, and more decorous, image-conscious, and narcissistic." (p. 257)
—Rodney A. Smolla, *Suing the Press,* New York: Oxford University Press, 1986

Libel plaintiffs can more easily establish *negligence*, the standard of proof required of private individuals since the *Gertz* decision, when the Supreme Court decided it was unfair to hold private individuals to the same strict standard of proof that applied to influential, visible and powerful persons.[21] By legal definition, there are various degrees of negligence, some more serious than others. Generally, the definition being applied in libel law is either *failing to exercise a degree of care that a prudent person would exercise under similar circumstances* or *doing something a reasonable person would not do.* Professional standards or ethical codes that govern reporting, interviewing, quoting and fact-checking can come into play as plaintiffs seek evidence of deviation by journalists from the norm.

Understandably, the standard of journalistic negligence is even more subjective than that of actual malice. Does failure to investigate defamatory charges establish actual malice? Apparently not. But failure to investigate *does* appear to constitute negligence. For example, a magazine writer was found to be negligent for not verifying information about fire hazards of wood-burning stoves. The court said the writer failed to examine two previously published sources for his article or contact the authors of either source, did not know about another article from a different publication that repudiated his claims, and failed to contact anyone in the stove industry for test results relevant to his article.[22]

Admittedly, the difference between public official-public figure and private individual is critical to the outcome of many libel cases. But media defendants who must pin their hopes on the plaintiff's status probably are fighting an uphill battle from the start. As always, journalists who are meticulously accurate and scrupulously fair in news coverage will not have to pray that the plaintiff is designated a "public figure."

REPORTER'S TIP FILE

Read the story draft carefully. Identify every potential plaintiff. Identity negative or possibly defamatory references. Justify the use of negative statements and the use of negative sources.

- Identify the source of possibly defamatory or negative references.
- Avoid high-risk phrases or labels in an article, such as "criminal behavior," "unethical behavior," "cheat," "liar," "misfeasance," "doublecrosser."
- A sentence—even a single word—can spell trouble.
- Rely on data and documents rather than opinion and remarks.
- Seek a response from the person or persons referred to in negative statements.
- Justify your journalistic and social purposes in reporting negative or potentially defamatory information.
- Know your stuff—for self-protection and the sake of accuracy. Double-check everything.
- Consult outside experts on the facts, findings and overall balance and accuracy of your story.
- Never break the law, or encourage others to break the law, in pursuit of a story.
- Keep your editors well informed at every stage of an important story.

Defenses

The constitutional libel defense provided by *New York Times v. Sullivan* is the journalist's principal protection. However, anyone facing a libel suit would prefer multiple layers of protection that include the defenses of *truth, consent, neutral reportage* and *privileged communications*.

Truth

Truth normally is an absolute defense in libel cases. If truth is on your side, victory and vindication *should* be yours, with an emphasis on *should*. Libel cases are exceedingly unpredictable. Whose version of the "truth" will the judge and jury believe? Despite the plaintiff's burden to prove, among other things, falsity, media defendants should be prepared to face an unofficial burden to prove truthfulness. Stories based on solid documentation notes, digital audio recordings, records and reliable, named sources are far easier to defend, if it comes to that.

Consent

When people talk to reporters, there is an assumption of implied consent. It is further assumed that news sources are talking freely without conditions, aware that what they say might later be broadcast or published. Dangers arise when a news subject withdraws consent prior to publication or broadcast, denies ever talking to the reporter or claims the reporter concealed his or her intent to publish what was said. A particularly self-damaging statement ought to be recorded verbatim, transcribed and accompanied by the subject's signed consent.

Neutral reportage

The defense of neutral reportage protects journalists who cover accusations and statements involving newsworthy public controversies. Neutral reportage is a promising development in libel law, but questions about its validity will remain until the Supreme Court addresses the issue. The defense, first recognized in 1977 by a U.S. Circuit Court of Appeals, has been endorsed by state courts in Illinois, California and Ohio, for example, but rejected in several other federal and state courts.

Where it is accepted, neutral reportage is a conditional or qualified defense intended to allow news organizations to disseminate the words of prominent, responsible persons or organizations regarding serious charges on an issue of public importance, provided coverage is disinterested and accurate.[23] Those conditions must be met for the defense to apply. It remains a viable defense even when reporters entertain doubts about the truthfulness of the charges.

Privileged communications

A broad category of public meetings, proceedings, pronouncements and records are considered *privileged communications* and immune from a lawsuit. In libel law, a *privilege* is an exemption from liability based on a premise that society's interests in unimpeded communication occasionally outweigh society's concern for an individual's reputation. The privilege is either absolute or conditional. *Absolute privilege* normally covers official acts of public officers and all judicial and legislative proceedings, such as city council meetings and court hearings. Lawmakers, for example, enjoy absolute privilege so they can freely debate and resolve public issues germane to their official duties. *Conditional* (or qualified) *privilege* applies to communication that falls outside absolute protection but nonetheless is related to important societal interests. Conditional privilege, for example, might protect a citizen who errs in identifying a holdup suspect in a good-faith attempt to assist police.

For the most part, the press enjoys a conditional privilege to report official meetings and communications with immunity, as long as coverage is accurate and free of any "extraneous" (outside) libelous material. Unfortunately, it is hard to know from state to state or jurisdiction to jurisdiction what is a privileged communication or situation and what is not. As a rule, information and statements emerging from open court proceedings and legislative sessions are privileged. Generally, so are public reports issued by governmental officials or offices. But more gray exists than black and white.

A few examples underscore the problem:

- Is an arrest report an official government document? In some jurisdictions, courts have ruled it is; in others, it takes issuance of a warrant before information of an arrest becomes privileged communication.
- Is a complaint or petition that initiates litigation a privileged communication? In a majority of states that have ruled on the question, privilege does not automatically commence with the initial filing; there must be either action by the court or a formal response by the other side before privilege clearly applies. One reason for such a policy is to protect people from damage done by a frivolous, unwarranted lawsuit.
- Is fair, accurate reportage of a legislator's attacks on another person privileged? This, too, is a hazy area. In most instances, the legislator's words must directly relate to official business, or, as the Supreme Court has said, to the "deliberative process" of the legislative body. Lawmakers do not enjoy absolute privilege every time they speak, so reporters may not be free of liability, for example, when they publish or broadcast a legislator's comments made during a corridor news conference or on a television talk show.

Obviously, reporters cannot always predetermine privileged communication. The safest course is never to spread any damaging accusation or comment without a serious effort to verify the charges and present the other side's story. When phone calls or messages fail to elicit a response, some news organizations will send certified letters to establish that the news source knew that his or her comments were sought.

Private Lives vs. the Public's Business

Reporters can invade someone's privacy by word, deed or both. By definition, libel centers on publication. Privacy poses a double danger. Publishing embarrassing details about someone's life might constitute one type of privacy action; a second privacy action might be based on the alleged deception a reporter used to obtain information.

Privacy actions fall under four categories:

- intrusion—violating someone's solitude by trespass, harassment, surveillance or other intrusive means
- embarrassing facts—publicly disclosing private facts, such as someone's confidential medical records
- false light—misrepresenting someone's views or characteristics in the public eye
- misappropriation—using someone's name or likeness for financial gain, which usually arises from advertising or promotion of products and services

Three of the four privacy actions—intrusion, embarrassing facts and false light— apply most directly to reporters. Each contributed to a prison guard's lawsuit against the *Dallas Times Herald*. The guard was one of 12 taken hostage and tortured during a 1980 riot at a New Mexico state penitentiary. According to the lawsuit, the reporter accompanied a visitor to the guard's hospital room. What happened in the hospital room is disputed. The guard claims the reporter eavesdropped on a private conversation, later producing a story that disclosed embarrassing facts about how he had been sodomized with an ax handle and placed him in a false light by referring to his "near-poverty" wages. A federal court jury awarded the guard $200,000 in damages.[24]

Privacy clashes are complicated because two constitutional interests are at stake— the public's right to know versus the individual's right to be left alone. Privacy is cherished, especially in an age when so little about our lives is hidden or protected. Yet the Supreme Court, employing much of the same reasoning it applied to libel law, has given the press considerable freedom to report and publish, even when reporters go where they are unwelcome and report on matters people dearly want to keep private. The Supreme Court's leading privacy case, *Time, Inc. v. Hill*, decided three years after *Times v. Sullivan*, stressed the importance of debate on all matters of public interest.[25] In subsequent cases, the court expanded rights to report about the private affairs of public officials and public figures. More recently, the Court rulings have given journalists the right to publish identities and details about society's most heinous assault on personal privacy—rape.[26]

While, indeed, there is considerable freedom to gather and report news, there are also limits, and when reporters exceed those limits, they can expect public scorn and dire legal consequences. Problems invariably arise when reporters expose private details in a manner and to a degree most people would find offensive.

Intrusion

Several privacy cases serve as warnings for journalists. One is *Dietemann v. Time*. In that case, a photographer and reporter for *Life* magazine posed as patients to secretly photograph and record what happened inside the home office of a man suspected of practicing medicine without a license. He was found guilty, but even guilty people have rights. Upholding a $1,000 award in the plaintiff's favor, the court said the First Amendment was not "a license to trespass, to steal or to intrude by electronic means into the precincts of another's home or office."[27]

Does *Dietemann* place reporters in jeopardy of litigation whenever they masquerade, conceal their identities, use hidden tape recorders or employ high-tech equipment to intercept private communication? No, partly because *Dietemann* represents the views of a single court. Additionally, federal law and statutes in some states require one-party consent (the journalist's) to electronically record conversations in person by use of an inexpensive suction-cup device that allows taping of telephone calls. But reporters who engage in trickery or subterfuge to enter private property or acquire confidential information ask for trouble, as *Dietemann* demonstrates.

A profession that resorts to lies and deception risks loss of public respect, trust and cooperation. Do not, for example, expect Patricia Martin, her family or friends to place much trust in the press. Martin, widow of a South Dakota state official, accused a local journalist of pretending to be an "old dear friend" of her husband, who said he wanted to express condolences. Only later did she realize she had been tricked into revealing her feelings about a painful situation that became known after her husband's death—he secretly had a second wife and separate family in another South Dakota city.[28] Few stories are so big or significant that they justify deceit and lies. Journalism is best served by honest, up-front reporting methods.

Galella v. Onassis sounds another alarm: Reporters who engage in aggressive tactics may cross the indistinct line that separates legitimate newsgathering from intrusion. Despite her public stature as a former first lady, Jacqueline Kennedy Onassis obtained an injunction that ordered freelance photographer Ron Galella to keep a distance from her and her children. In issuing the injunction, the court commented: "There is no general constitutional right to assault, harass, or unceasingly shadow or distress public figures."[29] When does reporting amount to harassment or cause distress? A reporter seeking information relevant to a legitimate news story is right to pursue a public official by telephone or other means, like camping outside the official's office. A reporter who calls at 3 a.m., when his questions can wait until a reasonable hour, hassles the official's spouse or children or engages in threatening tactics no longer is enterprising or determined. Such a reporter is abusive.

Intrusion can occur in public or semi-public places as well as private ones. Depending on the circumstances, people are entitled to a personal *zone of privacy* that invisibly encircles them. Courts have ruled that a privacy zone applies, for example, to a patient recuperating in a hospital room or an executive conducting private business in a public facility, such as a transaction at a bank. Reporters are not legally free to wander into any room or peer over shoulders, even when their snooping occurs in places generally accessible to the public. Nor are they free to use electronic devices (telephone bugs, scanners and hidden audio or video recorders) or high-powered lenses to intercept private communications or spy from afar.

REPORTER'S TIP FILE

To tape or not to tape

The Reporters Committee for Freedom of the Press provides an overview of what is at stake when journalists tape telephone interviews or use other means of electronic recording in their news coverage:

> At first, the question of whether or not to tape record a phone call seems like a matter of personal preference. Some journalists see taping as an indispensable tool,

while others don't like the formality it may impose during an interview. Some would not consider taping a call without the subject's consent, others do it routinely.

However, there are important questions of law that must be addressed first. Both federal and state statutes govern the use of electronic recording equipment. The unlawful use of such equipment can give rise not only to a civil suit by the "injured" party, but also criminal prosecution.

Accordingly, it is critical that journalists know the statutes that apply and what their rights and responsibilities are when recording and disclosing communications.

Although most of these statutes address wiretapping and eavesdropping—listening in on conversations of others without their knowledge—they usually apply to electronic recording of any conversations, including phone calls and in-person interviews.

Federal law allows recording of phone calls and other electronic communications with the consent of at least one party to the call. A majority of the states and territories have adopted wiretapping statutes based on the federal law, although most also have extended the law to cover in-person conversations. Thirty-eight states and the District of Columbia permit individuals to record conversations to which they are a party without informing the other parties that they are doing so. These laws are referred to as "one-party consent" statutes, and as long as you are a party to the conversation, it is legal for you to record it. (Nevada also has a one-party consent statute, but the state Supreme Court has interpreted it as an all-party rule.)

Twelve states require, under most circumstances, the consent of all parties to a conversa-tion. Those jurisdictions are California, Connecticut, Florida, Illinois, Maryland, Massachusetts, Michigan, Montana, Nevada, New Hampshire, Pennsylvania and Washington. Be aware that you will sometimes hear these referred to inaccu-rately as "two-party consent" laws. If there are more than two people involved in the conversation, all must consent to the taping.

Regardless of the state, it is almost always illegal to record a conversation to which you are not a party, do not have consent to tape and could not naturally overhear.

Federal law and most state laws also make it illegal to disclose the contents of an illegally intercepted call or communication.

At least 24 states have laws outlawing certain uses of hidden cameras in private places, although many of the laws are specifically limited to attempts to record nudity. Also, many of the statutes concern unattended hidden cameras, not cameras hidden on a person engaged in a conversation. Journalists should be aware, however, that the audio portion of a videotape will be treated under the regular wiretapping laws in any state. And regardless of whether a state has a criminal law regarding cameras, under-cover recording in a private place can prompt civil lawsuits for invasion of privacy.

In most cases, private places are strictly off limits to reporters; no matter how important the story, no matter how newsworthy the individual, trespassing or eaves-dropping on private property constitutes intrusion. An apparent exception is coverage of a disaster, such as a fire, tornado or plane crash, particularly if law enforcement personnel grant reporters permission to enter private property. An invitation by public officials is not, however, an unconditional passport to all news scenes. Reporters who accompanied authorities on a midnight raid of a private school for troubled youths learned that lesson when the Florida Supreme Court said, "In this jurisdiction, a law enforcement officer is not endowed with the right or authority to invite people of his choosing to invade private property."[30] The Supreme Court in two related decisions—*Wilson v. Layne*[31] and *Hanlon v. Berger*[32]—held that police violate the Fourth Amendment's prohibition on unreasonable searches and seizures when they allow members of the news media to accompany them during the execution of a warrant in private residence. Law enforcement agencies that invite journalists to participate in raids, ride-alongs (joining police on patrol) or the execution of arrests often do so for public relations benefits. The two Supreme Court rulings will likely cause law enforcement agencies to shy away from situations that might get them sued for violation of privacy or Fourth Amendment rights, particularly while on private property or residences. While reporters can be exploited by police for publicity purposes, there are advantages to a cooperative relationship so long as no ground rules restrict what can be reported. Even reporters believe they are within their rights to venture on private property, when covering emergencies, such as devasting hurricane like Katrina, reporters should show respect for the property and privacy of others and seek permission if the owner is present.

Embarrassing Facts

A critical point to remember about publication of embarrassing facts is that *truth offers no protection against litigation*. Some facts are simply too private, too intimate or too hurtful to be disclosed. There is no inclusive list of embarrassing facts, but many people, including journalists, would say at a minimum the list includes details about an individual's sexual life, family relationships and physical or mental health. Nonetheless, reporters still may be ethically correct and legally safe to report, for example, that a candidate for judge takes an antidepressant drug or that an ex-Marine who saved the president from a would-be assassin's bullet is gay. Privacy rights can be overcome by a nebulous, highly subjective, catchall defense called *newsworthiness*.

What, then, is newsworthy? There is no telling how a particular judge or jury is going to determine which published or broadcast stories are "newsworthy" and which are not, but the standard applied by various courts focuses on information of legitimate "public interest" or "public concern." In applying that loose standard, courts frequently have looked to the tastes and mores of the mythical "reasonable person." As one court put it, "The line is to be drawn when the publicity ceases to be giving of information of which the public is entitled and becomes a morbid and sensational prying into private lives for its own sake, with which a reasonable member of the public, with decent standards, would say that he had no concern."[33] Style or intent appears to be a factor. A breathless, *National Enquirer*-type presentation may suggest a "sensational prying into private lives."

A reasonable person probably would find much of the daily stream of information about public affairs—crime, accidents and litigation—"newsworthy." Less clear is how a reasonable person would categorize details about life's misfortunes, curiosities or oddities, such as the birth of Siamese twins. Most journalists would say, "That's news." But laypeople might respond, "Let the family decide whether it is news or not."

The question of newsworthiness is undoubtedly related to an individual's position or status in life. For celebrities and public officials, little is private and outside the realm of public interest or concern. The question of newsworthiness is less settled when a child or spouse of a public person becomes an object of media attention. The mayor's treatment for drug dependency is newsworthy. But what if the mayor's 24-year-old son is being treated privately? Is that newsworthy? Perhaps, depending on the circumstances. Are the son's problems preoccupying the mayor's thoughts, taking him away from city hall for long stretches of time and adversely affecting important city business? The mayor's absences and lack of attention must be explained, which invariably would mean reference to his son, but the focus should, it seems, remain on the public person—the mayor—and not the son.

Reporters need to be especially sensitive to the privacy of children, even children involved in stories with tempting human-interest appeal. For the most part, courts are protective about minors, particularly those who are considered "special" because of physical, mental or psychological needs. A reporter may feel proud after doing a story on an experimental program that has accomplished wonders for a group of fourth-graders with learning disabilities. But what if several sets of parents, while immensely gratified over their child's progress, have kept the learning disability a private matter? Even the neighbors do not know. Reporters are advised to proceed carefully with stories about children and, in most cases, to talk to the parents to discover whether they object to coverage. The parents may have compelling reasons for privacy that never occurred to the reporter.

Privacy rights generally yield when the information comes from public records. In several cases, the Supreme Court has upheld the press in privacy actions, holding in one of those cases, which involved publication of a rape victim's name, that the First Amendment "protects the publication of truthful information contained in official court records open to public inspection."[34] The public-records defense, however, is slippery because not all records held by government agencies and departments are open and accessible to the public. In fact, in many states, scores of records, such as identities of people receiving public aid, are exempt from disclosure for privacy considerations. Check with officials to ensure that the records in question are, indeed, "public."

Reporters should never, however, use availability of private information in public records as an *excuse* or *rationalization* to disclose embarrassing facts. Of special concern are rape victims. Although police records, available to reporters, might reveal names, nearly all news organizations voluntarily withhold the identity of rape victims to protect them from additional emotional trauma. Only the most reckless or thoughtless reporter would identify a rape victim when her assailant is at large. Nonetheless, that has happened in several instances, subjecting the victims to threatening telephone calls and other forms of harassment.

A handful of legitimate exceptions to the general policy of non-disclosure in rape cases allow the prominence of the victim and the circumstances surrounding the case to outweigh the individual's privacy rights. Still, the press goes to great lengths to protect identities. In 1989, a gang of youths confessed to brutally beating and raping a young investment banker who was jogging through New York City's Central Park. As *Newsweek* noted, "We've followed her remarkable recovery, from a shattered and comatose shell . . . to a walking miracle who returned to work. We seem to know everything except her name." For once, writer David Kaplan noted, the press "applauded itself for not doing its job" to report.[35]

In 2003, Trisha Meili identified herself in a memoir *I Am the Central Park Jogger*. About the same time, a convicted serial rapist and murderer told prison authorities he alone raped the jogger, and a judge dismissed all charges against the five men imprisoned in the Meili case.

At times, journalists' access to public records allows them to disclose facts that do more than embarrass, as the ordeal of Texas pediatrician Robert J. Huse illustrates. After Huse tested positive for the AIDS antibody, his former roommate began telling people the doctor had AIDS. Fearing the parents of his patients would react with needless alarm, Huse sought a restraining order to attempt to silence the former roommate, and Huse filed the petition under his actual name, not as "John Doe." By doing so, Huse made his medical condition a matter of public record, and before long several newspapers, including both Dallas dailies, had reported Huse's exposure to the AIDS virus.

Admittedly, there are no sure, easy answers to guide the press in handling stories like Huse's, partly because there are no sure, easy answers to AIDS. The fact remained that Dr. Huse did not have AIDS, and, as one newspaper reported, a "person with the AIDS virus has no more than a 30 percent chance of contracting the disease over the next five years."[36] Nonetheless, if the doctor felt there was no need to inform patients of his condition, did it fall to the press to do so? Many editors—and laypeople—would say, "yes." What about alternatives? Would withholding the doctor's name and using a reference such as a "local pediatrician" be an acceptable option? Perhaps not, because then all pediatricians in town would be suspect.

Normally, journalists strive to be precise and complete in covering stories and naming names. Should AIDS carriers be an exception? The publicity cost Dr. Huse his career in medicine. Do not look for easy answers. Ethical reporters, though, consider the range of consequences whenever a story poses the possibility of harming others. In the end, you may be faced with the painful task of determining where the *greatest* potential harm resides. In the aftermath of the Huse case, reports from Florida established that a dentist with AIDS had infected at least three patients. The deadly consequences of AIDS pressure journalists to inform the public of potential risks.

False Light

False light resembles libel. In privacy law, however, a false light often pertains to non-defamatory falsehoods—ones that may not necessarily damage reputation but cause embarrassment or distress. In one case, a man photographed standing in a line at a state unemployment office unsuccessfully sued for false light. It turned out that the man was not there to receive jobless benefits but to serve as a translator for a friend who did not speak English.[37]

Not any false statement or portrayal constitutes false light. Another requirement is for the published false light to be highly offensive to a reasonable purpose. Typically, courts will not base the degree of offensiveness on the embarrassment or bruised feelings suffered by the plaintiff, such as the homeowner who sued because a newspaper's photo caption described his home as "as a bit weatherworn and unkempt." Trivial indignities, one court said, are not meant to be grounds of a false-light lawsuit. On the other hand, a reasonable person might find offensiveness in a photo caption that said some fans "passed out early," showing a man stretched out asleep at an outdoor rock concert.

False-light cases also require that the plaintiff establish fault. For a plaintiff who is either a public figure or public official, the burden of proof in false-light cases is identical to the libel plaintiff's—the actual malice standard. What is not clear is whether the actual malice standard applies to *all* false-light plaintiffs, including private individuals. In libel law, the Supreme Court has declared that private individuals need only prove negligence to collect all but punitive damages. The Court has not, as yet, made a similar distinction in false-light litigation, although several state courts have applied the negligence standard in the false-light suits of private individuals, further clouding the waters.

False-light actions involving news reporters usually fall under one of two categories—fictionalization or distortion. With fictionalization, a reporter remakes a real-life person to sharpen features, invent dialogue or create scenes through a blending of fact and fiction. Fictionalization is most likely to occur when a reporter draws on the techniques of creative writing, such as characterization, scene-setting and internal dialogue, to produce a detailed profile or narrative. Reporters are right to borrow the style and devices of fiction to energize their writing as long as they remain true to journalism's tenets of accuracy and fairness. Occasionally, a reporter will go too far, swept away by unbridled imagination or ambition. Good stories, however, do not require fictionalized treatment. In the hands of a skilled, sensitive and honest writer, a mother's struggle to support seven children after her husband's death in a bridge collapse remains compelling without a need for embellishment.

False light by distortion most often occurs when a reporter intentionally quotes someone out of context; uses subjective, negative language to create a falsehood by implication; or omits crucial facts or details favorable to the subject of the news report. Because journalists often make hundreds of judgments as they decide how to best report and write a story, the possibility of inadvertent distortion is high. Of thousands of words spoken in an interview or the hundreds of facts and details collected during newsgathering, only a fraction usually end up in a story. Journalism inherently is a process of selectivity; reporters must remember that as they *choose* and, particularly, as they *discard* story material. Distortion can be accidental or calculated. Neither type of distortion is excusable, but deliberately misrepresenting someone's views or characteristics is a serious offense in journalism and evidence of actual malice in privacy law.

REAL-LIFE LESSONS

On being sued

Journalists might mistakenly assume the law is firmly on their side, as libel or invasion-of-privacy plaintiffs struggle to meet a heavy burden of proof. In the courtroom, though, lofty legal principles of free expression often get swept aside. When journalists face the opposing side's attorneys, a lawsuit can degenerate to a dogfight. Remember the statistics of libel and privacy trials; they suggest that the plaintiff's burden of proof can be met to the satisfaction of a majority of trial judges and juries. Journalists who fail to vigorously defend their actions increase the odds that already are heavily against them.

The fact is, any journalist sued for libel or invasion of privacy must be prepared to *prove* his or her innocence. If you face a deposition hearing or cross-examination on the witness stand, expect to be challenged and questioned by a skilled interrogator intent on making you look inept, reckless, malicious or all three. Here's a sample taken from an actual deposition of a reporter named in a false-light invasion of privacy case. The plaintiff's attorney persistently and aggressively questioned the reporter's adherence to her newspaper's ethical code on quoting.

Q. "See where it says, 'Quotations,' and I'll read it for you again. 'Readers should be able to assume that every word between quotations marks is what the speaker or writer said.' Do you see that?"
A. "Yes, ma'am."
Q. "Do you agree with that?"
A. "Yes, ma'am."
Q. "Do you follow that policy?"
A. "Yes, ma'am."
Q. "Is this a complete quote?"
A. "It left off the last word. . . ."
Q. "So it's not a complete quote, is it? It's not a complete quote, is it?"
A. "It doesn't appear to be."
Q. "So, once again, you made a mistake, right?"
A. "Yes."
Q. "Did you correct in anywhere?"
A. "No, ma'am."

Later, after going through several other examples of quotation "mistakes," the plaintiff's attorney returned to the first alleged mistake.

Q. "It's just missing a little piece, isn't it?"

A. "It's missing the last word."

Q. "It's not accurate then. It's not an exact quote, is it?"

A. "Yes, ma'am, it is the exact quote."

Q. "It's not the exact quote that's in your notes, is it?"

A. "It's from the memo but. . . ."

Q. "Did you answer?"

A. "The quote within the quotation marks is exact."

Q. "Just missed a little piece, isn't that right?"

Explanations of newsroom practices can be made to sound absurd or laughable: "Let me get this straight, Mr. Jackson. So you tried only two times to call Mr. Jones about a story that has wrecked his career? And that's what is considered responsible journalism in your newsroom?" The journalist's credentials will be fair game. "Ms. Evans, when's the last time you had a course on libel law? 'Not since journalism school'? That was 15 years ago, wasn't it Ms. Evans? Was it a full course on libel or a unit or just a week?" Your attorney might shout objections, and the jurors might be told by the judge to "disregard" the opposing attorney's remarks. By then, though, it might be too late. You have been portrayed as an ill-prepared, sloppy journalist.

The lesson: *Never underestimate the impact of your reporting. People who consider your story a personal attack or invasion of their privacy will fight back. Never assume the courts will be on your side. Prepare to defend yourself—your character and your performance.*

Privacy and Libel Danger Zones

Journalists seldom anticipate the mistakes that lead to libel or privacy lawsuits. One of the main danger zones in libel and privacy centers on *expunged* (erased) *record*. Most states, depending on the circumstances, permit courts to remove or expunge arrest records, particularly if charges have been dropped. Occasionally, even records of convictions are expunged. When that happens, it is as if the records never existed. As a result, a libel defendant cannot easily cite "truth" or "privileged communication" as defenses when the records to establish those defenses do not officially exist. Similarly, a privacy defendant may find newsworthiness no protection because expungement, after all, is meant to guard against disclosure.

Another set of legal problems arises when journalists routinely include arrest and conviction information lifted from previously published stories or obtained through unofficial sources. Journalists must consider the possibility that the court documents no longer are part of the public record. Suppose a reporter doing a routine check on a finalist for police chief calls the candidate's hometown newspaper for background information and learns that six years ago, the chief pled "no contest" to charges that he beat a girlfriend in a quarrel. Rather than settle for secondhand information, the reporter calls the court clerk's office to confirm details and obtain, if possible, a photocopy of records. (Failing to obtain confirmation from an official source is sloppy work and potentially reckless reporting, regardless of whether the records have been expunged.) A clerk tells the reporter there is no record of the case. Obviously, the reporter has encountered an obstacle, but it does not mean the story of the police chief's past problems must be killed. Considering the chief's stature and the importance of his position in the community, the odds of a successful suit are slim. Some stories are not risk-free. In this scenario, however, the reporter and his editors were able to anticipate the risks and figure the odds.

With both libel and privacy cases, passage of time diminishes the legal and ethical justification for the press to resurrect facts and information that continue to harm a person's reputation or feelings. In the opinion of some courts, public persons who purposefully shun publicity eventually revert to private-individual status. That is even truer of private persons who voluntarily or involuntarily became public figures for a short time—perhaps a five-minute act of heroism in a plane crash. How long must they be expected to pay the price of once being a news subject? Reporters cannot be oblivious to this problem or assume that the individual will not mind having his or her story retold.

Journalists should be particularly sensitive when reporting about people who occupied news for their misdeeds but now, after being punished, are trying to rebuild their lives. As one court explained, "One of the premises of the rehabilitative process is that the offender can rejoin that great bulk of the community from which he has been ostracized. . . . In return for becoming a new man, he is allowed to melt into the shadows of obscurity."[38] Remember, too, that no matter how well intended a story might be, it still may cause pain or troubles for the people it affects.

Computer-smart reporters face a newly emerging category of dangers when they search for electronic records, even public ones, without authorization. Today, anyone who illegally extracts information from private or public databases may face criminal charges for electronic trespassing. Certainly, those who break into computer files face civil action if the material they obtain discloses private facts or falsely injures a reputation. Medical records are a special problem, especially with new, tougher federal guidelines to protect against disclosure. When policyholders routinely sign consent forms that give the insurance company access to medical records, those records may be stored in information clearinghouses that share records with other insurance companies. Reporters with the means to obtain computerized records must never forget the power they possess. Extraordinary circumstances are necessary to justify disclosure of medical records or other private, potentially harmful details that are meant to be confidential under the law and public policy. Moreover, any record, especially those stored in huge electronic depositories, can be misfiled or contain incorrect information, adding further meaning to the computer-age expression of "garbage in, garbage out."

For reasons that go far beyond fear of litigation, journalists must always be vigilant for errors. Writer Martha Hume survived a libel suit, but the experience taught her a lesson. "Being sued . . . made me hypersensitive about every little fact," she said. "[I now] double-check and triple-check every last detail." Hume wrote about the dangers of fitness tests conducted by health clubs. Wired to a heart monitor, she took a test and reported that her pulse rate reached 178 beats a minute, what she described as a dangerously high rate without a doctor or emergency equipment standing by. Her notes included hundreds of details but no reference to the figure "178." It could have been, she said, an expensive omission if the plaintiff's attorney made it an issue.[39]

Precise, legible notes, digitally recorded interviews and thorough, careful, eyes-on examination of all documents and records help ensure against mistakes that lead to lawsuits. Never let deadline pressures force you to skim documents or take reporting shortcuts.

Journalists and Their Sources

Several years ago, a student interning at a small daily newspaper came by her journalism teacher's office to share some exciting news. "I'm going to get a byline on a story I did on some teenagers who break into homes." The teacher listened intently and then said, "Bonnie, are you prepared to go to jail over this story?" He never meant to shock her, but he did. Quickly, he explained what might happen if she refused a judge's orders to reveal the names of the youths. It turned out that a junior editor planned to use the story in a weekend edition, but he had not cleared the story with superiors. In the end, the newspaper's editor decided the story was not worth the grief it might cause for the intern. The intern and her teacher agreed.

Journalists who build stories on unnamed, confidential sources ought to understand the consequences. Among the legal entanglements are contempt citations, libel suits and reporter-source contractual disputes. The ethical problems include what columnist James Kilpatrick derisively calls "trust-me" journalism.[40]

Another set of reporter-source problems arises when reporters abuse, mistreat or deceive people in pursuit of the news.

Granting Anonymity: Risks and Rewards

Reporters need confidential sources; they provide tips, information and insights that lead to important stories. The classic confidential source is Watergate's "Deep Throat," the shadowy figure who helped Carl Bernstein and Bob Woodward investigate the Nixon administration. In 2005, the magazine *Vanity Fair* revealed Deep Throat as Mark Felt, who was assistant director of the FBI during the Watergate years. Over the years, reporters have courageously or stubbornly refused to reveal the identity of their confidential sources, enduring jail, fines and ostracism, even from colleagues.

At issue is a controversial legal concept called *journalists' privilege*. A privilege, in this context, is an exception to the law. Journalists have long argued that they are entitled to the same testimonial privilege traditionally reserved for lawyer-client, doctor-patient, priest-penitent and husband-wife. The argument is based on a reasonable premise: Forcing reporters to reveal confidences would dry up a major tributary of news, depriving people of their right to know about important issues. Journalists' privilege, however, clashes with another reasonable premise: For the courts (or other judicial bodies) to administer justice and seek the truth, they must be as unrestricted as possible to compel testimony and produce evidence.

The Supreme Court addressed the question of journalists' privilege just once, in the 1972 decision of *Branzburg v. Hayes*.[41] Although the Court's majority declined to recognize a constitutionally based journalists' privilege, the decision did not, as it might have done, strip the press of protection against forced disclosure of confidential sources. *Branzburg* proved to be a flexible opinion, offering courts room to maneuver. As lower courts attempted to resolve journalists' privilege disputes case by case, a number adopted a three-part standard urged by Justice Potter Stewart in his *Branzburg* dissent. Stewart said those seeking confidential information from journalists should (1) establish the relevancy of the information sought to the legal question at hand, (2) demonstrate that the information sought cannot be obtained by alternative means or from other sources and (3) show a compelling and overriding governmental interest in the information.

There are no guarantees when a journalist decides to protect a confidential source; some courts are more sensitive to the demands of newsgathering and the importance of anonymity than others. But certain situations leave reporters with little hope for protection. For example, a reporter who witnesses a serious crime or whose testimony can lead to an arrest can expect to be subpoenaed and ordered to disclose information. A similar fate probably awaits a reporter who possesses information crucial to determining guilt or innocence in a criminal trial or that goes to the "heart of the matter" in a civil case.

When a story based on anonymous sources results in a libel or privacy suit, one of the first steps the plaintiff's attorneys will take is to ask the reporter to name names. If the court agrees that the identity of the sources is central to the plaintiff's ability to establish fault, the reporter can further anticipate an order to disclose identities. Refusal may result in a contempt citation and possibly jail. Another possibility is that the judge will instruct the jury to assume that the anonymous sources do not exist.

In 31 states and the District of Columbia, reporters are protected to varying degrees by statutes commonly known as "shield laws." Many of those laws, however, include exceptions to a general policy of non-disclosure of confidential sources and information. In other words, there may be ways for those determined to force disclosure of sources to circumvent a shield law. In 2006, Congress considered several bills to establish a federal shield law, but as of early 2007, the legislation remained on hold.

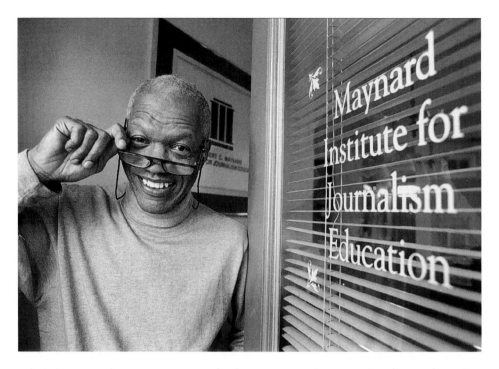

Earl Caldwell at the Maynard Institute Earl Caldwell battled government subpoenas seeking his grand jury testimony about the Black Panthers. He and two other journalists took their journalist's privilege cause to the Supreme Court in *Branzburg v. Hayes*. Caldwell chronicles his career in *The Caldwell Journals*, available online at http://www.maynardije.org/news/features/caldwell/. (Photo by Ray Chavez, courtesy the *Oakland Tribune*.)

Until 1990, journalists who revealed the names of confidential sources risked only professional ostracism. Now, however, they may be liable for breach of contract. In 1988, a Minnesota jury awarded $700,000 in damages to Dan Cohen, who had been identified in a *St. Paul Pioneer Press* story despite reporters' promises that his name would not be used. Six days before an election, Cohen, a spokesperson for a political candidate, gave reporters documents showing that a rival candidate had admitted to shoplifting $6 worth of merchandise in an incident dating back 12 years. Over objections of their reporters, editors at the newspaper decided Cohen needed to be identified to give readers the fullest information about the campaign.

The Minnesota Supreme Court overturned the damage award, arguing that enforcing a contractual agreement would violate the defendants' First Amendment rights. In 1990, the case went to the U.S. Supreme Court,[42] with little hope for journalists of a positive outcome. The Supreme Court ultimately upheld the contract argument, and reporters now face news sources who demand legal safeguards and written agreements before revealing sensitive information.[42] Had the Court supported the First

Amendment argument, then many news sources, concluding that a reporter's promise of confidentiality is meaningless, would decide to remain silent.

The *Cohen* case also demonstrates another important point about confidential sources: The decision to pledge anonymity to a news source is not the reporter's alone, and editors and reporters do not always share the same views. A reporter who disobeys an editor's order to reveal a source might retain his or her principles but lose the news organization's legal backing in the process.

Journalists are especially wary about confidential sources as a result of the Janet Cooke affair. Cooke, a *Washington Post* reporter, won a Pulitzer Prize in 1981 for her moving story of an 8-year-old heroin addict named Jimmy. The story was based on anonymous sources; no real names or addresses were used. The *Post's* editors did require Cooke to reveal her sources. It turned out the story was fiction, and Cooke was stripped of her Pulitzer Prize. No wonder many editors and news directors now insist on knowing the names of reporters' confidential sources.

A subpoena can be the ultimate test of a journalist's commitment to sources and the First Amendment. The experience of William Farr is an example. In 1970, Farr, covering the murder trial of Charles Manson, obtained a sworn deposition in which one of Manson's followers described how Manson planned to butcher several Hollywood stars. Farr's newspaper, the *Los Angeles Herald-Examiner*, published details in the deposition despite the objections of the trial judge, who earlier had ordered participants not to make any out-of-court statements. Apparently, either a defense or prosecution attorney leaked the deposition to Farr. Over the next 11 years, the case bounced from court to court—federal and state—with Farr either under threat of confinement or embroiled in court hearings and motions. Farr eventually spent 46 days in jail for refusing to identify the source of the deposition. Later, several attorneys connected to the Manson case sued Farr for libel, seeking to clear themselves of suspicion; they, too, wanted to know which attorney on the case violated the judge's order. Although, in a sense, Farr prevailed, the case left him financially and emotionally drained. But he remained true to his word; he died in 1987 at the age of 52 without naming his source.

Journalists' privilege involves more than complications over subpoenas, contempt citations and contract suits; it can also lead to a malady known as "sourcery." Some reporters, say critics, too quickly and too often grant anonymity. As a consequence, confidential sources are handed the means to spread accusations and plant information without accountability. The ultimate loser is the public, which is denied the opportunity to judge the credibility of these nameless, faceless "authorities."

Sourcery's roots are in Washington, D.C., where story after story cites "high-ranking officials" or "sources close to the White House." But sourcery has spread from big-city dailies to small-town weeklies, with rookie reporters and school board members engaging in the D.C. jargon of "deep backgrounders," "off the record" and "not for attribution."

The trial and conviction of I. Lewis (Scooter) Libby Jr., former chief of staff to Vice President Dick Cheney, opened the curtain on the questionable practice of allowing high-ranking officials to plant stories or attack enemies through reporters willing to grant them anonymity. In March 2007, a jury found Libby guilty of perjury and three related charges for lying about his role in the illegal leaking of the name of a covert CIA agent—the wife of a White House political foe—to several journalists. Testifying at Libby's trial, NBC journalist Tim Russert, moderator of *Meet the Press*, said he regards any conversation with a senior government official as confidential and would seek permission before ever reporting anything he or she said. In a reaction shared by a number of journalists, Dan Froomkin of the *Washington Post* said: "That's not reporting; that's enabling." The *Minneapolis Star Tribune* added: "A journalist who behaves as Russert did isn't working for the public; he's working for his sources."[43]

Actually, few stories require pledges of confidentiality. Reporters should first determine whether there is a genuine need for anonymity. Is the information so sensitive that exposing its source is dangerous? In many cases, there is no danger, only a reluctance to be identified as the source. Sometimes, with additional digging and legwork, the information can be obtained in other ways or from other sources willing to go on record. Indeed, many reluctant sources, if approached properly and persistently, ultimately will speak without conditions.

In those handful of cases where reasons for confidentiality appear strong and the story is important, the next step is to assess the reliability and motives of the source. Seek documentation and corroboration, especially if the sources are government officials, who may be using the press to plant a bogus story about an issue to test public reaction. Never agree to grant anonymity to someone whose intent is to launch a personal attack on a rival.

When reporters and editors agree that confidentiality is justified, the story should explain the reasons for not naming a source. Try to identify unnamed sources as precisely as possible, using a title or a job description. Finally, reporters should determine whether they and their sources speak the same language. To a reporter, "off the record" may mean, "Not to be used in any way." To a news source it may mean, "Quote my words, but don't attribute them to *me* in any way."

Reporting Rumors

Rumors ought to carry a warning sign: "Handle with Great Care." Many rumors that become news stories deal with what might be considered "scandalous" or "shocking" details of public figures and public officials, such as extramarital affairs, drug use, alcoholism and mental illness.

Asking a news source to confront a rumor in a public forum, such as a press conference, often does more harm than good. In 1986 on the *Today* show, an NBC reporter asked Rep. Jack Kemp if he had ever had a homosexual encounter. A *Today* official said the question enabled Kemp to put the rumor to rest. It did not. Other news outlets, including the *New York Times* and *Washington Post*, repeated the NBC reporter's question and Kemp's response, further spreading the rumor.[44] Prior to any thought of broadcast or publication, reporters should confirm significant rumors, learn who is spreading them and determine why they are being spread. Rumors tend to dry up when rumor-spreaders are pressed for details or asked to go on record.

Obviously, some rumors must be addressed by the press, but the objective should be a good-faith, non-judgmental attempt to either verify or dispel rumors, not spread or profit from them. Coverage of rumors calls for introspection: Do reporters too eagerly snap at the bait of gossip, forgetting that many rumors are spread out of ill will? And is the press too moralistic about the personal behavior of public persons? A *Newsweek* article made a point all journalists ought to ponder. By scrutinizing moral minutiae, such as ascertaining whether a congressional candidate ever smoked marijuana, the press may be overlooking issues or questions of far greater importance.[45] Moreover, coverage of rumors may unfairly put public persons on trial for an isolated indiscretion or mistake. Fair, serious journalism calls for a thorough examination of all available evidence and consideration of the individual's full record. Rushing into print or onto the air with a snippet of gossip might undermine or even destroy an entire career of good deeds.

Dealing with Sources

Janet Malcolm's book *The Journalist and the Murderer* explores the relationships between journalists and news sources.[46] Malcolm focused on the battle between writer Joe McGinniss, author of *Fatal Vision*, and his subject, Jeffrey MacDonald, the ex–Green Beret doctor who was convicted of murdering his wife and two daughters. But her commentary applies to everyone whose job is to draw stories and information out of others for publication or broadcast. Malcolm's stinging attack on journalists, first published in *New Yorker* magazine, is quoted in Chapter 2. Her words, however, bear repeating in a context of law and ethics: "Every journalist who is not too stupid or full of himself to notice what is going on knows that what he does is morally indefensible. He is a kind of confidence man, preying on people's vanity, ignorance, loneliness, gaining their trust and betraying them without remorse."[47] Critics accused Malcolm of exaggeration, yet her attack helped draw attention to what she called a "messy drawer" of legal and ethical issues.[48]

McGinniss spent a year cultivating a close relationship with MacDonald, presumably preparing to vindicate his friend in a forthcoming book. But when *Fatal Vision* was published in 1983, it portrayed MacDonald as a psychopathic killer. Feeling used and betrayed, MacDonald sued McGinniss for distorting the "essential integrity of his life story." MacDonald's lawyer framed the case as an issue of a "false friend" journalist who violated the trust of his interview subject by lying and deceit. McGinniss' lawyer argued that the case placed all journalists at risk of being sued "for writing truthful but unflattering articles should they ever have acted in a fashion that indicated a sympathetic attitude toward their interview subject."[49]

Although MacDonald and McGinniss settled out of court, the issues raised by the case remain disturbingly unsettled. As Martin Garbus, an attorney who handles press law issues, explains: "Taking Malcolm's argument at its extreme that nearly all journalists manipulate, seduce and even lie to get a story the question remains: Do we balance that ethical breach against the need to get out the truth, or do we 'forget the story'?"[50] Is the story—the Truth—of paramount importance? As Garbus correctly notes, "For those of us who hold both First Amendment values and honesty dear, there is a conflict." Of course, honesty and First Amendment values do not inherently conflict each time a reporter pursues a story. Conflicts are most likely to arise with stories of great significance. A few stories must be told, even if it takes lies and deception to do so. Nonetheless, once an ethical line is crossed, where is it to be drawn the next time and by whom? Moreover, what happens to a profession that tolerates and even encourages manipulation and lies in the name of truth-seeking? In the long run, will manipulation and lies only encourage manipulation and lies in return?

QUOTABLES

"I am continually surprised by the willingness of people to talk about great misfortune, even when they themselves caused it. They described what happened in detail. They, the accidental, regretful perpetrators of serious tragedies, the living victims, the survivors of plane crashes, house fires, tornadoes, floods, boating accidents, rapes, shootings, you name it. They were anxious to talk away their griefs, sorrows and guilt as though their words would erase the reality of the dreadful thing that had happened, not realizing how those words would sound on the air or appear in the paper. They were not politicians or spin-doctors. They didn't have the proper words to sway the public in their favor, or know what not to say to a reporter. They were the innocents. They did not choose or ever expect to see their likeness on a television screen or in a newspaper. . . . I felt I was an intruder on their private sorrows, but they did not treat me as one." (pp. 105, 106)
—Joseph P. Ritz, *I Never Looked for My Mother and Other Regrets of a Journalist*,
Bangor, Maine: Booklocker.com, Inc., 2006

Journalists rarely will feel compelled to hide, misrepresent or lie about their conclusions during an interview if they genuinely delay the mental process of "concluding"—which is what they should do—until it is time to write the story. Reporters who approach people with an open mind can expect to improve possibilities of openness from others.

Quoting Sources

With the McGinniss–MacDonald questions still reverberating within the journalism community, Malcolm ignited another debate within the profession. It stemmed from a libel suit brought against Malcolm by psychoanalyst Jeffrey Masson, central figure of another article she wrote for *New Yorker* magazine and later published as a book, *In the Freud Archives*. Masson accused Malcolm of putting words in his mouth, particularly when she quoted Masson as describing himself as an "intellectual gigolo." But the U.S. Circuit Court of Appeals in California dismissed Masson's libel suit. In a 2-to-1 vote, the judges said even fabricated quotations were permissible as long as they were either a "rational interpretation of ambiguous" comments or did not "alter the substantive content" of the speaker's words. The serious issues at stake brought the case to the U.S. Supreme Court in 1990 on appeal.

The Malcolm–Masson dispute opened a second messy drawer: Is it right for journalists to alter or invent direct quotations? Malcolm, in a defense that is almost convincing, argues that journalists not only are correct to modify direct quotations, it is their duty to do so: "When a journalist undertakes to quote a subject he has interviewed on tape, he owes it to the subject, no less than to the reader, to translate his speech into prose. Only the most uncharitable (or inept) journalists will hold a subject to his literal utterances and fail to perform the sort of editing and rewriting that, in life, our ear automatically and instantaneously performs."[51]

Once again, Malcolm brought a set of longstanding assumptions into question, leaving reporters even more unsure of what is right and wrong conduct in the use of direct quotes. Most news sources and journalists would say that direct quotations are "untouchables." Veteran AP editor Rene Cappon speaks for the majority of the profession when he says, "Once words are enclosed by quotation marks, they must be what the source said. Attempts to 'improve' that by reshuffling or even changing words are high crimes and misdemeanors. The furthest you can go is to fix minor grammatical errors and omit pure padding or meaningless repetition."[52]

The Masson–Malcolm libel suit challenged that venerable but mythical standard. The Supreme Court decided that tampering with direct quotations did not constitute actual malice unless the reporter altered the substance of the speaker's remarks. In the Court's opinion, *Masson v. New Yorker Magazine, Inc.*, Justice Kennedy described the complexities of quoting and explained quite well the difficulty of using verbatim quotes:

> Even if a journalist has tape recorded the spoken statement of a public figure, the full and exact statement will be reported in only rare circumstances. The existence of both a speaker and a reporter; the translation between two media, speech and the printed word; the addition of punctuation; and the practical necessity to edit and make intelligible a speaker's perhaps rambling comments, all make it misleading to suggest that a quotation will be reconstructed with complete accuracy. The use or absence of punctuation may distort a speaker's meaning, for example, where that meaning turns upon a speaker's emphasis of a particular word. In other cases, if a speaker makes an obvious misstatement, for example by unconscious substitution of one name for another, a journalist might alter the speaker's words but preserve his intended meaning. And conversely, an exact quotation out of context can distort meaning, although the speaker did use each reported word.[53]

Few journalists celebrated the *Masson* case as a First Amendment victory, but, in the context of *New York Times v. Sullivan*, the ruling appears legally correct and sensible. Holding journalists liable for the strict accuracy of direct quotations would chill coverage. Although strict accuracy should always be the goal, in practice, reporters often fail to quote news subjects verbatim. That is especially true of reporters who rely on handwritten notes instead of digital recorders. Reporters will make human mistakes as they gather and report the words of others, but relaxing standards of factuality, even if the courts give journalists additional breathing space, is dangerous.

As any examination of press law and ethics shows, the public's apparent predisposition against Big Journalism is reason enough for reporters to take every precaution in news coverage. Above all, however, common decency requires journalists to treat others as they themselves would want to be treated. Sometimes the profession is its own worst enemy, becoming excessively defensive when attacked for its behavior. At times, journalists must suppress the urge to be self-righteous, admit they have erred and say, "We're sorry." That may be all a victim of media malpractice requires to feel vindicated. Certainly, such a demonstration of humility would go far to restore goodwill between the press and the public.

Exercises

1. Check with a managing editor or news director to learn the company policy on use of confidential sources. In particular, find out how far the news organization will go to legally support a reporter who has been ordered to reveal a confidential source. Remember that court appeals are expensive.

2. Some public university officials have cited a federal law known as the Buckley Amendment, which ensures the privacy of student records, to deny reporters access to campus police reports. Find out the policy at your university or another public school nearby and discuss the policy with university officials.

3. Receive the *News Media & the Law* and make use of other legal resources by making a donation to the Reporters Committee for Freedom of the Press (www.rcfp.org). The magazine provides an overview of recent media law issues and court decisions. Your donation supports both the magazine and the organization's 24-hour advice hotline for legal emergencies.

Notes

1. See Thomas B. Littlewood, *Coals of Fire: The* Alton Telegraph *Libel Case* (Carbondale, Ill.: Southern Illinois University Press, 1988).
2. John Curley, "How Libel Suit Sapped the Crusading Spirit of a Small Newspaper," *Wall Street Journal*, Sept. 29, 1983, p. 1.
3. Littlewood, *Coals of Fire*, p. 190.
4. *New York Times v. Sullivan*, 376 U.S. 254 (1964).

5. "Libel Settlement a Record $34 Million," *St. Petersburg Times*, May 4, 1990, p. 11A.

6. See Rodney A. Smolla, *Suing the Press* (New York: Oxford Press, 1986).

7. "Michigan Daily Appeals $1 Million Libel Verdict," *Editor & Publisher*, Aug. 26, 1989, p. 26.

8. Steve Wilson, "How I Spent My Summer Vacation," *ASNE Bulletin*, November 1983, p. 36.

9. "Few Libel Damage Awards Are Sustained on Appeal," *Editor & Publisher*, Sept. 4, 1982, p. 16.

10. *Philadelphia Newspapers, Inc. v. Hepps*, 475 U.S. 767 (1986).

11. *Rosenblatt v. Baer*, 383 U.S. 75 (1966).

12. *Gertz v. Robert Welch, Inc.*, 418 U.S. 323 (1974).

13. *Time, Inc. v. Firestone*, 424 U.S. 448 (1976).

14. *Wolston v. Reader's Digest Association*, 443 U.S. 157 (1979).

15. *Garrison v. State of Louisiana*, 379 U.S. 64 (1964).

16. *St. Amant v. Thompson*, 390 U.S. 727 (1968).

17. *Curtis Publishing Co. v. Butts*, 388 U.S. 130 (1967).

18. *St. Amant v. Thompson*, 390 U.S. 727 (1968).

19. *Harte-Hanks Communication, Inc. v. Connaughton*, 491 U.S. 657 (1989).

20. *Herbert v. Lando*, 441 U.S. 153 (1979).

21. *Gertz v. Robert Welch, Inc.*, 418 U.S. 323 (1974).

22. *General Products v. Meredith*, 526 F. Supp. 546 (D.C. Va. 1981).

23. *Edwards v. National Audubon Society*, 556 F.2d 113 (2d Cir. 1977).

24. "Dallas Times Herald Loses $200,000 Suit," *Editor & Publisher*, Oct. 16, 1982, p. 57.

25. *Time, Inc. v. Hill*, 385 U.S. 374 (1967).

26. *Florida Star v. B.J.F.*, 491 U.S. 524 (1989).

27. *Dietemann v. Time, Inc.*, 284 F. Supp. 925 (C.D. Calif. 1968), 449 F.2d 245 (9th Cir. 1971).

28. "Widow of Man with 2 Wives Sues," *St. Louis Globe-Democrat*, Dec. 23, 1976, p. 10.

29. *Galella v. Onassis*, 487 F.2d 986 (2d Cir. 1973).

30. *Green Valley School v. Cowles Florida Broadcasting*, 327 So. 2d 810 (Fla. App. 1976).

31. *Wilson v. Layne*, 526 U.S. 603 (1999).

32. *Halon v. Berger*, 526 U.S. 808 (1999).

33. *Virgil v. Time, Inc.*, 527 F.2d 1122 (9th Cir. 1975).

34. *Cox Broadcasting Corp. v. Cohn*, 420 U.S. 469 (1975).

35. "Should We Reveal Her Name?" *Newsweek*, April 2, 1990, p. 48.

36. Deni Elliot, "Identifying AIDS Victims," *Washington Journalism Review*, October 1988, pp. 26–29.

37. *Cefalu v. Globe Newspaper Co.*, 391 N.E. 2d 935 (Mass. App. 1979).

38. *Norris v. King*, 355 So. 2d 21 (1978).

39. Quoted in Barbara Dill, *The Journalist's Handbook on Libel and Privacy* (New York: Free Press, 1986), pp. 76, 77.

40. James J. Kilpatrick. "'Trust-Me' Journalism," *Washington Journalism Review*, January–February 1988, p. 45.

41. *Branzburg v. Hayes*, 409 U.S. 665 (1972).

42. *Cohen v. Cowles Media Co.*, 501 U.S. 663 (1991).

43. Dan Froomkin, "Washington Journalism on Trial," washingtonpost.com, posted Feb. 8, 2007.

44. William Boot, "The Gossip Mill," *Ethics: Easier Said Than Done*, January 1989, p. 52.

45. "Trial by the Ethics Squad," *Newsweek*, Dec. 26, 1988, p. 25.

46. See Janet Malcolm, *The Journalist and the Murderer* (New York: Knopf, 1990).

47. Janet Malcolm, "The Journalist and the Murderer: I — the Journalist," *The New Yorker*, March 13, 1989, p. 38.

48. Janet Malcolm, "The Morality of Journalism," *New York Review of Books*, March 1, 1990, p. 20.

49. Malcolm, "The Journalist and the Murderer: I — the Journalist," p. 39.

50. Martin Garbus, "McGinniss: A Travesty of Libel," *Publishers Weekly*, April 21, 1989, p. 69.

51. Malcolm, "The Morality of Journalism," p. 20.

52. Rene J. Cappon, *The Word: An Associated Press Guide to Good News Writing* (New York: Associated Press, 1982), p. 71.

53. *Masson v. New Yorker Magazine, Inc.,* 501 U.S. 496 (1991).

Index